U.S. Marines in the Gulf War, 1990–1991

LIBERATING KUWAIT

BY
PAUL W. WESTERMEYER

HISTORY DIVISION
UNITED STATES MARINE CORPS
QUANTICO, VA
2014

Related History Division Publications

U.S. Marines in the Persian Gulf, 1990–1991:
Anthology and Annotated Bibliography

U.S. Marines in the Persian Gulf, 1990–1991: With the I Marine
Expeditionary Force in Desert Shield and Desert Storm

U.S. Marines in the Persian Gulf, 1990–1991: With the 1st Marine Division
in Desert Shield and Desert Storm

U.S. Marines in the Persian Gulf, 1990–1991: With the 2d Marine Division
in Desert Shield and Desert Storm

Humanitarian Operations in Northern Iraq, 1991: With Marines
in Operation Provide Comfort

U.S. Marines in the Persian Gulf, 1990–1991: Marine Communications
in Desert Shield and Desert Storm

U.S. Marines in the Persian Gulf, 1990–1991: With Marine Forces Afloat
in Desert Shield and Desert Storm

U.S. Marines in the Persian Gulf, 1990–1991: Combat Service Support
in Desert Shield and Desert Storm

U.S. Marines in the Persian Gulf, 1990–1991: The 3d Marine Aircraft Wing
in Desert Shield and Desert Storm

U.S. Marines in Battle: Al-Khafji, 28 January–1 February 1991

PCN 10600009700

ISBN 978-0-9911588-1-2

Contents

Foreword

In August 1990, Iraqi military forces invaded the neighboring nation of Kuwait. The invasion was part of an expansionist foreign policy that Saddam Hussein had established a decade earlier when he invaded post-revolution Iran. The Iraqi invasion of Iran failed, degenerating into nearly a decade-long war of attrition, but Kuwait was an easier target. Kuwait had financed the Iran-Iraq War for Iraq but refused to forgive the debt, and Iraq accused Kuwait of stealing oil from the Rumaylah oil field. Much smaller than Iran in terms of population and geography, Kuwait had focused its foreign and defense policies on negotiation and compromise rather than military force; inevitably, the large Iraqi army quickly overwhelmed the small Kuwaiti armed forces.

Inside Kuwait, Iraqi troops began wholesale pillaging as security forces acted to remove all those loyal to the Kuwaiti royal family. Iraq declared that Kuwait was now a province of Iraq, thus eliminating its debt and adding Kuwait's extensive oil fields to its own. Saddam stationed conscript infantry divisions in Kuwait and began building extensive defenses along the Kuwaiti-Saudi border.

While Saddam calculated the military balance between Iraq and Kuwait correctly, he underestimated the willingness of the world community, especially the United States and Great Britain, to intervene on Kuwait's behalf. His invasion set the stage for a military confrontation that was larger in scope than any similar circumstance since World War II. Under President George H. W. Bush, the United States assembled a global Coalition of concerned nations, first to defend Saudi Arabia against further Iraqi aggression, then to eject the Iraqi military from Kuwait. Early in this Gulf War, American military commanders designated the operation to protect Saudi Arabia as "Desert Shield," and the successive operation to free Kuwait as "Desert Storm." These military operations were massive undertakings, and they highlighted the paradigm shift from superpowers in precarious equilibrium during the Cold War to American global hegemony in the 1990s.

For the U.S. Marine Corps, the Gulf War was a test of its ability to perform quickly, under pressure, as advertised. A Marine expeditionary force was deployed rapidly and then reinforced, while two Marine expeditionary brigades were also deployed as the Marine Corps continued to support its peacetime commitments. Despite long months of tedium in the desert as the crisis played out, the Marines performed their duties with skill and élan, achieving a remarkable victory against the Iraqi Army in Kuwait and proving the Corps' strategic concepts, most especially the value of the Maritime Prepositioning Force. The impact of the war on American defense policy and the confidence the Gulf War's success gave to the Marine Corps continue to impact today's national security debates.

The author, Mr. Paul W. Westermeyer, joined the Histories Branch as a historian in 2005. Mr. Westermeyer is the author of *U.S. Marines in Battle: Al-Khafji*, published by Marine Corps History Division in 2008. He holds a bachelor's degree in history and a master's degree in military history from the Ohio State University.

Dr. Charles P. Neimeyer
Director of Marine Corps History

Preface

It was apparent very early that the Persian Gulf deployments of 1990 were of great historical significance to the Marine Corps, and in accordance with its mission, what was then the Marine Corps History and Museums Division began collecting and preserving evidence of the events for use by later historians. Command chronologies, oral histories, official records, and lessons learned reports were preserved in the Marine Corps Archives, providing the foundation for this official history of Marines in the Gulf War.

During the war, the History and Museums Division deployed five field historians to cover the conflict: Colonels Charles J. Quilter II and H. Avery Chenoweth and Lieutenant Colonels Charles H. Cureton, Dennis P. Mroczkowski, and Ronald J. Brown. In addition to collecting photographs, artifacts, and historically significant documents, they conducted a large number of oral history interviews with Marines deployed to the Gulf. These interviews form the core of the Gulf War oral history collection and are now stored in the Audio-Visual Information Repository of the General Alfred M. Gray Marine Corps Research Center, located in Quantico, Virginia. Without their work, this history would have been a pallid affair.

Following the conflict, the History and Museums Division produced eight monographs in the U.S. Marines in the Persian Gulf, 1990–1991 series. This excellent first pass at the history of Marines in the Gulf War provided the foundation for the current work.

I was assigned this project in 2006, shortly after joining the Marine Corps History Division. Writing such a history is a massive undertaking that required surveying the Marine Corps Archives (both the command chronologies and the extensive Southwest Asia collection) as well as the substantial secondary literature on the conflict. Several hundred oral histories had been preserved, but there were still noticeable gaps that could only be filled by new oral history interviews. In order to provide a fuller understanding of events, Iraqi sources had to be surveyed and translated as well.

This history could not have been published without the professional efforts of the History Division staff. I would like to thank the director of Marine Corps History, Dr. Charles P. Neimeyer; the chief historian of the Marine Corps, Mr. Charles D. Melson; and senior historian Mr. Charles R. Smith for their comments, advice, and support. Colleagues Dr. Nathan S. Lowrey, Dr. Nicholas J. Schlosser, and Ms. Annette D. Amerman provided unflagging professional advice and support. Dr. Thomas M. Baughn and Major David W. Kummer of Histories Branch supplied excellent editorial guidance.

Lieutenant Colonel David A. Benhoff and Chief Warrant Officer-4 Timothy S. McWilliams from the Field History Branch provided support and recommendations. Dr. Fred Allison and Mr. Anthony R. Taglianetti of our Oral History Branch were both essential to this project's success.

Our Editing and Design Branch, ably led by Ms. Angela J. Anderson, played an instrumental role in transforming the manuscript into a finished product. Ms. Jeanette L. Riffe coordinated the distribution and receipt of review drafts; Ms. Wanda J. Renfrow proofread the text; and Mr. Shawn H. Vreeland adeptly edited the manuscript and oversaw the production process. Maps, layout, and design were skillfully provided by Mr. W. Stephen Hill. Editorial interns Gabrielle Guillen and Elizabeth Dillard supplied necessary proofreading and fact-checking support.

The research for this project would have been impossible without the indefatigable aid and support of Dr. James A. Ginther at the Marine Corps Archives, as well as Mr. Danny A. Crawford, Mr. Robert V. Aquilina, Ms. Lena M. Kaljot, Ms. Kara R. Newcomer, and Ms. Beth L. Crumley of our Historical Reference Branch.

Many of the Iraqi documents used as sources for this project were translated by Ali al Saadee; the project could not have been completed without his excellent work. The finished manuscript also benefited from the aid and advice of Dr. David B. Crist, Mr. David J. Morris, Dr. Kevin L. Osterloh, Dr. Amin Tarzi, and Dr. Kevin M. Woods.

History Division interns Borislav V. Chernev, Alexander N. Hinman, Charles M. Kassir, Nicholas J. Ross, Evan Sills, Paul R. Zimmerman, and Brian Sperling provided invaluable research assistance and badly needed clerical and computer support.

A draft of this work was reviewed and commented on by Major General John H. Admire, General Walter E. Boomer, Brigadier General James A. Brabham Jr., Brigadier General Thomas V. Draude, General Carlton

W. Fulford, Colonel James A. Fulks, Colonel Richard W. Hodory, Major General Harry W. Jenkins Jr., General Charles C. Krulak, Lieutenant General John E. Rhodes, and General Michael J. Williams.

As with all of my historical endeavors, I am indebted to my doctoral advisor, Dr. John F. Guilmartin, whose advice and familiarity with the conflict were invaluable.

With a project of this size, it is impossible to recall all of those who made it possible and to whom I owe a debt of gratitude. My sincere apologies to anyone I might have inadvertently omitted.

Finally, although this work would not have been possible without the aid of so many, any errors or omissions are my own, and I take full responsibility for them.

CHAPTER 1

Background to a Flashpoint

On 2 August 1990, Iraq invaded Kuwait, sparking the largest armed confrontation in decades as the United States and a Coalition of Western democracies and Arab states demanded that Iraq remove its forces from Kuwait and return to the preinvasion status quo. It was the largest armed conflict to involve the United States since the Vietnam War, and the U.S. Marine Corps was intimately involved with the conflict even before it began.

The 1990–91 Gulf War symbolically marked the end of the Cold War, a period of tense bipolar struggles between symmetrical nuclear opponents. It inaugurated a period of asymmetrical struggles between Islamic and Western civilizations; even the events not directly related to the Gulf War occurred under the umbrella of American conventional military dominance that the war established. The Gulf War also established the context for several significant events of the 1990s and 2000s: the breakup of Communist Bloc Yugoslavia, the terrorist attacks on 11 September 2001, and the liberation of Iraq in 2003. In a similar fashion, the invasion of Kuwait and the subsequent liberation of Kuwait by Coalition forces occurred within the larger framework of Middle Eastern history.

A Brief History of Iraq

Mesopotamia, the region that generally corresponds to present-day Iraq, is often called the "cradle of civilization" because cities sprouted along the twin rivers of the Tigris and Euphrates before they developed anywhere else. Beginning with the Sumerians in the fourth millennium BC, then proceeding through the Assyrians, Babylonians, and Persians, Mesopotamia was the original center of civilization in the ancient Mediterranean world and within these earliest urban centers we find the oldest written law code yet uncovered alongside the roots of four of the world's major religions: Christianity, Judaism, Islam, and Zoroastrianism.[1]

Over time the centers of civilization shifted to both the west and the east, empires arose, and the fertile lands of Mesopotamia became a prize for foreign empires. By the beginning of the Roman Empire, the Tigris and Euphrates region was firmly established as a border region between the Roman Empire and the Parthian Empire (later replaced by the Sassanid Persian Empire). Control of the cities along the Twin Rivers often passed back and forth between these empires, but from 227 AD until 634 AD Mesopotamia was under the control of the Sassanid Empire.

In the seventh century AD, the prophet Muhammad began spreading his new religion, Islam, among the tribes of Arabia. Muhammad founded Islam on the same Abrahamic tradition as Judaism and Christianity, but he was equally influenced by the tribal culture of the nomadic Arabs. By the time of Muhammad's death in 632, the tribes and cities of the Arabian Peninsula were predominantly Islamic. These were impressive gains for a young religion, but Muhammad's last message—"Muslims should fight all men until they say, 'There is no god but God'"—foreshadowed the future militaristic, meteoric growth of Islam.[2]

His successor (the first caliph) Abu Bakr launched the campaigns now labeled the "Arab Conquest" against the Sassanid and Byzantine Empires (the Byzantines were the successors to the Roman Empire in the eastern Mediterranean). Abu Bakr's first two successors, Umar ibn al-Khattab and Uthman ibn Affan, successfully continued these campaigns. The Sassanians were decisively defeated in 637 at the Battle of al-Qadisiyah, opening the Tigris-Euphrates River valley to Islamic control. By the end of Uthman's reign as caliph, Muhammad's movement controlled the Arabian Peninsula, Egypt, the Tigris-Euphrates region all the way to the Armenian highlands, and the coastal lands between Egypt and Anatolia.[3]

Uthman's death in 656 led to the great schism in Islam between the Shia and Sunni. The larger Sunni movement coalesced from those who supported Muawiyah ibn Abi Sufyan, founder of the Umayyad Caliphate, while the Shia sect formed from those who supported Muhammad's cousin and son-in-law, Ali ibn Abi Talib. The Shiites lost both of the civil wars (661 and 680–92) that followed the split. During the second civil war, Ali ibn Abi Talib's son, al-Husayn, and his family were murdered, thus eliminating Muhammad's line. The Shia remained strong among the Persians of Iran and among some Arab tribes of the Tigris-Euphrates region, but the Umayyad Dynasty and the Sunni had secured the caliphate.[4]

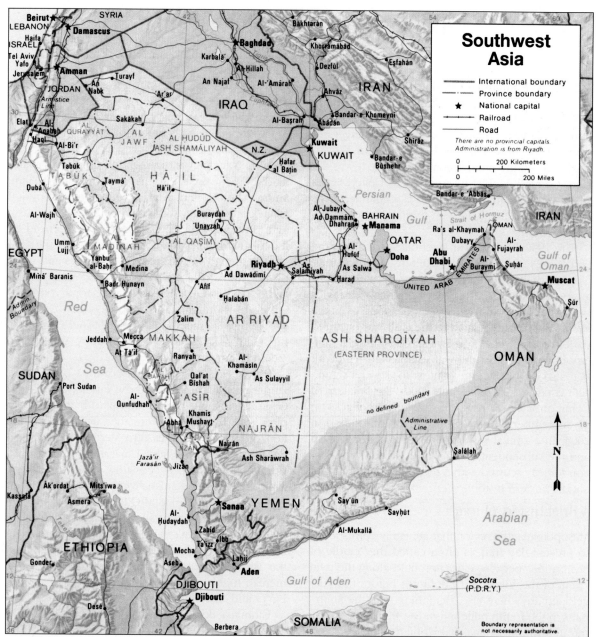

Adapted from a Central Intelligence Agency map by Marine Corps History Division

The Abbasids overthrew the last of Umayyad Dynasty in 750, establishing the Abbasid Caliphate. The Persians aided the Abbasids in their revolt, and the second Abbasid caliph, Abu Ja'far al-Mansur, founded Baghdad in 762, moving the capital of the caliphate from Damascus. The Abbasid Caliphate was a golden age for Baghdad and Iraq, as the region was the center of the Islamic Empire during the height of its scientific and cultural achievements. The Abbasids suffered reversals and setbacks on the periphery of their empire, but it was not until the Mongols sacked Baghdad in 1258 that the Abbasid Caliphate finally ended.[5]

Hulagu Khan, the Mongol leader who decimated Baghdad, formed a pyramid from the skulls of the intellectual and religious leaders of the city. The region's urban culture was effectively destroyed by the following century of rule by the Mongols; henceforth, Iraq would be dominated by its rural tribal culture. In 1509 the Shia Safavids conquered Iraq, beginning a period in which the Shia Persian and Sunni Ottoman empires would struggle for control of the region. Mesopotamia was again a border region caught between competing empires with different religious faiths. The conflict between the two empires exacerbated the differences between the

Reprinted from Mrs. Stuart Menzies, *Sir Stanley Maude and Other Memories* (London: Herbert Jenkins, 1920), p. 48
LtGen Sir Frederick Stanley Maude leads the British Army into Baghdad in March 1917. British influence in Iraq dates from the First World War, when the British drove Turkey, one of the Central Powers, from Iraq.

Shia and Sunni, who suffered or prospered as the pendulum of success swung between the two foes. The Sunni Ottomans gained control of the province in 1638, and Iraq formed three provinces (Mosul, Baghdad, and Basrah) of the Ottoman Empire until 1916. Throughout most of the seventeenth and eighteenth centuries, however, various local rulers dominated the region, and much of it was Ottoman in name only. This period of pseudo-independence encouraged ethnic and religious factionalism that would remain an issue, especially with the Kurds of northern Iraq.

In 1831, floods and plagues enabled the Ottomans to reassert their authority over Iraq, and in 1869 an Ottoman governor, Midhat Pasha, attempted to centralize and reform the government and economy of Iraq. Roads and schools were built, and Iraq began to develop a small core of native intellectuals and nationalists. The majority of these early Iraqi thinkers were Sunni, as the Sunnis enjoyed significant advantages in educational and economic opportunity throughout the Ottoman period.

Like most of the Ottoman Empire at the dawn of the twentieth century, Iraq was ready for change.

The nascent Young Turk movement's reforms had given the subject peoples a taste for independence and some experience in government but had excluded them from power. Turkish reforms were slow and strongly flavored with Turkish nationalism, and the Turks failed to fully stabilize the Iraqi provinces, which remained focused on insular local communities.

World War I

The Ottoman Turks favored the Germans during the opening decade of the twentieth century, and the Germans built rail lines throughout the Ottoman Empire, including lines connecting Baghdad and Basrah in 1902. When the First World War broke out, Ottoman neutrality was not expected to last, and the Turks soon entered the war on the side of Germany and the Ottomans' traditional European foes, the Austro-Hungarian Empire. British forces from India soon invaded southern Iraq, occupying the southern cities in 1915. The war in Iraq was considered a sideshow by the Allies and the Turks, but with the exception of the loss of al-Kut in 1916, the Allies were generally successful there. In 1918, when the war finally ended, the British occupied nearly all of present-day Iraq.

The British gained the support of Iraqi nationalists during the war by promising to end foreign rule over Iraq. The Paris Peace Conference awarded Iraq to the British as a League of Nations mandate, and the Iraqis saw this as a betrayal. Heavy-handed British administration of Iraq worsened the situation, and Iraq rebelled against the British in 1920. In Iraq, this rebellion is called 'Ath Thawra al Iraqiyya al Kubra (the Great Iraqi Revolution), and it has become the watershed event of modern Iraqi history. The British suppressed the revolt using troops from India and the Royal Air Force, but the revolt convinced them to prepare Iraq as soon as possible for self-governance.

The British Empire

Following the revolt, the British created a throne for Iraq (there had never been an Iraqi monarchy) and placed Prince Faisal of the Hashemite family of Mecca on it. Faisal was one of the leaders of the Arab forces that aided the British against the Turks in the war. He had been proclaimed king of Syria in 1920 by Syrian nationalists, but the French were given Syria as a mandate and removed him from power. The British felt that Faisal was strong enough to be king but only with British support.[6]

More important than the establishment of Faisal as king was the establishment of a constitutional monarchy with democratically elected representatives. Iraq would seldom, if ever, hold completely legitimate elections in the twentieth century, but the basic legitimacy of elected government was established. Despite their minority population status, the Sunnis continued to hold the positions of power in Iraq, in large part because of their higher levels of education.

Finally, failing to establish an independent Kurdistan in the face of Turkish opposition, the British added Kurdish areas to Iraq, thereby increasing Iraq's already considerable number of minority communities. This was to have serious consequences for Iraq later in the century as the Kurds revolted against the Iraqi government several times, first in the early 1930s; then throughout the 1960s and 1970s; and yet again in 1991, in the aftermath of the Gulf War.

In 1932, Iraq was declared a sovereign state. A 25-year treaty with Great Britain, which granted the British concessions on oil in exchange for British aid, remained as a "colonial vestige," but the new kingdom entered the League of Nations. Prince Faisal died unexpectedly in 1933 and was replaced by his son, Ghazi, an Arab nationalist. A weak ruler, Ghazi legitimized Iraqi's first military coup in 1936 before dying in a car accident in 1939. He was succeeded by an infant son, but the real power rested in the hands of Amir Abd al-Ilah, the regent and an Iraqi—as opposed to Arab—nationalist.

To facilitate the passage of Lend Lease supplies through Iraq and Iran to Russia, relatively small American logistics units served in Iraq after the United States entered World War II. The U.S. Army produced a guidebook for these servicemen that included Arab words and phrases, as well as pointed out cultural differences and provided instructions on how to avoid committing social blunders.

Reprinted from *Instructions for American Servicemen in Iraq during World War II* (U.S. Army, 1943)

The Baath Party

The Baath (Renaissance) Party is a secular party of Arab nationalists and socialists that first formed in Syria and then spread to Iraq. Essentially a fascist organization devoted to pan-Arabism, the Baath Parties of Syria and Iraq soon split, though they paid occasional lip service to the idea of Baathist unity. In the 1960s and 1970s, the party was popular as it seemed to cross sectarian lines and served as an alternative to the traditional Arab leaders who seemed impotent against Israel. Once in power, the fascist nature of the party became more pronounced, and it quickly became a totalitarian organization devoted to maintaining the dominance of its leaders.

Iraqi State Television

President Saddam Hussein ruled Iraq as a totalitarian dictator from 1979 to 2003. His régime was marked by violent conflict with internal and external enemies; he was finally removed from power by an American-led international Coalition in 2003.

The regent and the prime minister, Nuri as Said, supported Britain, but when Rashid Ali succeeded Nuri in 1940 as prime minister, the situation quickly changed. Rashid Ali was also an Iraqi nationalist, but he was very anti-British and his policies favored Nazi Germany. When the regent opposed him, Rashid Ali led another successful military coup and established an extremely nationalistic government in 1941. The British responded by occupying Iraq, forcing Rashid and his supporters to flee the country. They then reestablished the monarchy, but it was now a tainted institution that Iraqi nationalists rejected following the shame of this second British occupation.[7]

Rise of the Baathists

Like the rest of the Arab world, Iraq reacted forcefully to the 1948 creation of Israel. Thousands of Iraqi soldiers were sent to aid in destroying the fledgling nation, but they were poorly trained and equipped and contributed little to the Arab effort. Vigilante justice against Iraq's Jewish community led the vast majority of that wealthy minority to flee Iraq. Economic suffering, tribal and social changes, and foreign policy miscues all increased Iraqi discontent with the monarchy throughout the 1950s. In 1958, this finally boiled over and the monarchy was overthrown by a military coup inspired by Gamal Abdel Nasser's Arab nationalism movement, which resulted in the deaths of the king, Faisal II; his former regent, Abd al-Ilah; and the prime minister, Nuri as Said.[8]

The coup resulted in Abd al-Karim Qasim coming to power in Iraq. Qasim was unusual in Iraqi politics—he was of mixed Shia-Sunni background, and he had strong ties to Iraqi communists. Qasim was strongly supported by the urban poor of Iraq, but he was forced to balance the nationalists, the communists, and other power groups against each other in order to stay in power. Despite this he suffered several coups and assassination attempts, the most famous being the failed assassination in 1959 conducted by Iraq's future dictator, Saddam Hussein.[9]

Three events during Qasim's regime foreboded ominously for Iraq's future. First, despite their strong initial support, the Kurds revolted against his increasing despotism in 1961. Second, he increased tensions with Iran over the Shatt al-Arab waterway (this is formed by the confluence of the Euphrates and Tigris Rivers and drains to the Persian Gulf). Finally, also in 1961, he claimed Kuwait as part of Iraq, alienating the West and most of Iraq's fellow Arab states.[10]

In 1963, the nationalist Baath Party overthrew Qasim, but the Iraqi branch of the party was small and disorganized. Its leader, Ali Salih as Saadi, held power for less than a year before Abd as Salaam Arif overthrew him and took control. Arif filled his government with supporters of Egypt's charismatic pan-Arabian leader, Gamal Abdel Nasser, and flirted with joining Nasser's United Arab Republic. Arif died in a 1966 helicopter crash, but his brother Abd ar Rahman Arif succeeded him.[11]

There was an attempt to reassert civilian control over the government with the appointment of Abd ar Rahman Bazzaz as prime minister in 1965. Bazzaz worked to curtail the military's influence and negotiate an end to the ongoing Kurdish insurrection, but the military forced him to resign after only a year in office. Rahman Arif continued to try and juggle competing interests to stay in power, but he was overthrown by a military coup in 1968.[12]

The coup was carried out by two army officers, Abd as Razzaq and Ibrahim ad Daud, but they lacked a strong organization and the Baath Party quickly took control. Reorganized in the wake of their earlier failure, the Sunni Arabs from the city of Tikrit, joined by close tribal and family ties, had begun to dominate the party. The Baathists immediately began to purge Iraq of those who might oppose them. The senior Baathist leader was Ahmad Hasan al-Bakr of Tikrit, but he was merely first among equals in the senior leadership of the party. Throughout the 1970s Saddam Hussein gained power and prestige as Bakr's authority waned, and in 1979 Bakr resigned as president of Iraq and Saddam took his place.[13]

Saddam cemented his hold on Iraq with an extraordinarily brazen exhibition of power politics. Just days after Bakr resigned as president, during a televised meeting of the Baathist council, a Shia member publically confessed to being part of a conspiracy with Syria against Iraq and named others involved in the plot. Most of the accused were in the hall during the confession and were immediately arrested, and within days a series of show trials had led to 22 executions and the imprisonment of 33 other accused conspirators.[14]

Under the Baathists, Iraq's problems continued as tensions with Iran increased over the Shatt al-Arab and the Shah's suspicions of Iraq's socialist government. Also, the Kurdish insurrection continued despite more attempts to negotiate or force an end to the fighting. By 1976, however, massive Iraqi offensives and forced relocations had forced the insurrection into a temporary quiescence.[15]

A Brief History of Kuwait

Kuwait was formed from two former Ottoman provinces, al-Jarah and al-Ahmadi, but the future trading city was established in the eighteenth century by the Arab Utbi tribes. In 1752, these tribes selected the al-Sabah family as the emirs of Kuwait. The city of Kuwait became an important trading port, though the city and its surrounding provinces remained technically a part of the Ottoman Empire.[16]

In 1899, the al-Sabah sheikhs accepted status as a British protectorate and remained a de facto territory of the British Empire until 1961. The British fixed the modern boundary between Kuwait and Iraq in 1913, but neither the Ottoman Turks nor the Iraqis ever accepted this boundary. Turkish opposition was a moot point following the Central Powers defeat in 1918, but the boundary remained an ever-present issue between Iraqi and Kuwait throughout the twentieth century.

In 1958, when the Iraqi monarchy was overthrown, Abd al-Karim Qasim rejected the British-drawn boundary, and when Kuwait gained independence from Great Britain in 1961 Iraq attempted to assert its claim over the emirate. Though Kuwait was not invaded, British and Arab troops arrived quickly to defend the small, economically important state. Iraqi attempts to redress the perceived injustice of the British-mandated border continued; in 1973, Iraqi troops briefly occupied a Kuwaiti border post before withdrawing under international pressure.[17]

Kuwait was an extraordinarily prosperous country in the twentieth century because it supported a relatively small population on top of rich oil holdings. The al-Sabah sheikhs increased the health care, education, and living standards of the sheikhdom's population while maintaining the state's relatively conservative monarchy. In addition, they used their funds to support the regional powers they deemed most likely to act in Kuwait's best interests.[18]

A Brief History of U.S. Persian Gulf Policy

Official American involvement in the Middle East was sporadic prior to World War II and primarily limited to the occasional port visits by U.S. naval vessels. Americans were seen by the region's inhabitants as a sort of Englishman with similar interests but less power. During the war itself, the United States used the Middle East primarily as a highway to send supplies to China and Burma to the east and to the Soviet Union to the north. The British campaign to pacify Iraq occurred prior to American entry into the war, and the Americans followed Britain's lead in the region. The only notable event was the Tehran Conference of 1943, the first of the three conferences where President Franklin D. Roosevelt met with Prime Minister Winston Churchill of Great Britain and Premier Joseph Stalin of the Soviet Union.[19]

In the late 1940s and early 1950s, the United States shifted from an oil-exporting to an oil-importing economy as the postwar economic boom drove up demand for petroleum. This economic shift forced American politicians to pay closer attention to the Middle East, where large oil reserves and strong regional ethnic and religious tensions were conspiring to produce a devil's brew of instability. At first, the United States remained content to follow the lead of the region's traditional colonial powers, France and Great Britain, but this reticence came to an end in 1956 when President Dwight D. Eisenhower effectively vetoed the seizure of the Suez Canal by France, Israel, and Great Britain. Following this, Great Britain and France withdrew from the Middle East as major powers and have not attempted any intervention in the region since then without U.S. support and leadership.[20]

The United States found itself increasingly involved in the Mediterranean, and the U.S. Navy's, Sixth Fleet became an increasingly important force, shifting the Mediterranean from a "British" to an "American" sea and establishing a strong American presence on the western shores of the Middle East. Turkey's admission to the North Atlantic Treaty Organization (NATO) further strengthened the western flank, despite the constant Arab-Israeli conflicts, the Lebanese Civil War, and Egypt's political turmoil. At the same time, the British withdrawal from east of the Suez left a power vacuum in that region by 1971. The United States responded to this void with an increase in its own forces in the Indian Ocean and Persian Gulf, but these forces remained relatively small. From 1968–73, U.S. naval vessels spent significantly less time in the Indian Ocean than their Soviet Navy rivals.[21]

During the Cold War, the United States' prime concern in the Middle East was countering the influence of the Soviet Union. The region was generally seen as less important to American interests than Europe or Asia, and direct American involvement was to be avoided if possible. The solution was an alliance, the Central Treaty Organization. Originally comprising Iraq, Iran, Pakistan, Turkey, Great Britain, and the United States, it was never as firm or as formal as NATO. It did conduct some joint military exercises and provided a framework for defense against possible Soviet aggression in the region, however. This organization suffered its first blow in 1959 when Iraq withdrew from the alliance. Much later, Iran left in 1979 following the Iranian Revolution, and the Central Treaty Organization essentially collapsed at that point.[22]

Nixon and the Twin Pillars Policy

When President Richard M. Nixon took office in 1969, American foreign policy was understandably focused on the war in Vietnam. In that contentious period, one area of agreement was the idea that the United States had too many foreign entanglements. This general consensus was crystallized as the Nixon Doctrine in the president's 1970 State of the Union address. Henceforth, defending other nations would not be "exclusively or primarily an American undertaking."[23]

Putting this doctrine into practice meant finding other nations able to act as stabilizing influences in the various regions of the world. In the Middle East, the Nixon administration settled on the Twin Pillars policy, in which the "twin pillars" of Iran and Saudi Arabia would serve as the sources of stability in the region. On the surface, the two nations had a great deal in common. Both were Islamic monarchies with massive oil reserves and a history of friendship with the United States. In reality there were significant tensions between the two. Iran was predominantly Shiite and Persian, while Saudi Arabia was Sunni and Arab. Undeterred, the United States stepped up support for both nations during the 1970s with increased military and civilian aid.

Iran made use of this U.S. support in order to increase its role as a regional power. The Shah of Iran, Muhammad Reza Shah Pahlavi, doubled his arms imports in 1974, and then doubled them again in 1976, thereby threatening Iraq, which attempted to respond in kind. Rather than accepting U.S. hegemony in the region, the Shah appeared determined to become the dominant regional power. Of course, the Shah proved an unstable partner when the 1979 revolution in Iran overthrew him and further entangled the United States in Middle Eastern politics.[24]

In contrast, Saudi Arabia focused its aid package on infrastructure, dramatically increasing the capacity of its roads, ports, and airfields. Though Saudi Arabia spent nearly as much on defense as Iran, the size of its armed forces did not significantly increase. Instead, the United States increased the modernization efforts it had been making with the Saudi military for decades. The overall effect of the Saudi expenditures was to increase the ability of the Saudis to accept foreign aid while preventing Saudi Arabia from becoming a major regional military power. Of course, Saudi Arabia's economic, cultural, and religious importance in the Middle East remained strong.[25]

The Carter Doctrine

When President James E. "Jimmy" Carter Jr. assumed office in 1977, the comparative weaknesses of the United States in the Persian Gulf region had

Official U.S. Marine Corps photo

Gen Paul X. Kelley was appointed the first commander of the Rapid Deployment Joint Task Force (RDJTF) on 4 February 1980. An active proponent of the RDJTF, Gen Kelly was instrumental in its eventual transformation into U.S. Central Command. He became 28th Commandant of the Marine Corps on 1 July 1983.

been emphasized by the 1973 oil embargo and the relatively large Soviet naval deployments in the region. In addition, Israel's military strength was in some doubt following the unexpectedly strong Arab showing in the 1973 Yom Kippur War.[26]

The danger of the Twin Pillars policy became apparent in 1979 when the Shah of Iran was forced to abdicate to revolutionary Islamic forces. In November of that year, those same forces invaded the American embassy compound in Tehran and forced the crisis that set the dominant tone for American foreign policy through the end of the century all over the world, but most especially in the Middle East. Another portentous event in 1979 was the Soviet invasion of Afghanistan. Condemned immediately by the United States, the invasion seemed to pave the way for a Soviet move into the Middle East, especially when considered in tandem with the large presence in the Indian Ocean and Persian Gulf that the Soviet Navy then maintained.

President Carter responded to these events in his 1980 State of the Union address with the Carter Doctrine, which declared that the United States con-

sidered the Middle East vital to its national interests and would respond to any attempts to control the region by military force if necessary. The Carter Doctrine was expanded in 1981 with the Reagan Corollary, which stated the United States could allow no hostile group or nation to control Saudi Arabia.[27]

The Iranian hostage crisis demonstrated quite clearly that, despite the Carter Doctrine, the United States was relatively powerless in the Persian Gulf region. The attempt to rescue the hostages in April 1980 was a spectacular failure. Even before this tragedy, the Carter administration recognized that the United States needed a more credible military response capability in the Middle East, and in March 1980 had established the Rapid Deployment Joint Task Force. This concept was criticized almost immediately as being too weak, too impractical, or as needless interference in Middle Eastern affairs.[28]

Because the Rapid Deployment Joint Task Force was tasked with military intervention in a region devoid of American military bases, significant Marine Corps involvement in its development was inevitable. Many in Congress believed the Marine Corps was already such a force. Moreover, the Department of Defense's concentration on parrying the Soviets had left the Marine Corps struggling to show its utility in a defense of Western Europe. Marine Corps involvement in the Middle East presented the Corps with an opportunity to emphasize its utility in a Cold War context as part of the broader defense of regions that were peripheral yet critical to NATO's defense of Europe, much like the Marine Corps' assumption of a mission to defend Norway in the 1980s.[29]

The Commandant of the Marine Corps at the time, General Robert H. Barrow, felt that the Marine Corps should be at the heart of the Rapid Deployment Force despite the great difficulties involved in fighting in the region. This idea dovetailed with Secretary of Defense Harold Brown's[*] idea for the Maritime Prepositioning Ships program, and the Joint Chiefs of Staff decided that command of the Rapid Deployment Joint Task Force would rotate between the Marine Corps and the Army.[30]

The first commander of the Rapid Deployment Joint Task Force was General Paul X. Kelly, an officer with extensive experience on joint staffs and one of the Marine Corps' rising stars. The organization did not have permanently assigned forces; in-

---

[*]Dr. Harold Brown served as secretary of defense for President Carter from 1977–81.

stead, it was designed to draw on forces earmarked by various commands in the event of a major crisis in the Middle East, especially an invasion by the Soviet Union. The ambiguous notional assignment of forces was typical of joint organizations before the restructuring of the Goldwater-Nichols Department of Defense Reorganization Act in 1986.*

Kelley's task force was responsible for a truly vast area: Afghanistan, Bahrain, Djibouti, Egypt, Ethiopia, Iran, Iraq, Kenya, Kuwait, Oman, Pakistan, the People's Republic of Yemen (South Yemen), Qatar, Saudi Arabia, Somalia, Sudan, United Arab Emirates, and the Yemen Arab Republic (North Yemen). But the notional force structure was "so dependent upon non-existent airlift and sealift capabilities that the RDF [Rapid Deployment Force] was neither rapid, deployable nor a force." Despite the criticism and difficulties, General Kelley saw great value in the Rapid Deployment Force concept: "The unique characteristic of the [Rapid Deployment Joint Task Force] is that, for the first time I can recall, in peacetime we are pulling together the capabilities of all four services into one harmonized fighting machine with a permanent command and control headquarters."[31]

Kelley's conception of the Rapid Deployment Force would anticipate many of the reforms of the Goldwater-Nichols Act and provide the president with flexibility in the use of military force: "As I envision the [Rapid Deployment Joint Task Force], we will present the National Command Authority with a full range of options for any given crisis. Rather than going through the last-minute agony of what forces are available and who will command them, we will have done all the proper planning and force sizing beforehand. The National Command Authority can then rapidly deploy the correct force package before the crisis gets out of hand." In the end, it was obvious that a joint command was really needed for the region, as General Kelley recommended. The Rapid Deployment Joint Task Force was deactivated on 31 December 1982, and the U.S. Central Command was activated on 1 January 1983.[32]

*The Goldwater-Nichols Act of 1986 was the most far-reaching restructuring of the Department of Defense since it was established by the National Security Act of 1947. The act made many changes, but the most wide-ranging included establishing the chairman of the Joint Chiefs of Staff as the president's chief military advisor and streamlining the chain of command from the president through the secretary of defense, to the commanders of the various regional, united combatant commands. One of the act's primary goals was to encourage the services to act in a more "joint" manner.

United States Central Command

The U.S. Central Command was the first large, geographically unified command activated since the Korean War. It grew organically out of the Rapid Deployment Joint Task Force, being established in the same headquarters building on McDill Air Force Base in Tampa, Florida, that Kelley's command had occupied. The same forces were allocated to the new command, although later additional forces were added and all of the new command's forces were modernized throughout the 1980s.[33]

Lieutenant General Robert C. Kingston, USA, was the second commander of the Rapid Deployment Joint Task Force and the first commander in chief of U.S. Central Command. General Kingston's new regional command faced the difficulties that might be expected from a major reorganization of the U.S. military; in particular, neither U.S. European Command nor U.S. Pacific Command were eager to help the new organization made up of zones formerly in their areas of responsibility. It would take years for Central Command to be fully accepted as a joint command; Lieutenant General Kingston's promotion in November 1985 to four-star general was one step in this process. It established that the commander of Central Command would hold the same rank as the commanders of Pacific Command, European Command, Atlantic Command, and Southern Command.[34]

There was an understanding between the Army and the Marine Corps that command of the Rapid Deployment Joint Task Force would alternate between the two services, but the Joint Chiefs of Staff had subsequently decided that none of the joint commands should be officially or unofficially designated for specific services. General Kelley, former commander of the task force, was now Commandant of the Marine Corps, and he was determined that the Corps would not miss this first opportunity for one of its generals to hold a unified command. General Kelley fought for a Marine for the job, and as a result General George B. Crist took command of Central Command in November 1985.[35]

According to General Crist, Central Command headquarters was "covered with [General] Kingston's blood" because the first Central Command commander had to struggle with so many entrenched interest groups to get the command up and running. Despite the struggles, General Kingston successfully established the staff and building for Central Command, but when General Crist took command he felt it was still "a [Rapid Deploy-

Official U.S. Marine Corps photo

Gen George B. Crist was the first Marine appointed to head a unified command: U.S. Central Command. He commanded the Tanker War against Iran in the late 1980s and established the regional relationships and planning foundation that allowed Central Command to successfully intervene in the Gulf War.

ment Joint Task Force] wrapped in a unified command label" that "had never come to grips with the new area responsibilities." It remained focused too narrowly on its Cold War function and was "a retirement home, losing more people through retirement" than through permanent change of station orders.[36]

General Crist felt that the new command had to "have stature and credibility, and get a unified strategy, for the whole region, both peace and war." This meant establishing relationships with each of the nations within its area of responsibility despite the Department of State's suspicion of the new command. To accomplish this, Crist sent his staff on many trips to the Middle East, working directly with those in charge, because he knew that in the Middle East "rank or position meant absolutely nothing: it's man-to-man, a personal thing. If they like you, you can do almost anything. If they don't like you, forget it: you're not going anywhere." The strong relationships that Central Command formed in the Middle East, especially in Saudi Arabia, were very valuable during the crisis to come.[37]

The biannual Gallant Eagle exercises were begun

by Kelley's task force but continued by Central Command. Conducted in the deserts of California and Nevada, they provided an excellent rehearsal for the upcoming crisis in the Iraqi desert. Moreover, the Bright Star exercises conducted in Egypt since 1981 provided valuable experience in cooperating with Arab governments in the Middle East.[38]

The Iran-Iraq War

Shortly after consolidating his power in Iraq, Saddam Hussein ordered an invasion of Iran. He intended to take advantage of perceived Iranian instability following the 1979 revolution and the political isolation resulting from Iran's concurrent seizure of the American embassy in November of that year. On 22 September 1980, Iraq launched a series of air strikes against Iran, all self-consciously modeled on Israel's successful air strikes against the Egyptian Air Force at the start of the 1967 Six-Day War. Iraq's air force executed the attacks ineptly, however, and as a result the attacks were a failure. The very next day, the Iranian Air Force was able to launch strikes against Iraq and its invading columns.[39]

On 23 September 1980, Iraq invaded Iran, launching an offensive to take Khuzestan, push the border to the Zagros Mountains, and secure the Shatt al-Arab. The Iraqi ground offensive was not much more effective than the previous day's air strike, however. The Iraqis advanced very slowly, and only one of the targeted cities was captured—Khorramshahr on 24 October. Around the other cities the slow speed of the Iraqi attack allowed the Iranians to regroup and reinforce so that the Iraqi attack ground to halt. Attempting to put a good face on its failed offensive, Iraq offered terms to Iran, but the offer was ignored.[40]

In January 1981, the Iranians began their counterattack. One of the first battles was an armored clash between the Iranian 16th Armored Division* and the Iraqi *6th Armored Division* and the *10th Republican Guard Armored Brigade* at Susangerd. The Iranians employed approximately 300 M60A1 Patton and FV4201 Chieftain Mark V main battle tanks and lost approximately 200. The Iraqis, with

*The Marine Corps History Division's accepted style is to italicize enemy military formations within the text in order to aid the reader in differentiating them from American and allied units. Although Iran was the enemy during the Tanker War, which was a subconflict of the Iran-Iraq War, italicizing Iranian units in this chapter and then italicizing Iraqi units in subsequent chapters is needlessly confusing. Therefore, Iraqi units are italicized throughout this work, and Iranian units are not.

From Marine Corps Intelligence Activity, *Cultural Intelligence for Military Operations: Iran* (CD-ROM)
Iranian armor suffered badly in the initial battles of the Iran-Iraq War.

approximately 350 T-72, T-62, and T-55 tanks, lost around 100, despite the advantages of hull-down positions surrounding the Iranians on three sides along a single, narrow road.[41]

With this initial defeat, Iran's counterattacks—utilizing mass attacks by newly recruited but poorly trained and equipped religious volunteers backed by the regular Iranian army—were increasingly successful throughout 1981 and into 1982. In May 1982, Iran regained Khorramshahr and had essentially regained all of the territory lost to Iraq in the fall of 1980. Iran proceeded to invade Iraq in turn, pushing into southern Iraq and threatening the southern town of Basrah. During the first battle of Basrah in July 1982, Iraq finally stopped the Iranian offensive through excellent combat engineering and massive firepower.[42]

Iran's military successes shook the Iraqi military and the political leadership; this led directly to a series of military reforms, some immediate, others long term. In the aftermath of this first Iranian offensive, the Iraqis quickly realized that the only effective responses they possessed to Iran's mass attacks were massive fortifications and overwhelming firepower. As a result, Iraqi engineers became very good at building extensive fixed fortifications. These took the form of massive minefields and extensive barbed wire entanglements before high earthen berms designed as fighting positions. These positions were backed up by massive concentrations of artillery and extensive roads so that reinforcements and supplies could be quickly and easily shifted along the front. The Iraqis also began to employ larger and larger amounts of chemical weapons against Iranian attacks.[43]

The linear nature of these defenses also made it easier to control the Iraqi military, whose junior leaders remained startlingly incompetent. Moreover, defending Iraq itself was better supported by the troops than invading Iran, and Iraqi élan increased substantially, even among those troops drafted from the majority Shia population. With its own regular army greatly depleted, thus forced to rely increasingly on mass attacks alone rather than the combination of mass attacks backed by regular army forces with which it had initially been successful, Iran was unable to break through these tougher Iraqi defenses. Iraq in turn could still make no headway against the Iranians, resulting in a bloody stalemate on the ground from 1982 until 1986.[44]

The Iranian threat forced Saddam to reform military leadership as well. Like most totalitarian regimes, military advancement in Iraq had been predicated more on loyalty to Saddam Hussein and the Baath Party than on professional competence. Iraqi failures in the initial invasion of Iran highlighted the weaknesses involved and posed a threat to Saddam's hold on power in Iraq. Saddam began

Defense Imagery DN-SC-87-06413

The USS Stark *(FFG 31) listing to port after being struck by an Iraqi-launched Exocet missile during the Iran-Iraq War.*

the reforms by dismissing or executing 200–300 officers who had failed in various ways during the early years of the war while promoting those who did well. Former officers dismissed during the political purges were brought back, and the *Republican Guard*—the elite troops who reported directly to Saddam—was opened to new members based on ability rather than political loyalty. Finally, Saddam began promoting or leaving successful officers in place, rather than rotating them to prevent their building blocs of support. One officer who benefited from these policies was Salah Aboud Mahmoud, commander of the Iraqi *III Corps* and the Marines' primary opponent in the Gulf War.[45]

Like the ground war, the air war was also mired in stalemate. The Iraqi Air Force, including their numerous helicopters, did not perform well supporting the ground forces. In addition, Iraqi fighters did not aggressively engage Iranian aircraft and thus failed to achieve air superiority. In the early days of the conflict, the Iraqis conducted numerous air strikes against various strategic targets with little effect, dropping few bombs with great inaccuracy. Iraq's own air defenses were just as inadequate. On 7 June 1981, the Israeli Air Force destroyed the Iraqi nuclear reactor at Osirak, and Iraqi air defenses inflicted no losses on the Israeli aircraft. Iranian aircraft found it nearly as easy to make their own strikes against Iraqi targets, though the damage from those strikes was far less.[46]

The Iranian Air Force performed somewhat better, in part because Iraqi targets were significantly closer to their air bases, but they were handicapped by the American arms embargo, which left them unable to get spare parts or proper technicians to repair their American-built aircraft. The Iraqis attempted to end the standstill by attacks against Iranian population centers in what was called the "War of the Cities," but again the distance to Tehran blocked the Iraqi effort as it was beyond the range of the Iraqi SS-1/R-17 Scud-B surface-to-surface missiles.[47]

Iraq responded to its aerial impotence in three different ways. It hired the French to develop the Kari* integrated air defense command and control system, a system which came on line in 1986. The Iraqis also attempted to acquire longer range surface-to-surface missiles, but were unable to purchase these and were forced to begin to develop a long-range missile themselves by altering the Scuds they already possessed. Finally, like the Iranians, they shifted the attacks to oil production and transportation facilities.[48]

Like most Iraqi bombing efforts, attacks on Iranian refineries and pipelines were ineffective. Iraq also attempted to effectively blockade Iran's oil ports by firing on tankers entering or exiting these ports with Aérospatiale AM38 and AM39 Exocet

---

*Kari is not an acronym; the system was named by spelling the French word for Iraq, "Irak," backward.

anti-ship missiles. The Exocet proved ineffective at destroying the massive tankers, and Iraq's aircraft lacked the range to cover all of Iran's ports. Iraq's target identification methods were also poor, culminating in the unintentional launch of two Exocet missiles against the USS *Stark* (FFG 31) in May 1987. In the attack, 37 sailors died and 21 more were wounded, but the *Stark* did not sink. Iraq apologized for the incident, and Saddam took it as a sign of weakness when the United States responded with only a diplomatic note. Regardless, Iraq's attempts to close Iranian ports through airpower decreased.[49]

In February 1986, the Iranians made another attempt to break the deadlock, launching an amphibious assault across the Shatt al-Arab onto the al-Faw Peninsula. This amphibious assault managed to flank the Basrah defenses, and the Iraqis responded with increasing desperate counterattacks, including chemical weapons. The Iranian advance was stopped, but the Iraqi counterattacks failed to destroy the al-Faw salient. The Iranians launched their last serious offensive, the second battle of Basrah, in January 1987. This was a massive battle, with a combined total of at least a quarter of a million men contending for the small river city. The battle continued through March, with Iranian assaults and Iraqi counterattacks all failing, though the Iranians managed to get through five of the six Iraqi defensive lines. The end of this massive battle represented the end of Iran's offensive capabilities on the ground.[50]

With Iran's offensive capabilities depleted, the Iraqis planned a series of large, yet limited offensives designed to force the Iranians to accept peace terms. In April 1988, the Iraqis launched their first offensive since 1980 to drive the Iranians off the al-Faw Peninsula. In addition to the *Republican Guard* and the *VII Corps*, the Iraqi generals employed the *26th Naval Infantry Brigade* in an amphibious flanking attack. The Iraqis secured the peninsula in less than 48 hours of intense fighting following a massive bombardment. Beginning in May 1988, the Iraqis launched a series of four offensives. Each assault was carefully planned and meticulously rehearsed, and the attacks were preceded by massive artillery bombardments, including copious use of chemical weapons. Another significant factor was that the Iraqis outnumbered the Iranians by as much as 10 to 1 at the location of each attack. These offensives were very successful; Iraq destroyed much of Iran's remaining combat power in the Iranian province of

As the Iran-Iraq War dragged on, the Iranian Revolutionary Guard Corps (IRGC) became the predominant military force in Iran. The IRGC was formed from the urban guerrillas who unseated the Shah in 1979. The IRGC recruited and trained the Basij volunteers who conducted the human wave frontal attacks on Iraqi positions.

From Marine Corps Intelligence Activity, *Cultural Intelligence for Military Operations: Iran* (CD-ROM)

Khuzestan along Iraq's southeastern border, but it did not push to take large swaths of Iranian territory.[51]

Iraq's ground offensives in 1988 were matched by a renewal of the so-called War of the Cities, utilizing Scud surface-to-surface missiles the Iraqis had reengineered in order to dramatically increase their range. Over the next several months, Iraq launched over 200 missiles against a variety of civilian targets in Iran, bringing the Iran-Iraq War home to parts of Iran that had not previously experienced the war directly. Iran's response was weak because it now lacked the number of missiles required to retaliate fully against Iraq.[52]

The Tanker War

As noted earlier, the Iraqis responded to the stalemate of the early 1980s by striking at Iran's oil industry through air strikes on oil production facilities and ships. These attacks were not effective, but Iran retaliated against shipping heading for Iraqi ports

with its own relatively ineffective attacks. As the stalemate lengthened, the intensity of the war over each nation's oil lifeline increased, although neither state could effectively strike at the other. Iraq's air force lacked the capability to effectively strike the distant Iranian targets, yet much of Iraq's oil flowed through pipelines out of Iran's reach or passed through nonbelligerent Kuwait and sailed through the Persian Gulf in neutral tankers. Kuwait and other Gulf states provided extensive financial support to Iraq's war effort and provided neutral ports for war material bound for Iraq.[53]

Throughout 1986 Iranian attacks on Kuwaiti vessels increased, and the Iranians took the al-Faw Peninsula. The Kuwaitis responded in December 1986 by asking the United States if some Kuwaiti tankers could be reflagged as American vessels and escorted safely through the Persian Gulf by the U.S. Navy. In February 1987 the Iranians installed HY-2 Hai Ying "Silkworm" antiship missiles along the Strait of Hormuz, and in March President Ronald W. Rea-

Reprinted from Edward J. Marolda and Robert J. Schneller Jr., *Shield and Sword: The United States Navy and the Persian Gulf War* (Washington, DC: Naval Historical Center, Department of the Navy, 1998), p. 34

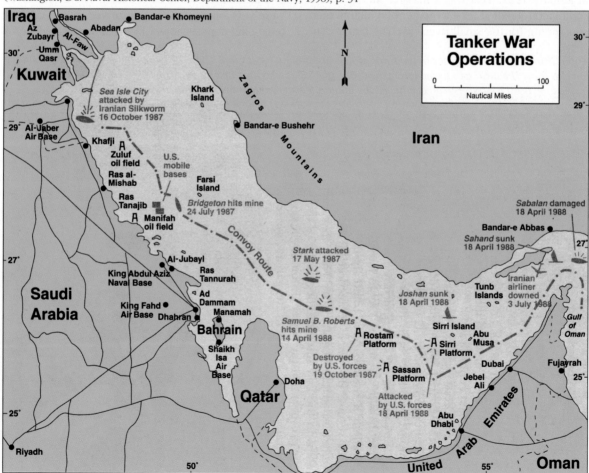

Photo by PO3 Henry Cleveland, USN. Defense Imagery DN-SC-87-12584
Naval contact mines aboard the captured Iranian minelayer, Iran Ajr. *Iran used mines extensively in the Iran-Iraq War. Iraq employed the same tactic during the Gulf War.*

gan decided to go forward with the reflagging operation. However, this was not publically announced until May, soon after the Iraqi attack on the USS *Stark.*[54]

In July 1987, the United States began the reflagging operation, which was designated Operation Earnest Will and later known as the Tanker War; it had an inauspicious start with one of the reflagged tankers, the *Bridgetown,* hitting an Iranian mine. The United States responded by rushing military forces to the theater. The threat to neutral shipping in the Persian Gulf was quite varied; it came from Iraqi aircraft, Iranian aircraft, Iranian mines, Iranian motor boats, Iranian surface-to-surface missiles, and Iranian naval vessels. The United States countered these diverse threats with an equally diverse combination of forces, including naval surface action groups, contingency Marine air-ground task forces, and special operations forces. In August, these forces were designated Joint Task Force Middle East under Rear Admiral Dennis M. Brooks, USN, under General Crist's U.S. Central Command. Operation Earnest Will would be Central Command's first combat operation, and the first combat operation

run by a theater combatant command under a Marine commander in chief.[55]

The first Marine unit to deploy for Operation Earnest Will was Detachment 2 from the 24th Marine Amphibious Unit on board the USS *Guadalcanal* (LPH 7); the detachment consisted of a composite helicopter squadron, a force reconnaissance platoon, and supporting attachments, as well as an infantry company that was off-loaded on Diego Garcia before deploying to the Gulf. Detachment 2 was replaced in November 1987 by Contingency Marine Air-Ground Task Force 1-88 on board the USS *Okinawa* (LPH 3); this task force comprised a composite helicopter squadron and an infantry company with supporting attachments. Contingency Marine Air-Ground Task Force 1-88 was in turn replaced in February 1988 by Contingency Marine Air-Ground Task Force 2-88 from the USS *Trenton* (LPD 14). It consisted of a composite helicopter squadron and an infantry company—Company B, 1st Battalion, 2d Marines—the same company left in Diego Garcia by Detachment 2 the previous year. Contingency Marine Air-Ground Task Force 2-88 was relieved by Contingency Marine Air-Ground Task Force 3-88 in June 1988.[56]

In order to better protect the northern sea lanes near Farsi Island, two barges (the *Hercules* and *Wimbrown VII*) were leased and used as semimobile bases from which special operations helicopters and patrol boats could counter the Iranian small craft threatening shipping and oil platforms in the northern Persian Gulf. Each of these bases embarked a small Marine security force from the rotating Marine air-ground task forces, in addition to U.S. Army and U.S. Navy special operations forces. The barges and their patrol craft were soon successful. On 21 September, Marines provided cover and support as U.S. special operations forces captured the Iranian vessel *Iran Ajr* engaged in clandestine mining in the Gulf. And on 8 October, the Marines provided the same support and cover as U.S. forces engaged four Iranian speedboats near Farsi Island.[57]

Operation Earnest Will continued throughout 1988 with U.S. Navy vessels escorting tanker convoys through the Gulf as other forces secured the passage from Iranian or Iraqi mines, air strikes, and missiles. For the Marines, the routine involved long days standing watch on the barges or the various Navy amphibious vessels on which they were deployed; Marine helicopter crews also flew patrols, transferred supplies, and escorted convoys while conducting visual searches for mines. Some 127 escort missions were completed during the operation,

Defense Imagery DN-ST-89-01414

An aerial view of the Dutch heavy lift ship Mighty Servant II *transporting the guided missile frigate USS* Samuel B. Roberts *(FFG 58). The frigate was damaged when it struck an Iranian mine while on patrol in the Persian Gulf.*

Photo by Cpl John Hyp. Defense Imagery DM-SN-93-00987

The main building of the Iranian Sassan oil platform burns after being hit by a BGM-71 tube-launched, optically tracked, wire-guided (TOW) missile fired from a Marine AH-1 Cobra helicopter as part of Operation Praying Mantis.

securing the sea lanes through the Persian Gulf for all the nonbelligerents along its coast during the vicious regional conflict. Despite the routine, the danger was real: on 12 February 1988, the Iraqis again mistakenly attacked a U.S. vessel, the USS *Chandler* (DDG 996), but this time the attack missed.[58]

On 14 April 1988, the frigate USS *Samuel B. Roberts* (FFG 58) found itself amidst several Iranian mines off the Qatar Peninsula. While attempting to avoid these mines, the ship struck an unobserved mine and suffered extensive damage below the waterline; 10 sailors were wounded. Over the next 10 days, eight more Iranian mines were discovered, and President Reagan ordered General Crist to retaliate. Two Iranian oil platforms, Sassan and Sirri, were to be destroyed, and an Iranian naval vessel was targeted. The retaliation strikes were named Operation Praying Mantis.

On 18 April 1988, Operation Praying Mantis began with U.S. Navy destroyers opening fire on the Sassan platform after repeated warnings to the Iranian crew to evacuate. The Iranians returned fire ineffectively but were suppressed, and they fled the platform. Marines of Company B, 1st Battalion, 2d Marines, and force reconnaissance boarded and secured the platform. After searching the platform, the Marines evacuated, and the platform was destroyed by explosive charges. Other U.S. Navy vessels bombarded and destroyed the Sirri oil platform.[59]

As the Iranian oil platforms burned, the U.S. Navy began its largest surface warfare action since World War II. The Iranian frigates *Sabalan* and *Sahand* stayed away from the battle at first, but Iranian speedboats attacked several neutral ships traversing the Gulf. U.S. Navy aircraft responded, sinking one speedboat and damaging several others. The Iranian Combattante II fast-attack ship *Joshan* unsuccessfully attacked U.S. naval vessels with a guided missile and was itself sunk in response. The Iranian frigate *Sahand* sortied out soon after and fired on U.S. Navy aircraft. Grumman A-6E Intruders and the destroyer USS *Joseph Strauss* (DDG 16) returned fire. The *Sahand* was stopped dead in the water and then sunk by an explosion when her magazines blew. Her sister ship, *Sabalan*, sailed out into the Strait of Hormuz and engaged American aircraft as well. A-6 Intruders from the USS *Enterprise* (CVN 65) bombed the *Sabalan*, which had a reputation for targeting the crew quarters of neutral merchantmen with concentrated machine-gun fire, leaving the Iranian frigate dead in the water and clearly taking on water. Iranian tugboats were allowed to tow her back to port.[60]

Operation Praying Mantis was not without cost for the United States, however. A Bell AH-1T Sea Cobra from Marine Light Attack Helicopter Squadron 167, flown by Captain Stephen C. Leslie and Captain Kenneth W. Hill, crashed during the afternoon while avoiding Iranian antiaircraft defenses. Both pilots perished in the crash and were awarded the Distinguished Flying Cross posthumously. Despite this loss, Operation Praying Mantis was a success, its impact magnified by the simultaneous successful Iraqi land offensive on the al-Faw Peninsula. As described above, Iraqi offensives continued through the spring and into the summer, as did the War of the Cities. From the Iranian perspective, the Iraqi offensives and the American naval operations appeared coordinated.[61]

http://www.imam-khomeini.com

Ayatollah Khomeini was the Supreme Leader of Iran from the 1979 revolution until his death in 1989. Upon accepting the end of the Iran-Iraq War, he said, "We must choose one of two alternatives—either martyrdom or victory, which we both regard as victory. . . . Happy are the disabled, the prisoners of war and those missing in action and the great families of the martyrs. And how unhappy I am because I have survived and have drunk the poisonous chalice of accepting the resolution, and feel ashamed in front of the greatness and sacrifices of this great nation."

Operation Earnest Will's closing act was a tragedy, and the final nudge toward peace that the Iran-Iraq War needed. On 3 July 1988, the cruiser USS *Vincennes* (CG 49) shot down Iran Air Flight 655, a civilian Airbus A300B2 passenger aircraft. All 290 passengers on board the flight were killed. The crew of the *Vincennes* mistakenly believed that they were firing on an Iranian Grumman F-14 Tomcat. Despite U.S. assurances that the attack on the civilian airliner was a tragic error, the Iranian government appears to have believed it was intentional, part of a pattern that included successful Iraqi land offensives, the increased intensity of the War of the Cities, and the destruction of much of the Iranian navy in Operation Praying Mantis. On 18 July 1988, the Iranians accepted a United Nations cease-fire resolution, ending the Iran-Iraq War and the Tanker War.[62]

Iraq ended the Iran-Iraq War in a seemingly strong position. Iran had been defeated after eight grueling years, and the Iraqi military was considered a powerful regional threat. Under Saddam Hussein's leadership, the Iraqis looked forward to increased leadership within the Arab and Islamic worlds as well as to economic growth. Iraq's considerable foreign debt and hostility toward the Western powers as well as Saddam's ambitions and paranoia now set the stage for the next large Persian Gulf conflict.[63]

• CHAPTER 2 •

Kuwait Invaded

The Decision to Invade Kuwait

The image of strength and influence that Iraq projected after the Iran-Iraq War masked a hollow reality. Perceived as the victor of the conflict, Iraq nonetheless faced a battered economy, a war-weary populace expecting to experience the benefits and rewards of peace, and a massive amount of foreign debt. The Saddam regime responded to these difficulties by retaining its massive conscript army (thereby staving off a surge in unemployment), planning further improvements to the nation's infrastructure, and attempting to increase oil production.[1]

During the Iran-Iraq War, Saudi Arabia, Kuwait, and the Gulf states supported Iraq politically and financially against Iran, primarily with loans. Iran was a traditional foe of the Arab states, and the fundamentalist revolution of the ayatollahs against the Shah threatened these monarchical Arab states. When the war ended, Saudi Arabia forgave most of the loans and signed a nonaggression pact with Iraq in March 1989, but the Kuwaitis were unwilling to forgive their loans without first coming to a permanent agreement with Iraq about border claims.[2]

Yet, the immediate cause of Iraq's financial crisis in 1990 was not the aftermath of the Iran-Iraq War, but a plunge in the price of oil. Saddam counted on oil to remain at $21 a barrel, the price in January 1990, but within a few months the price dropped to $11 a barrel. This drop in oil prices was an economic disaster for Iraq, and the cause of the drop was at least partly the unwillingness of Kuwait and the United Arab Emirates to stick to their assigned Organization of the Petroleum Exporting Countries (OPEC) quotas. At a meeting held in May 1990, in front of the emir of Kuwait, Saddam described this as a "war against Iraq."[3]

Iraq's continuing quest to build viable weapons of mass destruction was also coming under increased international scrutiny, and several events indicated the program's progress was not as secret as the Iraqis might have hoped. In March 1990, Canadian weapons designer Gerald V. Bull was assassinated, an event seemingly out of the pages of a bad espionage thriller. Bull was designing an extreme long-range, multistage artillery piece for the Iraqis, and the Iraqis believed he had been killed by the Israelis. A conspiracy was perceived when

parts for his weapon en route to Iraq were seized by the British. The Iraqis believed a repeat of the Israeli strike on Osirak was probable, and Iraq threatened to use chemical weapons against Israel in the event of such an attack.[4]

Further destabilizing the Middle East was the collapse of the Soviet Bloc. The fall of the Berlin Wall in November 1989 highlighted the Soviet Union's decreasing prestige and power. Conflict in the Middle East had been moderated by the larger Cold War conflict—as the various factions played the United States and the Soviet Union against each other, they were in turn held back from aggressive actions that might lead to a more general conflict. But the increasingly obvious weakness of the Soviets following their retreat from Afghanistan, the uprisings in eastern Europe, and the toppling of the wall convinced Soviet clients such as Saddam that they could no longer be trusted to counterbalance the Americans and the Israelis.[5]

Saddam's outsized view of the role in history that he and Iraq were to play is well established in records captured after the 2003 invasion. He imagined Iraq as the leader of a grand Arabic nation that would grow to rival, and eventually conquer, the various states that in his view oppressed the Arab peoples. As Kevin M. Woods noted in *The Mother of All Battles*, "In Saddam's view, unification of the Arab peoples, followed by the destruction of Israel and the expulsion of the 'colonial' powers from Arab lands was the predestined course of development for any Arab superpower of the future." This narrative of historical destiny was the bedrock of Saddam's political decisions, modified only by his own belief that he was the Arab leader destined to bring this to fruition.[6]

Saddam's view of Iraq's central role in history led directly to the other cornerstone of his historical narrative: a conspiracy between the United States and Israel to keep the Arab states generally weak and divided, and to destroy Iraq specifically. The Iran-Contra scandal in the United States, Kuwait's decision to overproduce oil, Israel's attack on Osirak, and the mysterious murder of Gerald Bull all added to his belief that the United States was determined to whittle away Iraq's power and influence. American concerns over Iraqi human rights abuses were "allegations that are designed solely for one aim which is to defame Iraq and dilute the efficacy of our victory." The United States had taken over the role of colonial oppressor that was previously held by the Ottomans and then the British; consequently, Saddam believed American meddling was at the root of all of Iraq's failures and tribulations.[7]

Saddam Hussein was prepared for a confrontation with the United States prior to the invasion of Kuwait, as evidenced by his comments to Palestinian leader Yasser Arafat in April 1990:

> We are ready for it. We will fight America, and, with God's will, we will defeat it and kick it out of the whole region. Because it is not about the fight itself; we know that America has a larger air force than us . . . has more rockets than us, but I think that when the Arab people see real action of war, when it is real and not only talk, they will fight America everywhere. So we have to get ready to fight America; we are ready to fight when they do; when they strike, we strike.[8]

Saddam's speech to Arafat may have been primarily political theater, but it also illustrates how a belief in an American conspiracy against Iraq was central to Saddam's worldview. Moreover, it shows how Saddam intended to resist this conspiracy as the means to unify the Arabs under his own leadership. In keeping with his background, Saddam intended to be ruthless: "When it comes to the region of the Middle East, we want to know where each American individual is, even those who come to do business. . . . This is the battle, so let us resist, and when we resist, let us be beasts."[9]

In the same meeting Saddam expressed a desire to use suicide bomb tactics against the United States:

> We mean all the things we say. Perhaps we cannot reach Washington, but we can send a strapped person [a suicide bomber] to Washington. Our rockets cannot reach Washington, but I swear to God that if it could reach Washington, we would hit Washington. . . . We can send a lot of people. Move them. Move a strapped [person] on to Washington and retaliate just [like] the old days. This is the thing. [A man] strapped with a bomb and throws himself on Bush's car. . . . Let us prepare ourselves on this level.[10]

Belligerent phrases aside, Iraq's president was convinced the United States would not fight, in part

U.S. Ambassador April C. Glaspie and Iraqi President Saddam Hussein meet on 25 July 1990. This meeting was intended by Saddam to pave the way diplomatically for the Iraqi occupation of Kuwait.

Reprinted from Kevin M. Woods, *The Mother of All Battles*, p. 49

because of the muted response to the Iraqi Exocet missile attack on the USS *Stark* in 1987 but also due to the American withdrawal from Lebanon following the Beirut bombing. Moreover, even if the United States desired military confrontation, the Soviet Union would intervene to prevent it, despite its reduced global influence.

If an attack did occur, Saddam was reportedly convinced that his massive military could inflict sufficient losses on the Americans to force them to abandon the struggle. He considered the 1975 withdrawal from Vietnam indicative of America's lack of resolve. The United States suffered over 58,000 dead in the Vietnam War; in comparison Iraq had lost 51,000 in a single battle with the Iranians on the al-Faw Peninsula in 1986. He believed then, as he stated after the war, "America is not in the prime of youth. America is in the last stage of elderliness and the beginning of the first stage of old age."[11]

Iraq had survived the long, eight-year slaughter of the "Khadisya Saddam," as the Iraqis termed the Iran-Iraq War, and Saddam believed that the conflict over Kuwait, if it came to blows, would follow a similar pattern. Airpower would be relatively ineffective; the main conflict would be a set piece battle as American forces impotently tried to breach the defenses built along the Kuwaiti-Saudi border. American losses would be severe; the American people would demand an end to the bloodshed; and the American government would then negotiate a peace. In the aftermath Iraq would become the undisputed regional power, while American and Western influence in the Middle East would suffer a near fatal blow.[12]

Convinced that the United States and Israel were engaged in a conspiracy against Iraq, and that they were using Kuwait as one of their tools in this conspiracy, Saddam had apparently decided by July 1990 to invade and annex Kuwait. While military preparations for the invasion were underway, Saddam laid the diplomatic groundwork as well.

On 25 July 1990, Saddam unexpectedly met with April C. Glaspie, the U.S. ambassador to Iraq. Though Glaspie had been ambassador for two years, this was the first time Saddam had personally met with her; the meeting was arranged quickly and obviously stage managed (at one point, Saddam's interpreters burst into tears as Saddam described Iraq's poor financial state). Saddam repeated his claims that Kuwait was waging economic war against Iraq, and implied that the United States was behind this, but promised that nothing would occur until after a meeting with Kuwait arranged by Egyptian leader Hosni Mubarak.[13]

The promised meeting with Kuwait occurred on 31 July 1990 in Jeddah, Saudi Arabia. Iraq's demands were extreme: "$2.4 billion in compensation for the disputed Ramalia [Rumaylah] oil field; $12 billion for Kuwait's role in depressing oil prices in general; forgiveness of Iraq's $10 billion war debt; and a long-term lease on Bubiyan Island." When the Kuwaitis refused these demands, the Iraqi response was ominous. Izzat Ibrahim al-Duri, Iraq's representative, told Kuwait's Crown Prince Sheikh Saad al-Abdullah as Salim that "you are driving me to kill you."[14]

The Plan to Invade Kuwait

The Iraqi military in the summer of 1990 appeared large and powerful. It boasted roughly 1 million troops; 5,000-plus main battle tanks; 3,500 or more artillery tubes; an estimated 6,000 armored personnel carriers; 600 or so surface-to-air missile launchers; some 500 aircraft; 500 helicopters; and 44 naval vessels. As the apparent victor of the eight-year-long Iran-Iraq War, many observers assumed that the Iraqi Army was battle tested and experienced, an impression the Saddam regime worked to maintain. The war forced the regime to promote officers more often for military competence than political loyalty, and there was a corresponding increase in professionalism and effectiveness. In fact, however, the Iraqi military was exhausted, its morale was questionable, and its training insufficient. The invasion of Kuwait would highlight the strengths and the weaknesses of the Iraqi military to the astute observer.[15]

Saddam Hussein continued to view the regular Iraqi Army with suspicion, so the *Republican Guard* had received the lion's share of the training and equipment. The *Republican Guard* was thus entrusted with the invasion of Kuwait, and planning was limited to its highest officers. Senior regular army officers were not even informed of the offensive until mere hours before it was launched. Throughout July 1990, the Iraqi Directorate of General Military Intelligence provided the *Republican Guard* commanders with reports on Kuwait, its armed forces, and its political leadership. The same reports indicated that Kuwait was likely to look for international support against an invasion and that the United States would help Kuwait.[16]

In mid-July, the *Republican Guard* forces chosen for the invasion began moving south in preparation for the assault. The units' officers were informed of the upcoming mission at this time, although regular military commanders continued to be kept in the dark.[17]

Reprinted from Kevin M. Woods, *The Mother of All Battles,* p. 68
*In July 1990, the Iraqi Air Force conducted several recon-
naissance flights over Kuwait. In this photograph, military
objectives in Kuwait City are noted.*

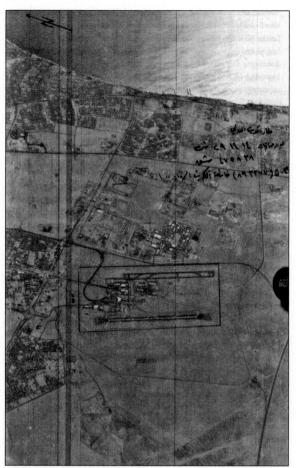

Reprinted from Kevin M. Woods, *The Mother of All Battles*, p. 85
*This Iraqi aerial reconnaissance photograph from July
1990 clearly shows Kuwait International Airport, the
major roads leading to and from it, and the shore south
of Kuwait City. The airport was a major Iraqi objective.*

Despite the Iraqi security precautions, its preparations were not unnoticed. As early as 21 July,
American intelligence began to detect signs of the
impending Iraqi attack on Kuwait. As the days
passed, American staff officers at U.S. Central Command were astounded to see Iraq virtually mirroring
the moves predicted in a training exercise, Internal
Look 90. That exercise tested Central Command's
Operations Plan 1002-90, the plan to defend the
Arabian Peninsula from an Iraqi attack.[18]

On 31 July, the *Republican Guard* division and
brigade commanders were informed that 2 August
would be the date of the attack. The Iraqi plan for
the invasion of Kuwait called for the *Republican
Guard* to invade in four columns, one from the
west and three from the north. Kuwait City and the
various civilian and military airports were the initial
targets, followed by a sweep to the southern coast.
Large helicopterborne commando raids would secure the Mutla Ridge choke point ahead of the advance and a raid on the palace would secure the
Kuwaiti royal family.[19]

Brigadier General Ra'ad Hamdani, commanding
general of the *17th Armored Brigade* of the *Republican Guard's Hammurabi Armored Division*, later
said that "speed was the most important factor to
achieving surprise and surprise was the most important factor in achieving mission success." The
Republican Guard planned to seize needed food
and supplies en route in order to achieve the required speed. There was also a desire to keep
Kuwaiti casualties, especially civilians, to a minimum, and so in a departure from the Iraqi military's
usual style, the invasion of Iraq was conducted
without artillery support. The lack of artillery in
Iraq's military buildup of late July was noted by
American intelligence and introduced some doubt
about Iraqi intentions.[20]

The Iraqi Air Force conducted several reconnaissance missions over Kuwait in late July, producing
photographs that, in conjunction with commercial

Iraqi Invasion of Kuwait
Phase I
2 August 1990

——	International boundary
★	National capital
+++	Railroad
═══	Expressway
——	Road
▨	Built-up area

0 10 20 30 Kilometers

0 10 20 30 Miles

Lambert Conformal Conic Projection, SP 26 23 N / 30 10 N

Adapted from a Central Intelligence Agency map by Marine Corps History Division

tourist maps, allowed the *Republican Guard* to locate its assigned targets. Once the attack was underway, the air force's mission was to establish air superiority, allowing the helicopterborne commando raids to proceed safely and to prevent the Kuwaiti Air Force from interfering with the invasion. Strikes on Kuwait's air bases and Raytheon Hawk (Homing All the Way Killer) MIM-23B surface-to-air missiles were intended to accomplish this.[21]

The smallest of the Iraqi military services was the navy, but Kuwait's coastal nature and extensive port facilities required a relatively robust naval component to the invasion plan. The commander of the Iraqi Navy, Staff Rear Admiral Gha'ib Hassan, was not informed of the invasion until a mere 36 hours before it was to be launched. He quickly composed a plan splitting Iraq's missile boat flotilla into two task forces, each carrying elements of the *440th Naval Infantry Brigade*. The first task force was to sail south and seize Kuwait's naval base at Ras al-Qulayah. The second was then to seize Faylakah Island.[22]

The Invasion of Kuwait

The Iraqi invasion of Kuwait began shortly after midnight on 2 August 1990 when the *Republican Guard* began seizing Kuwaiti border forts in preparation for the invasion. The invasion proper was set to begin at 0400.[23]

The Iraqi Air Force's initial strikes on Kuwait were delayed by poor weather over Iraqi airfields, and the first air strikes did not hit Kuwaiti airfields until 0625. As a result, the Kuwaiti Air Force's McDonnell Douglas A-4 Skyhawks were able to launch attacks against the advancing columns of the *Republican Guard* with effects that angered *Republican Guard* officers long after the battle had ended.[24]

The Iraqi Air Force also failed to secure air superiority for the helicopterborne commando missions that began the assault on Kuwait. Iraq's helicopter pilots were not trained in night or large formation flying, but with less than six-hours notice, 96 helicopters were ordered to fly elements of two *Republican Guard* commando brigades against two primary targets: the Kuwaiti royal family and the critical road junction at Mutla Ridge.[25]

Taking off in the early morning darkness of 2 August, the result was a predictable catastrophe. At least 40 of the helicopters were lost—20 most likely were downed by the Kuwaiti Air Force and Hawk surface-to-air missile batteries, but another 20 or so crashed into power lines or each other, sometimes while trying to avoid Kuwaiti missiles.[26]

The commando missions had little apparent success after landing. The *3d Republican Guard Special Forces Brigade* did not seem to have any appreciable impact on Kuwaiti forces rushing to hold Mutla Ridge. The *16th Republican Guard Special Forces Brigade* was landed at the royal palace and other sites in downtown Kuwait City but failed to capture the emir or any politically significant members of his family. They did manage to kill the emir's younger brother, Sheik Fahd al-Ahmed al-Sabah, as he defended the palace alongside the palace guard.[27]

After the Kuwaiti border forts were seized quickly and according to schedule, the *Republican Guard* columns moved quickly, driving for their ini-

tial objectives. The most important of these was Mutla Ridge, a natural barrier that the Kuwaitis intended to defend with two brigades, the 6th Mechanized Brigade and the 35th Armored Brigade. The *17th Armored Brigade, Hammurabi Armored Division*, arrived at Mutla Ridge at 0600 and blasted through a small force from the 6th Mechanized Brigade. They then engaged two forces from the 35th Armored Brigade in succession as they passed through Mutla Pass and descended on Kuwait City. By 0830, the *Hammurabi Armored Division's* lead elements were enmeshed in a traffic jam in Kuwait City as civilian traffic clogged the streets. In addition, fuel ran short and commanders commandeered additional fuel from civilian Kuwaiti filling stations in order to reach their final objectives on the Gulf.[28]

The *Nebuchadnezzar Division* secured its portions of Kuwait City by late afternoon on 2 August as well, but the *Medina Armored Division* ran into stiffer opposition from the Kuwaiti Air Force and the Kuwaiti Army as it tried to complete its mission of sealing the southern border.[29]

Colonel Salem Masoud Saad al-Sorour commanded Kuwait's 35th Armored Brigade, and his brigade placed itself at the Atraf road junction defending the Ali al-Salem Air Base and the roads into Kuwait City where they acted as the primary opposition to the *Medina Armored Division*. Throughout the day they fought a hard holding action against the Iraqi forces, stopping their tanks and forcing the Iraqis to make swarming attacks with their accompanying infantry. The brigade's stand had little hope, however. Colonel Salem later noted, "We were running short of ammunition, by three o'clock all the commanders notified me that their ammunition would be finished if we were to continue fighting and we had no means of replenishing our supplies." Colonel Salem requested air and artillery support, but none was available. Ordered to act on his own discretion, Salem took his brigade south to the border with Saudi Arabia, crossing over on the morning of 3 August after recovering as much of their equipment as they could from the brigade's barracks.[30]

Captain Martin N. Stanton, an American Army officer stationed in Saudi Arabia and trapped in Kuwait by the invasion, observed the Iraqi attack and was unimpressed by the *Republican Guard*. They lacked professionalism, in his view. Observing the odd placement of an artillery battery, he determined that "shade was the primary consideration; they put their battery where the men could get out of the sun. I had only to look at the artillerymen clustered around the trees to see that. Forget tactical considerations; these guys were going to be comfortable if they had to sit outside in the heat all day." He noted, "About the only thing the Iraqis seemed to be enthusiastic about was looting. They broke into food stores and at first took water, bread, meats, and fresh fruit; the latter seemed to be a particular favorite."[31]

The Iraqi Air Force struck Kuwaiti airfields again at 1220 and 1600, but the Kuwaiti Air Force continued to operate with some success by taking off from neighboring highways. The al-Jaber Air Base, according to *Republican Guard* officers, maintained Kuwaiti aircraft operations until the *Republican Guard* arrived there to shut the base down.[32]

The first of the two Iraqi naval forces, consisting of two missile boats carrying 160 troopers of the *440th Naval Infantry Brigade*, sailed at 2330 on 1 August, rendezvousing at the al-Bakr tanker platform in the northern Persian Gulf. This took longer than expected, pushing the assault on Kuwait's Ras al-Qulayah Naval Base until after daybreak. The vessels had numerous mechanical difficulties, and according to their commander, Naval Colonel Muzahim Mustafa, only overcame them due to "Russian experts on board for the purpose of training the crews."[33]

The two missile boats encountered a pair of Kuwaiti patrol boats as they neared al-Qulayah. Neither Iraqi missile boat had working weapons, and the Kuwaiti boats fired effectively, damaging the bridge of one of the boats, which subsequently ran aground and was unable to continue with the mission. Despite the setback Colonel Mustafa continued the amphibious assault with the remaining missile boat, landing the 75 men left to him at Ras al-Qulayah Naval Base. The naval infantry secured the base against confused Kuwaiti resistance; by 0830 on 2 August, the base was secured. The second Iraqi naval force was commanded by Lieutenant Colonel Saed Jalio and arrived off its target, Faylakah Island, late in the day on 2 August. The island was bombarded for six hours by the Iraqi boats, and the naval infantry subsequently landed in rubber boats. The Iraqi troops scoured the island but encountered no significant resistance, declaring the island secure at 1900 on 3 August.[34]

Early in the morning on 3 August the *Republican Guard* arrived at Ras al-Qulayah, a day later than expected and apparently unaware the base was held by Iraqi naval infantry. A friendly fire incident was avoided when the naval infantry raised the Iraqi flag over their prize. Over the next week the Iraqi Navy occupied the remaining Kuwaiti naval installations and the various small islands and oil platforms, and secured the captured Kuwaiti naval vessels.[35]

Faced with stiff Kuwaiti resistance, the *Medina Armored Division* did not reach al-Ahmadi until 3 August. Hit and run attacks by Kuwaiti forces operating in the southern desert would continue for two more days, but from this point Iraq completely controlled Kuwait. With their nation overrun, a significant proportion of Kuwait's military retreated across the border into Saudi Arabia in order to continue the fight against the Iraqi aggression. In the Iraqi invasion of Kuwait, the *Republican Guard* divisions suffered 100 or so casualties each in addition to the Iraqi Air Force and Navy casualties, but this was a practically bloodless operation by the standards of the Iran-Iraq War.[36]

Marines in the Iraqi and Kuwaiti Embassies

The first U.S. Marines involved in the Gulf War were the guards from the Marine Security Guard Battalion assigned to the embassies in Baghdad and Kuwait City. Ambassador April Glaspie had returned to the United States on 31 July, leaving Deputy Chief of Mission Joseph C. Wilson IV as the senior American official in the Baghdad embassy. The Baghdad Marines* stood security posts and destroyed classified documents during the early days of the crisis; they also helped collect Americans stranded in Iraq by the invasion.[37]

Of the Marines, Wilson later said:

> Their role was to protect classified material from falling into the hands of potential intruders and did not normally extend to protecting embassy personnel, except as directed by the chief of mission in the event of a riot or attack. I had already issued orders to the Marines that they were not to use their weapons to resist unless they felt their lives were threatened. I would have forbidden use of weapons even then, but the Marine Corps standard operating procedure was that they

---

*According to the Marine Security Guard Battalion (State Department) command chronology from January through December 1990 (on file at Gray Research Center, Quantico, VA), the following Marines were serving in the Baghdad security detachment in August 1990: SSgt G. E. Cudjoe (detachment commander); Sgt P. A. Lewis (assistant detachment commander); and Sgt H. L. Jones and Cpls P. C. Carver, T. D. Larson, and V. D. McMullan (security guards).

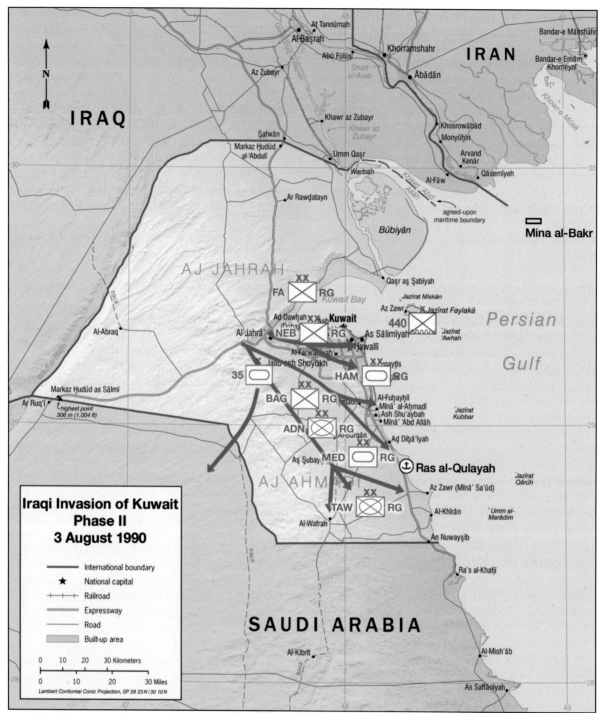

Adapted from a Central Intelligence Agency map by Marine Corps History Division

must always have the option to use their weapons in self-defense. My rationale was that if a breach of embassy security were to take place as a result of an extremely determined demonstration, the use of force by the one Marine normally on duty would be of limited effectiveness and would only further enrage the survivors of any armed confrontation.

Our chances of survival would be better if we were taken hostage than if an enraged crowd fought to avenge fallen comrades.

Wilson felt that once the vast majority of the classified material had been destroyed, there was little reason for the Marines to remain. But "it was all but impossible to convince these young patriots, whose

U.S. Chargé d'Affaires Joseph C. Wilson IV meets with Saddam Hussein on 6 August 1990. A career diplomat, Wilson led the U.S. State Department and embassy personnel remaining in Iraq until Saddam released the foreign hostages in December 1990.

loyalty to the mission was paramount, that their services were no longer required and they could leave. So long as any American official was in Baghdad, they wanted to stay to defend him."[38]

The decision to evacuate most of the families and nonessential embassy personnel provided his solution. Wilson ordered the Marines to accompany the first evacuation convoy from Baghdad across the western Iraqi desert to Jordan. The convoy crossed the desert to Jordan on 21 August with minimal problems, and the Baghdad Marines subsequently returned to the Marine Security Guard Battalion at Marine Corps Base Quantico on 23 August.[39]

The Marines of the Kuwaiti embassy* experienced a longer odyssey. In the early morning hours of 2 August, word of the Iraqi invasion of Kuwait reached the embassy. At 0520, the Marines were called to duty, and within 10 minutes they were all armed and at their posts. Small-arms fire could be heard in the distance, and calls from frightened Americans

stranded within Kuwait City began to come in. Sergeant Paul G. Rodriguez later reported, "One of the calls I took was from a woman who was staying in a hotel in Kuwait City. She reported to me that something hit the ground in the cemetery which was next to the hotel. I asked her to describe it and all she could say was that it made a small cloud of dust. She reported a second impact and by then I knew they were mortars coming down range." In addition to their other duties, the Marines notified U.S. Army Major John F. Feeley Jr., an officer from U.S. Central Command in Kuwait, to brief the ambassador on the invasion, and they worked closely with Feeley to report on Iraqi movements within Kuwait.[40]

The primary duty of the Marines was the destruction of classified material; the task was complicated because the burn barrels were outside the embassy walls, and the civilian personnel would not leave the embassy to enter the chaos of Kuwait City on 2 August. Staff Sergeant J. B. Smith, the detachment commander, and two of his Marines carried out the destruction of the classified information. Smith recalled, "One Marine covered the other two. Post 1 also had a camera mounted on the outside of the wall to help with the monitoring of possible dangers to the Marines outside. The use of the burn barrels lasted approximately two hours." It took a

---

*According to the Marine Security Guard Battalion (State Department) command chronology, the following Marines were serving in the Kuwait guard detachment in August 1990: SSgt J. B. Smith (detachment commander); Sgt Gerald W. Andre (assistant detachment commander); and Sgts Mark T. Ward, David K. Hudson, and Paul G. Rodriguez and Cpl Mark E. Royer (security guards).

total of six hours for all of the classified material to be properly destroyed (material not burned was shredded and disintegrated); when the burning was complete, the Marines returned to defensive positions around the embassy.[41]

The violence of the invasion raged around the embassy all day on 2 August. Iraqi tanks fired on buildings near the embassy, and Sergeant Rodriquez reported that

> Kuwait National Guard forces still stood their ground outside the compound. Some firefights broke out the back gate with the Kuwaiti forces taking cover behind their vehicle barriers. Iraqi forces were stopping cars and taking them for "joy" rides. Once the Kuwaitis found out at the back gate, they began to check all the cars going by. The back gate local guards reported that the Kuwaitis found two Iraqi troops in a car and pulled them out and reported that they were going to take the Iraqis away from the embassy area. So the report we got later was that the Kuwaitis took them somewhere else and shot them.[42]

The chaos continued on the second day; a burned-out Kuwaiti tank stood at the back gate, and Americans stranded and scattered throughout the city called the embassy for aid and advice. With little sleep, the Marines stood watches and responded to occasional alerts concerning potential Iraqi attacks on the compound. Rumors of these attacks swept through the disorganized city. On 4 August, approximately 50 Iraqi soldiers were dropped off behind the embassy by trucks. The Kuwaiti National Guard troops that had been positioned around the embassy had disappeared.[43]

Major Feeley later remembered that the Iraqis were expected to assault the embassy on the fourth night after the invasion: "And so we were all set up, as the Marines said, to rock 'n' roll. We hadn't had any sleep, and we pretty much thought that the majority of the military folks weren't going to make it through the night." The Marines were expected to defend the embassy with small arms and tear gas while the civilians were barricaded behind a steel door. In the end, however, the Iraqis never attacked the compound.[44]

Throughout their remaining time in Kuwait, the Marines continued to man defensive positions and otherwise assist the embassy staff by finding Americans lost in the city and relaying intelligence reports on Iraqi activities through Major Feeley to U.S. Central Command. Staff Sergeant Smith noted in his

after action report that "this was vital information that CentCom [Central Command] relied upon for its intelligence on Iraqi forces that were heading south to the Kuwait/Saudi Arabian border along [the] Arabian Gulf Road, which passes between the embassy and the Persian Gulf."[45]

On 7 August, the Marines were ordered out of their uniforms and into civilian clothing, and on 8 August garbled orders had them mistakenly destroy their weaponry. Both events had a demoralizing effect, but the Marines were permitted back into uniform on 10 August and they acquired some pistols from various sources to replace the destroyed weapons.

Staff Sergeant Smith summarized the Marine embassy guards' time in Kuwait during the invasion in the following manner:

> The embassy walls were never breeched while

Marines of the Kuwait embassy security detachment form a color guard in July 1990. From left to right, then-Cpl Paul G. Rodriguez, Sgt Gerald W. Andre, then-Cpl David K. Hudson, and Cpl Mark E. Royer. These Marines escorted embassy personnel and civilians from Kuwait following the invasion but were then trapped in Iraq until December 1990.
Photo courtesy of Sgt Gerald. W. Andre and the
Marine Embassy Guard Association

the Detachment was in Kuwait. The embassy itself did take fire from small arms into the buildings on the compound including the Chancery and the Marine House. Tank and artillery rounds also were fired over the embassy compound; two tank rounds hit a building adjacent to the compound. The Marines were still in defensive positions during the firing of these rounds, except on occasions during the second through sixth days [when they had] to locate civilians that were off the compound taking refuge and escort them to safe buildings on the compound. SSgt J. B. Smith, Sgt Paul G. Rodriguez, and Cpl Mark E. Royer were involved in these actions.[46]

On 23 August 1990, the U.S. ambassador to Kuwait ordered the Marines to escort a convoy of all nonessential embassy personnel and other civilians from Kuwait City to Baghdad. The Iraqis would not permit the embassy personnel to drive south into Saudi Arabia. The 30-vehicle convoy departed Kuwait City with the Marines spread among the convoy in an attempt to keep all the vehicles together.[47]

Travel was slow, with a great deal of traffic, and a serious accident occurred just outside Kuwait City:

> In one vehicle an elderly woman was thrown under the front seat; her hip was broken and she received lacerations on the face and leg. The other two elderly occupants of the vehicle received facial bruises and lacerations. [Sergeant David K.] Hudson, upon seeing this, proceeded to the accident site and performed first aid on the elderly woman with the broken hip. He proceeded to help her by talking to her and administering to her medical needs. The tail vehicle was used to transport her back to a hospital in Kuwait, and Sgt Hudson accompanied her back to the hospital. She was admitted and Sgt Hudson then proceeded to return to the convoy at the Kuwait/Iraq border. The decision and initiative of Sgt Hudson to accompany the woman back to the hospital took great courage and sacrifice because of the possibility of not being able to return to the convoy or quite possibly loss of life.[48]

In the early morning hours of 24 August, the convoy reached Baghdad and discovered that they would not be able to depart Iraq from Baghdad as intended. The Marines from Kuwait assumed Marine Security Guard duties at the Baghdad embassy but "were not permitted to use mace, handcuffs, [or] ammunition . . . all of which were to be secured in a safe." The Marines were handicapped by this policy until the arrival of a State Department inspector, James J. "Jim" Blystone, in Baghdad. Blystone recommended the Marines take up their proper security duties, and on 1 October they assumed these duties, conducting security sweeps in addition to standing post.[49]

Life in Baghdad settled into a routine for the Marines, despite the uncertainty and tension. Iraqi soldiers were stationed near the embassy, and Iraqi secret police followed the Marines whenever they left the embassy, but no incidents occurred. The Marines performed their assigned duties, conducted physical training and security drills, and watched the unfolding Kuwait crisis from Baghdad throughout the fall of 1990.

Finally, in early December, Saddam Hussein decided that no further benefit could be gained from holding the foreign hostages he had taken. On 9 December, the Marines were relieved of their duties at the Baghdad embassy and returned to the United States via Germany.[50]

The World's Response

The international response to Iraq's invasion of Kuwait was overwhelmingly negative. On the day of the invasion, the United Nations (UN) Security Council passed Resolution 660, which condemned the invasion and called for Iraq to immediately withdraw all of its forces from Kuwait. Providing convincing evidence that the Cold War was well and truly over, the United States and the Soviet Union issued a joint statement condemning the invasion.[51]

The United States took the lead early, alarmed at the prospect of Iraq controlling such a large percentage of Middle Eastern oil reserves, as well as the blatant violation of international norms in place since the close of World War II. Both Kuwaiti and Iraqi overseas assets were frozen, and extensive diplomacy to isolate Iraq from potential allies was begun. Great Britain and France supported the United States in diplomatic efforts to reverse the conquest; British Prime Minister Margaret H. Thatcher met with President George H. W. Bush urging that Iraq's action be reversed, by military means if necessary, and that no compromise be accepted.[52]

The Arab world was shattered by the Iraqi invasion; no Arab state had invaded another in modern history. Saudi Arabia and the Gulf states were di-

Defense Imagery DN-SC-89-05558

George H. W. Bush fought as a Navy pilot in World War II and served as the director of the Central Intelligence Agency prior to becoming President Ronald W. Reagan's vice president in 1980. He was elected the 41st president in 1988. President Bush assembled and led the largest international Coalition since World War II in opposition to Saddam Hussein's invasion of Kuwait.

rectly threatened by Iraq's aggression (Iran is a Persian, not an Arab, state). Militarily these states were no more prepared for conflict than Kuwait had been, and they shared similar political and economic systems with Iraq's victim. Iraq remained a Baathist state, and Saddam's political rhetoric over the previous two years had combined increasingly strident calls for opposition to Israel with denunciations of the oil-rich Gulf states' economic policies.

Egypt and Syria shared Baathist histories with Iraq, as well as some of Iraq's hostility toward the oil-rich Gulf states. Nevertheless, the Egyptians had been viciously denounced by Saddam following the Camp David Accords and the resulting truce with Israel, and they had helped broker the 31 July meeting at Jeddah, which appeared in retrospect to have been merely an Iraqi ploy. Moreover, Syria and Iraq had a long history of antipathy that simmered just below the boiling point for most of the two nations' modern history. Iraq, Syria, Egypt, and Saudi Arabia were the top contenders for leadership of the Arab world, and none of the four were inclined to see any of the others succeed on a scale as large as the Iraqi conquest of Kuwait.

On 6 August, the UN Security Council passed

Resolution 661, an economic embargo of Iraq. That same fateful day, American and Saudi Arabian discussions resulted in the Saudis agreeing to a deployment of American military forces to defend Saudi Arabia against the perceived Iraqi threat. The remarkable international Coalition that would eventually coalesce to drive Iraq from Kuwait was now taking shape.

Iraq responded to the outrage and admonishments of the international community with defiance. On 7 August, Saddam declared that Iraq had deposed Kuwait's monarchy and that Kuwait was now a republic. On 10 August, the Arab League met in Cairo to debate Iraq's invasion. After an acrimonious meeting, 12 of the 20 states voted for Iraq to withdraw from Kuwait and to allow the al-Sabah monarchy to return. They also called for troops to defend Saudi Arabia from Iraq. Iraq in turn linked its invasion of Kuwait to a resolution of the Arab world's open sore, Israel and Palestine.

Many of Iraq's diplomatic and military strategies throughout the crisis would turn on Saddam's understanding of the Arab world. By invading Kuwait, he believed, Iraq was not making an opportunistic land grab, but rather striking at the Middle Eastern status quo. Saddam argued that most Arab governments were corrupt remnants from the Age of Imperialism and that while he worked for the favor of Arab popular opinion, the opposition of the Arab governments was expected. "Any state that takes us further and brings our enemies closer to their evil goals," he asserted, "we must refuse, even if our blood reaches our chest."[53]

Iraq had begun making conciliatory diplomatic overtures to Iran prior to the invasion of Kuwait. Following the invasion Saddam offered to give up all of Iraq's gains from its minor victory in 1988, securing Iraq from Iranian interference in the unfolding crisis. Iran responded cautiously to Iraq's proposals during the early weeks of the situation, and despite the hesitation of some of Iraq's senior leaders, Saddam continued to pursue a conciliatory policy toward Iran throughout the crisis.[54]

Iraq's most brutal method of shaping international reaction involved the use of hostages. Thousands of foreigners were trapped in Kuwait and Iraq by the invasion. The Iraqis refused to allow most of them to depart the country; they were collected in hotels in Baghdad and released on a country-by-country basis only after delegations from individual states arrived and provided proper "respect" to the Iraqi government. The goal was to buy time and build a community of nations committed to "peace" who were willing to allow Iraq to retain Kuwait. Hundreds of male hostages were even spread among strategic targets throughout Iraq to deter bombing of those sites.[55]

Though the hostages dominated news reports and much of the diplomatic maneuvering throughout the fall of 1990, in the end Saddam apparently decided that they were not going to help him achieve his goals. He announced their impending release on 6 December, and they had all departed Iraq by mid-December.

On 28 August, Saddam formally annexed Kuwait as Iraq's 19th province, thus "restoring the branch to the tree." There would be a great deal of talk and discussion over the next five months, but Iraq refused to withdraw, attempting instead to split the international community and subvert the Coalition opposing its invasion. Iraqi intransigence and the international community's refusal to allow Iraq to benefit from its aggression drove events toward a military conclusion. As diplomacy continued over the coming months, the United States built up the forces required for the impending confrontation.

The American Military Response

At the time, the Iraqi Army was commonly judged to be the fourth-largest military force in the world, and it was considered battle-hardened by the nearly decade-long Iran-Iraq War. The invasion of Kuwait had been extremely swift, and surprisingly effective; the problems the Iraqi military encountered were not widely known. In fact, events would prove the Iraqi military was largely a hollow shell, with demoralized, poorly trained troops greatly outnumbering the better-trained and better-equipped *Republican Guard* units. But in August 1990, this was not obvious, and Iraq's historical willingness to use poison gas against its enemies increased the threat it represented.

In contrast, the American military in 1990 was relatively untested. The 1970s had been the nadir of American military effectiveness, with drug use and racial conflict reportedly common among American servicemembers. The military had an abundance of advanced weaponry, and service personnel had undergone a decade-long revitalization, but neither the equipment nor the troops had been tested in combat on a large scale.

The fiasco of the rescue attempt during the Iranian hostage crisis and the failure of the Marine deployment to Lebanon in the 1980s added to the specter of defeat lingering from the American experience in Vietnam, but there were some small-scale

Defense Imagery HD-SC-00-02946
Secretary of Defense Richard B. "Dick" Cheney gave military leaders great leeway in conducting the Gulf War. He later served as vice president under President George W. Bush.

conflicts that offered a glimpse of American capabilities. The invasion of Grenada in 1983, the invasion of Panama in 1989, and the air conflicts with Libya in the mid-1980s had all been successful operations despite some setbacks. Events would prove that the American military of the 1990s was the best-trained, best-equipped, and most professional large military in the world at that time, but those events were in the future as American military commanders considered how to make President Bush's promise that Iraq's aggression would not stand a military reality.

The American military was operating under a new organizational plan following the Goldwater-Nichols Act of 1986. Prior to the act, the chain of command had flowed from the president through the service secretaries down to the service chiefs and on to the individual services. Interservice rivalry was built directly into the system. A direct response to the perceived failures in the system demonstrated during the Iran hostage crisis, the

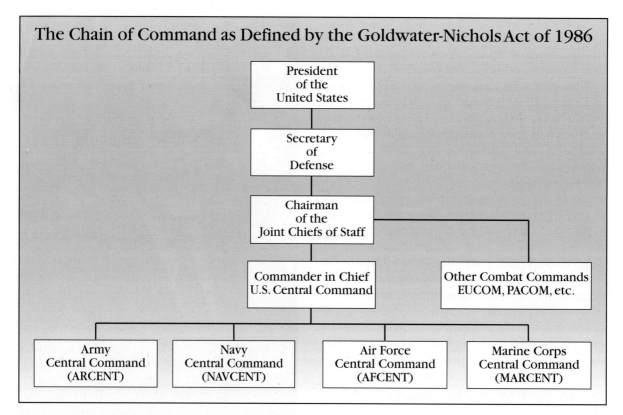

The Chain of Command as Defined by the Goldwater-Nichols Act of 1986

President of the United States

Secretary of Defense

Chairman of the Joint Chiefs of Staff

Commander in Chief U.S. Central Command

Other Combat Commands EUCOM, PACOM, etc.

Army Central Command (ARCENT)

Navy Central Command (NAVCENT)

Air Force Central Command (AFCENT)

Marine Corps Central Command (MARCENT)

act's most relevant changes impacted the chain of command.

The new system created a chain of command that ran through the secretary of defense to the chairman of the Joint Chiefs of Staff (now designated as the president's chief military advisor) to the geographic joint combatant commands (Pacific Command, European Command, Southern Command, and Central Command). The service chiefs were effectively removed from the chain of command; they were now "force providers" tasked with training, supplying, and supporting the forces dispatched to the geographic commands in order to fight the war. The Gulf War was the first test of this new system in a major conflict.

Three large personalities held the top positions under the president for the Persian Gulf conflict. Secretary of Defense Richard B. "Dick" Cheney was the senior civilian leader. A former congressman and the White House chief of staff under President Gerald R. Ford, Cheney was a strong proponent of the use of force to reverse the Iraqi invasion. He worked closely with General Colin L. Powell, USA, chairman of the Joint Chiefs of Staff.

Like most of the senior military officers involved in the Gulf War, General Powell was heavily influenced by his experiences in the Vietnam War. He was the developer of what has been dubbed the

"Powell Doctrine," which might fairly be described as the military philosophy that underpinned the American military effort in the Gulf War. In theory, the doctrine set very high standards for the use of American military force, requiring massive domestic and international support for any military intervention and specifying a massive expenditure of military might to overwhelm any resistance.[*]

The direct military commander, and the man who came to represent the Gulf War to the American public, was General H. Norman Schwarzkopf Jr., USA. In addition to his service during the Vietnam War, Schwarzkopf had been the senior Army officer for Operation Urgent Fury, the 1983 invasion of Grenada. In late 1988, he replaced General George Crist as the commander of U.S. Central Command.

The end of the Iran-Iraq War had led Central Command to reconsider likely threats in its theater, and under General Schwarzkopf this resulted in Internal Look, Central Command's annual training exercise, examining the problem of defending the region from an aggressive Iraq in 1990. As already

---

[*] In practice, Michael R. Gordon and LtGen Bernard E. Trainor assert in *The Generals' War* that Gen Powell insisted on extremely high force estimates in an attempt to dissuade the president from any military intervention over Kuwait.

Defense Imagery DA-SC-91-07109

The first African American chairman of the Joint Chiefs of Staff, Army Gen Colin L. Powell's two tours in Vietnam shaped his views on military affairs and the subsequent "Powell Doctrine." Powell later served as secretary of state for President George W. Bush.

Defense Imagery DA-SC-91-04130

Gen H. Norman Schwarzkopf Jr., USA, commanded U.S. Central Command during the Gulf War. After the war, Gen Walter E. Boomer recalled that there was a "tremendous amount of trust" on the part of Gen Schwarzkopf, who "always felt that he didn't have to worry about us . . . he knew that part of his campaign, that part of his theater was okay."

mentioned, this produced an odd sense of déjà vu in Central Command planners during the summer of 1990 as Iraq's actions mirrored the conditions established in the exercise. Secretary of Defense Cheney took General Schwarzkopf with him to brief King Fahd bin Abdul Aziz al-Saud in the 6 August meeting that led to Saudi Arabia agreeing to allow American forces to deploy to the Desert Kingdom to defend it against Iraq. Suitably modified, the plan Schwarzkopf put into play for building up forces in Saudi Arabia was essentially the plan from Internal Look 90.

Removed from the operational chain of command by Goldwater-Nichols, the Commandant of the Marine Corps in 1990 was General Alfred M. Gray Jr. As Commandant, General Gray had aggressively continued the reform efforts of the 1980s and added new training initiatives of his own. He preferred to be seen in combat fatigues and promoted a combat culture in the Marine Corps that made him popular with junior officers and enlisted men. He was also determined to create an intellectual culture in the Marine Corps by expanding officer and noncommissioned officer training and in 1989 publishing Fleet

Marine Force Manual 1 (FMFM1), *Warfighting*, perhaps the most well-known Marine Corps manual published since the earlier *Small Wars Manual*.

The senior Marine operational commander for the Gulf War, Lieutenant General Walter E. Boomer, had recently been assigned as the commanding general of both U.S. Marine Forces Central Command and I Marine Expeditionary Force. General Boomer was a Vietnam War veteran like his fellow Gulf War commanders and was the commanding general of the 4th Marine Division, the Marine Corps Reserve command, in New Orleans, Louisiana, prior to his Gulf War command.

General Boomer and his family were traveling in two cars from New Orleans, his previous duty station, to Camp Pendleton, California, when he heard the news of Iraq's invasion on 2 August. In a 2006 interview, he recounted the day's events:

We were somewhere in west Texas, when I heard on the radio that Kuwait had been invaded. When we reached our planned desti-

Defense Imagery DM-SC-95-00050

As Commandant of the Marine Corps, Gen Alfred M. Gray reformed and revitalized Marine training. Gen Gray fought in the Korean and Vietnam Wars and served as Commandant during the Gulf War.

Official U.S. Marine Corps photo

Then-LtGen Walter E. Boomer commanded U.S. Marine Forces Central Command as well as the I Marine Expeditionary Force. LtGen Boomer served two tours in Vietnam prior to his Gulf War command.

nation that night, I asked Sandi [his wife] if she had been listening to the radio or the news, and she said, no they had been talking. She asked, "What happened?" I said, "Iraq invaded Kuwait." Having been a Marine wife for a while she looked at me and said, "What does that mean?" I said, "Well, I don't know but it probably doesn't bode well in that the I Marine Expeditionary Force will probably be involved," and it obviously was.[56]

CHAPTER 3

Desert Shield

In the late twentieth century, it became increasingly difficult for the Marine Corps to live up to its World War I recruiting poster slogan "First to Fight." Modern aircraft and midair refueling techniques enabled U.S. Army light infantry forces, instead of Marine forces, to deploy with unheard of speed anywhere in the world where friendly airstrips awaited them, and Saudi Arabia's airfields had been improved for precisely this situation.

The first land-based aerial unit to arrive in Saudi Arabia was the 1st Tactical Fighter Wing of the U.S. Air Force, which deployed from Langley, Virginia, on 8 August 1990. On 9 August, they began conducting combat air patrols. The first American ground troops to arrive in Saudi Arabia were the men of the 2d Brigade, 82d Airborne Division; this was the duty "ready" brigade of the division. They began deploying to Saudi Arabia by air on 8 August, and the brigade was fully deployed on 14 August. The rest of the 82d Airborne Division was fully deployed to Saudi Arabia on 24 August. The U.S. Navy already had the Joint Task Force Middle East on station in the Persian Gulf. This task force consisted of the guided missile cruiser USS *England* (CG 22); the destroyer USS *David R. Ray* (DD 971); the frigates USS *Vandegrift* (FFG 48), USS *Reid* (FFG 30), USS *Taylor* (FFG 50), USS *Robert G. Bradley* (FFG 49), and USS *Barbey* (FF 1088); and the command ship USS *La Salle* (AGF 3). In addition, carrier task forces built around the USS *Dwight D. Eisenhower* (CVN 69) and USS *Independence* (CV 62) were within striking range.[1]

These formidable forces might not have been able to stop a determined Iraqi armored assault into Saudi Arabia, however. The 82d Airborne's brigades were light infantry units with little in the way of supporting arms, and their mission was initially limited to defending the Saudi airfields and acting as a "trip-wire" force should Iraq invade the Desert Kingdom. The Marines were not the first forces to deploy to Saudi Arabia, but their deployment provided the muscle needed to make Operation Desert Shield

MV PFC DeWayne T. Williams *(AK 3009), part of Maritime Prepositioning Ship Squadron Three, unloads AAV-7 amphibious assault vehicles. The Prepositioning Program allowed the Marines to quickly build up combat power in Saudi Arabia.*

Photo by PO2 (SW) Joe Bartlett, USN. Defense Imagery DN-ST-91-11215

Marines from 7th Marine Expeditionary Brigade headquarters at Marine Corps Air Ground Combat Center in Twenty-nine Palms, California, board buses en route to Desert Shield in August 1990. After flying to Saudi Arabia, the Marines of this brigade met ships of Maritime Prepositioning Ship Squadron Two, which carried their heavy equipment.

a reality. Moving combat power rapidly ashore has long been a Marine capability, but Marine power in the Gulf War was not projected by amphibious assault. Instead, it was projected through a new program, Maritime Prepositioning.[2]

Marines and Maritime Prepositioning

The Gulf War would be the largest deployment of Marines since the Vietnam War. It challenged the entire warfighting establishment of the Marine Corps—aviation, ground, and logistics—and forced a generation of Marines to put two decades of planning and training to the test. The Corps would see many of its tactical and operational philosophies justified under combat conditions. The Military Sealift Command's Prepositioning Program proved its worth, enabling Marines to be the first combined-arms task force in Saudi Arabia.

Prepositioning ships are civilian crewed vessels with a squadron staff of U.S. Navy personnel, and the vessels supporting the Marines are named after Marine Corps Medal of Honor recipients. Maritime Prepositioning Ship Squadron One usually serves the Mediterranean Sea and eastern Atlantic Ocean;

Squadron Three usually serves the western Pacific; and Squadron Two is normally based at Diego Garcia and covers the Indian Ocean and Middle East. Squadrons Two and Three deployed in support of Operation Desert Shield, with Squadron Two deploying from Diego Garcia on 8 August.

There was some controversy over the relatively late departure of the squadron. After the war, Generals Alfred Gray and Joseph P. Hoar[*] both argued that the prepositioning ships should have been deployed sooner, allowing the Marine brigade to deploy more quickly after the Saudis agreed to accept American forces to aid their defense. Though the ships were discussed at high levels prior to 7 August, they were not ordered to sail.[3]

General Hoar later said, "It's an important lesson for us as Marines that when a crisis begins that we, and our Navy partners, do not have to wait until

---

[*]In August 1990, then-LtGen Hoar was deputy chief of staff for plans, policies, and operations at Headquarters Marine Corps. As a major general, he served as chief of staff, U.S. Central Command, from 1988 to 1990, and he later succeeded Gen Schwarzkopf as commander in chief of Central Command in August 1991.

Birth of the Maritime Prepositioning Ship Squadrons

In 1979, Secretary of Defense Harold Brown put the Prepositioning Program into place. General Robert H. Barrow, 27th Commandant of the Marine Corps, later recalled how Dr. Brown first brought the concept up to him:

I think it was at an Armed Forces Policy Council meeting. That would be on Monday morning at eleven o'clock. Harold Brown said to me, "Bob, could I see you for a minute?" I've already described Hal Brown. I like him very much, but he's not given to small talk so I knew it was something apart. He got me aside, and he said, and I'm paraphrasing obviously, "Do Marines always have to storm a shore?" Isn't that a strange question? He's not given to such small talk. I read a lot into it.

So, I fired back. I said, "No, sir. They surely do not. An amphibious operation is but a means to an end. Marines do most of their fighting after they have gotten ashore. Getting ashore—we want that to be as little fighting as we can possibly make it, but knowing that you cannot always expect to go for some undefended place, somebody has to know how to do it, and we call that amphibious warfare, but it's a mean to an end. So, to answer your question, no, sir, we don't."

He said, "In other words, Marines, if you had their equipment aboard some other kind of ship that could be brought into a port or somehow moved over to the shore in an environment that was not threatening, the Marines would do that, do you think?" I said, "We would do that extremely well because it still has a maritime character about it, and we're accustomed to having one foot on the beach and one foot in the sea." He said, "Well, that's very interesting."[4]

The Prepositioning Program was a response to a perceived weakness in America's strategic posture; the Iran hostage crisis put a spotlight on America's inability to project power into the Persian Gulf region, despite the region's relative importance. In Europe and the Pacific, the United States maintained large bases on the territory of allies, but this was neither practical nor feasible in the Middle East (see chapter 1).

The new program was tied into the creation of the Rapid Joint Deployment Task Force. The Prepositioning Program put all of the equipment for a Marine expeditionary brigade as well as enough supplies for the brigade to fight for 30 days on a squadron of purpose-built vessels of the U.S. Military Sealift Command. The personnel and personal equipment of the brigade would be deployed by the Military Airlift Command to the region where it could rendezvous with a Maritime Prepositioning Ship Squadron. The concept required a friendly host nation with well-developed airfields and ports; a great deal of aid was given to the various Gulf states and Saudi Arabia to build up the infrastructure required to support a rapid military deployment in the region if required.[5]

the same day that aviation and ground forces are loaded into a theater; that naval ships, MPS [Maritime Prepositioning Ships], can be moved before the decision is made. And it is a very prudent decision, in our belief, to move those forces earlier so they are available to the National Command when the time comes. We believe that we would have been better positioned to have operated had those ships been moved, say, on the second or third day of August."[6]

7th Marine Expeditionary Brigade

Marines of the 7th Marine Expeditionary Brigade, commanded by Major General John I. Hopkins, arrived in Saudi Arabia in mid-August, where they joined with the equipment from Maritime Prepositioning Ship Squadron Two.[7]

General Hoar later noted:

The 7th Marine Expeditionary Brigade was the first ground element that had tanks and armored personnel carriers. It was the first element that was capable of meeting the threat that existed in Kuwait. But it was more than that; it was an air-ground team as we all know, that had fixed wing, rotary wing . . . had an air-ground task force headquarters. It had its full suite of logistics for 30 days, so it was self-sustaining for 30 days. . . . Marine forces were arriving not only with that combat power, ready to be put into operation, but in addition to that brought [their] logistics as well.[8]

The 7th Marine Expeditionary Brigade, like all Marine air-ground task forces, was a tripartite formation, with a ground, air, and logistics component. Logistical support for the brigade was provided by Colonel Alexander W. Powell's Brigade Service Support Group 7, comprising Combat Service Support Detachments 71, 72, and 73. The ground component was the 7th Marines (Reinforced) under the command of Colonel Carlton W. Fulford Jr. This regimental combat team contained four infantry battalions (1st Battalion, 7th Marines; 2d Battalion, 7th Marines; 3d Battalion, 9th Marines; and 1st Battalion, 5th Marines); the 3d Light Armored Infantry Battalion; the 3d Amphibious Assault Battalion; the 3d Tank Battalion; and artillery of the 3d Battalion, 11th Marines (Reinforced), as well as other, smaller associated units. The 7th Marines was well trained in desert warfare; it served as part of the garrison of the Marine Corps Air Ground Combat Center at Twentynine Palms in the Mojave Desert of southern California.[9]

The aviation combat element was Marine Aircraft Group 70, commanded by Colonel Manfred A. Ri-etsch. This composite air group included fixed-wing, helicopter, and air-defense missile squadrons in addition to its supporting units. Fixed-wing aircraft included McDonnell Douglas F/A-18A and F/A-18C Hornets in Marine Fighter Attack Squadrons 314, 235, 333, and 451. A-6E Intruders came with Marine All-Weather Attack Squadron 224. McDonnell Douglas AV-8B Harrier IIs from Marine Attack Squadrons 311 and 542 rounded out the complement of strike aircraft. Helicopter transport was provided by Boeing Vertol CH-46E Sea Knight medium-lift helicopters of Marine Medium Helicopter Squadron 161 and Sikorsky CH-53D Sea Stallion and CH-53E Super Stallion heavy-lift helicopters of Marine Heavy Helicopter Squadrons 462, 465, and 466. Bell-Textron AH-1W Super Cobras and UH-1N Iroquois (more commonly known as "Hueys") were provided by Marine Light Attack Helicopter Squadrons 367 and 369.[10]

The brigade deployed very quickly; the first Marines debarked from their military airlift flights in Saudi Arabia on 14 August. After the long transoceanic air flight, arrival in Saudi Arabia was memorable for most Marines. Sergeant James I. Mabus of Marine Aircraft Control Group 38 described "the back hatch of the plane opening . . . and the hot air shooting into

M60A1 tanks from the 1st Tank Battalion fire rounds on 11 September 1990 as the battalion conducts live-fire training during Operation Desert Shield in Saudi Arabia. Finding time and space to conduct needed training on ranges was difficult throughout the deployment.

Defense Imagery DM-SN-92-01310

Warehouses provided temporary billeting for Marines newly arrived in Saudi Arabia during the early days of Operation Desert Shield. These quarters were hot and uncomfortable, and consequently most Marines were glad when they deployed to defensive positions in the desert.

the aircraft, stifling with the strong scent of jet fumes. Someone in the plane said, 'This might not be hell, but we can see it from here.' . . . It took a while for the mind to accept . . . that you are now in a truly foreign place that remains this hot all day long."[11]

General Hopkins's brigade was the first to use the Maritime Prepositioning Ship Squadrons as intended. Three of the ships of Maritime Prepositioning Ship Squadron Two were present at Diego Garcia when the order to move arrived: MV *Cpl Louis J. Hauge Jr.* (T-AK 3000), MV *1stLt Alexander Bonnyman Jr.* (T-AK 3003), and MV *PFC James Anderson Jr.* (T-AK 3002). These three set sail at once for al-Jubayl, Saudi Arabia, which they reached on 15 August. MV *Pvt Harry Fisher* (T-AK 3004) was rerouted to Florida for scheduled maintenance when the call came; it changed course for Saudi Arabia as well, arriving on 24 August. MV *PFC William B. Baugh* (T-AK 3001) was already in Florida undergoing scheduled maintenance; it departed Florida and arrived in Saudi Arabia on 5 September. In addition the aircraft maintenance ship USNS *Curtiss* (T-AVB 4) deployed to support Marine Aircraft Group 70, but unexpected engine problems en route delayed the *Curtiss* and it did not arrive in Saudi Arabia until 30 September.[12]

Conditions in al-Jubayl remained harsh for the Marines of the brigade. Billeting was limited to four warehouses with inadequate sanitation facilities, and the Saudis were reluctant to allow the Marines the spaces needed for ranges and training—all of the large caliber weapons coming out of storage on the ships needed to be bore-sighted before deploying to the field. The Saudis were uncomfortable with the large American military force descending on their nation and strove to minimize the impact by restricting training areas and troop movements as much as possible.

Unloading proceeded briskly, but it was not a flawless process. In some cases the proper maintenance had not been performed regularly on the equipment stored on the ships, and some spare parts or required tools were missing as well. The Iraqi Army in Kuwait was only 150 or so miles from al-Jubayl along the coast road, and aside from light Saudi units stationed at the border, al-Jubayl was undefended until the 7th Marine Expeditionary Brigade unloaded its heavy equipment. In order to present a credible deterrent, combat units arrived prior to logistics units, and this further slowed unloading and distribution of equipment. In the initial rush to get their units ready for combat and deployed to the field, many employed the traditional Marine Corps art of scrounging, creating a somewhat chaotic situation.

The Marines of Regimental Combat Team 7 were eager to leave the deplorable conditions of the warehouses. Major Michael F. Applegate of the 3d Assault Amphibian Battalion's opinion was held by many: "The time we spent in those warehouses was the worst experience of my life. At least in the desert you can move around, and you have the morning and evening breezes." General Hopkins's efforts with the Saudis eventually paid off, and the brigade's ground combat forces began deploying to defensive positions north of al-Jubayl.[13]

General Hopkins later described his initial defensive plan:

> There were only about three or four defensible pieces of terrain between the Kuwaiti border and [al-]Jubayl. I went up to Manifa Bay, which is about 70 miles south of the Kuwaiti border. We decided to screen there with the light armored vehicles, and then Colonel [later Brigadier General Carlton W.] Fulford could deploy the mechanized units and the greater part of the Regimental Combat Team by the cement factory, which was 40 miles north of Jubayl and 27 miles or so south of Manifa Bay, where there was some relief in the desert. It was the best defensible terrain and Fulford deployed his Regimental Combat Team there.
>
> That was our concept. We would screen as far forward as possible, delay and attrit the Iraqis with airpower, then defend in a main battle area along what became known as "cement [factory] ridge." The Iraqis had two possible attack routes. We thought they'd either come down the coast or use a route a little bit to the west, but both these routes come together at a junction near the cement factory. If they kept coming, we had drawn a line in the sand by the cement factory. We were going to stay there.[14]

The performance of the Iraqi military in the Iran-Iraq War (see chapter 1) and its later performance against light armored vehicles of the Marines and Saudis backed by strong air support in the Battle of al-Khafji (see chapters 6 and 7) indicate that the soldiers of the 82d Airborne might have been more than a speed bump, although the Air Force initially did not have the assets or munitions in theater to support the paratroopers as thoroughly as the Marines and Saudis were supported during al-Khafji. But certainly once the 7th Marine Expeditionary Brigade was in position on 25 August, Iraq's window of opportunity for conquering a significant portion of Saudi Arabia was gone.

The maritime prepositioning system had worked as designed. The only apparent flaw in the system involved the deployment of aviation assets. General Hopkins later said,

> The fixed-wing was stalled at MCAS [Marine Corps Air Station] Beaufort [South Carolina] and at MCAS Cherry Point [North Carolina]. The Air Force didn't give us the tankers that we needed to get across the Atlantic. That was my biggest concern, because basically the concept calls for us to be combat ready in about ten days. We were ready on the ground, with the MEB [Marine expeditionary brigade] declared combat ready on 25 August; but the F/A-18s didn't arrive until around the 23rd, because they were delayed. The Air Force was moving its own aircraft, and that's one of the weaknesses of the MPF [Maritime Prepositioning Force] concept—it's not tied together at the Joint Chiefs of Staff level.[15]

Marines Afloat

The 13th Marine Expeditionary Unit (Special Operations Capable) deployed on a scheduled cruise of the western Pacific Ocean in June 1990. These "WestPac" cruises were an annual six-month deployment that rotated between West Coast Marine units; the deployed units served as the landing force of the U.S. Seventh Fleet. The expeditionary unit was commanded by Colonel John E. Rhodes. It comprised Battalion Landing Team 1/4, Marine Medium Helicopter Squadron (Composite) 164, and Marine Expeditionary Unit Service Support Group 13. These Marines were embarked on the ships of Amphibious Squadron 5, an amphibious ready group that included USS *Okinawa* (LPH 3), USS *Ogden* (LPD 5), USS *Fort McHenry* (LSD 43), USS *Cayuga* (LST 1186), and USS *Durham* (LKA 114). The cruise was planned for six months, but the deployment was extended by the crisis in the Gulf by nearly four months. As a consequence, the Marines began calling themselves the "Raiders of the Lost ARG* [amphibious ready group]."[16]

The 13th Marine Expeditionary Unit was designated "Special Operations Capable." Prior to getting underway, the unit went through a training cycle designed to prepare it to conduct different types of special operations that might be encountered dur-

---

*A humorous play on the title of the popular 1981 movie *Raiders of the Lost Ark*.

Photo courtesy of LtCol Marshall K. Snyder

Amphibious Squadron 5 underway in the Persian Gulf. This squadron carried the 13th Marine Expeditionary Unit (Special Operations Capable) on the USS Fort McHenry *(LSD 43), USS* Durham *(LKA 114), USS* Cayuga *(LST 1186), USS* Ogden *(LPD 5), and USS* Okinawa *(LPH 3).*

ing its deployment.* These special operations included recovering lost aircraft, rescuing hostages, evacuating civilians from hostile environments, and training local forces.[17]

The 13th Marine Expeditionary Unit (Special Operations Capable) began its cruise of the western Pacific with a training exercise in the Philippines in July 1990. An earthquake on the island of Luzon on 16 July led to a disaster relief operation that lasted through the end of the month. A scheduled port visit to Hong Kong followed in August, but the "Raiders of the Lost ARG" were then ordered to the Persian Gulf, arriving in the region on 7 September.[18]

In August 1990, the 4th Marine Expeditionary Brigade was commanded by Major General Harry W. Jenkins Jr., and the brigade was preparing to train with NATO forces in two exercises, Teamwork and Bold Guard 90, in northern Europe. Stationed on the East Coast, primarily at Camp Lejeune, North Carolina, the brigade was traditionally oriented toward Europe and Africa. In addition to preparing for the upcoming exercises, the brigade kept an eye on civil war–torn Liberia, where the 22d Marine Expeditionary Unit was conducting a noncombatant evacuation and defending the U.S. embassy

throughout August 1990. The focus of the brigade abruptly shifted on 10 August when it was ordered to the Persian Gulf, forcing units that had trained for operations in Norway to turn in their cold weather gear for desert warfare garb.[19]

The ground combat element of Jenkins's brigade was Regimental Landing Team 2, commanded by Colonel Thomas A. Hobbs. Major units of the regimental combat team included 1st Battalion, 2d Marines; 3d Battalion, 2d Marines; 1st Battalion, 10th Marines (Reinforced); Companies B and D, 2d Light Armored Infantry Battalion; Company A, 2d Assault Amphibian Battalion; and Company A, 2d Tank Battalion.

The logistics element was Brigade Service Support Group 4, commanded by Colonel James J. Doyle Jr., and it included the 2d Military Police Company, 2d Medical Battalion, 2d Dental Battalion, 2d Maintenance Battalion, 2d Supply Battalion, 8th Communications Battalion, 8th Motor Transport Battalion, 8th Engineer Support Battalion, and 2d Landing Support Battalion.

The 4th Marine Expeditionary Brigade aviation combat element was Marine Aircraft Group 40, commanded by Colonel Glenn F. Burgess. Because the group was deploying on board amphibious warfare vessels, the only fixed-wing aircraft in the group were the Harriers of Marine Attack Squadron 331. Marine Medium Helicopter Squadrons 263 and 365 brought Sea Knights; Marine Heavy Helicopter Squadron 461 was equipped with Super Stallions;

---

*These predeployment training programs were the Marine reaction to the creation in the 1980s of the joint U.S. Special Operations Command that included Army, Navy, and Air Force special operations forces. The Marine Corps did not join Special Operation Command until 2006.

Marines and sailors on board the amphibious transport dock USS Raleigh *(LPD 1) watch as their ship and the amphibious assault ship USS* Okinawa *(LPH 3) conduct underway replenishment operations with the fleet oiler USNS* Andrew J. Higgins *(T-AO 190). The Marine amphibious forces spent most of the Gulf War at sea, deploying in August 1990 and returning to the United States in the spring of 1991.*

and Marine Light Attack Helicopter Squadron 269 flew Sea Cobras and Hueys.[20]

The brigade was embarked on the ships of the U.S. Navy's Amphibious Group 2, commanded by Rear Admiral John B. LaPlante, USN. The vessels were divided into three transit groups: Transit Group 1 consisted of USS *Shreveport* (LPD 12), USS *Trenton* (LPD 14), USS *Portland* (LSD 37), and USS *Gunston Hall* (LSD 44). Transit Group 2 comprised USS *Nassau* (LHA 4), USS *Raleigh* (LPD 1), USS *Pensacola* (LSD 38), and USS *Saginaw* (LST 1188). Transit Group 3 included USS *Iwo Jima* (LPH 2), USS *Guam* (LPH 9), USS *Manitowoc* (LST 1180), and USS *LaMoure County* (LST 1194). In addition, Military Sealift Command supported the brigade with a squadron that included USNS *Wright* (T-AVB 3), MV *Cape Domingo* (T-AKR 5053), and MV *Strong Texan* (T-AK 9670). Three additional vessels were leased for the duration of the deployment; these nonnaval vessels were MV *Bassro Polar*, MV *Pheasant*, and MV *Aurora T*.[21]

The 4th Marine Expeditionary Brigade was intended to deploy on two dozen amphibious warfare vessels, but only a dozen were available in time for the brigade's deployment. As a result, some of the brigade's assault equipment and supplies were loaded on board the Military Sealift Command vessels. The brigade loaded the available shipping at Morehead City and Wilmington, North Carolina. The dispersed loading sites and rushed embarkation created confusion that required the brigade's shipping to reorganize and reload in al-Jubayl in November 1990. Transit Group 1 departed on 17 August; Transit Group 2 departed on 20 August; and Transit Group 3 departed on 21 August, each passing across the Atlantic and Mediterranean and through the Suez Canal to the Persian Gulf.[22]

Amphibious Group 2 arrived in the Gulf in early September, with the transit groups arriving in the same order they had departed, on 3 September, 6 September, and 9 September, respectively. The brigade's Military Sealift Command vessels arrived from mid-September through mid-October. Because they were not present when these vessels were loaded, the brigade's logistics officers had to physically board each vessel and then find and record the location of all their cargo in person.[23]

Following Navy–Marine Corps amphibious doctrine, the 4th Marine Expeditionary Force and 13th Marine Expeditionary Unit (Special Operations Capable) fell under the control of U.S. Naval Forces Central Command, rather than under Lieutenant General Walter Boomer's Marine Forces Central Command. Through December 1990 Vice Admiral Henry H. Mauz Jr. commanded Central Command's naval forces. Amphibious Group 2 and Amphibious Squadron 5 formed the Amphibious Task Force (TG 150.6), commanded by Rear Admiral LaPlante, and the two Marine expeditionary forces formed the Landing Force (TG 150.8), commanded by Major General Jenkins.[24]

The Marine expeditionary forces in the Amphibious Task Force were intended as a theater reserve, and their employment was controlled directly by General Schwarzkopf. During Desert Shield, they were prepared to reinforce the troops defending Saudi Arabia if needed, or to launch amphibious assaults or raids against the enemy's rear if the Iraqis

attacked Saudi Arabia. Their presence was also intended to divert Iraqi forces toward defending the coast, thus reducing the number of troops faced inland.[25]

Admiral Mauz saw the terminal end of the Persian Gulf as particularly inhospitable for naval forces, with Iran a constant danger on the flank of any naval force passing through the Strait of Hormuz and up the Gulf to Kuwait. Admiral Mauz later declared: "I wanted to see an amphibious landing as much as anybody. . . . [T]he trouble was, there was no good place to do a landing." Mauz believed that Desert Shield would shape interservice competition in the post-Soviet world and that the Army and Air Force were looking to replace their NATO missions with traditional Navy/Marine Corps expeditionary missions; therefore, he wanted the naval forces to have an impact on the conflict. Despite this, he made "insistent and repeated" requests to General Schwarzkopf to halve the number of am-

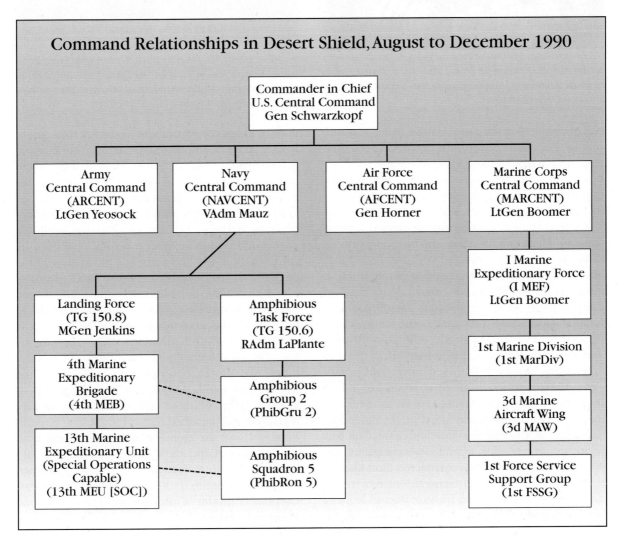

Command Relationships in Desert Shield, August to December 1990

VAdm Henry H. Mauz Jr. commanded U.S. Naval Forces Central Command from the start of the Persian Gulf crisis through December 1990.

MajGen Harry W. Jenkins Jr. (left), landing force commander, and RAdm John B. LaPlante, USN, amphibious task force commander throughout the deployment to the Persian Gulf, during Exercise Sea Soldier.

phibious ships in the area. Mauz's belief that amphibious operations were not practical in the Gulf likely led General Jenkins to conclude that the commander of U.S. Naval Forces Central Command "displayed little interest in developing a naval campaign that went beyond the level of presence."[26]

General Schwarzkopf repeatedly denied Admiral Mauz's request to reduce the amount of amphibious shipping under his command because the Marines afloat were already being used as a threat and a feint against the Iraqis, who could never rule out the possibility of an amphibious assault. General Jenkins and his staff prepared various amphibious options for the 4th Marine Expeditionary Brigade and the 13th Marine Expeditionary Unit (Special Operations Capable), both separately and in tandem. These options included landings behind an Iraqi thrust into Saudi Arabia as well as reinforcement of the American and allied forces defending Saudi Arabia. Because the shoreline of the Gulf was relatively unsuited for amphibious operations, the reinforcement mission was considered most likely.[27]

The hasty departure of General Jenkins's troops and their previous training for exercises in Norway left the brigade ill prepared for amphibious opera-

tions in a desert environment. To rectify these problems, a series of amphibious exercises were planned in the friendly nation of Oman. There would be four of these exercises, each dubbed "Sea Soldier." Sea Soldiers I and II took place in October and early November, respectively. In addition to practicing amphibious landings, the exercises gave the Marines a chance to conduct maintenance that could not be completed on ship and rearrange the loading of the amphibious vessels to better suit the staff's planning. The 13th Marine Expeditionary Unit worked with the brigade in these exercises as well, highlighting the unity of the amphibious task force.[28]

Maintaining and training large amphibious forces at sea is not without risk, however. On 8 October, two UH-1N helicopters operating from the USS *Okinawa* collided during a training flight. Both aircraft from Marine Light Attack Helicopter Squadron 267, attached to the 13th Marine Expeditionary Unit's air element, were lost along with their Marines: Captains William D. Cronin Jr., Gary S. Dillon, Kevin R. Dolvin, and William J. Hurley; Sergeants Kenneth T. Keller and John R. Kilkus; Corporal Timothy W. Romei; and Lance Corporal Thomas R. Adams.[29]

Three of the ships assigned to the brigade's Military Sealift Command support squadron were leased vessels with foreign flags, and they were unable to be employed in a combat zone. With the prepositioning ships now emptied of gear, two vessels from Maritime Prepositioning Ship Squadron Two—the *PFC William Baugh Jr.* and the *1stLt Alex Bonnyman Jr.*—were assigned to the brigade's support squadron instead. Throughout October and November, the three leased vessels—the *Bassro Polar, Pheasant,* and *Aurora T*—were off-loaded in al-Jubayl, and their cargos were combat loaded onto the two roll-on/roll-off* prepositioning ships. Major General Jenkins explained, "This was the first time that [Maritime Prepositioning] ships had ever been combat loaded to support a general landing plan for the amphibious force."[30]

While the amphibious forces trained and reorganized themselves, they also had a more active maritime mission to prosecute against Iraq. UN Security Council Resolution 661 established an embargo on exports from Iraq and Kuwait, as well as on imports of most cargo except medical supplies and food. The U.S. Navy took the lead in an international naval effort to enforce this embargo, but the 13th Marine Expeditionary Unit (Special Operations Capable) was tasked, per doctrine, with providing a maritime special purpose force for conducting opposed boarding operations against underway vessels. The USS *Ogden* detached to conduct these operations with a heliborne force from 1st Force Reconnaissance Company and a Naval Special Warfare Command (Sea, Air, and Land [SEAL]) detachment.[31]

The first interdiction occurred on 13 October against the Iraqi vessel *Al-Mutanabbi*, and the next on 22 October against the *Al Sahil Al Arabi*. On 28 October, the 13th Marine Expeditionary Force's maritime special purpose force made its last interdiction against the *Amuriya*, an Iraqi vessel that refused to stop despite warning shots fired by U.S. and Australian frigates and low-level passes by U.S. Navy aircraft. The successful boarding party insertion finally persuaded the vessel to stop and allow an inspection. None of the boarding actions resulted in any casualties.[32]

A Line in the Sand: Planning to Defend Saudi Arabia

With Lieutenant General Walter Boomer at the helm

of both Marine Forces Central Command and I Marine Expeditionary Force, Marines continued to deploy to the Gulf and to solidify the defenses of Saudi Arabia. The 1st Marine Expeditionary Brigade deployed to Saudi Arabia by air and met the ships of Maritime Prepositioning Ship Squadron Three at al-Jubayl. The brigade did not operate independently when it arrived in Saudi Arabia, however. Instead, it combined with the 7th Marine Expeditionary Brigade upon arrival, as planned, forming the I Marine Expeditionary Force, the primary combat arm of Marine Forces Central Command.[33]

I Marine Expeditionary Force officially took over as the controlling Marine air-ground task force in Saudi Arabia on 3 September. The staff of the 7th Marine Expeditionary Brigade was combined with incoming staff to form the new headquarters, and Major General John Hopkins became the deputy commander, I Marine Expeditionary Force. Major General Jeremiah W. Pearson III was the deputy commander, Marine Forces Central Command. He remained in Riyadh at Central Command headquarters, serving as the senior Marine on staff there and coordinating with the other services.

The ground combat element of the I Marine Expeditionary Force during this initial phase of Operation Desert Shield was the 1st Marine Division, commanded by Major General James M. Myatt. The division's regiments were initially the 7th Marines, led by Colonel Carlton Fulford; 3d Marines, commanded by Colonel John H. Admire; and 11th Marines, led by Colonel Patrick G. Howard. In addition, the division had the 3d Tank Battalion, 3d Assault Amphibian Battalion, 1st Combat Engineer Battalion, 1st Tank Battalion, 1st Reconnaissance Battalion, and the 1st Light Armored Infantry Battalion. Because the division deployed in waves, several of its regimental units were comprised of battalions from different regiments. This lack of unit coherence extended to the company level for some of the attached battalions. Lieutenant Colonel Clifford O. Myers III of the 1st Light Armored Infantry Battalion responded to having companies from multiple battalions by designating the light armored infantry force as Task Force Shepherd; later this practice would spread to the entire division.[34]

The I Marine Expeditionary Force air combat element was the 3d Marine Aircraft Wing; it initially comprised three air groups and their supporting logistics and air defense units. Colonel Manfred Rietsch commanded Marine Aircraft Group 11, which controlled most of the fixed-wing squadrons of the wing at Shaikh Isa Air Base and Bahrain Interna-

---

*Roll-on/roll-off ships are designed to carry wheeled cargo such as trucks, automobiles, or railroad cars that are driven on and off the ship.

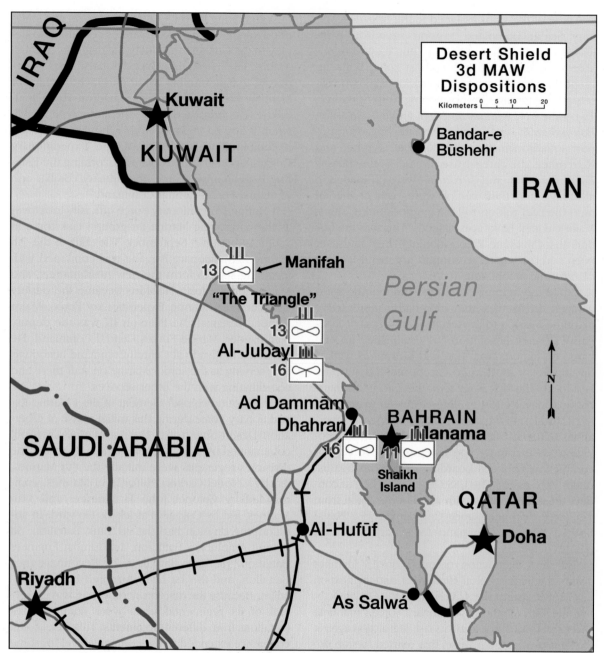

Adapted from a Central Intelligence Agency map by Marine Corps History Division

tional Airport. These squadrons included F/A-18 Hornets, A-6E Intruders, Grumman EA-6B Prowlers, and Lockheed KC-130 Hercules. Eventually the group would total 10 squadrons. Colonel John R. Bioty Jr. commanded Marine Aircraft Group 13 at King Abdul Aziz airfield. Colonel Bioty commanded the rest of the wing's fixed-winged squadrons, flying AV-8B Harrier IIs and North American OV-10 Broncos. By the end of Desert Storm, Bioty's group comprised four Harrier squadrons and two Bronco squadrons. Colonel Larry T. Garrett commanded

Marine Aircraft Group 16 with its rotary-wing squadrons based at the al-Jubayl Naval Air Facility. His seven squadrons flew CH-46E Sea Knights, CH-53D Sea Stallions, CH-53E Super Stallions, AH-1W Super Cobras, and UH-1N Hueys. Later Garrett's group would expand their operations to Ras al-Ghar and Manifah Bay.[35]

The 1st Force Service Support Group was commanded by Brigadier General James A. Brabham Jr. and provided the logistics element of I Marine Expeditionary Force. When the two brigades were combined, General Brabham, a veteran of service in the Middle East who had been working in Saudi Arabia preparing for the Marines' arrival since early August, organized the support group into a direct support group, a general support group, and a headquarters and services group. Colonel Alexander W. Powell, the former commanding officer of Brigade Support Group 7, commanded the direct support group, which was charged with sustaining the 1st Marine Division and the 3d Marine Aircraft Wing. Colonel Thomas E. Hampton commanded the general support group, which provided general support to I Marine Expeditionary Force. The Headquarters and Support Group was commanded by Lieutenant Colonel Henry T. Hayden. Among other duties, it coordinated port security.[36]

In addition to the three large units, I Marine Expeditionary Force controlled several smaller units, including the 1st Radio Battalion commanded by Lieutenant Colonel Thomas A. Flaherty and the 1st Surveillance, Reconnaissance, and Intelligence Group commanded by Colonel Michael V. Brock. Colonel Brock's group was a new organization, adopted in the late 1980s and based on concepts developed during the Vietnam War; it served as a regimental-sized umbrella organization that brought together previously independent intelligence collection and analysis organizations that served the expeditionary force.[*] During the course of the Gulf War deployment, the group would double in size as new units arrived from the United States, including the Marine all-source fusion center, fleet imagery intelligence unit, and topographic platoon as well as communications battalions, remotely piloted vehicle companies, air and naval gunfire companies, an intelligence company, and force reconnaissance companies.[37]

When I Marine Expeditionary Force began deploying its forces to Saudi Arabia, the need for the naval mobile construction battalions, better known as "Seabees," to reinforce the engineers of the 1st Force Service Support Group was apparent, and the commander of Naval Construction Battalions, U.S. Pacific Fleet, ordered four battalions to Saudi Arabia for this purpose. Captain Michael R. Johnson, USN, commanded this force, which ultimately became the 3d Naval Construction Regiment. From August 1990 until June 1991, the regiment completed 6 million square feet of aircraft parking; built 9.9 million square yards of ammunition storage; erected camps

for 37,500 people; set up mess halls that fed 100,000 people; maintained 400 kilometers of road; and laid out two airstrips, in addition to myriad smaller tasks. The close cooperation of Captain Johnson's Seabees and the Marines of the 1st Force Service Support Group continued the long tradition of Marine and Seabee cooperation and comradeship, as well as the important doctrine of Navy support for Marine Corps operations.[38]

General Boomer also received tactical command over an allied contingent, the British Army's 7th Armored Brigade, the famed "Desert Rats" of the North African campaign of World War II. Commanded by Brigadier Patrick Anthony John Cordingley, this brigade provided a boost to the Marine tank battalions with 170 FV4030/4 Challenger I main battle tanks. The 1st Force Service Support Group provided logistics for the British brigade, which formed an additional maneuver element for the Marine defense sector.

On the ground, Saudi Arabia was defended from a possible Iraqi invasion in September and October 1990 by the I Marine Expeditionary Force; the XVIII Airborne Corps, commanded by Lieutenant General Gary E. Luck, USA; and Saudi Arabian and allied forces. The Arab forces, which were arranged along the frontier, acted as a buffer and trip wire against any Iraqi movement south, but the primary defense of the Desert Kingdom lay with the American forces. The U.S. Army's primary troop contribution to the defense of Saudi Arabia—the XVIII Airborne Corps—consisted of the 82d Airborne Division, the 101st Airborne Division (Air Assault), the 24th Infantry Division (Mechanized), and the 1st Cavalry Division.

There were three potential avenues of approach for an Iraqi force invading Saudi Arabia. One route lay out of Iraq and Kuwait along the Wadi al-Batin (a "wadi" is the Arabic term for a shallow desert depression, often a dry river- or streambed) and directly across the desert to Riyadh. The next route passed from Kuwait and down the "Tapline Road" (so named because it followed a pipeline) across the desert to the Gulf, and the third route lay along the coastal highway south from Kuwait. The Tapline Road and coastal highway routes formed what was commonly referred to as the "Triangle," whose southern point was near Abu Hadriyah and whose two northern points were near an-Nuayriyah and Manifah Bay, respectively. Both Marine and Army planners saw the Triangle as the key region for the defense of Saudi Arabia.

The Army's plan for defending Saudi Arabia called for the 101st Airborne to screen to the west, while

---

[*]By the end of the 1990s, the Marine Corps had abandoned the surveillance, reconnaissance, and intelligence group concept.

the 24th Infantry Division covered the central desert region and I Marine Expeditionary Force covered the eastern region around the port of al-Jubayl. The 1st Cavalry Division was established behind the 24th Infantry Division; the Marines prepared to launch a counterattack; and the 82d Airborne was deployed around Dharhan, ad-Dammam, and Abqaiq in order to secure the rear areas from commando and terrorists attacks. The Army intended to engage Iraqi forces early with its attack helicopters and armored forces while conducting a mobile defense.[39]

Primarily concerned with the coastal highway route, the Marine plan, in contrast, called for utilizing the terrain to hinder and disperse the Iraqi forces as they drove south. The highway was bordered by *sabkhas* or salt marshes; by mining the highway, blowing up highway culverts, and destroying gas stations, the Marines hoped to channel the Iraqis off the road and into these desert sand traps where close air support and naval gunfire could destroy them. Lacking the Army's vehicular mobility and high numbers of armored vehicles, the Marines intended to hold just south of the tip of the Triangle, at what was called "Cement Factory Ridge" (the same piece of high ground that 7th Marines had initially defended in August). This was considerably removed from where the Army intended to engage the Iraqis, and the Marines worried that the Iraqis passing down the Tapline Road might flank them. This caused some tension between the Marine and Army tactical commanders, though in the actual event the Iraqis did not invade and the defensive plans were thus never tested.[40]

Meeting of Cultures: Marines and Saudis

The United States began providing the Kingdom of Saudi Arabia with military assistance in the 1940s, and as the decades passed the relationship grew. The United States assisted the kingdom as a bulwark first against communism and secular ethnic

Adapted from a Central Intelligence Agency map by Marine Corps History Division

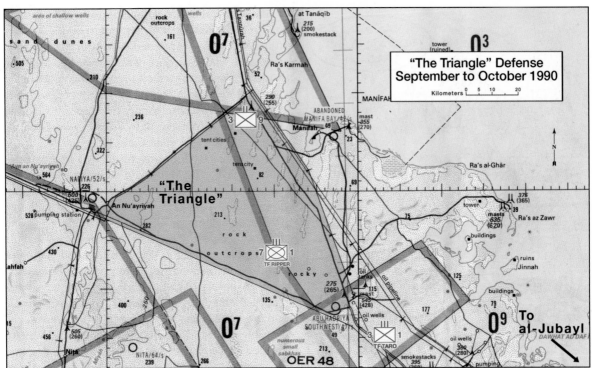

Adapted from a 1991 Ministry of Defence (United Kingdom) map by Marine Corps History Division

Arab nationalist movements, and later against radical Islamic movements. In addition, a strong, stable Saudi Arabia was seen as the key to preventing a general war in the Middle East. For the House of Saud (as the royal family is known), the close relationship and military assistance of the United States acted as a counter to Saudi Arabia's more powerful neighbors Iraq and Egypt, as well as an aid in the suppression of internal rebellious movements.[41]

As the decades passed, however, and hostility against the United States increased in the broader Islamic world, American military assistance became nearly as much of a liability as it was an asset. This paradox was neatly summarized by leading Egyptian journalist Mohamed Heikal: "The first responsibility of a Saudi monarch is to keep intimate relations with Washington, and the second is to do all he can to hide it."[42]

The Iraqi invasion of Kuwait produced a near catastrophe in foreign relations for the Saudis, because it was clear they could not stop any Iraqi encroachment into their territory without American aid, yet that aid would have to be very public. The intimate relationship between the United States and Saudi Arabia had long been an open secret, but now it would truly be exposed. The presence of a massive "infidel" army on Saudi soil, home to Mecca and Medina, the two holiest cities in Islam (and forbidden to nonbelievers), was a potential public relations disaster. On the other hand, Sad-

dam had invaded Kuwait, a fellow Arab country that had materially aided Iraq in its war against Iran. Moreover, Saddam's own Baathist Party was an avowedly secular organization devoted in part to ethnic Arab nationalism. Both of these facts helped Saudi Arabia maintain its image in the Islamic world while accepting American aid. But the situation required constant, careful manipulation. There were many tensions between the Saudis, who naturally wished Coalition forces would disrupt Saudi life as little as possible, and the Coalition forces, who often felt unappreciated by the Saudis they were ostensibly in the desert to protect.

General Schwarzkopf took steps as soon as American forces began to arrive in the Saudi Arabia to mitigate the impact of hundreds of thousands of Americans pouring into the Desert Kingdom. Alcohol and pornography were forbidden to American forces deploying to the region, and chaplains were renamed "morale officers." In some areas, however, Saudi beliefs had to bend to American mores, especially in regard to American servicewomen. Women were firmly integrated into the American armed forces, and it was difficult if not impossible to deploy without them, regardless of the Saudi dislike for women in roles the Saudis perceived as masculine. This led to one of the few issues the Marines had with Saudi customs when a Saudi commander complained about a televised broadcast of

Reprinted from Eliot A. Cohen et al., eds., *Gulf War Air Power Survey*, vol. IV, *Weapons, Tactics, and Training and Space Operations* (Washington, DC: U.S. Government Printing Office, 1993)
Iraq worked hard to drive a wedge between Saudi Arabia and the United States throughout the Gulf crisis. This cartoon from an Iraqi propaganda pamphlet highlights the thrust of their argument. Drunken American soldiers (one wearing a Star of David around his neck) and two scantily clad females cavort in front of an oil well, while a corpulent King Fahd says, "Our holy things, our land, and our honor are in safe hands." American military policies in Saudi Arabia were designed to prevent incidents that might validate this propaganda.

a touch football game between Navy and Marine women in shorts and T-shirts while male Marines were watching.[43]

Once in the kingdom, liberty was severely curtailed, and most Marine units lived a monastic desert life for most of the deployment. Captain Michael J. McCusker, commander of Company I, 3d Battalion, 3d Marines, later said, "We never had an air-conditioned place like people saw on TV in the States. We were not authorized to go to town. That p——d a lot of us off because people in the States thought we were seeing civilians. We were stuck in the desert, nowhere near a town. We didn't even have electricity. It was all flashlights and candles and chem[ical] lights."[44]

Although unpopular with the troops, some of the restrictions had very positive effects. General Boomer later recalled, "CENTCOM [Central Command] General Order Number One: prohibits drinking in Saudi Arabia. It turned out to be the greatest thing that's ever happened. I've been in a combat situation where alcohol was allowed and one in which it wasn't allowed and I will tell you, it's better when there is no alcohol. It's just better. So many fewer problems. Disciplinary problems. It's hard to keep it out. Marines want to drink, as did I, but we didn't and it was a great thing."[45]

Saudi military forces were divided into two distinct services. The Ministry of Defense and Aviation consisted of the regular Saudi ground and aviation forces, whose mission was to protect the kingdom from external threats. The Saudi aviation forces were folded, along with other Coalition air forces, into the air campaign, but the Royal Saudi Land Forces or Saudi Army operated separately as nine brigades.[46]

The Ministry of Defense and Aviation units were supplemented by the Saudi Arabian National Guard, comprising two mechanized brigades. Ostensibly, the Saudi Arabian National Guard was intended to reinforce the Ministry of Defense and Aviation forces in the event of a war, but in reality its primary role was to protect the royal family from internal rebellion. Staffed with personnel loyal to the House of Saud specifically through family and tribal ties, the Saudi Arabian National Guard was descended from the Ikhwan,* a Wahhabite tribal militia that formed the main body of Ibn Saud's forces during World War I. The government employed the Saudi National Guard to protect the holy cities of Mecca and Medina and to counter the regular armed forces in the event of an attempted coup. It received the lion's share of training and equipment that was available to Saudi forces, although it did not possess tanks.[47]

Overall, the Saudi National Guard was favored over the Ministry of Aviation and Defense; the royal family kept the two forces separated; and neither force trained with the other. Nevertheless, oil-rich Saudi Arabia did not lack resources, and both services were lavishly equipped with modern military hardware. Despite the massive amounts spent on modernization, many Saudi soldiers lacked professional standards or competence, and the officer corps granted the noncommissioned officers neither authority nor responsibility.

---

*Named after the Arabic term for "brotherhood," the Ikhwan became known as the White Army because they wore traditional white robes instead of military uniforms. Wahhabism, the dominant form of Islam in Saudi Arabia, aims to purify Sunni Islam of any practices that deviate from the teachings of Muhammad and his compatriots.

In 1990–91, direct American military assistance to Saudi Arabia centered around two organizations. Officially, there was the U.S. Department of Defense's Office of Program Manager for the Modernization of the Saudi National Guard, which assigned American officers as advisors to the Saudi National Guard. In addition, the Vinnell Corporation provided the Saudi National Guard with military contract advisors, most of whom were American veterans of the Vietnam War. In both cases, the personnel assigned to train the Saudi National Guard prior to the invasion of Kuwait fought with the National Guard forces, greatly increasing their effectiveness. The military advisors and Vinnell contractors worked closely together in supporting the Saudi National Guard.[48]

Since neither Saudi Arabia nor the United States was willing to have its forces under the other's command, a joint structure was set up. Joint Forces Command, a parallel organization of Central Command, was composed of most of the Arab contingents and was led by Saudi General Khaled bin Sultan. A nephew of King Fahd, he was a graduate of the Royal Military Academy, Sandhurst, and the Air War College at Maxwell Air Force Base, Alabama. In 1986, after 25 years in the armed forces of his country, General Khaled was appointed commander of the Royal Saudi Air Defense Forces.

Originally the Arab forces were organized into the Eastern Area Command stationed along the northern border, but eventually the command was further subdivided into Joint Forces Command–North and Joint Forces Command–East. Joint Forces Command–North, although dominated by two Egyptian divisions, also contained Saudi Arabian Ministry of Defense and Aviation, Kuwaiti, and Syrian brigades. It controlled the territory from the "elbow" at al-Manaqish to the Kuwait-Iraq border. Saudi National Guard units and Ministry of Defense and Aviation forces, as well as Kuwaiti forces and a Qatari mechanized brigade, made up Joint Forces Command–East. It controlled the territory from the eastern border of the al-Wafrah oil fields to the Persian Gulf coast, including al-Khafji and the surrounding territory. The assignment of Saudi National Guard units under the command of General Khaled was out of the ordinary and indicated how seriously the House of Saud took the crisis. The placement of the subcommands was due to Arab pride, which dictated that they hold positions in the front line to ensure theirs would be the first blood shed.[49]

Although well-equipped and provided with professional military advisors, the Saudi forces were still not up to Western military standards. Islamic holidays, daily prayers, and familial obligations dramatically decreased the amount of training. The troops generally averaged an eighth-grade education, and there was no noncommissioned officer corps. The officers were often well educated, and most spoke at least some English, but they were discouraged from independent thought or action until given a battalion-level command. They faced tremendous pressure to keep their superiors happy.

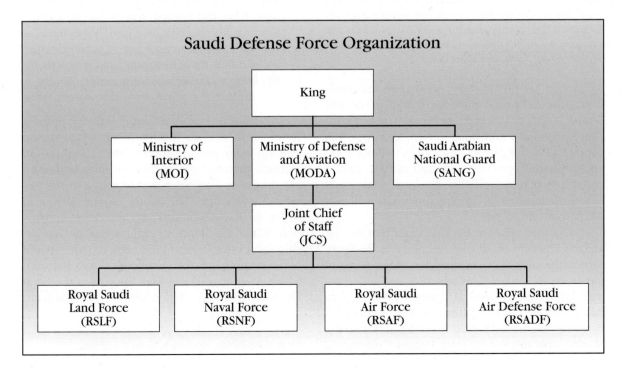

Defense Imagery DA-ST-92-08034

Gen Khaled bin Sultan bin Saud, a prince of the Saudi royal family, was the Joint Forces commander and Gen Schwarzkopf's opposite number. Joint Forces Command was composed of the Coalition's Islamic forces from Saudi Arabia, Egypt, Syria, and other states.

As Captain Joseph Molofsky, 3d Marines liaison officer to the 2d Brigade of the Saudi Arabian National Guard, noted: "It's all make or break. You displease your senior and you're done forever. You make him happy and he sends you on vacation to Europe, literally." Saudi forces were untested in 1991, having last seen action in the 1920s. Because of these factors, there was serious concern about how well they would perform in battle.[50]

In October, when it became clear that the 1st Marine Division would be fighting beside Saudi forces, the division's commander, Major General James Myatt, ordered his assistant division commander, Brigadier General Thomas V. Draude, to take primary responsibility for liaison duties.[51] Brigadier General Draude used 3d Marines, the Marine unit nearest to Joint Forces Command–

East units, as the primary focus of his liaison effort. As Colonel John Admire, commanding officer of the 3d Marines, remarked:

> We were the only U.S. combat force located on the eastern coast [of Saudi Arabia]. Now the significance of that of course is that we continued to train with Coalition forces. We were the division's primary instrument from October-November-December and through January of training with the Saudis and training with the Qatari forces.[52]

Colonel Admire assigned Captain Molofsky, an officer with previous experience in the Middle East who had served with the UN on the Sinai Peninsula, as the Marine liaison officer to the Saudi National Guard.[53]

In addition to liaison and training work, the air and naval gunfire company fulfilled its doctrinal role and attached fire control teams to the 2d Brigade, Saudi Arabian National Guard. Major General Myatt later recalled:

> What was really interesting was we got a lot of pushback, because at that point there was a bit of interservice rivalry and the Special Forces folks were looking for a mission, and they said, "It's our mission to be training indigenous forces[.]" They would resist us training the 2nd SANG [Saudi Arabian National Guard] and I just simply ignored it, and I told General Boomer that, "We have got to give them the confidence that we can do it." Because what the Special Forces role is, is to train them to use their own gear, not to interface with our gear and our capabilities. It caused a little bit of heartburn, and wasn't the only thing to cause heartburn in the alliance, but I did it.[54]

The Marines began working with the nascent Royal Saudi Marines* in September. A U.S. Marine training team was attached to them, and the 3d Marines shared some of their facilities and training ranges as they prepared to move to the Cement Factory line. The Saudis taught classes on desert tactics, desert survival, and desert navigation, while the Marines taught weapons, leadership, and equipment maintenance. One benefit of the training was the enhanced contact between Saudi Arabian officers and their men. General Draude explained, "When you got into the tech-

---

*The Royal Saudi Marines today comprise two battalions within the Royal Saudi Navy and are based at Ras al-Ghar.

nical description, you needed someone who spoke Arabic and we just simply couldn't strip away what few Arabic speakers that we had. So the Saudi officer, who in most cases spoke English, became the guy who was translating, and therefore his status in the eyes of his men was raised considerably."[55]

In December, General Draude described the training as successful up to that point, noting that

we found, as always, our best ambassador is a U.S. Marine. It's something that we kind of take for granted and I started thinking about it and came to the conclusion that in the Marine Corps, we deploy. I mean, you don't stay around home for very long if you're going to be in the Marine Corps. You go overseas. If you go overseas you're going to have contact with folks from another country. That, of course, usually means the military. . . . We just have an experience base of working with soldiers of other countries. It's not a big deal for us to come up to a soldier of a different nation, different color skin, different language, different everything, and out comes the poncho, his weapon is on the poncho, your weapon is on the poncho, disassemble and you show me yours, I'll show you mine, and without any translation needed, without any interpreter needed. It's just two soldiers who will work together very well. A U.S. Marine is also guileless: what you see is what you get. Our Marines will share whatever they have with another soldier. You can't train someone to be that way. I mean he just is or he isn't, and that basic goodness—without trying to bring tears to your eyes—that basic goodness of a Marine comes through and it

Members of the Saudi Arabian National Guard pose in their V-150 armored personnel carrier.

Photo courtesy of Capt Joseph Molofsky

make us different and it makes us better in this regard of working with soldiers of other countries. I'm absolutely convinced of it and have told the Commandant so and the State Department folks and others just how good of an ambassador a U.S. Marine is.[56]

◆ CHAPTER 4 ◆

Preparing for War

Throughout the fall of 1990, diplomacy continued as the Coalition focused on convincing Iraq to release the hostages it had taken during the invasion and to withdraw from Kuwait. Iraq veered between defiance and attempts to end the crisis but focused on splitting the Coalition by applying diplomatic pressure to its traditional ally, the Soviet Union, and its greatest trading partner, France. But Iraq's understanding of the changed international situation in the wake of glasnost was consistently wrong. France remained a reasonably firm member of the Coalition, sending troops and aircraft to the fight. Russia attempted to broker multiple peace deals, but Iraq's intransigence and the firmness of the Coalition's position that Iraq must depart Kuwait without preconditions precluded each of them, making a military conflict seem more likely each week.[1]

Despite the threat of a Coalition military intervention, Iraq refused to withdraw from Kuwait. Saddam was convinced that the United States could neither maintain the Coalition nor intervene militarily in a meaningful way. A military struggle to free Kuwait thus became inevitable.

Operation Desert Shield was a success at the beginning of November. Sufficient military force was in the Persian Gulf to prevent an Iraqi attempt to take Saudi Arabia or the Gulf states.* Now the political decision over whether or not the Coalition would attempt to forcibly eject Iraq from Kuwait had to be made. On 8 November 1990, President Bush indicated this would happen when he announced the American military force in the Gulf would nearly double in size. Thereafter, U.S. Central Command proceeded to reinforce the troops in the Gulf and began serious planning for an offensive to evict Iraq from Kuwait.

Imminent Thunder and Amphibious Operations

The 13th Marine Expeditionary Unit (Special Operations Capable) had been deployed since June 1990, when it had departed on its scheduled cruise of the Pacific. On 4 November, the expeditionary unit departed the Persian Gulf region and sailed for Subic Bay in the Philippines, with orders to rearm and train, preparing to possibly return to the Gulf at a later date. The departure of Colonel John Rhodes's Marines left the 4th Marine Expeditionary Brigade as the sole amphibious landing force available in the Persian Gulf region.

Operation Imminent Thunder was conducted from 15 to 21 November 1990. Conducted by Central Command at General Schwarzkopf's orders, this training exercise was conducted in order to test the plan for defending Saudi Arabia and to determine what issues would arise from the large joint/combined* force working together in the Desert Kingdom. It was a five-phase operation that focused on air and amphibious exercises paired with tests of command, control, and communications. The exercise also served to strengthen General Walter Boomer's I Marine Expeditionary Force staff. Although Marine expeditionary forces were an established part of Marine Corps doctrine, there was little expectation that they would be employed. The Marine expeditionary units deployed annually to the Mediterranean and the Pacific, and the Marine expeditionary brigades exercised regularly, but few expected the Corps to deploy an expeditionary force outside a major war. Operation Imminent Thunder provided an opportunity for the Marine expeditionary force staff to practice controlling the battle in a joint/combined environment.[2]

The exercise's amphibious landings were originally planned for Ras al-Mishab, but its proximity to the Kuwaiti border and the possibility of unintentional conflict with Iraqi forces led to General Schwarzkopf shifting the exercise south, to Ras al-Ghar. The new site was much more accessible to the media, which was eager for any new footage as the confrontation continued into its third month. Marine amphibious capabilities received great deal

---

*In retrospect, it seems unlikely that Iraq intended to invade Saudi Arabia, but the secretive and unpredictable nature of Saddam Hussein's government prevented that contingency from being ruled out at the time.

*In American military parlance, joint operations are conducted by two or more services (Navy-Army, Air Force-Marine Corps, etc.), while combined operations are conducted by American forces in conjunction with allied foreign military forces. Operation Desert Shield, conducted by forces from all U.S. Armed Services as well as the military forces of several other nations (including Saudi Arabia, Great Britain, France, etc.), was therefore a joint/combined operation.

Marines of 2d Marine Division move out on a mission after disembarking from a Marine Medium Helicopter Squadron 263 CH-46E Sea Knight helicopter in Saudi Arabia during Exercise Imminent Thunder, which was part of Operation Desert Shield.

During Exercise Sea Soldier III in the Persian Gulf, the bow ramp of a utility landing craft from the amphibious assault ship USS Nassau *(LHA 4) descends as troops and vehicles prepare to hit the beach in support of Operation Desert Shield.*

of press attention as a result, and the Amphibious Task Force commander, Rear Admiral John La-Plante, later described it as "beating our chest for the press." Ironically, most of the amphibious landings were canceled because of dangerous seas, but the extensive air and communication operations were a success.[3]

The exercise also marked the end of one of the earlier Marine air innovations. In response to the difficulties involved in defending Saudi Arabia from

Call Waiting *by Col H. Avery Chenoweth, head of the I Marine Expeditionary Force combat art team during the Gulf War. The painting depicts patient Marines at one of many telephone facilities set up near U.S. compounds during Operation Desert Shield.*

an Iraqi attack in the early days of Operation Desert Shield, Marine planners had developed Task Force Cunningham. They designed it as a task-organized, aviation-only task force that would stop Iraqi ground maneuver forces with concentrated fire from the air, covering the withdrawal of Saudi and Marine forces along the coastal highway. UH-1N Huey and AH-1W Super Cobra helicopters would operate alongside OV-10D Bronco and AV-8B Harrier fixed-wing aircraft in the task force. The intent was for this task force to cover the western flank of the Marines. Marine commanders viewed the concept with some skepticism; they were worried that Marine air assets could be used up in this manner. Brigadier General Granville R. Amos, assistant wing commander of the 3d Marine Aircraft Wing during the Gulf War, summed it up succinctly: "If you shoot your wad at one time, you don't really have anything to follow-up." In November, it was concluded that the general support of the divisions precluded

the ability of the wing to maintain a separate, massed task force, but Task Force Cunningham influenced staff concepts of massed aerial forces throughout the planning for Operation Desert Storm.[4]

From 8 to 18 December, another amphibious landing exercise was conducted: Sea Soldier III. This brigade-sized exercise included helicopter and surface landings at night, and ended with the Marine Forces afloat conducting much needed maintenance and logistics operations ashore.[5]

The UN-sanctioned embargo of Iraq and Kuwait continued throughout November and December. After the 13th Marine Expeditionary Unit departed, the 4th Marine Expeditionary Brigade was tasked with providing a heliborne maritime special purpose force for conducting opposed boarding operations against underway vessels. USS *Trenton* detached to conduct these operations with force reconnaissance Marines and a Navy SEAL detachment comprising the boarding force. After forming in late October, the special maritime force practiced boarding operations throughout November.[6]

In late December, the 4th Marine Expeditionary Brigade's boarding force conducted its first maritime interdiction, the most complicated interdiction undertaken during the crisis. The Iraqi vessel *Ibn Khaldoon* was known as the "Peace Ship" and was intended as direct challenge to the UN embargo. It sailed from Tripoli, Libya, with female peace activists, children, and journalists from a variety of countries on board, and the vessel's cargo was listed as milk and medicine. In accordance with the UN embargo, the *Ibn Khaldoon* was interdicted on 26 December. The Marines and sailors of the boarding force subdued the ship's crew with minimal force; one Swedish peace activist who suffered a heart attack during the boarding was saved by the *Trenton*'s medical personnel. The swift, professional interdiction denied Iraq a propaganda victory. The final Marine boarding operation of Desert Shield came on 30 December when the brigade's boarding force took an Iraqi tanker, the *Ain Zallah*, again with minimal force.[7]

Happy Holidays from Saudi Arabia

The president's 8 November announcement that American forces in the Persian Gulf would be reinforced in anticipation of liberating Kuwait led to a series of visits by senior civilian and military leadership throughout the month. These culminated in the Thanksgiving visit of President Bush and his wife, First Lady Barbara P. Bush, accompanied by several senators and congressmen as well as Army General Colin Powell, chairman of the Joint Chiefs of Staff. On 22 November the president and his wife enjoyed Thanksgiving dinner with the Marines, and the president gave a speech warning Iraq again that it must withdraw from Kuwait. On 23 November the presidential couple visited with Marines and sailors on board the USS *Nassau*.[8]

Marines celebrated the Marine Corps birthday on 10 November with cake and food; the customary toasts were given using nonalcoholic beverages. Many Marines later recalled this birthday celebration in a war zone as one of the most memorable of their careers. Thanksgiving was celebrated in a similar manner, although the presidential visit dominated the holiday. Christmas was very sparse as preparations for the upcoming offensive kept all the Marines in the Gulf occupied, and Christmas religious observances were muted in deference to Saudi sensibilities. Despite these conditions, Marines were showered with packages from the Red Cross as well as myriad parcels from home addressed to "any Marine." In fact they received so many of these packages that carrying them was difficult.[9]

Officers and noncommissioned officers worked hard to maintain troop morale during the holidays. Captain Michael J. McCusker of Company I, 3d Battalion, 3d Marines, later described one of his own efforts:

Jay Leno performs a stand-up routine for the Marines in the desert during a holiday USO tour. The unusual environment notwithstanding, Marines remember he was quite funny.

Photo courtesy of Maj Thomas P. Simon

Photo by Sgt Jeff Wright. Defense Imagery DF-ST-92-07519

Entertainer Bob Hope performs for military personnel at the USO Christmas tour during Operation Desert Shield.

It was something to keep their minds off of being so far away and to make some sort of Christmas there in the desert, and it worked. The Marines use to give me s——t about it: "Gee, sir, this Christmas tree is so ugly that we are going to burn it." But it gave them something to look at, and I think it did what I wanted it to do. We decorated it with engineering tape and tinsel and little Christmas ornaments that school kids made and sent to us. I took chem. [chemical] lights and hung them on the tree on Christmas Eve and made a big cross on top. It was round like a big bush. It was five or six feet tall, and the camels used to come and chew on it and we had to shoo them away. It served its purpose.[10]

Despite the best efforts of the officers and noncommissioned officers, however, it was inevitable that Christmas 1990 would have a melancholy tinge to it for Marines in the Gulf. Most were convinced that they would be liberating Kuwait by force soon, and this expectation of combat was never far from the troops' minds.[11]

As it has since 1941, the United Service Organizations (USO) sent tours of performers to the war zone in order to entertain the troops in the Gulf during the crisis of November and December. The headliner of the tours was the venerable Bob Hope, who entertained American troops in a war zone for the final time in his storied career. Other entertainers included comedians Steve Martin and Jay Leno; all three visited with Marines both ashore and afloat. In 1990, CBS ran a popular sitcom called *Major Dad* that centered on the life of a Marine major and his family. The star of the series, Gerald McRaney (and his wife, actress Delta Burke), also visited Marines in the Persian Gulf on USO tours, even as his character on the series lamented not being assigned to the Gulf.[12]

Brigadier General Thomas Draude recalled Bob Hope's visit with the Marines on 26 December:

> Bob and Delores Hope arrived to entertain the Marines of the First Marine Division. I was assigned as the escort officer and was amazed how this couple hopped on and off our helicopter at the various stops. His daughter was concerned about tiring him, so the last show, to one of the assault elements going into Kuwait, was cancelled by her. I asked if we could at least let him fly over so the Marines would see his helicopter—she agreed. I then asked if we could land so he could see what their living conditions were—she reluctantly agreed. I then asked if she would allow him to take a jeep ride to see where the troops were waiting—she was not pleased with me at this point, but gave her OK. When Bob Hope saw the stage and all

the thousand or so Marines, it was "show-time!"

He proceeded to put on a show with De-lores, who was a great singer (she was one of the few women the Saudis would allow in country—Gladys Knight and the Pips re-mained outside the country). Also joining them were [baseball player] Johnny Bench and [country music singer] Aaron Tippin. It was a performance I'll never forget!

When it was over, there was a mass move-ment forward by the Marines to thank Bob and Delores for coming. One of the most moving sights was Delores hugging Marine after Marine, as if she was a surrogate mother, as Bob shook hands—and also hugged.

Bob and Delores became my heroes that day—and remain so ever since.[13]

Building an Offensive Capability

On 18 November 1990, the 2d Marine Division was ordered to join I Marine Expeditionary Force in the Persian Gulf. Commanded by Major General William M. Keys, the 2d Marine Division had not deployed overseas as a division since the Second World War. It had already contributed the majority of the ground combat element to the 4th Marine Expeditionary Brigade and was also committed to providing two battalions to maintain Marine expeditionary units in the Mediterranean. As a result, the regimental com-bat teams of the 2d Marine Division had a somewhat patchwork quality, with each containing battalions

---

A Marine Christmas

Marines responded to the holidays with characteristic "grunt" humor, as this carol composed in theater illustrates.

The Twelve Months of Exile

(Heard on Armed Forces Radio "Oasis Station 99.9" on the Desert Shield Network on Christmas Eve 1990)

In our 12th month of exile,
My jarhead gave to me:
A 12 month extension,
11 months of waiting,
10 cans of near beer,
9,000 sandbags,
8 days in gas masks,
7 gallons of water,
6 miles of cammie netting,
5 MREs [meals, ready to eat],
4 weeks of guard duty,
3 hours of sleep,
2 pairs of cammies,
and a camel burger in a plastic bag.[14]

---

from various regiments. The division's major units were the 6th Marines, commanded by Colonel Lawrence H. Livingston; the 8th Marines, led by Colonel Larry S. Schmidt; and the 10th Marines, com-manded by Colonel Leslie M. Palm. Additionally, the

The vehicle cargo ship SS Maj Stephen W. Pless *(T-AK 3007) of Maritime Prepositioning Ship Squadron One offloads equipment for the 2d Marine Division during Operation Desert Shield.*

Photo by SSgt J. R. Ruark. Defense Imagery DM-ST-92-00102

M1A1 Abrams tanks of the 2d Tank Battalion in the desert. The arrival of the 2d Marine Division and its Abrams tanks greatly increased the firepower available to LtGen Walter Boomer.

division included the 2d Light Armored Infantry Battalion, 2d Tank Battalion, 8th Tank Battalion, 2d Assault Amphibian Battalion, 2d Combat Engineer Battalion, and 2d Reconnaissance Battalion.[15]

Much of the division's equipment was brought by Maritime Prepositioning Ship Squadron One, and the squadron's arrival in Saudi Arabia on 13 December was much less chaotic than the August and September debarking. The squadron's four vessels, SS *Sgt Matej Kocak* (T-AK 3005), SS *PFC Eugene A. Obregon* (T-AK 3006), SS *Maj Stephen W. Pless* (T-AK 3007), and MV *2dLt John P. Bobo* (T-AK 3008), were unloaded in 10 days.[16]

The 2d Marine Division headquarters was established on 14 December in Saudi Arabia, and the first division order was issued on 25 December. From this point the division moved its units forward and prepared for offensive operations, although the last of the division's units, 2d Tank Battalion, did not complete unloading its equipment and moving forward until 17 January.[17]

There was never any doubt that the 2d Marine Division would deploy and fight as a separate division, but the organization of the air and support legs of the I Marine Expeditionary Force was less certain. For the air element, there was some dis-

agreement between Headquarters Marine Corps and the Marine commanders in the Gulf over whether the 2d Marine Aircraft Wing should deploy as a separate unit or send its subordinate groups and squadrons to reinforce the 3d Marine Aircraft Wing in place in Saudi Arabia. Major General Royal N. Moore Jr., the 3d Marine Aircraft Wing's commander, felt that "it is cleaner, [with] less overhead, to place the additional squadrons under existing groups. . . . More importantly, the operational lines are simpler, which translates to a more responsive aviation combat element." In the end, General Moore's view prevailed.[18]

The result was that additional squadrons were added to Marine Aircraft Groups 11, 13, and 16. These additional squadrons were drawn from the 1st, 2d, and 4th Marine Aircraft Wings on both the East and the West Coasts. A second helicopter group, Colonel Michael J. Williams's Marine Aircraft Group 26, also deployed to the Gulf. Its seven squadrons of CH-46E Sea Knights, CH-53D Sea Stallions, Sikorsky RH-53D Sea Stallions, CH-53E Super Stallions, AH-1J Sea Cobras, and UH-1N Hueys were drawn from the 2d Marine Aircraft Wing and the 4th Marine Aircraft Wing.[19]

The combat service support leg of the I Marine

Expeditionary Force had a similar problem. Supporting two Marine divisions and two wings worth of Marine aircraft required the resources of two force service support groups, but General Boomer wanted the unity of command that one force service support group provided. Brigadier General James Brabham, commanding general of the 1st Force Service Support Group, and Brigadier General Charles C. Krulak, commanding general of the 2d Force Service Support Group, reached a solution that provided for both issues. Brigadier General Krulak deployed his unit deployed to the Gulf as the Direct Support Command. Direct Support Command was further divided into Direct Support Group 1, commanded by Colonel Alexander W. Powell, and Direct Support Group 2, commanded by Colonel Thomas P. Donnelly Jr. Brigadier General Brabham commanded the General Support Command, divided into Colonel Paul A. Pankey's General Support Group 1 and Colonel Thomas E. Hampton's General Support Group 2. Captain Michael R. Johnson, USN, continued to command the 3d Naval Construction Regiment. By doctrine, combat service support units provide rear area security, but General Boomer wanted those Marines focused on supporting the combat units and provided the reservists of Colonel George E. Germann's 24th Marines to provide rear area security instead.[20]

In practice, the 2d Force Service Support Group's headquarters operated the Direct Support Command, and the 1st Force Service Support Group's headquarters continued to operate the General Support Command, but their subordinate units were mixed and matched to best support their differing missions. Direct Support Command received the tactical motor transport, engineers, and landing support assets as well as Direct Support Group 1, while the General Support Command contained the supply, maintenance, and service units and ran the Marine services at the ports. By the end of December, General Krulak had selected Kibrit, Saudi Arabia, as the site of the forward combat support area for the offensive to liberate Kuwait, and construction on the new base had begun.[21]

In October 1990, the 5th Marine Expeditionary Brigade, commanded by Brigadier General Peter J. Rowe, was told to prepare to ship to the Persian Gulf in order to replace the 4th Marine Expeditionary Brigade. President Bush's early November announcement that U.S. forces in the Gulf would be dramatically reinforced shifted that mission from replacement to reinforcement. Brigadier General Rowe's brigade was normally the designated sea-deployment brigade of the I Marine Expeditionary Force (just as the 7th Marine Expeditionary Brigade was designated as the Maritime Prepositioning Force brigade), but many of the units that would normally be called on to fill out the brigade had al-

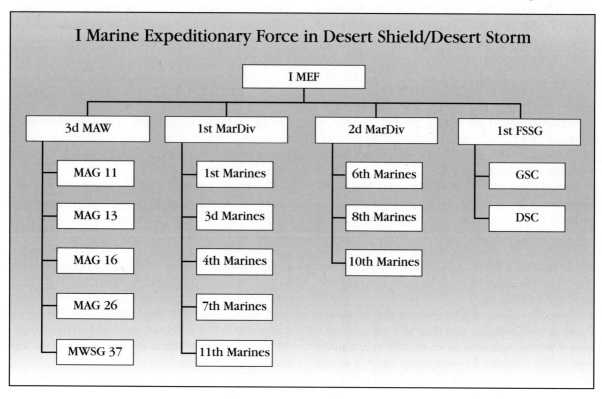

A bow view of the amphibious assault ship USS New Orleans *(LPH 11) underway. During the Gulf War, the* New Orleans *served in Amphibious Group 3, carrying the 5th Marine Expeditionary Brigade. After the war, she became the flagship of Amphibious Squadron 1, carrying the 11th Marine Expeditionary Unit, which broke from the rest of the brigade to conduct its scheduled Pacific cruise.*

ready been gutted when filling out the forces deploying for Desert Shield. As a result, the brigade's elements all had large numbers of reservists operating alongside their active-duty Marines.[22]

The brigade's ground combat element was Colonel Randolph A. Gangle's Regimental Landing Team 5 comprised of the 2d Battalion, 5th Marines; 3d Battalion, 5th Marines; the 3d Battalion, 1st Marines; the 2d Battalion, 11th Marines (Reinforced); Company B, 1st Reconnaissance Battalion (Reinforced); Company A, 4th Tank Battalion (Reinforced); Company A, 4th Assault Amphibian Battalion (Reinforced); and Company D, 1st Light Armored Infantry Battalion (Reinforced).[23]

Colonel Randall L. West commanded Marine Aircraft Group 50, which made up the air element of the brigade. His squadrons included Marine Medium Helicopter Squadron (Composite) 268, Marine Medium Helicopter Squadron 265, Marine Light Attack Helicopter Squadron 169, and Marine Reserve Attack Helicopter Squadron 773.[24]

Lieutenant Colonel Robert E. Lupton commanded Brigade Service Support Group 5, the combat service support element of the brigade. Although des-ignated a brigade support group, this was really only a reinforced Marine expeditionary unit service support group. The brigade lacked many of its required logistics assets, and while this was not an issue while at sea, the brigade would have difficulty sustaining itself once it deployed ashore.[25]

Rear Admiral Stephen S. Clarey's Amphibious Group 3 was designated to carry the 5th Marine Expeditionary Brigade to the Gulf, but initially it included only nine amphibious vessels, far less than the two dozen required for a brigade. More vessels were added after high-level conferences so that when the brigade departed on 1 December, Amphibious Group 3 comprised the amphibious assault ships USS *Tarawa* (LHA 1), USS *Tripoli* (LPH 10), USS *New Orleans* (LPH 11), USS *Denver* (LPD 9), USS *Juneau* (LPD 10), USS *Mobile* (LKA 115), USS *Vancouver* (LPD 2), USS *Anchorage* (LSD 36), USS *Barbour County* (LST 1195), USS *Frederick* (LST 1184), USS *Mount Vernon* (LSD 39), USS *Germantown* (LSD 42), and USS *Peoria* (LST 1183). In addition, Maritime Sealift Command provided SS *Flickertail State* (T-ACS 5) and SS *Cape Girardeau* (T-AK 2039) to carry sustainment supplies.[26]

Colonel Robert J. Garner's 11th Marine Expeditionary Unit was originally intended to replace the 13th Marine Expeditionary Unit in the Gulf, but its units formed the core of General Rowe's brigade instead. Loading and organization were designed so that Colonel Garner could break his unit out from the brigade and operate independently if required, however. It comprised Battalion Landing Team 3/1, Marine Medium Helicopter Squadron (Composite) 268, and Marine Expeditionary Unit Service Support Group 11 and was embarked on Amphibious Squadron 1, commanded by Captain Michael D. Barker, USN. The vessels earmarked for Captain Barker's squadron were the *New Orleans, Denver, Germantown, Peoria,* and *Mobile*. In the event, 11th Marine Expeditionary Unit and Amphibious Squadron 1 did not break off from the brigade until March, after hostilities in the Gulf were over.[27]

The 5th Marine Expeditionary Brigade set sail on board Amphibious Group 3 from the West Coast on 1 December. The group traveled west to Hawaii and then to the Philippines on its way to the Persian Gulf, conducting extensive training on board to make up for the training precluded by the hurried departure. The 13th Marine Expeditionary Unit was ordered to return to the Gulf from the Philippines in company with the brigade, rendezvousing at sea, and the two amphibious forces joined Central Command's forces in the Arabian Sea on 14 January 1991.[28]

As the landing force of Naval Forces Central Command, the two Marine expeditionary brigades and a Marine expeditionary unit formed a very large amphibious force. Major General Harry Jenkins, the senior Marine afloat, suggested to General Alfred Gray that the forces be formally designated as the IV Marine Expeditionary Force, with an appropriate staff deployed. General Gray approved the idea, but the war was over before this change could be made.[29]

The Marine Corps was not required to activate any of its Reserves for the Desert Shield deployment, aside from a few individual billets filled voluntarily. But the president's 8 November reinforcement order required a Reserve call up that would eventually number 30,000 reservists. Of these, over 11,000 would serve in the Persian Gulf region. As noted above, most of these reservists were activated with their units, and these companies, battalions, and squadrons were assigned to Marine air-ground task forces as needed. One regiment, the 24th Marines, deployed as well. Other reservists were assigned individually to fill out units already deployed or preparing to deploy, especially in the 5th Marine Expeditionary Brigade. Over 99 percent of the Marines recalled to active duty responded to the call and entered hurried training and orientation courses prior to deployment; they then deployed and served with enthusiasm, despite early administrative issues that left many reservists facing temporary financial hardship at the beginning of their tours. The Reserve Marines proved the value of the Reserve program, and Colonel Gangle of the 5th Marines spoke for many when he reported that after a few weeks' time he could not tell the regulars from the reservists.[30]

Iraq's Defenses

Throughout the fall of 1990, Iraq responded to the international condemnation of its invasion of Kuwait with bluster and counterclaims. Saddam Hussein believed that Iraq could outlast the UN sanctions imposed on it in the wake of the invasion and that the Coalition of Western and Arab states that opposed him would inevitably break part. Nonetheless, Iraq prepared for the confrontation to turn violent and readied its defense in Iraq and Kuwait. In that event, Iraq expected a prolonged "prewar bombardment" by Coalition air forces, which Saddam expected to endure successfully based on his Iran-Iraq War experience, followed by a Coalition assault into Kuwait.[31]

As noted in chapter 1, the Israeli air strike on the Osirak in 1981 inspired Iraq to upgrade its air defenses, centered on the French-made Kari integrated air defense command and control system activated in 1986. This system organized four of Iraq's five air defense sectors (the fifth was Kuwait), consisting of over 7,000 pieces of air defense artillery and over 100 surface-to-air missile batteries. Iraq's surface-to-air missiles were, like most Iraqi weapons, primarily supplied by the Soviet Union. Iraqi surface-to-air guided missiles included the S-75 Dvina (SA-2 Guideline*), Isayev S-125 Neva/Pechora (SA-3 Goa), 2K12 Kub (SA-6 Gainful), 9K33 Osa (SA-8 Gecko), 9K31 Strela-1 (SA-9 Gaskin), and 9K35 Strela-10 (SA-13 Gopher). The French-made Roland was Iraq's only non-Soviet surface-to-air guided missile. Iraq's air defense artillery included many diverse types, but the most dangerous was the ZSU-23-4 Shilka self-propelled, radar-guided antiaircraft weapon system. Iraq also fielded thousands of portable, shoulder-fired surface-to-air missiles, all 9K32 Strela-2s (SA-7 Grails) and 9K34 Strela-3s (SA-14 Gremlins). Despite this quantita-

---

*The names in parentheses for these missiles are their NATO reporting names.

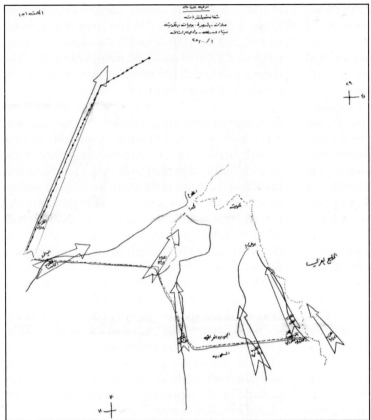

Reprinted from Kevin M. Woods, *The Mother of All Battles*, p. 139
*This sketch map, created by Iraq's III Corps headquarters in August 1990,
indicates the routes the Iraqis expected a Coalition offensive into Kuwait to
follow. This plan is remarkably close to the "one corps" plan described in
this chapter.*

tively impressive antiaircraft defense network, the Iraqis expected that they would have to suffer a prolonged aerial bombardment by the Coalition that would best be met by endurance, deception, and bunkered defenses.[32]

In theory the Iraqi Air Force could field over 700 aircraft and more than 500 helicopters, but the skill and effectiveness of its crews were questionable, as their performance during the invasion of Kuwait indicated.[*] An Iraqi aircraft had managed to inflict serious harm on the USS *Stark* during the Iran-Iraq War,[**] however, so the possibility of a "lucky shot" from an Iraqi aircraft inflicting a mass casualty event could not be discounted. The Iraqi Air Force planned strikes against Coalition ground forces, naval vessels, and Saudi oil terminals. A study was conducted on how to defeat an American aircraft carrier. The study's conclusions were pessimistic,

stating that only a 34-aircraft strike had a chance of disrupting the operations of an American aircraft carrier and that "the loss of 34 advanced ground attack planes to disrupt one aircraft carrier out of [the] nine carriers mobilized by the enemy in the region was ineffective." Hence, Iraqi Air Force plans were more focused on preserving itself than on winning the impending conflict.[33]

Iraq's navy was small even with the addition of captured Kuwaiti vessels, containing around a dozen missile boats, some minelayers, and small craft. Naval defense plans focused on mine warfare, intending to deny the Coalition the ability to operate close to the coast of Kuwait as well as making the Persian Gulf itself a danger to Coalition vessels. Iraq deployed over 1,300 naval mines during the conflict. The Iraqi Navy also intended to use oil as a naval weapon, employing intentional oil spills from shore facilities, oil platforms, and tankers. The *440th Naval Infantry Brigade* garrisoned Faylakah Island, and Iraq's navy also occupied several of the smaller islands and oil platforms, but the navy's plans focused on evacuating these positions (as well as the Kuwaiti naval ports it occupied) if attacked. Notably, Iraqi naval defense plans indicate no specific plan for the missile boats.[34]

Saddam Hussein and the senior Iraqi leadership expected that the offensive to liberate Kuwait would be much like the combat experienced in the Iran-Iraq War—a slow, bloody battle of attrition along fixed lines with neither side able to gain a true advantage. Such a battle was to Iraq's advantage, since Saddam believed mass Coalition casualties would splinter public opinion and the Coalition itself. Iraq's plans for conducting the ground war were based on these assumptions.

In November, Iraq's Directorate of General Military Intelligence sent a series of reports to the Iraqi military forces in the Kuwaiti theater detailing expected Coalition invasion routes and operational intentions. The report was remarkably prescient. The authors expected that "the enemy will use the indirect approach to achieve a rapid decision and avoid a large number of losses. This approach [rests] on

[*]See chapter 2.
[**]See chapter 1.

exploitation of intense aerial strikes and a rapid advancement on primary axes to threaten as many of our troops as possible by attacking from unexpected directions and carrying out deep penetrations that target headquarters and road intersections." The report also showed that the Iraqis were keenly aware of American amphibious capabilities: "The enemy will conduct naval landing operations simultaneously with land and air operations to isolate as many troops as possible and support land operations from the sea with heavy artillery fire." Comparing the expected avenues of approach to Central Command's initial, "one corps" plan for liberating Kuwait (described below), Iraqi intelligence was remarkably accurate.[35]

The *Republican Guard* departed Kuwait on 7 September and established itself in southern Iraq near Basrah as a mobile theater strategic reserve. The guard's commander, Lieutenant General Ayyad Fateeh al-Rawi, ordered his troops to disperse in order to blunt the expected Coalition air attacks while hoping to remain ready to conduct a swift counterattack against the expected Coalition assault.[36]

Iraq's Regular Army was left to confront the Coalition forces directly and defend Kuwait. As in the Iran-Iraq War, the Iraqi Army assigned its corps to geographic locations. Individual divisions and separate brigades were assigned to these corps but could be shifted between the corps if required; each corps controlled several armored and mechanized divisions supporting a larger number of entrenched infantry divisions.

During the Gulf War, the Marines primarily faced the Iraqi *III Corps* and *IV Corps*. The *III Corps*, commanded by Major General Salah Aboud Mahmoud, held southeast Kuwait from the coast to the elbow of the Saudi-Kuwaiti border, including Kuwait City proper. The *III Corps* was one of Iraq's better formations, with several successes in the Iran-Iraq War to its credit. Its primary fighting power came from the *5th Mechanized Division* and the *3d Armored Division*. Both of these divisions employed T-55/54 and T-62 main battle tanks. The *III Corps* also controlled 9 to 16 infantry divisions.[*] These infantry divisions were arrayed along the border and the coastline. The *IV Corps*, commanded by Major General Yaiyd Khalel Zaki, defended the southwest portion of Iraq, from the elbow to the Wadi al-Batin basin (from there, southern Iraq was defended by

the *VII Corps*). The mobile formations of the *IV Corps* included the *1st Mechanized*, the *6th Armored*, and the *10th Armored Divisions*. These too employed T-55/54 and T-62 main battle tanks. The corps controlled five to seven infantry divisions, entrenched along the border.[37]

Iraqi engineers became very good at building extensive fixed fortifications during the Iran-Iraq War. These took the form of massive minefields and extensive barbed-wire entanglements before high-earthen berms designed as fighting positions and backed up by concentrations of artillery. Expecting air attacks, the Iraqis concealed their positions and placed large numbers of decoys to draw attacks away from their functional equipment and to increase the apparent strength of the units defending Kuwait. Inside the *III Corps* fortifications that the Marines faced, "Decoy tanks and camouflaged nets were deployed as a cover up. Destroyed vehicles were used so that no tank would be withdrawn unless a decoy tank was placed in the same position. And no cannons were pulled away unless a decoy one was placed in that same position." Junkyards and tank boneyards in Kuwait and Iraq were ransacked for the appropriate inoperable vehicles, equipment, and dummy parts.[38]

The original deployment massed the troops in the front areas, but in November orders were given to shift to a defense in depth. General Salah Aboud Mahmoud later explained the reasoning behind the change: "We had to consider the possibility that the enemy could be airdropping Marines. So we had to dedicate part of our resources to carry out that mission or we could face an airdrop deep against our bases. Thus, some of our formations would not deploy unless there was a grave necessity to do so."[39]

The Iraqis did not limit their plans to conventional operations; in any case it is clear that Saddam saw his defense as a bluff that would convince the West not to challenge Iraq's actions for fear of massive casualties. Inflicting large numbers of casualties was a primary means of accomplishing these goals, and Saddam pursued unconventional means of doing this. For example, he spoke often in public and private about guerilla and terrorist operations against Coalition forces both in the theater and without. None of these plans appears to have come to fruition—very few terrorists attacks were launched outside of Iraq, despite threats to do so—but they represented Saddam's strategy of bluff and blackmail.[40]

More dangerous were Saddam's SS-1 Scud-B al-Hussein surface-to-surface medium range missiles

---

[*]Iraq created many new infantry divisions during the fall of 1990 and assigned them to Kuwait. Some of these divisions may have only existed on paper, and they are therefore difficult to track.

U.S. Marine Corps Armored Vehicles

Vehicle	Type	Armament	Crew	Top Speed	Weight
	M1A1	• 1 x 120mm smooth-bored gun • 1 x 7.62mm coaxial machine gun • Antiaircraft commander's cupola: 12.7mm machine gun • Antiaircraft loader's hatch: 7.62mm machine gun	4	66.7 km/h	57,154 kg
	M60	• 1 x 105mm M68 rifled gun • 1 x 7.62mm coaxial machine gun • Antiaircraft: 1 x 12.7mm machine gun	4	48.7 km/h	52,617 kg
	AAV-7	• Carries 25 Marines • Mk 19 40mm automatic grenade launcher or M2HB .50-caliber machine gun	3	32 km/h	26,399 kg
	LAV	• 2 x 7.62mm machine gun and 25mm main gun • Carries 4 troops or TOW-2 ATGM or 81mm M252 mortar	4 to 7	100 km/h	11,612 kg

and his chemical weapon arsenal. Less obviously, but still a worry, were his biological and nuclear weapons programs. Saddam's use of chemical weapons during the Iran-Iraq War indicated he was capable of using them again, and in fact Iraqi records show that preparations were made to use these weapons again during the Gulf War (the records do not explain why they were not used).

Iraq's nuclear program had not yet developed a weapon, though it was further along than anyone knew at the time. The Scud missiles, however, had been used to some effect during the Iran-Iraq War and offered Iraq a way to appear strong and to strike back, despite the Coalition's expected control of the air.[41]

Although Iraq did not expect to win a conven-

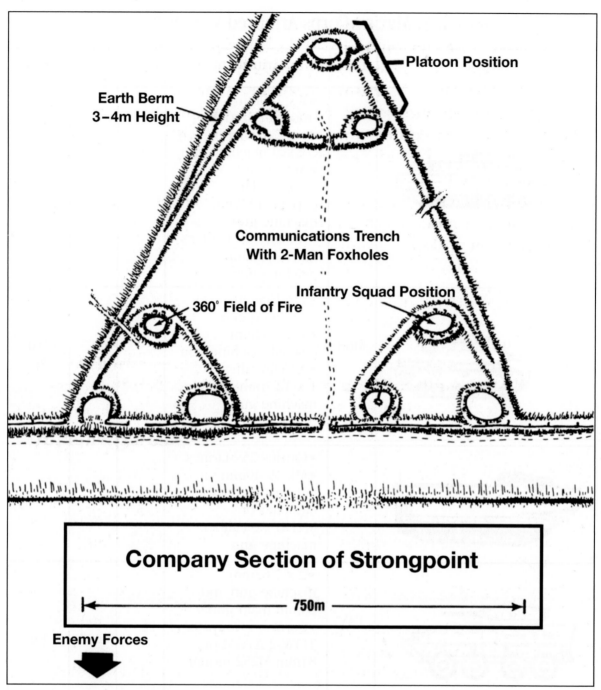

Reprinted from U.S. Army Intelligence Agency, *How They Fight: Desert Shield Order of Battle Handbook* (1990)
Diagram of an Iraqi company subsection of a triangular strongpoint.

tional war over Kuwait, it ended the year reasonably confident that its plans and defenses would lead to a negotiated settlement and that it could prevail against the untested American military forces and unstable Coalition facing them. Saddam declared to his staff in November 1990 that "as long as our blood is less, as long as our breath lasts longer, and at the end we can make our enemy feel incompetent." He was certain that it would be a long war, and that a long war would play to Iraq's strengths and the United States' weaknesses.[42]

Planning a Storm

Planning for an offensive against Iraq actually began in August. In the immediate aftermath of the invasion of Kuwait, General Schwarzkopf asked the Air

Force to provide a plan for an air campaign against Iraq because this was the only offensive option that could be employed if the president wanted to strike Iraq immediately. Central Command's staff was busy with the complicated business of deploying forces to Saudi Arabia and forming plans to defend the Desert Kingdom. The job of creating this campaign plan was given to Colonel John A. Warden III, USAF, then the Air Force's deputy director of warfighting concepts and head of its "Project Checkmate" wargaming office in the Pentagon. Colonel Warden developed a "ring" targeting model that he believed could defeat an opponent through airpower alone. He quickly developed an air campaign dubbed "Instant Thunder" that was presented to General Schwarzkopf and the U.S. Air Forces Central Command commander, Lieutenant General Charles A. Horner, in mid-August in Riyadh. Unlike Colonel Warden, neither General Schwarzkopf nor General Horner believed the air campaign alone could defeat Iraq.[43]

After hearing Colonel Warden's briefing on the Instant Thunder campaign, General Horner appointed Brigadier General Buster C. Glosson as director of campaign plans for Air Forces Central Command, a department often referred to as the "Black Hole" due to its extreme secrecy. General Glosson took the original Instant Thunder campaign plan and reworked it into the plan that was eventually used against Iraq. Colonel Warden returned to the United States, but one of his deputies, Lieutenant Colonel David A. Deptula, USAF, became a key member of the Black Hole. Although the plan was adjusted to better fit local conditions and made more practical, Warden's guiding principles and targeting priorities heavily influenced the final version of the Gulf War air offensive plan.[44]

Once the early, Wild West days of Operation Desert Shield were over, Marine and Air Force air combat doctrines began to clash. The Air Force had pushed through its concept of a joint forces air component commander in the 1986 Goldwater-Nichols Act. This joint air commander would control all fixed-wing* air assets in the command; during the Gulf War General Horner held this position. Under Air Force doctrine he would control these forces through the air tasking order, a daily document that was intended to contain all of the fixed-winged sorties planned for each day. The intention was to allocate aerial resources according to theaterwide

priorities, subordinating all of a theater's airpower to a single commander. After the war General Horner succinctly explained the concept in the following way: "The ATO [air tasking order] is the JFACC [joint forces air component commander]."[45]

The history of the 3d Marine Aircraft Wing's operations in the Gulf War aptly summed up the Air Force position:

> Given the appropriate resources and wide latitude from political leaders, Air Force leaders argued that an air campaign focusing on strategic targets could break the enemy's will and compel him to surrender or desist without the U.S. having to resort to a costly and possibly unpopular ground campaign. This form of nearly unrestricted air warfare against deep or strategic targets demanded that ground officers who favored using airpower primarily against tactical targets be kept at arms' length. To ensure that the air commander in a joint operation possessed the authority to direct or redirect strikes across the length and breadth of the theater in pursuit of campaign objectives, Air Force doctrine also demanded that airspace not be ceded or parceled out to other services or allies.[46]

In contrast, the Marine doctrine was focused on close air support for the Marine ground forces; air and ground were combined in the same team, the Marine air-ground task force. Rather than a daily, planned sortie list, the Marines emphasized flexibility and rapid response to the ground commander's needs and a geographic organization similar to the Vietnam-era "route packages" (which the Air Force vociferously rejected). Marines felt that under the Air Force theaterwide system response times to close air support requests would increase dramatically. Although Goldwater-Nichols established the basic authority of the joint forces air component commander, the 1986 Omnibus Agreement for Command and Control of Marine Tactical Aviation in Sustained Operations Ashore stated that the Marine commander would maintain operational control of his organic air assets.[47]

In September, the Solomon-like solution was that all of the 3d Marine Aircraft Wing's Intruders and Prowlers would be devoted to "JFACC mission," while half of the sorties flown by the Hornets would be similarly tasked. The Marines' Harriers and all of their helicopters would be retained entirely for Marine directed missions. General Boomer later said, "It made no sense to me to not allow the

---

*For the most part, the Air Force is disinterested in helicopter operations.

Photo by MSgt Jose Lopez Jr. Defense Imagery DF-ST-92-07542

Civilian and military decision makers during a conference for Operation Desert Shield. Bottom row, from left: Paul D. Wolfowitz, under secretary of defense for policy; Gen Colin L. Powell, USA, chairman of the Joint Chiefs of Staff; Richard B. Cheney, secretary of defense; Gen H. Norman Schwarzkopf, USA, commander in chief, U.S. Central Command; LtGen Calvin A. H. Waller, USA, deputy commander, U.S. Central Command; and MajGen Robert B. Johnston, chief of staff, U.S. Central Command. Back row, from left: LtGen Walter E. Boomer, commander, Marine Forces Central Command/I Marine Expeditionary Force; LtGen Charles A. Horner, commander, Air Forces Central Command/Ninth Air Force; LtGen John J. Yeosock, USA, commander, Army Forces Central Command/Third Army; VAdm Stanley Arthur, Commander, Seventh Fleet; and Col Jesse Johnson, Special Operations Command Central.

Marine air wing to be used by the joint commander to help prosecute the campaign. That's what our doctrine says will happen. Marines always tended to wrap around the axle here, in my view. Some felt no one could task Marine air except the Marine commander. I don't think that's true and I don't think it's wise." In contrast, a later Air Force study concluded the agreement was acceptable "in the interest of harmony," primarily because the Air Force had enough resources in the theater that it could afford to be generous.[48]

Planning for the ground war began in September when General Schwarzkopf assembled a small team of Army officers on his staff in Riyadh—all of whom were graduates of the Army's School of Advanced Military Studies—and charged them with planning

for a ground offensive to liberate Kuwait. Led by Lieutenant Colonel Joseph H. "Joe" Purvis, this team kept its work secret and self-contained; it was officially called the Special Plans Group but was known informally as the "Jedi Knights."* Initially charged with creating a plan based on the forces earmarked for Operation Desert Shield, the Jedi Knights provided a one corps plan that called for Coalition forces to advance into Kuwait from the elbow to the Wadi al-Batin while Navy and Marine forces staged an amphibious feint on the coast. Neither the Jedi Knights nor General Schwarzkopf liked this plan, and it can be seen how closely it mirrored the approach routes that Iraqi intelligence antici-

---

*A reference to a mystical military order in the popular *Star Wars* movie franchise.

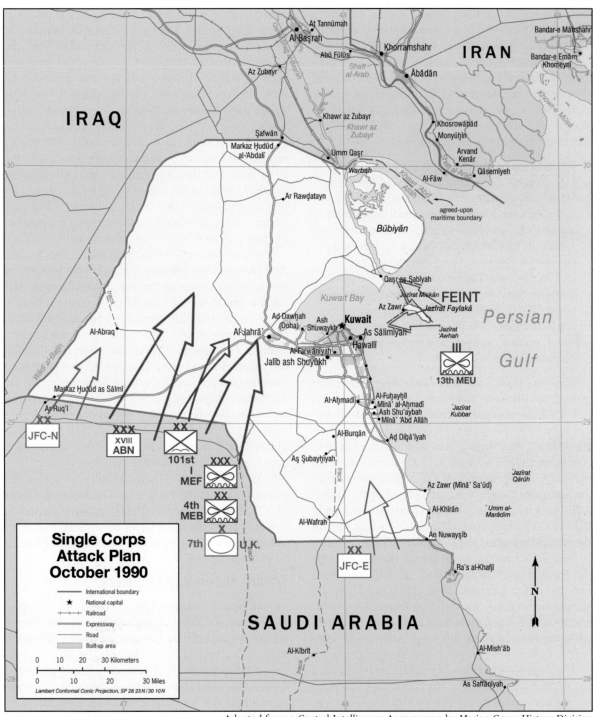

Adapted from a Central Intelligence Agency map by Marine Corps History Division

Kuwait is a small state, and there are limited avenues of advance into the nation from Saudi Arabia. The "one corps plan" depicted here is remarkably close to the Iraqi map of expected Coalition offensives seen earlier.

pated, as noted above. Nonetheless, Marine Major General Robert B. Johnston, the Central Command chief of staff, and Lieutenant Colonel Purvis briefed the Joint Chiefs on this plan on 10 October and the president on 11 October.[49]

General Boomer and his staff were surprised to discover that an Army cell was developing plans for a ground offensive to liberate Kuwait. The Jedi Knights had no Marine members, and General Boomer was not informed that the planning cell even existed. More disturbing, the plan called for using the Marines in a manner similar to an Army corps, rather than in a way consistent with Marine Corps doctrine. General Boomer quickly formed a team on his own staff and instructed them to work closely with the Army staff as the new plans were developed. Colonel James D. Majchrzak was the I Marine Expeditionary Force plans officer; he later summarized the mission as follows:

> When directed by U.S. CinCCent [commander, U.S. Central Command], U.S. MarCent [U.S. Marine Forces Central Command] conducts U.S. CentCom [Central Command] supporting attack to fix and destroy Iraqi operational reserves in southeastern Kuwait to preclude their employment against USCentCom main attack in the west; isolate Kuwait City for EPAC [Eastern Province Area Command]/multinational MOUT [military operations in urban terrain] operations. Be prepared to continue the attack north to support USCentCom offensive operations.[50]

President Bush's announcement on 8 November shifted the planning paradigms as the U.S. Army's heavy VII Corps deployed from Europe to Saudi Arabia in order to increase the forces available to liberate Kuwait. The unpopular one corps plan was consequently abandoned, and Lieutenant Colonel Purvis's Jedi Knights now produced a two corps plan that called for a wide, westward sweep of the Army's XVIII Airborne Corps as the mechanized divisions of the VII Corps swept through southern Iraq toward Basrah and smashed the *Republican Guard*.[51]

General Schwarzkopf chose the Marines to evict the Iraqis from Kuwait proper, fighting with Arab members of the Coalition on either side. On the Marines' west flank, the Saudi Arabians, Egyptians, and Syrians formed Joint Forces Command–North, while on the east flank the Saudi Arabians of Joint Forces Command–East advanced along the coast.[52]

The Jedi Knight two corps plan originally had the Marines executing a "fixing" attack, holding Iraqi forces in place as the two Army corps enveloped them on the left. But the Marine plan called for evicting the Iraqis from Kuwait directly. General Boomer later said, "There was never any doubt in my mind that that's what we were going to do. We weren't going to play around with them on the border in some sort of fixing attack; we were going to retake Kuwait, and General Schwarzkopf didn't have a problem with that."[53]

On 10 December, General Boomer's staff and senior commanders received a briefing on the Iraqi military from retired Lieutenant General Bernard E. Trainor (see appendix G). He had retired from the Marine Corps in 1985 after a career that included combat service in Korea and Vietnam, and then he went on to become a war correspondent for the *New York Times*. Lieutenant General Trainor went to Iraq in the winter of 1987–88 to report on the Iran-Iraq War, and his status as a retired senior officer convinced the Iraqis to grant him unusual access to the front lines and their operational units. His briefing focused on his direct observations of the Iraqi military's capabilities. Most of the briefing proved prescient, especially when he predicted that the number of Iraqi prisoners would be "enormous."[54]

General Trainor's lecture was useful, but for Marine planners the primary question was how many breeches to create in the Iraqi fortifications. The ideal solution would have been to create a breech for each division, allowing for a broader advance, but the Corps lacked the required amounts of engineering equipment to force two breeches through the minefields and obstacles. Instead, the 1st Marine Division would breach the Iraqi defenses, while the 2d Marine Division followed. After the fortifications were passed, the 2d Marine Division would pass through General Myatt's Marines and advance to the al-Jahra road crossing while the 1st Marine Division continued on to Kuwait International Airport. The 4th and 5th Marine Expeditionary Brigades remained afloat in the Persian Gulf on board the ships of U.S. Navy amphibious ready groups, providing a seaborne threat in order to tie up Iraq resources along the shoreline as well as a strategic reserve for Central Command.[55]

Trading Desert Rats for Tigers

Throughout Operation Desert Shield, the I Marine Expeditionary Force was paired with the initial British contribution to the ground forces, Brigadier Patrick Cordingley's 7th Armored Brigade, the famous Desert Rats. This brigade's tanks provided General Boomer with an armored punch that complemented the 1st Marine Division's traditionally high percentage of infantry. The Marines and the British troops trained together for months, and built a great deal of camaraderie. When the assault on Kuwait happened, General Boomer was counting on the British tanks to help counter the large Iraqi armored formations in Kuwait.

Not everyone was happy with the British forces being linked to the Marines, however. The Jedi Knight planners thought the British tanks should

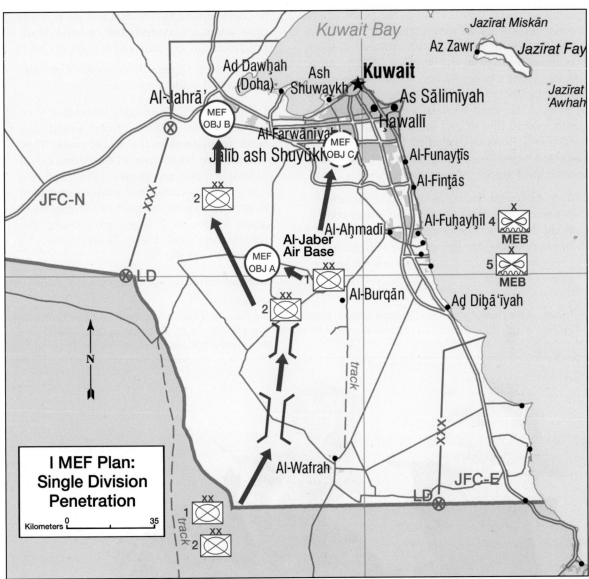

Al-Jahrā'

Ad Dawḥah
(Doha)

Ash
Shuwaykh

Kuwait Bay

Az Zawr

Jazīrat Miskān

Jazīrat Fay

Kuwait

As Sālimīyah

Ḥawallī

Jazīrat
'Awhah

Al-Farwānīyah

Jalīb ash Shuyūkh

Al-Funayṭis

Al-Finṭās

JFC-N

MEF
OBJ B

MEF
OBJ C

2

Al-Aḥmadī

Al-Jaber
Air Base

Al-Fuḥayḥīl 4

MEB

5

MEB

MEF
OBJ A

1

2

Al-Burqān

Aḍ Dibā'īyah

LD

track

N

I MEF Plan:
Single Division
Penetration

Kilometers 0 ———— 35

1

2

Al-Wafrah

track

JFC-E

LD

Adapted from a Central Intelligence Agency map by Marine Corps History Division

be devoted to the "left hook" that would face the *Republican Guard* rather than the "holding attack" that they intended the Marines to perform. Lieutenant General Sir Peter Edgar de la Cour de la Billière, commander in chief of British forces in the Persian Gulf, agreed with them.

General de la Billière believed that the British forces—which were being reinforced for the attack, forming the British 1st Armored Division—should be employed to the west as the Jedi Knights wished. He had three reasons for this. First, he felt the terrain was "not at all suitable for the far-ranging fire-and-manoeuvre [maneuver] tactics in which they specialized" because there were "far too many man-made obstacles—principally oil installations."[56]

Beyond not allowing the British tankers to fully utilize their training, he didn't think supporting the Marine attack would fully showcase the British Challenger main battle tank's capabilities for foreign sales. As he put it in his memoir of the Gulf War, "We must at least be given a chance to show what our armour could do in an environment which suited it."[57]

Casualties were the third and largest worry for General de la Billière. He believed that the Marines were "exceptionally gung ho" and that they would suffer casualties as high as 17 percent in attacking Kuwait, in part because he believed the Marine commanders were eager to use the war to illustrate the Corps' value and avoid budget cuts. In the end, de la Billiére said, "I did not believe that we should commit the main British effort at the point where the heaviest casualties were expected."[58]

On 24 December, the British armored division was transferred from the Marines to U.S. Army Forces Central Command and shifted to the west. During the liberation of Kuwait, this division acted as part of the great western sweep through the desert toward Basrah and the *Republican Guard*. As General Boomer explained later, he was not surprised when word came that the British were leaving the I Marine Expeditionary Force:

> This move did not occur overnight. General Schwarzkopf talked to me about it and confided that he was getting a lot of pressure to move the Brits. He intimated he was getting pressure even from London. I think we both knew that it was inevitably going to happen.

So, between the two of us it was no real surprise when it occurred, just extreme disappointment on my part and I think on his.[59]

Moreover, General Boomer felt that de la Billiére had made a mistake:

> I think General Cordingley knew that if he stayed with us, the British forces would have been spotlighted in the world press. They would have taken part in the liberation of Kuwait. I was going to give them a hell of a lot of credit because they were so important to us, and I knew the kind of job they were going to do. As it were, who knows the British were even there. Does anybody? I mean they got lost.[60]

General Schwarzkopf ordered Lieutenant Gen-

A British soldier from the Queen's Dragoon Guards shows a Marine from 7th Platoon, 1st Force Reconnaissance Company, how to operate a British L1A1 rifle as they take part in weapons training during Operation Desert Shield.

Photo by SSgt J. R. Ruark. Defense Imagery DM-ST-91-11998

Photo by Maj Andres Ortegon, USA. U.S. Army
John B. Sylvester (shown here as a lieutenant general) commanded the 1st (Tiger) Brigade, 2d Armored Division, as an Army colonel during the Gulf War. His brigade was attached to the 2d Marine Division for the liberation of Kuwait.

eral John J. Yeosock, the Army Central Command's commanding general, to send the Marines a replacement for the British 1st Armored Division that was a "like force." General Yeosock sent the 1st (Tiger) Brigade, 2d Armored Division, commanded by Colonel John B. Sylvester. General Boomer later noted that trading a division for a brigade was hardly trading like for like, but the Tiger Brigade was "a very professional brigade led by a very professional leader" and that "when they understood what an important, critical role we had for them, using them as an Army brigade should be used, they just fell right in and did a terrific job." Colonel Sylvester and his brigade joined the Marines on 10 January 1991 and were assigned to General Keys's 2d Marine Division.[61]

General Boomer thought that the loss of the British forces helped spark the minor controversy that accompanied the December visit to the Gulf by the Commandant, General Gray. This was General Gray's third, and final, visit to the war zone. He received a briefing on I Marine Expeditionary Force's then-current one breech plan for the assault on Kuwait, but he was reportedly not happy with the plan. He felt that the Marine amphibious forces were not being properly employed, and he blamed this,

along with the loss of the British forces, in part on General Boomer wearing "two hats" as commanding general of I Marine Expeditionary Force and commander of Marine Forces Central Command. He believed that the Marines were not well represented in Schwarzkopf's headquarters in Riyadh. In contrast, Boomer felt that he and his Marines were well represented in Central Command's headquarters by his deputy commander at Marine Forces Central Command.[*] Beyond that, Boomer also felt "there was a tremendous amount of trust, in my view, on the part of General Schwarzkopf for the Marines and our capability."[62]

In December, General Gray asked General Schwarzkopf about splitting the two commands, leaving General Boomer in command of the field forces while another general would be placed over General Boomer in command of Marine Forces Central Command. General Schwarzkopf did not want another senior officer inserted into Central Command, however, especially since he and General Boomer had a good working relationship. At General Boomer's suggestion, Major General John J. Sheehan joined the amphibious forces as commander, U.S. Forces Central Command (Forward) in January. General Sheehan acted as liaison with Vice Admiral Stanley A. Arthur and helped General Jenkins's amphibious forces get the command planning guidance they desired.[63]

General Gray made no more trips to the Persian Gulf, but the idea of an umbrella command for the Marines in the region apparently did not completely die. The Corps' History and Museums Division produced a "point paper" on 30 January 1991 that commented on the historical precedent for designating "the present Marine Corps organization in Southwest Asia" as the I Marine Expeditionary Corps. The paper points out that both historically and by Marine Corps order these expeditionary corps were designed for situations that required more combat power than was normally available to a Marine expeditionary force. The point paper's recommendation was never put into

---

[*]MajGen Jeremiah W. Pearson III held this position until 17 January, when MajGen Norman E. Ehlert took over the position.

effect, and there is no record of who requested it.[64]

Commenting on these command politics after the war, General Boomer stated that "all of this wasted my time and mental energy and did absolutely nothing to help I MEF [I Marine Expeditionary Force] defeat the Iraqis."[65]

CHAPTER 5

The Air War

Marine Air in the Assault

There was a flurry of last-minute diplomatic activity in the days leading up to the 15 January 1991 deadline for Iraq's voluntary evacuation of Kuwait that was established by the UN Security Council on 29 November 1990. On 12 January, the U.S. Congress voted President Bush the authority to militarily eject Iraq from Kuwait if the UN deadline was ignored. Despite last-minute attempts by the Soviet Union to negotiate a settlement, Iraq's ultimate refusal to withdraw prevented any peaceful solution to the crisis.[1]

On 17 January 1991, Operation Desert Storm began with massive air strikes throughout Iraq and Kuwait. Although the operation had an expected ground component, U.S. Air Force strategists who believed that bombing alone could compel Iraq to relinquish Kuwait drove the first phases. As a result, the primary focus of the campaign was on achieving air superiority (accomplished the first evening), suppressing air defenses, striking strategic (especially leadership and communications) targets inside Iraq, and annihilating Iraq's elite *Republican Guard* centered in southern Iraq. Only after the first three objectives were accomplished did the Air Force plan to shift to hitting Iraqi forces in Kuwait proper. All of the strikes for the first three days of the assault were planned out in an air tasking order that was 700 pages long. To make up for the relative lack of targeting in Kuwait proper, the 3d Marine Aircraft Wing used its AV8-Bs, and the F/A-18 sorties that were not promised to the joint air commander, to hit targets deemed important by General Boomer. The primary targets in Kuwait for the first weeks of the air war were the air defense and artillery weapons, both of which were present in large quantities.[2]

During the air campaign, Marine aviation conducted hundreds of sorties against Iraqi positions in Kuwait and Iraq. Aircrews of the 3d Marine Aircraft Wing struck Iraqi command and control centers, antiaircraft defenses, and strategic targets deep inside Iraq, as well as later performing traditional reconnaissance, battlefield interdiction, and close air support missions in Kuwait.

Some of the pilots had given up hope that the attack would be launched, believing that some compromise or deal would be made, and they were

Photo by SSgt Scott Stewart, USAF. Defense Imagery DF-ST-92-07396
U.S. Marine Corps F/A-18 Hornet strike-fighter aircraft from Marine Fighter Attack Squadron 212. These capable aircraft split their missions between strategic targets chosen by the air component commander and tactical targets selected by Marine commanders.

pleasantly surprised to find the launch proceeding as planned. In his memoir *Hornets Over Kuwait,* Captain Jay A. Stout expressed the basic views of most pilots eager to prove their hard-earned skills: "Most of us were not eager to kill. To destroy, yes. But as far as killing the individual, or the masses of individuals, was concerned, we were not bloodthirsty. But we knew we would kill—without hesitation. It was the nature of the beast."[3]

17 January: The First Night

Operation Desert Storm began with a task force of Army and special operations helicopters destroying Iraq's early warning radar sites. Not long after that, the first wave of aircraft and cruise missiles struck at targets all across Iraq. Over 100 General Dynamics BGM-109 Tomahawk cruise missiles were fired from U.S. Navy surface vessels and submarines at large radar installations and communications centers. The Tomahawk missiles and Lockheed F-117A Nighthawk bombers struck air defense targets, the Baath Party headquarters, the Iraqi Ministry of Defense, strategic weapons targets such as Scud missile storage, and infrastructure targets like electrical power generating plants. One of the most famous images of the air assault on that first day came from a BBC reporter in Baghdad who saw "a 20-foot Tomahawk glide quietly down a deserted street for several blocks, then turn left and explode into a building."[4]

Conventional Coalition aircraft flew in waves against Iraq as well; they were met by a disorganized but vigorous Iraqi air defense that lit up the sky with tracers and surface-to-air missiles. Most Iraqi officers found out about the air strikes in the same manner as Brigadier General Ra'ad Hamdani of the *Republican Guard,*[*] who was informed of the Coalition air strikes by a soldier shouting, "The planes are above us! The planes are above us!"[5]

Aircraft for the first Marine air strike of the war took off at 0400. In this strike, Marine Aircraft Group 11 sent 48 aircraft against Scud missile support facilities at Tallil and Qurnah, as well as against a power plant at an-Nasiriyah and surface-to-air missile sites at Shaibah Air Base. The strike's F/A-18 Hornets and A-6E Intruders were supported by EA-6B Prowlers and KC-130 Hercules as the strike force flew north under radio silence alongside Air Force McDonnell Douglas "Wild Weasel" F-4G Phantom IIs and British Royal Air Force Panavia Tornado GR.1s.[6]

Some of the Hornets and the Wild Weasels fired AGM-88 high-speed antiradiation missiles at Iraq air defense radars (over half of the antiradiation missiles fired by Marines in the Gulf War were fired in the first day of the war). The strike force crossed into Iraqi territory in the face of impressive, if inaccurate, antiaircraft fire.[7]

Lieutenant Colonel Waldo B. Cummings Jr., of Marine All-Weather Attack Squadron 533, later described the mission:

> As we penetrated Iraqi airspace, I looked down and saw the biggest light show I had ever seen. Continuous lines of red and orange tracers cov-

ered the black void below us. It seemed that every Iraqi who could put his finger on a trigger had pressed down and wouldn't let go. Most of the airbursts were below us, but some were going off near us as well. We soon lost count of the numbers of small white dots of fast moving light that continually arched over our canopies. They were surface-to-air missiles fired blindly in the hope that one would hit something. We could also see the small blue flames that our escorts' high-speed anti-radiation missiles let out as they went streaming by us to seek out the enemy radars. Several miles from the target, I pushed the nose of my aircraft down into a 30-degree dive as "Condor," my bombardier/navigator, picked out his aim point on the radar. Passing 13,000 feet I started our recovery to make time on target 0409 and banked hard left as I felt the aircraft suddenly get 6,000 pounds lighter when all three of our bombs were released. . . . I saw two bright blue flames, which highlighted one of our escort fighters as he lit afterburners and began to climb away. The target below was engulfed in flames and secondary explosions.[8]

The first strike was a success, despite its complicated nature, and all of the aircraft returned safely with a great deal of damage done to the targets. After the war, the lead bombardier/navigator, Captain David W. Deist of Marine All-Weather Attack Squadron 224, was awarded the Distinguished Flying Cross for having "conceived, planned, briefed, and led a 48 plane strike package" that was "confronted by a formidable array of enemy antiaircraft artillery, surface-to-air missiles, and air to air threats. . . . In the face of intense enemy defensive fires, [he] successfully prosecuted the target, [and] his attack severely damaged the storage facilities used to support the missiles."[9]

Later in the day, Marine F/A-18s led by Major Robert E. Schmidle, the executive officer of Marine Fighter Attack Squadron 333, flew a large strike against the Basrah oil refinery. Like Captain Deist, Major Schmidle received the Distinguished Flying Cross for the successful attack.[10]

On the same day that the largest Marine air strike since the Vietnam War was flying into Iraq, another Marine was also making history. Captain Charles J. Magill, an exchange pilot flying with the Air Force's 58th Tactical Fighter Squadron, 33d Tactical Fighter Wing, scored what is still the most recent Marine air-to-air combat victory. Magill, call sign "Zerex

---

[*]BGen Hamdani was the commander of the *17th Armored Brigade, Hammurabi Armored Division,* of the *Republican Guard.*

U.S. Marine Corps Aircraft for the Gulf War

Aircraft	Type	Armament	Crew	Top Speed	Range
	Bell AH-1T Sea Cobra Bell AH-1W Super Cobra	• TOW, Hellfire Sidewinder, and Sidearm missiles • 2.75- and 5-inch rockets • 20mm gun	2	152 to 189 knots	311 to 317 nautical miles
	Grumman A-6E Intruder	• 18.000-lb payload • Assorted rockets missiles, and bombs	2	563 knots	2,819 nautical miles
	McDonnell Douglas AV-8B Harrier II	• 25mm cannon • 13,200-lb payload • Assorted rockets missiles, and bombs	1	584 knots	1,200 nautical miles
	McDonnell Douglas F/A-18 Hornet	• 20mm Gatling gun • 13,700-lb payload • Assorted rockets missiles, and bombs	1	795 to 1,034 knots	1,800 nautical miles
	North American Rockwell OV-10 Bronco	• 4 x M60 machine guns • Assorted rockets missiles, and bombs	2	250 knots	1,114 nautical miles

71," was flying a McDonnell Douglas F-15C Eagle all-weather air-superiority fighter when he and his wingman, Captain Rhory R. Draeger, USAF, locked their radars on a pair of Iraqi Mikoyan MiG-29 "Fulcrum" air-superiority fighters flying at an altitude of around 1,500 feet. The two F-15 pilots fired AIM-7 Sparrow radar-guided missiles at the MiGs, destroying them both. Captain Magill was thus the first Marine pilot to score a kill since the Vietnam War.[11]

The first day of the air war highlighted Marines' fears about the unresponsiveness of the air tasking order. Heavily focused on striking strategic targets deep inside Iraq, and controlling all of the Marines' EA-6 aircraft due to the joint air agreement from September, the Air Force did not allocate any electronic warfare aircraft to support the Marines' planned AV-8B missions along the Saudi-Kuwaiti border. The planned missions targeted the Iraqi artillery and rocket batteries that had the range required to target Coalition ground forces. Rather than going into Kuwait, Marine Aircraft Group 13's Harriers stood ready on alert on the strip at their forward airbase, King Abdul Aziz airfield in Saudi Arabia, loaded with munitions for close air support missions.

The Iraqi artillery units along the Saudi-Kuwaiti border were undeterred by their relatively low priority on the Air Force targeting lists and responded to the launching of the air campaign by shelling al-Khafji and the Coalition forces inside the evacuated Saudi town. The town's oil refinery and desalination plant were both hit and caught fire. An OV-10 Bronco from Marine Observation Squadron 1 spotted the Iraqi artillery after dawn, and Colonel John Bioty, commanding officer of the Marine Aircraft Group 13, recalled: "General Moore called . . . 'We have an OV-10 reporting Iraqi shelling in the al-Khafji area. . . . Launch the ready Harriers.'" Bioty

launched four aircraft on the Harrier's first close air support mission of the war, led by Major Richard C. Branch of Marine Attack Squadron 311. The forward air controllers in the OV-10 observed artillery tubes tumbling through the air following the Harrier strike.[12]

From this point onward, Colonel Bioty said that the Harriers turned southern Kuwait into a "Harrier hunting ground." Lieutenant Colonel Richard M. Barry of the 1st Surveillance, Reconnaissance, and Intelligence Group and his detachment of Marine and allied troops at a border outpost north of al-Khafji benefited from the quick Harrier response as they were being shelled later that day. Harriers promptly answered their calls for close air support and soon destroyed the Iraqi battery.[13]

In a later letter, Lieutenant Colonel Barry credited the Harriers with saving his outpost:

> On 17 January 1991, hostilities commenced and Iraqi artillery began firing on my command post at the desalination plant (grids TM475572). I was outside friendly artillery range and thus began looking for air support. The enemy had a 152mm self-propelled bat-

U.S. Marine Corps AV-8B Harrier II attack aircraft from Marine Attack Squadron 513 fly in formation. Harriers were restricted to missions in direct support of the Marine mission and destroyed many targets in Kuwait.

Photo by SSgt Scott Stewart, USAF. Defense Imagery DF-ST-92-07395

Photo by Don S. Montgomery. Defense Imagery DD-ST-91-11904

Ground crews painted a small bomb for each mission flown on the side of U.S. aircraft, and at the end of the war they painted the total number of missions flown inside the larger bomb outline. The 31 mission markings on the nose of this Marine All-Weather Attack Squadron 533 A-6E Intruder at the end of the war demonstrate the intense effort Marine air put into preparing the way for the ground advance.

tery at grids (TM445632) and was firing flat trajectory into my position with effect. At approximately 0930, two [Fairchild Republic] A-10s were diverted by the Air Force Airborne Command and Control Center to support me. The A-10s checked in and indicated a cloud cover and a briefed SA-8 [9K33 Osa surface-to-air missile system*] threat were causing them to return to base. Essentially, they left me and my force without any support.

Next, four Harriers checked in and were "looking for work." I identified the target and indicated that they were firing and to look for the smoke. The Harriers attacked the target with extreme bravery and aggressiveness, dropping 12 to 16 250-pound bombs, setting off all stored ammunition. They repeatedly attacked the battery coming straight from the top dropping one bomb at a time for accu-

racy. Several hundred antiaircraft artillery rounds were fired at the Harriers, but they continued to press the attack, expending all ordnance and firing their internal guns. The battery was completely destroyed as I could see pieces of artillery flying backwards into the air. Later, we took 11 prisoners—they were bleeding from the ears and noses, indicating their battery had been wiped out by airplanes. All their guns were destroyed and the commander had been killed.

. . . Not only was it a superlative display of airmanship and bombing accuracy, but [it] took a lot of plain "old guts" as the fire was intense. I feel compelled to chase this one down as they saved my group of 34 combined forces personnel from further bombardment, as we already had sustained 2½ hours of the same and enemy accuracy improving.[14]

The Harriers were not the only close air support asset employed along the Kuwaiti border; AH-1W Super Cobras also responded to calls for support

---

*The NATO reporting name for this missile system is the SA-8 Gecko.

from the Marines in the border outposts, though there was some problem with radio frequencies that reduced their effectiveness in at least one instance.[15]

Back at the airfields, the tempo of operations began to increase as incessant Scud alerts sent the overworked ground crews into their bulky, awkward (and single use) chemical warfare protective gear. Continuing through the night, these alerts made it impossible for the air and ground crews to get the required sleep. "I finally ordered the loud speakers to be disconnected in the sleeping areas," said Colonel Manfred A. Rietsch, commander of Marine Aircraft Group 11.[16]

18 January: The Scuds

On the second night of the war, Marine Hornets and Intruders continued to strike targets listed on the three-day, preplanned air tasking order that Central Command's Air Force planning cell (aka the Black Hole) had created for the first phase of the air campaign. They attacked Tallil Airfield and *Republican Guard* units in southern Iraq. Iraq's air defenses continued to produce impressive amounts of fire, both surface-to-air missiles and antiaircraft artillery fire. In his memoir, Captain Stout of Marine Fighter Attack Squadron 451 described the surface-to-air missiles: "What we saw was a brilliant flash at launch, and then a brilliant bluish white or yellow streak as the missile climbed toward us. The most terrifying moments followed rocket motor burnout when, unsure of whether I was being tracked or not, I scrunched down in the cockpit and waited for the SAM [surface-to-air missile] to hit. Or miss. Some of the missiles would self-detonate after a certain period. The explosions looked just like giant, cheap, molten bursts from a roman candle."[17]

Captain Stout was flying an F/A-18 in a strike against a power plant in southern Iraq, a complicated mission much like the previous night's strikes. It was his first combat mission. "About forty miles out as we approached the coast near Bubiyan Island," he recalled, "the airspace in front of us was filled with an incredible barrage of SAMs and AAA [antiaircraft artillery]. It was much more intense than anything I thought the Iraqis could manage." The sky was also crowded with Coalition aircraft attacking their targets: "We were all using the 'Big sky, little airplane' maxim to keep us from running in to each other. The scene around me was terrifying. I could see the flash of bombs from under the clouds below, as jets from other flights hit their targets." But their training prevailed, and the pilots continued their mission: "For just an instant I felt indignant.

These guys were shooting at *me*. . . . I honestly had my feelings hurt. I was really a pretty nice guy, not the sort of person you'd want to kill. . . . Approaching my release point I mashed down on the red bomb pickle button . . . then selected full afterburner and started climbing. . . . Looking back I got some satisfaction in seeing the flash from my bombs as they exploded below the thin layer of clouds."[18]

On 18 January, Iraq began firing Scud-B al-Hussein surface-to-surface medium range missiles against Israel and Saudi Arabia. The first eight missiles were launched at Tel Aviv and Haifa, as planned. The Scuds were very inaccurate and did not have the political impact that Saddam had hoped (he expected the Scuds would tear the Coalition apart), but the missile force operated with great efficiency. As Kevin Woods later described, "The missile force quickly settled into a routine of confirming target guidance with Saddam, cycling launch vehicles through missile storage and fueling locations, establishing a secure firing position, and finally launching."[19]

The political and military consequences of the Scud attack forced Central Command to begin what was called the "Great Scud Hunt." Although the hunt was largely unsuccessful, it diverted large numbers of aircraft and reconnaissance resources away from Kuwait and into the western Iraqi desert. In particular, the hunt required the use of the two prototype Grumman E-8C Joint Surveillance Target Attack Radar System (Joint STARS) aircraft. The E-8C had arrived in Saudi Arabia after Christmas and was a new, untested battlefield technology. Central Command used this new technology to track mobile Scud launchers in the western desert, although originally it was designed to track large-scale troop movements such as those that would precede a major offensive.[20]

In Kuwait, Marine Harriers were joined in attacks on Iraqi artillery and rocket batteries by Air Force Fairchild Republic A-10 Thunderbolt IIs (more commonly referred to as "Warthogs"). Along the border, Cobras from Marine Light Attack Helicopter Squadron 369 responded to calls for close air support from the reconnaissance teams stationed in the observation posts and destroyed Iraqi mortars under intense antiaircraft and artillery fire. Captain Steven G. Springer and First Lieutenant Gregory D. Anderson were each awarded the Distinguished Flying Cross for leading the destruction of the Iraqi positions after the original lead helicopter lost the use of its radios.[21]

At 0910 on 18 January, the first Marine aircraft of the conflict was shot down. Flying their second

The OV-10 Bronco's last combat service with the Marine Corps was in the Gulf War. Two Bronco squadrons deployed to the Gulf, and each squadron had one of its aircraft shot down during the conflict.

combat mission of the war in an OV-10 Bronco over Kuwait, Lieutenant Colonel Clifford M. Acree, squadron commander of Marine Observation Squadron 2, and his aerial observer, Chief Warrant Officer-4 Guy L. Hunter Jr., were looking for Iraqi artillery when they spotted a rocket launcher battery. As they banked above the Iraqis, Colonel Acree saw "a horrifying sight: glinting metal followed by an incredibly fast gray-white vapor trail snaking toward us. A heat-seeking surface-to-air missile had locked on to our aircraft and was tracking us. The missile, pointed right at my face, was coming fast to blow us out of the sky. With less than 6,000 feet of altitude, I had no more than a second warning to dodge the missile streaking toward us. . . . It's the same feeling you get in a car crash when you've hit the brakes hard and so has the other guy. You know the impact is coming all the same."[22]

Initially, the aircrew was believed to have been killed. As Colonel Bioty remembered, "We did not know that they were alive until we saw them on TV. . . . [The aircraft going down] was really a shocker and that squadron took a real significant

hard swallow, . . . because there was a lot of leadership and experience in that airplane and here it got hit on the second day of the war." Acree and Hunter were captured by the Iraqis, the first of five Marines eventually taken prisoner. Like the others they would be beaten, mistreated, and used as human shields until after the war.[23]

19 to 27 January

The third day of the air campaign, 19 January, marked the end of the preplanned, initial air tasking order. The 3d Marine Aircraft Wing flew two successful major missions to complete the preplanned missions: one against bridges at Basrah and the other against *Republican Guard* units. Other Hornets and Intruders joined the wing's Harriers in attacking Iraqi units in Kuwait, continuing to concentrate on artillery.[24]

Now Marine air began to focus more heavily on targets in Kuwait of concern to the Marines, steadily flying fewer joint missions each day. Each morning Major General Royal Moore held a 0600 breakfast meeting with the four Marines who commanded

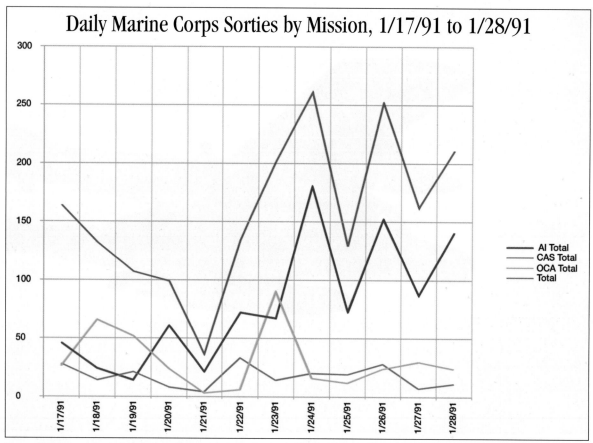

Daily Marine Corps Sorties by Mission, 1/17/91 to 1/28/91

Data culled from *A Statistical Compendium and Chronology—Gulf War Air Power Survey*, vol. 5 (Washington, DC: U.S. Government Printing Office, 1993), pp. 260–268

Air Interdiction (AI): missions to delay, divert, disrupt, or destroy the enemy's military potential beyond the fire support coordination line. Close Air Support (CAS): missions requested by a ground commander for support of, and close to, friendly ground forces. Offensive Counter Air (OCA): missions to destroy or neutralize enemy air power. In the Gulf War these included, for Marines, air-to-surface attacks on enemy airfields and attacks to destroy or disrupt enemy surface-to-air defenses or integrated air defense systems. A sortie is an individual aircraft mission from takeoff to landing.

watches in the wing's tactical air control center: assistant wing commander Brigadier General Granville Amos, chief of staff Colonel William A. Forney, Colonel William D. Can Jr., and Colonel Melvin W. DeMars Jr. General Amos later recalled, "We would meet every morning at seven to kind of go through the day's evolution. Then, at 1300 we would meet with the plans side of G-3 [operations division] to look at the next 12-, 24-, 48-, 72-hour plan, and that is where General Moore made his input into changing . . . the frag[mentary order] process."[25]

As can be seen on the chart detailing Marine Corps sorties from 17 January to 28 January, the number of sorties dipped dramatically on 20 and 21 January, when poor weather forced the cancellation of many missions. Intruders from the all-weather attack squadrons did manage to launch, however, striking Iraqi multiple rocket launchers that were firing toward Mishab.[26]

As the weather improved, the number of sorties increased exponentially, and the targets of the Marines continued to shift. Fewer Marine strikes were launched against power plants or airfields (the "offensive counter air" sorties on the chart), and a larger percentage of Marine strikes were aimed at interdiction. In some cases, this meant strikes on bridges or *Republican Guard* units, but it also meant strikes on Iraqi units in Kuwait. Air Force A-10 Warthogs and General Dynamics F-16 Fighting Falcons also launched strikes at Iraqi units inside Kuwait proper. Close air support missions were flown in small numbers as Marine Harriers and helicopters supported the Marines manning the observation posts along the border.[27]

There were some internal difficulties with command and control for Marine air, specifically a struggle for control between the wing's tactical air control center and the direct air support center located with the I Marine Expeditionary Force headquarters in Safaniya. As Colonel Manfred Rietsch later explained, "The DASC [direct air support center] wasn't used in its doctrinal role. . . . The MEF [Marine expeditionary force] absorbed the DASC and it became almost a competition between the TACC [tactical air control center] and the DASC as to who was going to control airplanes and the flow of airplanes. . . . They [the DASC] attempted to control airplanes where their job was really coordination, not control, and a couple of times they actually put some airplanes into some situations that they shouldn't have been. Telling them to go after some ridiculous target in a dangerous situation. It didn't work the way it was intended." By the end of the first two weeks of combat, the conflict had been resolved.[28]

The Marine air campaign continued steadily after the bad weather of 20 and 21 January, and the war began to become routine. Colonel Donald A. Beaufait, executive officer of Marine Aircraft Group 11, described typical missions for F/A-18 Hornet pilots flying into Iraq:

The very first ones obviously took a lot of detailed planning because we had, first of all, to gather the intelligence on where the defenses were. We always wanted to avoid them as much as possible; if we couldn't avoid them we would come up with a detailed plan to suppress them and then we'd have a strike leader who would coordinate all of the suppression efforts along with the detailed bomb aim points for each of the airplanes on a strategic target. Then they'd sit down probably three hours before the mission and then start briefing it so they could brief the overall concept of how it's going to work, with an intelligence brief and that type of thing.

Then each of the elements whether they were the strike airplanes or the suppression airplanes or the combat air patrol elements would then break down further and brief their section or their element, division, on what the plan was. And then pretty much everyone would go out and we'd get started up and take off. They'd have a tanker plan, they would go and refuel. We had huge numbers of airplanes, both Marine Corps and Air Force tankers, KC-10s [McDonnell Douglas KC-10 Extenders] and

An F/A-18C Hornet strike-fighter aircraft of Marine Fighter Attack Squadron 232 taxis on the runway before takeoff for a mission in support of Operation Desert Storm.

Photo by Sgt Jeff Wright. Defense Imagery DA-ST-92-07701

those types of airplanes, KC-135s [Boeing KC-135 Stratotankers], C-130s. Refuel the airplanes prior to going across the border into either Iraq or into Kuwait so they had a full combat load of fuel. Then execute the mission, come back out, and normally there would be another tanker waiting as soon as we got back into Saudi Arabian airspace to be able to refuel airplanes in case we had any combat damage. We'd also have an element of airplanes which would be designated as a rescue combat air patrol in order if we had to pick up some pilots that were downed somewhere along the mission. Then we'd land, we had hot refueling pits that were set up with fuelling stations at Shaikh Isa [Bahrain]. Come back and refuel the airplanes and then they'd go back, park the jets, go through maintenance control, and come back and have a major debrief with the intelligence on what happened.[29]

Lieutenant Colonel William R. Jones commanded Marine Attack Squadron 231, an AV-8B squadron operating out of King Abdul Aziz airfield in Saudi Arabia. In an interview, he described a typical mission in Kuwait during this period:

A lot of the delivery was roll-in at 18/20,000 feet; get your nose on the target; use the angle rate bombing system, which is a magnified TV camera in the nose so you could lock on to a dot with the TV camera and then call the TV display in the cockpit and you could look at it and see is that a shadow or is that a truck. . . . We're dropping at 550 [knots] in a 45 to 60 degree dive and of course the sensation in the cockpit once you got even past 45, but certainly at 60, you feel like you're actually kind of coming out of your seat. You do and you're still at 1.0G. That's what the meter tells you on the airplane, but it sure doesn't feel that way.

This Kuwaiti police post, which was opposite Observation Post 4, was occupied by Iraqi forces. It was destroyed by Marine Harrier attack aircraft on 27 January 1991.

Photo courtesy of MGySgt Gregory L. Gillispie

You feel like you're just barely hanging in there, coming straight down. It seems like straight down. You pickle off your bombs and then pull off. . . . You're at 550 knots at 60 degrees nose down so the pull off is really just: "Ugh, how low am I going to go on this bottom out!?" Of course that's when you start worrying about getting back up above 10,000 feet and getting the flares off on the climb out so they don't catch you with a cheap shot on the way out.[30]

Iraq's broadest response to the air campaign was to "hunker down" and simply outlast the onslaught, preserving what it could for after the campaign rather than attempting to defeat Coalition air power. On 21 January, Saddam ordered his air defenses to "maintain the weapons and equipment and to cut down on the use of ammunition." Saddam had determined that "the enemy is planning to shorten the battle, which we planned to prolong, the opposite of their expectation. Therefore, according to our calculations, the most important requirements of the long war are to conserve everything."[31]

In Kuwait, the common Iraqi soldier was unsure what to believe. Aside from the border artillery units and the air defense sites, there had been relatively few strikes on Iraqi targets in Kuwait proper. There were rumors about the Coalition's air attacks but few facts, and rumor ran rampant in a military that treated official news as suspect. One young Iraqi soldier serving in the *III Corps* kept a diary that was found abandoned after the war. His entry for the fourth day of the campaign illustrates the uncertainty the bombing of Iraq was producing in the soldiers in Kuwait:

One says they have destroyed Baghdad and demolished it and another says there is no water, electricity or telephone lines. Some of them turn the world black in your eyes. Others come to pacify you saying nothing has happened there—they have only bombed the military installations. Others say they have bombed the civilian buildings. You don't know who to believe and who is lying. All news [reports] are hallucinations. They are all lying. The truth is lost.[32]

The missions were increasingly familiar and that familiarity was also a danger. Colonel Jones described how he warned his Harrier pilots to stay focused and avoid flying too aggressively as the air war continued: "There're no bad guys in the wire.

There's no reason to be pressing the attack. There's no reason to get down and expose you or your aircraft to damage." He added that "this part of the war really was mechanical and it was basically go in high and find the target, take it out, go home, come back and do it again."[33]

A more direct warning of the dangers of routine came in the form of two friendly fire incidents. On 23 January, an Air Force A-10 strafed Marines at Observation Post 6; luckily there were no casualties. On 24 January, a convoy of 1st Force Reconnaissance Company driving near Observation Post 2 on the Saudi-Kuwaiti border was repeatedly strafed by an Air Force A-10. Two vehicles were damaged, and a Marine and a sailor were wounded. General Walter Boomer responded to this incident—the first involving casualties—by shifting the fire support coordination line several thousand meters farther into Kuwait and placing Marine liaison officers with the Air Force's A-10 squadrons.[34]

Also on 24 January, the only known Iraqi offensive air sorties of the war occurred when a pair of Iraqi Dassault Mirage F-1s attacked the Saudi oil terminal of Ras Tanura. They were targeted by Marine MIM-23 medium-range surface-to-air missiles but were both shot down by a Saudi Arabian F-15C's AIM-9 Sidewinder air-to-air missiles.[35]

Multiple strikes were launched by Marine aircraft against the Iraqi *III Corps'* headquarters. Captain Stout flew in one on 24 January that left the place "in a shambles." On 25 January, Marine aircraft destroyed the Ahmadi ammunition storage facility; the resulting smoke pillar rose to 30,000 feet. A later strike against *III Corps* headquarters was postponed after the Iraqis began pumping oil into the Persian Gulf. The strike was diverted to destroying the pumps at the refinery in an attempt to slow the flow of the oil.[36]

As part of Saddam's plan to try and preserve his forces and endure the air assault, on 26 January he ordered the Iraqi Air Force to start fleeing to Iran, where the aircraft might sit out the war unharmed by Coalition attacks. Many Iraqi aircraft made the dash over the coming weeks, but neither aircraft nor crews returned to Iraq after the war in significant numbers.[37]

Marines and the Air Tasking Order

Under the pressure of combat, the differences between Air Force and Marine Corps air doctrine began to strain the agreement reached in September. As noted in chapter 4, the Air Force used its control of the air tasking order to control targeting

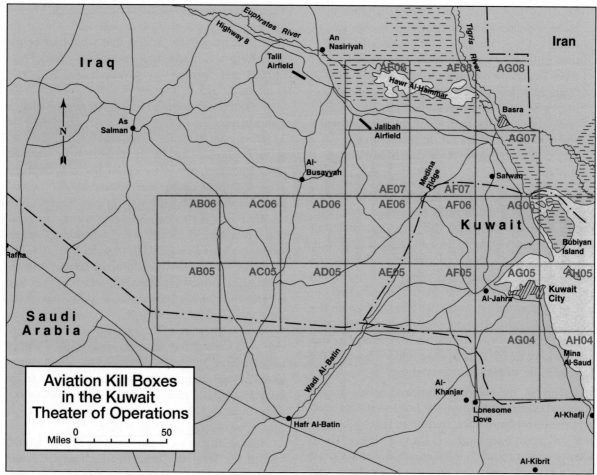

Reprinted from Edward J. Marolda and Robert J. Schneller Jr., *Shield and Sword: The United States Navy and the Persian Gulf War* (Washington, DC: Naval Historical Center, Department of the Navy, 1998), p. 239

"Kill boxes" allowed the Coalition aircraft to hunt in predesignated regions in search of targets of opportunity.

priorities, thus attempting to control the use of all air power in the region. The Air Force saw no problems with this approach and felt the Marine worries were groundless. Air Force Lieutenant Colonel Deptula explained this way: "Their [the Marines'] concern is so dogmatic that we want to take their air away from them, and that's not true. . . . If they get into a major ground battle, or a ground battle period, we're not going to hold that air away from them. That's the way they act, and that's why they kept their AV-8s, which is fine. We had enough F-16s to compensate."[38]

Despite the Air Force's confidence, there were problems during the Gulf War in targeting priorities; the Air Force invariably gave a higher priority to targets inside Iraq itself, or to air defense targets. And those sorties that were not aimed at Air Force priority targets were distributed to the Army corps as well as to General Boomer's Marines. This led to targets that directly targeted Marine priorities getting

postponed or denied. For example, General Boomer's staff tried multiple times to get the headquarters of the Iraqi *III Corps* on the "JFACC"* targeting list, but it never made passed muster as a "strategic" target. Instead, the Marines targeted it with the sorties withheld from the joint forces air component commander by the September agreement. Because the first three days were dominated by JFACC sorties (aside from Harrier close air support missions for Marines under fire), the Iraqi corps headquarters was not targeted for days.[39]

Another issue lay with the daily air tasking order itself, which was several hundred pages long each day. It overwhelmed the communication facilities of the Marine (and Navy) units that needed it, di-

---

*JFACC (pronounced "Jay-Fack") is short for "Joint Forces Air Component Commander." It was used as slang in the Marine headquarters to designate targets and sorties that were generated by Air Force Gen Horner's staff, rather than those generated by the Marine staff.

verted other message traffic, and clogged the system. It was drawn up by General Horner's staff, which was dominated by Air Force officers (calling into question the so-called joint nature of his command), and it followed Air Force doctrine. Each day's tasking was planned days in advance, and Marines and sailors both felt the system would be unresponsive to the fast-paced changes the air campaign would require. The Navy was unhappy with the way the Air Force dominated the process, with Vice Admiral Stanley Arthur, General Boomer's Navy counterpart, remarking after the war that "we've had many examples of . . . fleeting moments of opportunity, without being able to get back to them. We had an enemy that crumbled on us this time, but if we had an enemy that was very tough and a lot smarter, we can't let those little windows of opportunity ever disappear."[40]

In an interview from March 1991, Colonel Rietsch expressed the views of many Marines on the air tasking order:

> We were able to do our job in spite of the ATO [air tasking order] process and that's really true. From the Air Force point of view this thing will probably come out as a big success—the ATO—because they are going to say "yes it worked." Well, my answer: it worked— we did our job in spite of it. It was not flexible, [and] most days we got the ATO after the ATO day had already started. I mean we were launching airplanes before we got the ATO.[41]

The 3d Marine Aircraft Wing responded to the air tasking order's flaws by "opting out." The Marines stuffed the order with planned sorties, then cancelled or diverted them as needed on the day in question. This gave General Moore the flexibility he needed to respond to General Boomer's priorities in preparing the Kuwaiti battlefield for the liberation.[42]

28 to 31 January

On 28 January, 3d Marine Aircraft Wing lost its second aircraft when Captain Michael C. Berryman's Harrier was shot down by an infrared surface-to-air missile. Flying with Marine Attack Squadron 311, Berryman was leading his section as they were diverted to an Iraqi rocket battery when he was hit. He ejected safely but was captured by the Iraqis, joining Acree and Hunter as the third Marine aviator captured in the war. Like them, he would be tortured and mistreated by the Iraqis. Unlike Acree and Hunter, the Iraqis did not publicly acknowledge Berryman was their prisoner until after the war. He

was originally listed as missing in action and was presumed killed.[43]

Also on 28 January, Marine F/A-18s of Marine Aircraft Group 11 participated in a strike at a rocket fuel factory near Baghdad, the deepest penetration into Iraq by Marine aircraft during the Gulf War. The factory was heavily damaged, and none of the Hornets were damaged on the mission.[44]

Marines continued to hunt for *III Corps* headquarters, which they believed had been split between a permanent and a mobile headquarters. On 29 January, General Boomer was informed that an Iraqi prisoner of war claimed the headquarters was located at a racetrack. Marine intelligence officers in the 1st Surveillance, Reconnaissance, and Intelligence Group combined this and other collected information with reports from the Kuwaiti resistance, and they determined that the site of the headquarters was on a former military base in southern Kuwait and that a meeting for Iraqi officers was scheduled there for the evening of 31 January.[45]

The resulting air strike illustrates the way the Marines worked around the strictures of the air tasking order. Two A-6Es from Marine Aircraft Group 11 were taken from a cancelled JFACC mission and directed to strike the small building identified. They hit it with two laser-guided GBU-10 2,000-pound bombs, demolishing the target. The Marines believed they had killed General Salah Aboud Mahmoud, the *III Corps* commander, but this was not the case.[*] It is difficult to determine what exactly this strike hit; Iraqi sources do not describe any direct attacks on General Salah Aboud, but he did later say, concerning his headquarters in this period, that it "consisted of a small shelter and of a building that belonged to Kuwait's Army. . . . It was badly damaged because the enemy had started attacking it daily. . . . There were many big impact craters from the bombs dropped at the entrance of the shelter. For the entrance, we had to provide signs from these roads to our entrance to avoid any unexploded ordnance."[46]

As January came to a close, the 3d Marine Aircraft Wing had done considerable damage to the Iraqi military, but most of the damage had been done to strategic targets. Inside Kuwait itself there had been relatively few strikes, as the following chart indicates.

---

[*]It is strongly suggested on pages 51–52 in Col Charles Quilter II's monograph *U.S. Marines in the Persian Gulf, 1990–1991: With the I Marine Expeditionary Force in Desert Shield and Desert Storm* that Gen Salah Aboud died in this strike. This is incorrect; the general was later present at the Safwan cease-fire talks and spoke often to the Iraqi War College in the mid-1990s.

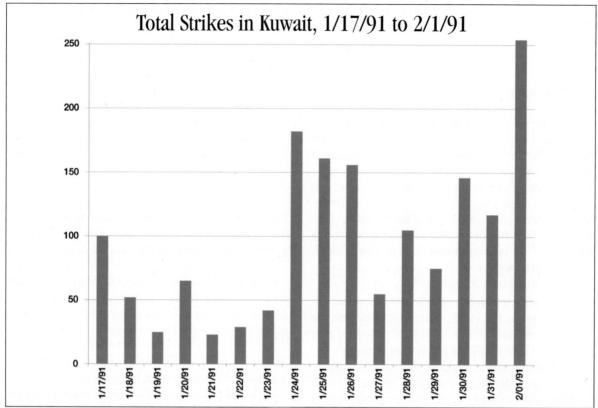

Total Strikes in Kuwait, 1/17/91 to 2/1/91

Data culled from *A Statistical Compendium and Chronology—Gulf War Air Power Survey*, vol. 5 (Washington, DC: U.S. Government Printing Office, 1993), pp. 466–467

This chart shows the number of strikes by Coalition aircraft carried out each day against Iraqi forces in Kill Boxes AF6, AG6, AH6, AF5, AG5, AH5, AG4, and AH4. These kill boxes contained the Iraqi forces most likely to engage Marine ground forces. A strike is defined as a weapon employed by a single aircraft against a target. Aircraft often made multiple strikes on each sortie.

The end of the initial phase of the air campaign and 3d Marine Aircraft Wing's decision to increasingly opt out of the air tasking order process resulted in an increase in missions into Kuwait from 24 January onward, with a sharp spike occurring on 31 January when Coalition aircraft caught a large convoy of Iraqi forces north of al-Khafji. Nonetheless, it would be fair to say that that Iraqi forces in Kuwait, in particular the *III Corps* and *IV Corps,* who were defending the area through which the Marines would be advancing, had not yet suffered a prolonged, broad, intensive air bombardment.

At the 28 January daily staff briefing, General Boomer expressed his frustration with the air campaign in Kuwait proper:

I don't know how to address this very well because if you don't feel it in your bones, it's very hard for me to get the point across. But we are in a full-court press now for everything to be working, all of our assets to be utilized, and you can't accept any bull s——t reasons

for why this can't happen. . . . Time is getting short. Every sunlit day that we have we must take maximum advantage of it. Every asset must be up. I am concerned that we don't have enough sorties today. . . . Our planning and our system should be such that their every pilot should fly today. . . . If they are not, it's our fault; it's our fault, pure and simple. That monkey's on our back, guys, and the backs of the other staffs; the wing staff and the division staff. None of you are going through that wire; none of you are going through that breach system. I sense that if you were, then you wouldn't be accepting some of these "nos."[47]

That is not to say that Coalition air power was not impacting those Iraqi units, however. It is true that the Iraqi entrenchments and decoys had been somewhat effective in minimizing damage, and very few of the Iraqi armored vehicles had been damaged or destroyed in the attacks. But vehicle readi-

Marine Corps Art Collection

Fly Over *by Col H. Avery Chenoweth*

ness was now a major issue for the Iraqis, mostly because the increase in Coalition flights from 24 January onward combined with the steady presence of Coalition aircraft over Kuwait kept the Iraqis hiding in their bunkers rather than performing needed maintenance. Iraqi supply vehicles were no longer able to move, so ammunition, food, and water were also beginning to become issues for the Iraqis. Iraqi commanders attributed this to the Coalition aircraft "flying continuously over our forces [just] beyond 75mm antiaircraft artillery range" rather than just "dropping bombs and leaving." General Salah Aboud ascribed these difficulties to the destruction of his corps' air defense command headquarters.[48]

The Iraqis responded by employing innovative supply solutions such as slaughtering local cattle for food or collecting camels as an alternative method of supply transport. Vehicle maintenance, never an Iraqi strong suit, was shifted to the hours of darkness. Nevertheless, little could be done for the unit most heavily targeted during January, the *III Corps'* artillery, which was "experiencing trouble with

some of [its] artillery pieces due to [over]use or because [it] had been bombed."[49]

One measure of the success of the campaign in Kuwait is that after the war, Iraqi War College studies focused heavily on defeating or avoiding air attacks. Burning oil fires, deception, decoys, and dispersal were all techniques that were tried in Kuwait and that the Iraqis would later perfect in the decade of tense peace following the war.[50]

The success of the air campaign was also apparent on a more individual level. After the first week of bombing, the aforementioned anonymous Iraqi soldier made the following entry in his diary: "I haven't slept a wink and I don't know anything about my family. No news about them for seventeen days. I don't know if they are safe and I don't know about my brother Hussain who is in the Alexandria Institute or about my brother Abbas who is in the Air Force Supply and Transportation Unit. I pray to God that they may be safe."[51]

Despite the Scud distraction and the focus on strategic rather than operational targets, the air campaign had an obvious and significant impact on Iraqi forces inside Kuwait. It isolated units from the national command authority; degraded troop morale; and made even simple movements difficult, often requiring days of detailed planning for routine operations. With its diplomatic options exhausted, and enduring the effects of an air campaign much longer than anticipated, Iraq began planning a large spoiling attack centered on the Saudi town of al-Khafji on 29 January 1991. Now known as the Battle of al-Khafji, it was the first major ground combat action of the Gulf War.

Chapter 6

Preludes to al-Khafji

Building Kibrit

Brigadier General Charles Krulak, commanding general of Direct Support Command, had chosen Kibrit as the location of Combat Service Support Area 1 on 17 December. From this forward supply point, the command was to supply the logistics needs of two Marine divisions in the assault. The location was chosen as the best geographic location to support the original one breech attack plan. Approximately 50 kilometers south of the Kuwaiti border, Kibrit was out of range of Iraqi artillery but close enough to support the assault, and its topography concealed the camp's silhouette.[1]

Commanded by Captain Brian J. Hearnsberger, Company B, 8th Engineer Support Battalion, arrived at Kibrit and began construction on 27 December. This engineer battalion ended December 1990 as the closest Marine unit to Iraqi forces as they provided their own security and worked on the massive complex.[2]

On 4 January, Company C, 1st Battalion, 3d Marines, arrived at Kibrit and began to provide security so that the engineers could focus on constructing the complex rapidly. The 7th Engineer Support Battalion arrived on 6 January to reinforce its sister battalion. Major Steven M. Zimmeck later recorded that, when construction was completed on 15 January, the 8th Engineer Support Battalion and the 7th Engineer Support Battalion had "built a 73-cell ammunition support point, improved the 3,000-foot air strip, established a 1.8-million-gallon fuel dump, stored 500,000 gallons of water, dug in two field hospitals, and surrounded the entire complex with a blast berm." The complex sprawled over 40 kilometers as a defense against Iraqi air or artillery attack.[3]

On 6 January, Seabees of Captain Michael R. Johnson's 3d Naval Construction Regiment arrived at Kibrit. They attempted to build a new well, restored a 1,200-foot-deep well already in place, and began maintaining heavily used desert road between Kibrit and Mishab.[4]

Sea Soldier IV

Although the air campaign had already begun, most

An aerial view of some of the facilities at the Marine Corps combat service support area in Kibrit in late February 1991. Kibrit was intended originally as the primary logistics support for the liberation of Kuwait.

Photo by SSgt George. Defense Imagery DM-SN-93-02252

An African Distraction: Operation Eastern Exit

In January 1991, the U.S. Navy and Marine Corps demonstrated the flexibility and versatility of naval forces by undertaking Operation Eastern Exit—the evacuation of the U.S. embassy in Mogadishu, Somalia—in the midst of the preparations for Operation Desert Storm during the Gulf War.

The ongoing Somalian civil war created an unsafe situation in the capital of Mogadishu as order crumbled and various militias began fighting openly throughout the city. The U.S. ambassador's request to evacuate the embassy was approved on 2 January 1991. The Navy and Marine amphibious forces in the Persian Gulf, who were preparing to help liberate Kuwait, were given this task.

Colonel James Doyle Jr., commanding officer of Brigade Service Support Group 4, was appointed the Marine commander of the evacuation, and Captain Alan B. Moser, USN, commander of Amphibious Squadron 6, was appointed commander of the amphibious task force. Both the USS *Guam* and USS *Trenton* sailed immediately south with elements of the 4th Marine Expeditionary Brigade on board to conduct the evacuation.

On 4 January, the U.S. ambassador reported the embassy was under siege by looters, and that night Marine helicopters flew 450 miles (being refueled twice en route by Marine C-130s) and landed a security detail of Navy SEALS and Marines from Company C, 1st Battalion, 2d Marines. They evacuated 61 civilians and returned to the amphibious task force. The next night, while the Marines provided perimeter security, the helicopters evacuated over 200 more civilians. By the morning of 6 January 1991, less than four days after receiving the order, the evacuation was complete. Two hundred eighty-

one civilians from 31 countries, including Great Britain, Germany, Kenya, Kuwait, Nigeria, Oman, the Soviet Union, Sudan, Turkey, and the United Arab Emirates, were evacuated (the wife of the Nigerian ambassador gave birth on board the USS *Guam* en route to Oman, increasing the number of evacuees to 282).

Thanking the sailors and Marines for the swift, efficient evacuation, the U.S. ambassador said, "Few of us would have been alive today if we had been outside your reach. . . . We will take a part of each of you with us for the rest of our lives."[5]

Adapted from a Central Intelligence Agency map by Marine Corps History Division

of the Marines serving on board the amphibious task force spent the end of January participating in Sea Soldier IV, the last amphibious exercise conducted for the Gulf War. Both the 4th and 5th Marine Expeditionary Brigades participated in this huge exercise, marking it as the largest Marine amphibious exercise since 1964.[6]

The sea is dangerous, even when one is merely practicing to go in harm's way, and flying military aircraft is an inherently dangerous occupation as well. This was made clear even before the exercise

officially began. On 22 January, an AV-8B of Marine Attack Squadron 331 was lost, and its pilot, Captain Manuel Rivera Jr., was killed in the crash. Captain Rivera was making a night landing on the USS *Nassau*, using an instrument approach. Three miles from the ship, his Harrier suddenly dived into the beach and exploded.[7]

Despite this ominous beginning, the two-brigade amphibious landing was a success. Three battalions of the landing force were lifted ashore by the brigade's helicopter squadrons, training to handle prisoners of war occurred, and the brigades underwent a week of desert training and equipment maintenance before conducting a tactical withdrawal exercise from the beach back to the ships. For most of the Marines in the 4th Marine Expeditionary Brigade, floating in the North Arabian Sea since early September, this would be the highlight of their monotonous Desert Shield and Desert Storm deployment.[8]

Artillery Raids and Reconnaissance Patrols

Very early on 17 January, Major General Salah Aboud Mahmoud of *III Corps* received orders to begin the preplanned sabotage of the oil fields at al-Wafrah and al-Burqan. He was also ordered to begin artillery strikes against Coalition forces south of the border, the shelling of al-Khafji in particular. The Marines responded to the shelling with air strikes, and it was several days before the fires in the oil fields grew to the point that they were noticeable. Neither tactic spurred the ground combat the Iraqis sought.[9]

On 20 January, the commander of *III Corps* was ordered to send troops to raid across the border in order to "capture as many prisoners as they can." The goal of these raids was to "force the enemy to engage in a major ground battle [where we hope] that the enemy will suffer great losses." None of these raids captured any Americans, and they certainly did not have the intended impact. In fact, many appear to have led to Iraqis surrendering to the Americans. The largest such operation detected by the Marines occurred on the night of 22 January, and while unsuccessful it appears to have been cleverly planned and executed with more enthusiasm than the Iraqi forces usually displayed.[10]

Marine intelligence received word that a "mass defection" of a company of Iraqi soldiers would occur near Observation Post 6 on the night of 22 January. The 1st Reconnaissance Battalion had a team holding the post who prepared to receive the prisoners, and the 1st Light Armored Infantry battalion prepared a "tactical recovery of aircraft and personnel" force of trucks, High Mobility Multipurpose Wheeled Vehicles (HMMWVs, better known as "humvees"), and General Dynamics LAV-25 light armored vehicles to extract the prisoners or aid the outpost as needed. Near midnight, the Marines at the post received small-arms fire and rocket-propelled grenades instead of Iraqi defectors. They temporarily evacuated the position with the aid of the LAV-25 force. After the evacuation, the Iraqis shelled the empty outpost and fired some illumination rounds. There were no Marine losses in the action, and in the morning they reoccupied Observation Post 6.[11]

After the air war against Iraq began, I Marine Expeditionary Force began a series of artillery raids

An AAV-7A1 amphibious assault vehicle is driven off a utility landing craft from the amphibious assault ship USS Nassau *(LHA 4) in an amphibious beach assault exercise. Sea Soldier IV was the last amphibious exercise conducted by 4th Marine Expeditionary Brigade during the Gulf War.*

Photo by PO1 Ken Mark O'Connell, USN. Defense Imagery DM-ST-92-06923

against Iraqi forces in Kuwait. The raids served multiple purposes. First, they were aimed at specific Iraqi artillery forces; second, they were designed to confuse and bewilder the Iraqis by making the ultimate Marine breaching points unclear; and third, they permitted Marine air to strike against the Iraqi artillery (considered Iraq's most dangerous conventional asset), which inevitably replied with counterbattery fire.

Each raid followed the same basic pattern, with some variations. A Marine artillery battery would advance to the border and fire a carefully planned barrage. As soon as the shells cleared the barrels, they would limber the artillery pieces and drive away. Within minutes, the firing location would be empty desert. When Iraqi artillery attempted counterbattery fire, it would fall on the abandoned position, and then waiting Marine aircraft would pounce on the revealed Iraqi artillery and destroy it.[12]

The composition of the raid forces followed a pattern as well. The ground element consisted of a battery or two of artillery with a small security force and a company of light armored vehicles from one of the light armored infantry battalions. The 3d Marine Aircraft Wing would provide an aviation element: this usually comprised an OV-10 Bronco acting as an airborne forward air controller, a McDonnell Douglas F/A-18D Hornet* and two A-6E Intruders to strike the enemy artillery sites, an F/A-18D and two F/A-18s to suppress enemy air defenses, and an EA-6B Prowler to provide electronic countermeasures support.[13]

The first artillery raid (unprotected by a light armored infantry force) occurred on the night of 21 January and was fired from a location just north of al-Khafji against Iraqi artillery positions north of the border. The 1st Battalion, 12th Marines, part of Task Force Taro, launched the raid using two of its batteries of M198 155mm howitzers. The hope was to find an Iraqi rocket system, but none fired. Instead, 80 rounds of dual-purpose improved conventional munitions were fired at suspected Iraqi artillery positions, and Marine aircraft bombed the positions as well.[14]

The next raid was on 26 January near the elbow of the Saudi-Kuwaiti border at al-Jathathil. It was conducted by Batteries Q and S of 5th Battalion, 11th Marines, and screened by Company B, 1st Light Armored Infantry Battalion. The Iraqis attempted to counterbattery fire this time, but it was

inaccurate. Marine artillery fired on three different targets, and Intruders and Hornets bombed and rocketed the Iraqi positions as well. While the artillery retired as planned, B Company destroyed an Iraqi vehicle on the Kuwaiti side of the border berm. Unfortunately, this raid was not without casualties. Two of the light armored vehicles of Company B collided as the company left the area. Three Marines were killed in the crash: Staff Sergeant Michael R. Connor Sr. and Lance Corporals Arthur O. Garza and Michael A. Noline.[15]

The 2d Marine Division conducted its first combat action of the conflict with an artillery raid on the night of 27–28 January. Security for this raid was provided by 2d Light Armored Infantry Battalion, and the raid was conducted by Battery Q and Battery R of the 5th Battalion, 10th Marines. The 5th Battalion's commander, Lieutenant Colonel Andrew F. Mazzara, was the raid force commander. In support of the raid was Battery A, 92d Field Artillery Regiment of the U.S. Army, commanded by Captain Edward L. Hughes, USA. This multiple-launch rocket system battery was prepared to conduct counterbattery fire against Iraqi artillery fire. In the event, there was no return fire from the Iraqis. Battery Q, armed with M109A1 155mm self-propelled howitzers, fired 72 rounds, and Battery R, armed with M110A2 8-inch self-propelled howitzers, fired 36 rounds on their targets: a vehicle park and a logistics site. Then the raid force returned to its staging area.[16]

On the night of 28–29 January, Task Force Shepherd, made up of companies from the 1st Light Armored Infantry Battalion and the 3d Light Armored Infantry Battalion, conducted a raid on the Kuwaiti police station at Umm Hujul, across the border from Observation Post 4. The light armored vehicles of Company A, 1st Light Armored Infantry Battalion, fired their 25mm cannon and Emerson 901A1 TOW 2 (tube-launched, optically tracked, wire-guided) antitank guided missiles at the police post. There was no Iraqi return fire, so the two batteries from 5th Battalion, 11th Marines, that had been assigned to conduct counterbattery fire withdrew without firing.[17]

Iraq's al-Khafji Plan

With its diplomatic options exhausted, and enduring the effects of an air campaign much longer than anticipated, Iraq determined to launch a large spoiling attack centered on the Saudi town of al-Khafji. This attack signaled the beginning of the Battle of al-Khafji, the first major ground combat of the Gulf War.[18]

---

*The F/A-18D was a two-seat version of the F/A-18. It was often used to perform coordination duties or to act as an airborne forward air controller.

Marines of Task Force Shepherd plan their next operation. In addition to screening duties, the light armored infantry battalions also provided security for the Marine batteries conducting artillery raids on Iraqi forces in Kuwait.

Saddam expected the air campaign to last a week and then be followed by the ground war, what he claimed would be the "Mother of All Battles," which would produce the desired massive American casualties. Instead, the bombing showed no sign of stopping and was inflicting serious damage on the Iraqi forces without any corresponding ability to produce the desired Coalition casualties. In the Iraqi view, something needed to be done in order to goad the United States into the planned Kuwaiti "meat grinder."

An Iraqi War College study completed after the war highlighted the Iraqi understanding of the situation in late January 1991:

> In military practice, there are principles. One of the important principles is that the attack is the best defense. In the Mother of Battles this principle is particularly important, because the enemy of Iraq and the Arab nation has deployed a large number of airplanes, rockets and modern equipment, from which it seems they are prepared for a total war. They deployed the most modern equipment for their field forces, which consist of the armies of 28 nations totaling half a million

Artillery Mission *by Sgt Charles G. Grow*

men. But for all this great power, they hesitate to attack the Iraqi field forces because they realize how well the Iraqi forces can defend against a ground attack. And, they know already, the military genius of Iraq's leader, Saddam Hussein.[19]

The Iraqis believed they understood American intentions: "Like we say, they intend to destroy our

ونية راس النفجي
الإماليات ١٥؟٢٨؟ ش
؟٨؟١١٠ شد

An Iraqi Air Force reconnaissance aircraft photographed the Saudi port of al-Khafji in mid-August 1990. Al-Khafji's oil refinery is visible in the upper left of the photograph.

forces and the infrastructure of our country through the air attack, by airplanes and long-range missiles. And they want to avoid the losses of a ground war as much as they can." Moreover, they claimed, "George Bush will not be able to handle the heavy responsibility of heavy casualties in front of Congress and public opinion." In this case, the Iraqis understood American intentions, although they underestimated American resolve, and they gravely overestimated the ability of the Iraqi military to inflict losses on the attacking Coalition forces.[20]

The al-Khafji operation was intended to spark the ground battle of the "Mother of All Battles," which Saddam felt was the prerequisite for his eventual victory. It was intended as a provoking raid that would draw the Americans into a hasty and massive military response and result in significant American casualties. Despite his deficient military acumen, he correctly identified that the center of gravity in the Coalition war effort was the willingness of the American people to suffer casualties, and he designed his operational plans to strike directly at that willpower.

Saddam chose al-Khafji as the target of the attack

for several reasons. The Iraqi War College analysis noted that the town had two harbors: one designed specifically for exporting oil, and the other believed by the Iraqis to be a base for Coalition forces. In Saddam's view, an Iraqi force occupying the town would be able to threaten Coalition naval forces in the Gulf. Al-Khafji was also within range of Iraqi supporting artillery in Kuwait. The attack also would force the Saudis to respond; Saddam knew they could not permit him to hold any part of their kingdom for long. It seemed likely that the attack would force the Coalition into the bloody ground war that Saddam desperately wanted.[21]

The operational plan for implementing Iraq's strategic goal was relatively straightforward. Five Iraqi infantry divisions defended the Saudi-Kuwaiti border from the coast to the elbow: from east to west, they were the *18th Infantry, 8th Infantry, 29th Infantry, 14th Infantry*, and *7th Infantry Divisions*. These commands would not take part in the offensive; instead they would continue to defend the fortifications along the border. These border fortifications, called the "Saddam Line" by U.S. forces, consisted of a belt of minefields, antitank obstacles, and triangular brigade strongpoints. Iraqi engineers had designed and constructed the belt based on lessons learned in their 10-year war with Iran.

The actual raid forces would be drawn from the *3d Armored* and *5th Mechanized Divisions* of *III Corps*, under General Salah Aboud Mahmoud, and the *1st Mechanized Division* of *IV Corps*, under Major General Yaiyd Khalel Zaki. Major General Salah Aboud had overall command of the operation; *III Corps*, considered one of the better organizations in the Iraqi Army, had successfully conducted similar operations during the Iran-Iraq War, as well as performed successfully while defending the Iraqi city of Basrah.[22]

The armored battalions of these divisions were equipped with a combination of T-54/55 and T-62 main battle tanks, while their mechanized infantry battalions were equipped with BMP-1 armored personnel carriers supported by BRDM-2 scout vehicles. Their divisional artillery was lavishly equipped with various models of 152mm and 155mm howitzers.[23]

The plan called for the *1st Mechanized Division* to pass through the lines of the *7th* and *14th Infantry Divisions* between the border's "heel" just south of Umm Hajul and the elbow at al-Manaqish. This maneuver was intended to protect the flank of Brigadier General Hussan Zedin's *3d Armored Division* as it traversed the al-Wafrah oil fields and the lines of the *8th* and *29th Infantry Divisions*. The *3d Armored Division* would then take up a blocking position to the west of al-Khafji. Al-Khafji itself was the target of the *5th Mechanized Division*, which was to seize and fortify the town. Once the *5th Mechanized Division* had secured al-Khafji, the *1st Mechanized* and *3d Armored Divisions* would withdraw back into Kuwait. In theory, after the Coalition ground response was provoked, the *5th Mechanized Division* would retire from al-Khafji and move safely behind the massive fortifications along the Saudi-Kuwaiti border. The attack was set to be launched at 2000 on 29 January 1991, and al-Khafji was to be occupied by 0100 on 30 January.[24]

General Salah Aboud ordered that the forces be "dug in" and "hidden underground" by the morning of 30 January. He provided some insightful tactical advice as well: "I emphasized the use, and the im-

Part of the Iraqi plan for the Battle of al-Khafji, as shown in an official Iraqi history of the battle. This sketch indicates that 6th Armored Brigade's *attack on Observation Post 4 at the "heel" of the Kuwaiti–Saudi border was not intended as the main Iraqi effort.*

Harmony Document Folder ISGQ-2003-00054592

Iraqi Armored Vehicles

Vehicle	Type	Armament	Crew	Top Speed	Weight
	T-54/55	• 1 x 100mm D10T2S gun w/43 rounds • 1 x 7.62mm SMGT coaxial machine gun w/3,500 rounds • 1 x 12.7mm DShK or NSVT antiaircraft w/500 rounds	4	50 km/h	36,000 kg
	T-62	• 1 x 115mm 2A20 gun w/40 rounds • 1 x 7.62mm PKT coaxial machine gun w/2,500 rounds	4	45.5 km/h	40,000 kg
	T-72	• 1 x 125mm 2A46 gun w/45 rounds and 6 ATGW • 1 x 7.62mm PKT coaxial machine gun w/2,000 rounds	3	60 km/h	44.500 kg
	BMP-1	• 1 x 73mm 2A28 low velocity gun w/40 rounds • 1 x 7.62mm PKT coaxial machine gun w/2,000 rounds • 5 x Sagger ATGM	3 to 8	65 km/h	13,500 kg
	BMP-2	• 1 x 30mm 2A42 gun w/500 rounds • 1 x 7.62mm PKT coaxial machine gun w/2,000 rounds • 1 x 30mm AG-17 grenade launcher w/350 rounds • 1 x AT5 launcher w/4 rounds	3 to 7	65 km/h	14,300 kg
	BRDM-2	• 1 x 14.5mm KPVT w/500 rounds • 1 x 7.62mm PKT coaxial machine gun w/2,000 rounds	4	100 km/h	N/A

portance of shoulder fired anti-aircraft weapons in ambush in the front and flanks of the fortified positions. And I emphasized how the snipers should be active and effective against the helicopters of the enemy." He instructed his men to light tire fires because the smoke would confuse the infrared sensors of the Coalition forces. Finally, he ordered his troops "to be economic with the ammunition which is in the tanks and the carriers. Because the enemy air will be focused on the battle territory, especially the transportation, so movement will be very limited." However limited Saddam's understanding of the battle was, at least one of his generals anticipated the difficulties the Iraqis would face trying to maneuver against overwhelming Coalition air superiority.[25]

The capture of American personnel was a high priority. Saddam had determined from the American prisoner of war experience during the Vietnam War and the Iranian hostage crisis that the United States was vulnerable to hostage taking. This led him to hold many westerners hostage early in the Gulf crisis, but he released them in December 1990 to little obvious advantage. Nevertheless, he felt that American soldiers would still be excellent bargaining chips in the confrontation. An Iraqi prisoner from the battle later told American interrogators: "The sole purpose of the raid on al-Khafji was to capture Coalition personnel. The loss of all Iraqi equipment and personnel involved in the raid was of no importance as long as POWs [prisoners of war] were captured."[26]

When giving orders for the attack to his corps commanders, Saddam summed up Iraqi goals in this way: the "enemy in front of us, if he faces this time our willingness to cause severe damage to him, he won't be able to handle it. He will be destroyed and the news will be heard. And all the chairs of the enemy governments will shake." For Iraq, the Battle of al-Khafji was not intended as a skirmish; it was intended to win the war by destroying the Coalition's will to fight. At the heart of the Coalition was the alliance between the United States and Saudi Arabia.[27]

Saudi-Marine Relations

As mentioned in chapter 3, 1st Marine Division commander Major General James Myatt ordered his assistant division commander, Brigadier General Thomas Draude, to take primary responsibility for liaison duties with the Saudi Arabian military. Brigadier General Draude in turn used 3d Marines (commanded by Colonel John Admire), the Marine unit nearest to Joint Forces Command–East units, as the primary focus of his liaison effort.[28]

Colonel Admire assigned Captain Joseph Molofsky, an officer with previous experience in the Middle East, as the 3d Marines liaison officer to the 2d Brigade, Saudi Arabian National Guard. From the beginning, there was tension between the Marines and the Saudis. "The Marines felt that they needed to get their own eyes on [things]," Captain Molofsky explained. "They couldn't trust the Saudis. The Saudis were insulted that the Marines didn't trust them." This situation was exacerbated in January 1991 when 3d Marines was given the duty of protecting the town and airfield of Mishab. Previously Mishab had been part of Joint Force Command–East's area of operations; placing it within the Marine area of operations, especially as the United States began to use the airfield, implied a lack of faith in Saudi military capabilities on the part of Marine commanders.[29]

In addition to the U.S. Army advisors and Special Forces teams assigned to the Saudi forces, commanders attached air-naval gunfire liaison teams to coordinate Marine air and artillery support for the Saudis. Specifically, 1st Air-Naval Gunfire Liaison Company (1st ANGLICO) was attached to Joint Forces Command–East, and in turn the company assigned supporting arms liaison teams to Saudi brigades and fire control teams to Saudi battalions. These teams worked closely with their Saudi counterparts, developing excellent working relationships.[30]

On the eve of the battle of al-Khafji, American and Saudi forces had worked and trained together for five months. There was some unease between the two forces, but both sides had made a concerted effort to overcome it. The Iraqi invasion would put those efforts to the test.

Ra's al-Khafji

The Saudi coastal town of Ra's al-Khafji, more commonly known as al-Khafji, lies approximately seven miles south of the Saudi-Kuwaiti border. Before the war, the primary industries in the town were oil and tourism, but now it was essentially deserted. Saudi General Khaled bin Sultan had ordered the town evacuated in August because it was too close to the Kuwait border to be properly defended. North of the town there was a water desalination plant, and to the south there was an oil refinery, a pier, and a small airstrip. Southeast, beyond the town's outskirts, was a Saudi Arabian National Guard compound.[31]

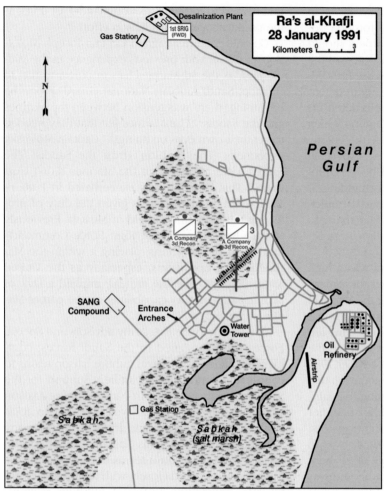

Map by W. Stephen Hill

Ra's al-Khafji was particularly difficult to defend because the town lay to the north of extensive *sabkhas* (salt marshes). As Captain Molofsky explained, "A sabkha is a patch of desert that has some kind of underlying moisture that causes a thin, mudlike crust to develop on the top, which cracks in the heat, but it's easily penetrated by a vehicle and very soft underneath—you get stuck in it in a huge way." The sabkhas served to channel traffic onto the coastal highway, especially the heavy vehicles needed to support the logistics of large military forces.[32]

Coalition Dispositions

Covering deployed Coalition forces were a series of observation posts strung out along the Kuwaiti-Saudi border. Each post was situated near a Saudi border fort, described by virtually every eyewitness as a "*Beau Geste** fort." U.S. Navy SEALs, Army Spe-

*Beau Geste is a 1939 film starring Gary Cooper as a French legionnaire stationed at a fort in the Sahara Desert.

cial Forces soldiers, and Marine reconnaissance teams manned these posts in order to gather intelligence on Iraqi forces in Kuwait. Placed at 10 to 20 kilometer intervals, Observation Post 8 was set on the coast; Observation Post 7 was farther to the west; and Observation Posts 1, 2, 4, 5, and 6 followed the border until the elbow was reached at al-Jathathil.*

Nearest to the coast, the Marine Corps' 1st Surveillance, Reconnaissance, and Intelligence Group controlled Observation Posts 2, 7, and 8.** The coastal highway ran between Observation Post 7 and Observation Post 8, which gave those two posts overlapping oversight of the most likely route into al-Khafji. In addition to the special operations teams, air-naval gunfire supporting arms liaison teams also occupied these observation posts. The 1st Surveillance, Reconnaissance, and Intelligence Group had a headquarters at the desalination plant located to the north of al-Khafji. The 1st ANGLICO, attached to Joint Forces Command–East, was a subordinate unit of the 1st Surveillance, Reconnaissance, and Intelligence Group, which coordinated closely in and around al-Khafji with the various units in the Kuwaiti border area.[33]

Task Force Shepherd*** of the 1st Marine Division had companies on a screening mission near Observation Post 4 (Company D), Observation Post 5

*Most works on the Battle of Khafji list the observation posts slightly differently from east to west: OP-8, OP-7, OP-1, OP-2, OP-4, OP-5, and OP-6. Two important primary sources—the command chronology of the 2d Light Armored Infantry Battalion and the after action report of 1st ANGLICO/1st Surveillance, Reconnaissance, and Intelligence Group—both make clear that the order should be the one given in the text.
**The 1st Surveillance, Reconnaissance, and Intelligence Group was a unit responsible for coordinating intelligence gathering operations, and was subordinate to the I Marine Expeditionary Force rather than the 1st Marine Division. Its primary headquarters was with the I Marine Expeditionary Force headquarters, but it maintained a forward headquarters in al-Khafji.
***The 1st Marine Division's 1st Light Armored Infantry Battalion was actually a composite organization with companies from two separate light armored infantry battalions. To encourage a sense of identity in the ad hoc battalion, it was designated Task Force Shepherd.

Photo courtesy of Capt Charles G. Grow

Saudi soldiers move through the evacuated border city of al-Khafji. Although the city's architecture was relatively monotonous, it offered civilized amenities and was a popular stop for Coalition commanders and journalists.

(Company B), and Observation Post 6 (Company C). Only Observation Post 4 had a Marine reconnaissance platoon in place when the Iraqi attack occurred on 29 January. The 2d Marine Division's 2d Light Armored Infantry Battalion established a similar screen to the east directly in front of the al-Wafrah oil fields and Observation Post 1, between Task Force Shepherd and the Joint Forces Command–East area of operations along the coast.[34]

Under the command of Major General Sultan 'Adi al-Mutairi, Joint Forces Command–East was further divided into task forces. Abu Bakr Task Force was responsible for al-Khafji and the surrounding desert; it comprised the 2d Saudi Arabian National Guard Brigade and an attached Qatari armored battalion. The 2d Saudi Arabian National Guard Brigade's 5th Battalion established a screen north of al-Khafji and west of the coastal highway, behind Observation Post 7. Tariq Task Force, comprising the nascent Saudi Arabian Marines as well as a battalion of Moroccan infantry, was along the coast south of al-Khafji. Further west was Othman Task Force, built around the 8th Mechanized Brigade of the Ministry of Defense and Aviation. A battalion of the 8th Brigade served as a screening force behind Observation Posts 2 and 7. In addition, further west in Joint Forces Command–East's area of operation was Omar Task Force, built around the 10th Mechanized Brigade of the Ministry of Defense and Aviation, with a battalion serving as a screen behind the border. The Saudi mechanized screens were approxi-

mately 3 kilometers behind the border, while the main Saudi defensive positions were approximately 20 kilometers behind the screen.[35]

The I Marine Expeditionary Force's area of operations at this time was shaped somewhat like a fat "L." The leg of the "L" extended along the bend of the Saudi-Kuwaiti border from al-Jathathil to just east of the oil fields at al-Wafrah, and the foot of the "L" extended south of Joint Forces Command–East's area of operations to Mishab and the airfield. Mishab and the surrounding area were held by Task Force Taro, built around the 3d Marines. The pillar of the "L" was held by Task Force Shepherd and the 2d Light Armored Infantry Battalion, which stretched along the border in a light armored screen. Behind this screen was the massive Marine logistical base at Kibrit, which Lieutenant General Boomer, commander of I Marine Expeditionary Force, decided to place forward of the main Marine combat forces in order to speed the eventual attack into Kuwait. Kibrit was relatively vulnerable, and during the Iraqi attack on al-Khafji Brigadier General Krulak, commander of the Direct Support Command and the Kibrit logistics base, would quickly call for armored forces to establish positions north of the base. There is little indication, however, that the Iraqis were ever aware of the base, or its importance to future Marine operations in the region.[36]

Colonel Admire's 3d Marines was responsible for the defense of Mishab. In January, he began to run

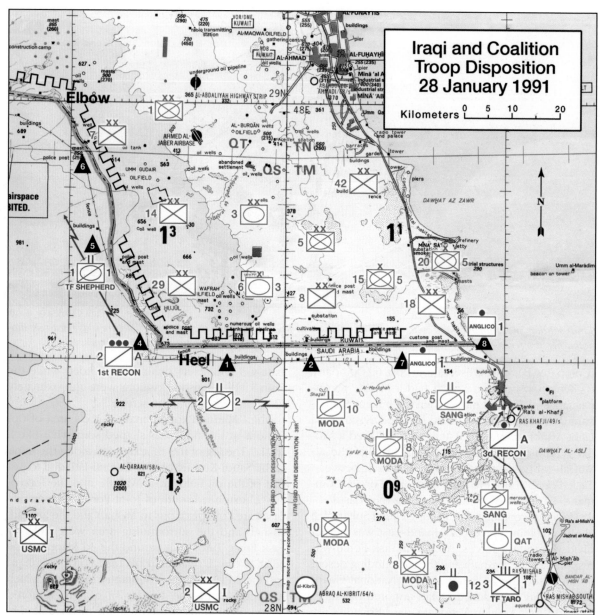

Adapted from a 1991 Ministry of Defence (United Kingdom) map by Marine Corps History Division

reconnaissance training missions into the town of al-Khafji. Teams from the 3d Platoon, Company A, 3d Reconnaissance Battalion, then attached to Task Force Taro, would infiltrate the city by vehicle, usually humvees, establish an observation post, and then leave a day or so later. Unfortunately, these missions were not coordinated with the Coalition forces in al-Khafji. This would have a dramatic impact during the Iraqi invasion, as Captain Molofsky later noted: "I was unaware, [1st ANGLICO's Captain James R.] Braden was unaware, and the Saudis were unaware, that the Marines had reconnaissance teams up in al-Khafji."[37]

Other Marine operations would lead to the

Coalition's success at al-Khafji, however. In response to the difficulties involved in defending Saudi Arabia from an Iraqi attack in the early days of Operation Desert Shield, Marine planners had developed Task Force Cunningham. They designed it as a task-organized, aviation-only task force that would stop Iraqi ground maneuver forces with concentrated fire from the air, covering the withdrawal of Saudi and Marine forces along the coastal highway. Huey and Super Cobra helicopters would operate alongside Bronco and Harrier fixed-wing aircraft in the task force. Joint Forces Command–East liked the plan, and it would serve as the model for air support during the battle.[38]

27 to 28 January

Despite the danger of Coalition air attacks, Saddam Hussein journeyed from Baghdad to the southern Iraqi city of Basrah on the morning of 27 January, where he met with two of his senior Iraqi officers in Kuwait, General Aeeid Khlel Zaki, commander of *IV Corps*, and General Salah Aboud Mahmoud, commander of *III Corps*. Among others at the meeting was the Iraqi minister of defense; the chief of staff; their deputies; other members of the general staff; and Colonel Aboud Haneed Mahoud, commander of Saddam's bodyguard.[39]

Basrah's infrastructure was in ruins. "It was apparent on the road, which had big holes from the bombs and some destroyed military vehicles on both sides of the road," General Salah Aboud remembered. "In al-Basra region all the damage was clear and we noticed it on the bridge, railroads, on the roads, on the facilities. . . . And the streets were very dark, compared to before the war, when they were glowing." At the military headquarters, there was no power, and small candles dimly lit the rooms. General Salah Aboud did not realize that he was to meet Saddam until he "saw the faces of the special guards."[40]

At the meeting, the Iraqi president presented the plan for the attack on al-Khafji and then gave his officers some words of inspiration. As General Hashem Sultan later recalled, Saddam began by discussing Iraqi military successes in the Iran-Iraq War. He said that success had come from Iraqi willpower, despite Iran's advantages in personnel and material. Then he discussed the Coalition air campaign against "our factories, cities, and roads." The air attacks had already lasted two weeks, he explained, because the Coalition did not have as much willpower as the Iranians and was afraid to fight a ground war against Iraq.[41]

He then told his officers that by inflicting casualties on the Coalition they would win the war and save the lives of thousands of Iraqi citizens. Waiting was not to Iraq's advantage, Saddam insisted, they must do something now, implying that Iraq could not survive the continuous air bombardment. He concluded with an old Iraqi proverb: "In order to be ready to fight the fox, you must prepare to fight the lion."[42]

The crew of a Marine LAV-25 scans the desert. The LAV-25 was the backbone of the light armored infantry battalions, an untried concept prior to the Battle of al-Khafji. These battalions were used in a cavalry role, providing a screen in front of the main body of the I Marine Expeditionary Force.

Official U.S. Marine Corps photo

General Salah Aboud, given command of the al-Khafji mission, informed Saddam that he would present him with the city as a present on the morning of 30 January. The meeting then broke up and the Iraqi president returned to Baghdad, surviving an attack by two U.S. Air Force F-16 Falcons. Ironically, the Air Force did not realize they had hit Saddam's convoy until after the war.[43]

General Salah Aboud returned to Kuwait and met with his division and brigade commanders at the *5th Mechanized Division's* headquarters, then at the oil facility of al-Maqwa. He instructed his commanders in tactics for countering Coalition airpower and ordered them to dig in quickly after reaching their objectives. He then passed on Saddam's inspirational words and told them of his promise to make Saddam a present of al-Khafji on the morning of 30 January. Finally, he approved *IV Corps'* request for artillery fire against the sector opposite the *7th* and *14th Infantry Divisions*. The Iraqi forces then began to move into position for the upcoming battle.[44]

Warnings

The Coalition did have some indications that the Iraqis were planning something. One of the E-8C surveillance aircraft reported large-scale Iraqi vehicle movements on the night of 22 January and again on 25 January. These were only preliminary Iraqi maneuvers, but the aircraft also noted the Iraqi movement on the night of 28 January, which was the direct preparation for the upcoming offensive.[45]

All three of the observation posts manned by air-naval gunfire liaison Marines (Observation Posts 2, 7, and 8) reported unusually heavy Iraqi activity on the nights of 27 and 28 January. In addition, according to one account, "Sporadic Iraqi rocket and artillery fires were directed at the city of al-Khafji, the forward Saudi defensive belt, and the border observation posts, often with illumination rounds mixed in." On the night of 27 January, Marines at Observation Post 7 called in a strike on Iraqi "mechanized reconnaissance forces" moving in front of their position, reporting two Iraqi armored personnel carriers destroyed as a result. Some Marine officers considered the Iraqi movements to be a response to the Marine artillery raids that had taken place on 21 and 26 January.[46]

On the night of 28 January, the reported Iraqi mechanized movements coincided with another Marine artillery raid. The teams at the desalination plant north of al-Khafji and at Observation Post 8 each called for air strikes on Iraqi forces they observed, but the artillery raid just to the west had the priority for air support. By 0315 on the 29th, the artillery raid had concluded and air support was again available to the observation post teams. At Observation Post 7, the air-naval gunfire supporting-arms liaison team under Captain John C. Bley II called in a flight of A-10 attack aircraft on a column of Iraqi armored vehicles moving west across its front toward the al-Wafrah oil field. The Iraqi column suffered heavy damage; Bley's team reported nearly a dozen vehicles destroyed. The team observed Iraqi soldiers trying to recover vehicles at sunrise. The team at Observation Post 2 also observed a large Iraqi force moving from east to west, which Coalition airpower engaged. All three observation posts heard the movement of the Iraqi vehicles for the rest of the night.[47]

One Coalition officer who realized at the time that the Iraqis were preparing for an offensive was Lieutenant Colonel Richard Barry, commander of the forward headquarters of the 1st Surveillance, Reconnaissance, and Intelligence Group. He closely monitored Iraqi radio traffic during the air strikes on 28 January and decided that "the Iraqis put probably 150 sappers out there to try and clear that road. [I] sensed they really wanted it opened. They were obviously using that road as some sort of interior line like at Gettysburg." The information was passed on to higher headquarters. Lieutenant Colonel Barry was right; the air attacks against the *3d Armored Division* as it tried to pass through the Iraqi minefields of al-Wafrah paralyzed much of the division, and General Salah Aboud spent much of 29 January trying to fix the scheduling problems these attacks caused. When the division's attacks finally did fall on Observation Post 4 and Observation Post 1, they would be far weaker as a result.[48]

Despite Lieutenant Colonel Barry's warning that "this is it . . . the Iraqis want Khafji," Central Command thought the possibility of an Iraqi ground attack remote as attention was focused on the air campaign and the expected ground offensive to liberate Kuwait.[49]

29 January

On the morning of 29 January, General Salah Aboud inspected the assembly areas of the *5th Mechanized Division* and found fewer vehicles moving than he expected, many being broken down alongside the road. He also found that the division's deception operations were working well, and he saw no sign that Coalition forces knew of

Photo courtesy of MGySgt Gregory L. Gillispie

The arches into the Saudi city of al-Khafji proclaim, "The municipality and residents of Khafji welcome the honorable visitor." Because the city was within range of Iraqi artillery in Kuwait, it was ordered evacuated on 18 August 1990.

its movements. He believed this was because "the order was given to take cover under the smoke clouds of the burning oil, and also the tanks, the armored personnel carriers, and the support weapons' vehicles were all deployed under the trees of al-Thal and were hard to see."[50]

Things were going worse with the *3d Armored Division*, especially with the division's *6th Armored Brigade*, which was commanded by Colonel Ibdil Raziq Mahmoud. The brigade had been pounded by Coalition aircraft the night before, and it had lost at least two tanks. "On the morning of 29 January, the enemy started screaming and shouting after we completed deploying our forces in the desert area; although the enemy had their reconnaissance technologies they were not able to notice our forces," recalled Brigadier General Hussan Zedin, commander of the *3d Armored Division*. He added: "[Coalition aircraft] started to attack our troops during the daylight, in their concealed locations. They tried to affect our morale and cause damage in order to make us too weak to execute the mission."[51]

The air attacks led General Salah Aboud to conclude that the Coalition had discovered his brigade,

and he expected it would face stiff resistance at its objectives. He told the *3d Armored Division* commander, Brigadier General Hussan Zedin, that the *6th Armored Brigade* could expect to face "tanks, anti-tank weapons, and armored cars." He ordered the brigade to employ "a reconnaissance assault a suitable distance ahead of the main convoy to get information about the strength of the resistance of the enemy."[52]

General Salah Aboud was wrong, however. Aside from Lieutenant Colonel Barry at 1st Surveillance, Reconnaissance, and Intelligence Group, the Coalition was not expecting an Iraqi attack, missing much of the Iraqi movement and interpreting the movement that it did observe as either training exercises or reactions to the Marine artillery raids. On the morning of 29 January, the Iraqi *III Corps* and *IV Corps* had moved to their assembly areas successfully. Coalition airpower had already inflicted significant losses, but those losses resulted from routine strikes in Kuwait and chance attacks against Iraqi forces caught moving in the open. The bulk of the Coalition's air effort remained focused elsewhere.

At al-Khafji the various special operations and

reconnaissance forces occupying the city were proceeding with what had become their normal day. For the air-naval gunfire liaison Marines, this meant routine relief of the forward positions. Captain Douglas R. Kleinsmith's supporting arms liaison team relieved Captain Bley and his team at Observation Post 7 in the early morning, and Bley's team returned to the group headquarters at the water desalination plant north of al-Khafji.

Less routine, but not surprising, was the capture of three Iraqi soldiers by Marines at Observation Post 8. All three were in clean uniforms and appeared to be in good health, despite two weeks of Coalition air strikes. Lieutenant Kurtis E. Lang, commander of the air-naval gunfire team at the post, thought they were forward observers; the Iraqis carried maps that detailed Iraqi and some Coalition positions, including Observation Post 8. A U.S. Navy SEAL unit took charge of the prisoners and sent them to the rear. Approximately 30 minutes after

the team captured the prisoners, the Iraqis fired a single tank shell at the position, causing no damage.[53]

Along the coastal highway there were also indications of increased Iraqi activity. At Observation Post 7, Captain Kleinsmith reported Iraqi artillery six to eight kilometers in front of his position, while at Observation Post 8 Lieutenant Lang reported heavy vehicle noises. At 2000, as evening fell, Captain Kleinsmith directed a successful A-6 Intruder attack on the two Iraqi artillery positions, eliminating at least one of the sites.[54]

Outposts

Observation Post 4 was a two-story Saudi police post known as Markaz al-Zabr. To the north, along the border, ran a large berm approximately 15 feet high. The fort protected one of the few openings in the embankment. On 29 January, Observation Post 4 was the only post this far west that was manned;

The Saudi border fort at Observation Post 4 was known as "OP Hamma" to some Marines. This painting by Sgt Charles G. Grow depicts the fort and the burning oil fields at al-Wafrah following a Coalition bombing raid on 24 January 1991.

Marine Corps Art Collection

OP HAMMA OCCUPIED BY A CO 1ST RECON BN
0615, 24 JAN 91 AFTER B-52 BOMBING OF AL-WAFRA

Photo courtesy of MGySgt Gregory L. Gillispie

Maj Keith R. Kelly (on right), executive officer, 1st Reconnaissance Battalion, and then-SSgt Gregory L. Gillispie, platoon sergeant, 2d Platoon, Company A, 1st Reconnaissance Battalion, pose at the southern end of the platoon's position on the berm at Observation Post 4. One of the platoon's bunkers can be seen to the right.

it was held by 2d Platoon, Company A, 1st Reconnaissance Battalion, and a company of light armored vehicles.[55]

The reconnaissance platoon had originally been Deep Reconnaissance Platoon, Company C, 3d Reconnaissance Battalion, based on Okinawa. Comprised of volunteers, it had shipped out to the Middle East in the initial rush to get Marines to Saudi Arabia in September 1990. With its parent battalion remaining on Okinawa, the platoon was absorbed into 1st Reconnaissance Battalion.[56]

Nearly two weeks before, the platoon, led by First Lieutenant Steven A. Ross, was assigned to Observation Post 4. Working as a platoon was a welcome change, since it had been previously assigned to various observation posts in smaller groups alongside other Marine reconnaissance and Army Special Forces teams. Supplies were running low, however, and the platoon was to be relieved on 30 January. Lieutenant Ross had dispersed his men along the berm, divided into three teams along a 500-meter front. Armed with M16 rifles, M249 squad automatic weapons, M60 machine guns, and M136 AT4 antitank weapons, the Marines were not equipped to stop a major Iraqi assault. Lieutenant

Ross stationed the platoon's vehicles—four humvees and a 6x6 5-ton truck—behind a U-shaped berm approximately 500 meters to the rear of the observation post. In the event of a serious Iraqi attack, the plan was for the platoon to withdraw to the U-shaped berm, mount up, and move to the rear while calling in air strikes on the Iraqis.[57]

Captain Roger L. Pollard's Company D, 3d Light Armored Infantry Battalion, was attached to the 1st Light Armored Infantry Battalion, which was designated Task Force Shepherd. It had 19 LAV-25 light armored vehicles divided into two platoons and a company headquarters element.[*] Each LAV-25 was armed with an M242 Bushmaster 25mm cannon and carried a four-man infantry fireteam. A section of seven General Dynamics LAV-AT antitank light armored vehicles from 1st Light Armored Infantry Battalion's Headquarters Company was attached to Pollard's company. Each LAV-AT was equipped with a 901A1 TOW 2 antitank guided missile

---

[*]Standard light armored infantry company organization was three platoons and a headquarters element, but Company D had only four assigned officers. To compensate for the lack of officers, Capt Pollard organized the company into two platoons and trained the company to operate as two elements.

launcher and a thermal imaging system, and was manned by a crew of four. They were the company's primary antitank asset.[58]

At 1200, Company D was ordered to move to Observation Post 4 and act as a screen for the evening. Captain Pollard conducted a reconnaissance and established his company and its attached LAV-AT section northwest of Observation Post 4 at around 1500. He created his fire plan, used a global positioning satellite device to precisely note his unit's locations, and met with Lieutenant Ross. The liaison with Lieutenant Ross was incomplete, as Captain Pollard did not know that 2d Platoon had its own vehicles. This oversight would lead to misunderstandings during the engagement.[59]

Operation Desert Sting

During the Gulf War of 1991, the Navy–Marine Corps team was charged with creating a credible amphibious feint in the Persian Gulf, drawing Iraqi forces away from the Iraq–Kuwait–Saudi Arabia frontier. When the Allied air attacks against Iraq began on 17 January 1991, the seaborne feint needed reinforcement in order to remain credible. Amphibious raids were one method of reinforcing that threat.[60]

On 23 January 1991, Captain Thomas L. McClelland, USN, commanding Amphibious Squadron 5, and Colonel John Rhodes, commander of the 13th Marine Expeditionary Unit (Special Operations Capable), were ordered to plan for an amphibious raid on several Iraqi-held Kuwaiti islands; this raid was code named Operation Desert Sting. Iraqis on one of the targeted islands, Qaruh, surrendered on 25 January to the USS *Curts* (FFG 38). On 26 January, the Iraqis garrison on another of the targeted islands, Umm al-Maradim, created a sign indicating they wished to surrender to U.S. Navy reconnaissance aircraft that photographed the island. The plan for Operation Desert Sting was modified accordingly.

Heavily supported by Navy aircraft, Company A, Battalion Landing Team 1/4 (Reinforced), landed on the north end of Umm al-Maradim Island at noon on 29 January. They encountered no enemy fire or other resistance and found the island had been deserted by its garrison. The Marines captured or destroyed a large quantity of small arms, machine guns, and mortars as well as several Iraqi antiaircraft guns and missiles. After three hours on the island the raid force departed, leaving a Kuwaiti flag raised over the island and the words "Free Kuwait" and "USMC" on several of the buildings.

Meanwhile, the Iraqis dispatched 15 fast patrol boats from Ras al-Qulayah, apparently intending to land commandos at al-Khafji in support of the Iraqi *5th Mechanized Division*, but Allied commanders misinterpreted the movement as an attempt to retake Umm al-Maradim. Despite this, the Iraqi boats were intercepted by Royal Air Force SEPECAT GR-1A Jaguar fixed-wing aircraft and Royal Navy Westland HMA.8 Lynx helicopters from HMS *Brazen* (F91), *Cardiff* (D108), and *Gloucester* (D96). Other Coalition aircraft then continued the attack, destroying or severely damaging all of the Iraqi vessels and landing forces.

With a Cobra attack helicopter hovering protectively nearby, a Marine from Company A, Battalion Landing Team 1/4, takes cover behind an abandoned Iraqi fighting position on Umm al-Maradim during Operation Desert Sting. Despite prepared fighting positions and large amounts of ammunition, the Iraqis had deserted the island prior to the Marine landing on 29 January 1991.

Photo courtesy of LtGen John E. Rhodes

CHAPTER 7

The Battle of al-Khafji

Night, 29–30 January

At the Observation Posts

The first serious ground combat in the Battle of al-Khafji occurred at Observation Post 4, which was manned by 2d Platoon, Company A, 1st Reconnaissance Battalion, and Company D, 3d Light Armored Infantry Battalion. The Iraqi *6th Armored Brigade* of the *3d Armored Division* was assigned to strike through the gap in the berm,

drawing attention away from the movement of the *5th Mechanized Division* to the east. As General Salah Aboud Mahmoud later recalled, "The *6th Armored Brigade* was ordered to move forward from the heights above the al-Zabr [Observation Post 4] and they crossed the line at eight o'clock at night. And at nine o'clock and thirty minutes they encountered enemy resistance at al-Zabr, in Saudi Arabia."[1]

At 2000, Lieutenant Steven Ross, commanding the reconnaissance platoon, heard the clank of treads and then observed Iraqi armored vehicles ad-

Adapted from a 1991 Ministry of Defence (United Kingdom) map by Marine Corps History Division

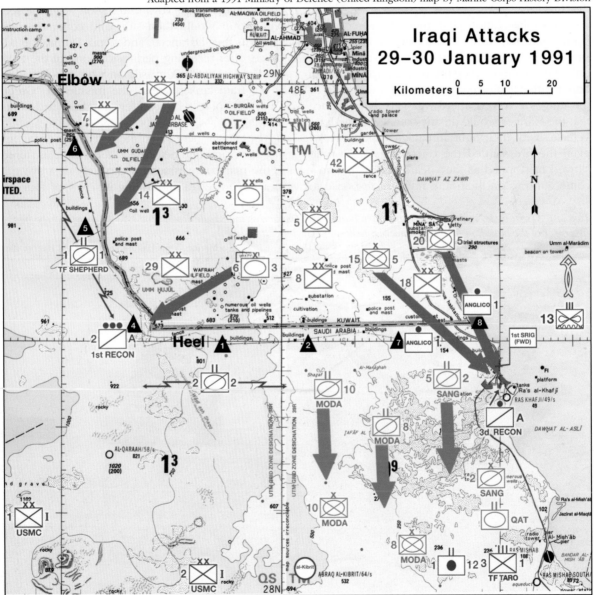

vancing through his night-vision device; it was a sizable force. He attempted to contact his outlying teams as well as Company D and the reconnaissance battalion headquarters by radio but got no response. Since contact earlier was no problem, there was a strong presumption that the reconnaissance platoon's radios were being jammed. Using runners, Lieutenant Ross alerted his platoon and continued trying to get through and inform higher headquarters and Company D of the oncoming Iraqi force. Finally, at 2030, he made radio contact and informed Company D that a large mass of Iraqi vehicles, tanks, and armored personnel carriers was advancing on Observation Post 4. Captain Roger Pollard, Company D's commander, informed Task Force Shepherd and prepared his company to face the threat.[2]

At the observation post, there appeared to be some confusion within Ross's platoon. Rather than simply retreating to the U-shaped berm as planned, one of the teams opened fire on the oncoming Iraqi armor with machine guns and antitank weapons. At the ranges involved, there was very little chance that the Marines would do any damage to the Iraqi vehicles with their light antitank weapons. However, the fire startled the oncoming Iraqis, who slowed or stopped as they heard the ping of machine gun fire on their tank hulls. In response to

the reconnaissance platoon's fire, the Iraqis began to fire back. Their fire was random and inaccurate, but the volume was impressive. At the same time, Iraqi communications jamming appeared to have stopped, and Lieutenant Ross was able to reestablish radio contact with all three of his teams. He promptly ordered everyone to fall back to the U-shaped berm as previously arranged.[3]

To cover the reconnaissance platoon's withdrawal, Captain Roger Pollard led his 2d Platoon's light armored vehicles forward, along with half of the LAV-ATs. The plan was for 2d Platoon to advance in line to aid the reconnaissance platoon." The LAV-ATs had to stop when they fired, in order to provide cover for the advancing LAV-ATs and LAV-25s, half of the LAV-ATs would stop ready to fire while the others advanced a short way. The second group would then stop and cover the first group as they advanced, and so on. During the advance, after receiving permission, one of the LAV-ATs fired its antitank missile on what it believed to be an Iraqi tank. Instead, the missile hit "Green Two," one of its fellows, a few hundred yards to its front.[4]

The missile penetrated the rear hatch of the armored vehicle and detonated the 16 missiles stored in the rear compartment, completely destroying it in a huge fireball and killing its crew of four. "It

Two LAV-ATs from 1st Light Armored Infantry Battalion drive across the Saudi desert. The LAV-AT provided the heavy firepower of the battalion with its antitank missiles.

Photo by LtCol Charles H. Cureton

During the fight at Observation Post 4, LAV-AT "Green Two" was struck in the rear by an antitank missile fired by one of its fellow LAVs, causing the armored vehicle's magazine of 16 missiles to detonate with catastrophic results. Four Marines were lost with the vehicle: Cpl Ismael Cotto Jr., PFC Scott A. Schroeder, LCpl David T. Snyder, and LCpl Daniel B. Walker.

came through the bottom, right troop hatch on this one," First Lieutenant David Kendall of Company D later said. It "hit all the other missiles, I guess, and it was all a spontaneous detonation. There were no secondary explosions. Nothing. This whole thing just went up."[5]

There was confusion at this point, with some Company D Marines believing the vehicle had been destroyed by Iraqi tank fire and others not certain the vehicle had actually been destroyed. The explosion obliterated it so completely that there was not enough wreckage left to register on night vision devices. The crew did not respond to radio calls, but it was common for a radio to cease working. The fate of the LAV-AT would not be confirmed until the next morning.[6]

Captain Pollard and his 2d Platoon continued forward, leaving the LAV-ATs behind. He was finally informed that Ross's platoon had sufficient vehicles to withdraw. Pollard's platoon halted and began firing on the Iraqi vehicles with their 25mm guns. The reconnaissance platoon had observed the incident, and Lieutenant Ross was convinced that Company D would soon fire on his troops by mistake as well. He ordered the platoon to mount their vehicles and withdrew from the battlefield.

After Ross's platoon had completed its withdrawal, Company D's 1st Platoon shifted south of the 2d Platoon in order to support 2d Platoon's fire against the Iraqi forces advancing on the now-abandoned observation post. Pollard's company then backed away from the border but continued to engage the Iraqi armor with missile and 25mm cannon fire. Although the fire had little hope of damaging the Iraqi vehicles at the ranges involved, it served to disorient the Iraqi tanks, which stopped and buttoned up as the rounds ricocheted off their armor. The fire was also useful for marking Iraqi vehicles for incoming aircraft. Lieutenant Scott P. Williams (the company's executive officer) and Corporal Russell T. Zawalick acted as forward air controllers for a series of air strikes against the Iraqi forces utilizing this method of marking enemy positions.[7]

The battle at the observation post was now under control as Coalition air support arrived in large numbers. "At that point, everything was going pretty well." Lieutenant Kendall later noted, "We started getting the air [support] in. It was hitting the tanks down there, and we were just marking for the air by firing our main guns at the tanks and they were following the tracer rounds to them and hitting them with the air." Hearing reports of some Iraqi tanks attempting to cross the berm farther south, Captain Pollard withdrew the company approximately 5,000 meters from the observation post.[8]

Photo by TSgt Rose Reynolds, USAF. Defense Imagery DF-ST-92-07825

An Air Force A-10A Warthog patrols over the desert during the Gulf War. The aircraft carried AGM 65 Maverick air-to-ground missiles and was one of the primary providers of close air support during the Battle of al-Khafji.

Photo courtesy of Sgt Mark S. McDonnell

An American flag flies from the burned-out hulk of "Red Two," which was destroyed by a malfunctioning air-to-surface antitank missile during the fight at Observation Post 4. Seven Marines were lost with the vehicle: LCpl Frank C. Allen, Cpl Stephen E. Bentzlin, LCpl Thomas A. Jenkins, LCpl Michael E. Linderman Jr., LCpl James H. Lumpkins, Sgt Garett A. Mongrella, and LCpl Dion J. Stephenson.

A section of Air Force A-10s now arrived over the battlefield. Corporal Zawalick was controlling air support with live ammunition for the first time, but under Lieutenant Williams's guidance, he directed the incoming aircraft to their targets. The A-10s were finding it difficult to identify the Iraqis, however. After two failed attempts, one of the Warthogs dropped a flare that landed next to "Red Two," one of the company's LAV-25s. Corporal Zawalick informed the A-10 the flare had marked a friendly position and directed him toward the enemy from the flare. Meanwhile, a rifleman

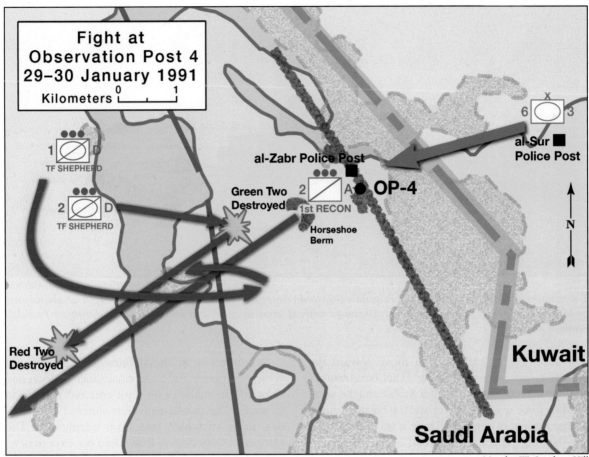

Fight at Observation Post 4 29–30 January 1991
Kilometers 0 1

al-Zabr Police Post

Green Two Destroyed

2 A OP-4

1st RECON

Horseshoe Berm

Red Two Destroyed

1 D TF SHEPHERD

2 D TF SHEPHERD

6 X 3

al-Sur Police Post

N

Kuwait

Saudi Arabia

Map by W. Stephen Hill

jumped from "Red Two" to bury the flare, but as he did the A-10 fired an AGM 65 Maverick air-to-ground missile that struck the LAV-25, destroying it and killing all of the crew that remained inside except the driver, who was ejected from the vehicle. An investigation conducted by I Marine Expeditionary Force after the battle determined that the most likely cause of the incident was a malfunction by the Maverick missile.[9]

Again there was confusion as Pollard tried to determine if "Red Two" had been destroyed by friendly or enemy fire. "That's the first time, the first time I got scared," he later remembered. "I didn't know what had happened. I didn't know where the bad guys were." There was some worry that the Iraqis had penetrated the berm and succeeded in outflanking the company. As a result, Pollard reorganized the company into a screen line and pulled it back slowly.

"The Marines, of that company, as the whole battalion, were calm," said the commander of Task Force Shepherd, Lieutenant Colonel Clifford O. Myers III. "All of my conversations with Captain Pollard . . . were extremely calm and in total control. Even after the Maverick hit 'em."[10]

Despite the calm demeanor that Lieutenant Colonel Myers observed, Pollard's company had lost one vehicle to fire from its own air support and another was missing. With massive amounts of air support moving to the border, and other companies ready and able to move into contact, Lieutenant Colonel Myers ordered Company D to withdraw to the west and link up with Task Force Shepherd's Company A, commanded by Captain Michael A. Shupp. Company D accomplished the maneuver shortly after midnight on the 30th. The remaining six LAV-ATs were transferred to Company A, and Company D was reorganized and resupplied behind Shupp's company, which moved forward to screen Observation Post 4.[11]

The Iraqi perspective on the battle's outcome at the observation post differed considerably from the American view. "Now this small [enemy] force consisted of armored vehicles equipped with a large number of the anti-tank weapons and the brigade informed us they had destroyed a number of tanks, stopping the brigade convoy," General Salah Aboud recalled. "So, I ordered those fighting the enemy, to stop the enemy forces and let the brigade pass this

The remains of two of the 6th Armored Brigade's T-62 tanks destroyed on the night of 29 January 1991 lie abandoned on the sand in front of Observation Post 4. The Iraqis suffered severe matériel and equipment losses during the four-day Battle of al-Khafji.

resistance to the east, and to move toward the brigade target without stopping. [The] *6th Armored Brigade* moved deep into Saudi Arabia and the small resisting force was rolled over and the brigade caused a large amount of damage." There is no evidence that the flanking movement General Salah Aboud described penetrated more than a few hundred meters into Saudi Arabia, and the *3d Armored Division's* commander did not mention it. Salah Aboud continued, "Although, our troops continued by moving toward the targets, we faced a very strong ground resistance at al-Zabr supported by the Air Force and helicopters from the enemy." As Brigadier General Hussan Zedin reported: "At 8 o'clock on 29 January, we executed our duty and we stayed in the area until the forces of Mohammad al-Qasim[*] completed their duty and mission to occupy al-Khafji."[12]

Whether or not they entered into Saudi Arabia, the *6th Armored Brigade* had accomplished its primary mission. "All the airplanes of the enemy were over the brigade convoy and attacking the area," General Salah Aboud explained. "The brigade had succeeded in capturing completely the attention of the enemy. And the enemy didn't observe any movement of our troops to occupy al-Khafji so at midnight, I instructed the *3d Armored Division* to order the *6th Armored Brigade* to go back toward al-Wafra and their original positions."[13]

Supported by air, the Marines of a light armored vehicle company and a reconnaissance platoon had stopped the attack of an Iraqi armored brigade in its tracks. The two Marine units suffered 11 casualties, none of which was from enemy fire. The Marines at Observation Post 4 had not experienced combat before the attack on 29 January.

While the fight at Observation Post 4 was taking place, a brigade of the *5th Mechanized Division* attempted to cross into Saudi Arabia through the berm near Observation Post 1, then screened by Company A, 2d Light Armored Infantry Battalion, commanded by Captain Dennis M. Greene. At 2115, members of the company observed "60–100 BMPs [armored personnel carriers] . . . moving south with arty [artillery]."[*] The company called in air support, reporting that AV-8s and A-10s engaged the Iraqi forces. Members of the company then observed a 29-vehicle column of Iraqi armor arriving

---

[*]"Mohammad al-Qasim" was the honorific name for the Iraqi *5th Mechanized Division.*

[*]Most sources confuse Observation Post 1 and Observation Post 2, but according to both the 2d Light Armored Infantry Battalion's command chronology and the 1st ANGLICO's after action report, Observation Post 1 was in 2d Light Armored Infantry Battalion's area of operations and Observation Post 2 was in the Joint Forces Command–East area of operations. Most likely, this confusion resulted from the use of two conflicting methods of numbering the border observation posts. Originally U.S. Army Special Forces teams numbered the observation posts as they occupied them in chronological sequence rather than in geographic sequence. The Marines later attempted to regularize the observation post designations, but the new system did not stick and only served to confuse the issue.

at the berm. At 2320, Corporal Edmund W. Willis III knocked out one of the Iraqi T-62 tanks with an antitank missile.[14]

Greene's company continued to act as forward air controllers for strikes on the Iraqi forces moving across the berm throughout the evening. It received a significant amount of airpower—five A-6s, two F-16s, two A-10s, and eight AV-8s—and reported 11 destroyed vehicles. Corporal Willis fired another missile at 0157, hitting the same T-62 as the Iraqis attempted to move it to the rear. At around the same time, the Iraqis halted their attack and retreated back into Kuwait.[15]

Further north, Company C, 1st Light Armored Infantry Battalion, established a screen between Observation Post 5 and Observation Post 6. Commanded by Captain Thomas R. Protzeller, this company had a section of LAV-ATs attached, making it similar to Pollard's company at Observation Post 4. But unlike Company D, it had a section of General Dynamics LAV-Ms (a light armored vehicle variant armed with an M252 81mm mortar) attached. Originally, Protzeller's company screen line centered on Observation Post 5, but early on the evening of 29 January the company had fired its mortars at suspected Iraqi forward observers. As a result, Major Jeffrey A. Powers, Task Force Shepherd's operations officer, ordered the company to withdraw from the berm in order to forestall any retaliatory Iraqi artillery fire.[16]

Protzeller's company observed the fighting taking place to the south around Observation Post 4 but did not take part in the fight until around 1030 when it was ordered to occupy Observation Post 5 as a blocking force. Shortly thereafter, the company was informed that approximately 70 enemy vehicles were moving toward Observation Post 6, and it was ordered to block that position. Traveling along the berm, Protzeller's company advanced north cautiously; each platoon took turns covering the other. As it advanced, the company fired antitank missiles at a group of Iraqi vehicles it spotted on the Saudi side of the berm. Once the company reached Observation Post 6, at around 0100, it settled in and called air strikes on the Iraqi infantry who had occupied the post and on their vehicles that had retreated back to the Kuwaiti side of the berm. In the morning, many of the demoralized Iraqi soldiers surrendered with little fuss, others having apparently withdrawn.[17]

The 2d Light Armored Infantry Battalion's fight at Observation Post 1 and Company C of the 1st Light Armored Infantry Battalion's fight at Observation Post 6 both ended early on the morning on 30 January, but the enemy made one last gasp at Observation Post 4 just after the sun rose at 0720. There, Task Force Shepherd's Company A, under Captain Shupp, called in air strikes from Air Force A-10s and Marine Corps F/A-18s. The air attack smashed this final Iraqi advance at the outpost.[18]

At dawn, Company A established a screen on the berm while Company D recovered its dead and secured Iraqi prisoners. The morning light fully revealed the destruction caused in the previous evening's fight. Pollard's company and its attached LAV-AT section had lost 11 Marines and two vehi-

A Marine LAV-AT is positioned behind the sand berm that separated Saudi Arabia from Kuwait. Built to control the wanderings of nomadic Bedouin tribesmen, the berm offered a convenient demarcation of the border between Saudi Arabia and Kuwait. Observation Post 5 can be seen in the background.

Photo courtesy of Cpl Kenneth J. Lieuwen (www.1ofthefew.com)

Photo courtesy of Cpl Kenneth J. Lieuwen (www.1ofthefew.com)

Iraqi prisoners of war huddle near a fire to keep warm, while Marines of Task Force Shepherd examine the prisoners' weapons: an AK-74, RPK-74, two pistols, and two grenades. Although some prisoners were captured by Marine and Saudi forces during the Battle of al-Khafji, they did not surrender in the vast numbers captured during the later advance into Kuwait.

cles in the five-hour battle at Observation Post 4, but it destroyed approximately 22 Iraqi tanks and armored personnel carriers as well as killed scores of Iraqi soldiers. When the recovery effort was complete, Company A withdrew and Company D reestablished its position at Observation Post 4, which it was to hold for another 10 days.[19]

Assault on al-Khafji

At Observation Post 2, Captain David W. Landersman and his air-naval gunfire team heard a large number of vehicles approaching their position. Keenly aware of the fight at Observation Post 4 to their west, the team requested air support but abandoned the outpost before the air support could be diverted from the fight at the western observation post. Meanwhile, Iraqi artillery began firing on Captain Douglas Kleinsmith and his team at Observation Post 7, as well as south along the coast road. The two teams reported the artillery fire was a combination of illumination and high explosive rounds.[20]

As Captain Kleinsmith's team was being shelled by the Iraqis, a mechanized Iraqi force attacked Observation Post 8 and Lieutenant Kurtis Lang's team

with "intense direct machine gun, recoilless rifle, and tank main gun fire." Three different groups were stationed at Observation Post 8: Lang's fire control team, a Navy SEAL detachment, and a team from 3d Force Reconnaissance Company. They all began taking heavy fire: "after numerous illumination rounds, pop-up flares, and mortar rounds[,] Fire Control Team 9 [FCT], south of OP-8 [Observation Post 8], was overrun by APCs [armored personnel carriers] with the SEALs from OP-8 retreating just in front of the enemy APCs." Despite the heavy fire, all three teams managed to evade the Iraqi assault and fell back without suffering casualties. The SEAL and reconnaissance teams pulled back to al-Mishab, and Lieutenant Lang's team joined 1st Surveillance, Reconnaissance, and Intelligence Group at the desalination plant.[21]

Three Saudi battalions had formed a screen along the Kuwaiti border in Joint Forces Command–East's area of operations. Their orders, according to General Khaled bin Sultan, were clear: "to observe the movement of Iraqi troops and report the approach of hostile columns. They were not to engage the enemy or risk being taken prisoner. I did not want to give Saddam a propaganda victory. If the

Iraqis crossed the border, they were to rejoin our main force further south."[22]

The 5th Mechanized Battalion of the 2d Saudi Arabian National Guard Brigade, commanded by Lieutenant Colonel Naif, had responsibility for the coast road and the surrounding area. The road itself was not covered; the vehicle assigned to it was repositioned closer to the rest of the unit, and the battalion was not in communication with the various American forces station in al-Khafji and the border observation posts. As the battalion advanced down the coast road, it came under enemy artillery fire and pulled back before the Iraqi advance without offering any resistance. Two battalions from the 8th and 10th Saudi Arabian National Guard Brigades, screening further inland, executed similar movements. Unopposed by ground forces, the Iraqi *15th Mechanized Brigade* drove south into al-Khafji, although it was struck by a U.S. Air Force Lockheed AC-130 Spectre gunship and Marine AH-1W Super Cobras.[23]

"As the APCs overran the forward position tank main gun and mortar rounds began impacting in the area of the desalinization plant that SALT 5 [Supporting Arms Liaison Team 5] and SRIG [surveillance, reconnaissance, and intelligence group] forward occupied," Captain James R. Braden of 1st ANGLICO explained, "SRIG forward ordered all teams in the city to pull out and head for the 'safehouse' in al-Khafji. A hasty meeting was held just south of the desalinization plant between FCT 9 [Fire Control Team 9] and SALT 5 to conduct a head count and confirm the rendezvous at the safehouse in the southern part of the city of al-Khafji."[24]

Lieutenant Colonel Richard Barry's group and Lieutenant Lang's team withdrew from the desalination plant to the southern outskirts of al-Khafji and established an observation post in a water tower, but the advancing *15th Mechanized Brigade* forced the units to withdraw again. Barry's group headed south to al-Mishab, while Lieutenant Lang's team rejoined other 1st ANGLICO teams with the Qatari mechanized brigade.[25]

Stationed on the east side of al-Khafji, near the beach, was a unit of Saudi Marines. Designed to emulate U.S. Marines, this newly formed Saudi force lacked equipment, and their American Marine advisors had not yet joined them. As Captain Joseph Molofsky later explained, they were "camped out—basically functioning at very low ebb." Joint Forces Command–East ordered the unit to withdraw just after midnight to al-Mishab, and they took no further part in the Battle of al-Khafji.[26]

At this point in the battle, some bitterness arose on the part of the Saudis concerning the amount of air support being allocated to Joint Forces Command–East forces. In the face of the Iraqi advance, Major General Sultan 'Adi al-Mutairi "repeatedly called on the U.S. Marine Corps for air strikes to stop them." As General Khaled later recounted: "He was in close touch with the Marines because they shared a sector. They had trained together and an American liaison officer was attached to his headquarters. But in spite of his pleas, no air strikes had taken place. Coalition aircraft had not moved." The resentment can be attributed in part to poor communications. Shortly after midnight, General Sultan had called for air strikes against the *15th Mechanized Brigade* as it drove south to al-Khafji. He claimed "that there had been no air attack," when in fact an attack had taken place against the Iraqi column. But primarily the Saudi impatience arose from differing priorities. The Americans viewed the Iraqi occupation of al-Khafji as a minor inconvenience that would soon be rectified, but for the Saudi kingdom it was an assault on their own sacred soil.[27]

Saudi impatience could explain the perception of lack of air support, as well as inexperience in modern air-ground cooperation that the battle required. However, the Marines working alongside Joint Forces Command–East also supported the Saudi belief. As Captain James Braden later wrote, "Little air support was available to the [Joint Forces Command–East] forces as the priority of effort was with the Marines to the west in repulsing the attack of the Iraqi *1st Mechanized Division* and elements of the *3d Armored Division*. The Marine fight had preceded the JFCE [Joint Forces Command–East] fight by a couple of hours and would remain the focus of effort throughout the night."[28]

The fight at Observation Post 4 attracted the attention of Coalition aircraft right away. A later Air Force study found that "Marine and Air Force CAS [close air support] began to arrive in front of OP-4 [Observation Post 4] by 2130 local time. By 2300, three AC-130 gunships, two F-15Es, two . . . F-16Cs, and four A-10s had joined the battle at OP-4." Despite the rapid response to the fighting at Observation Post 4, all sources agree that the tactical air control center did not respond promptly to the initial Iraqi attacks. By most accounts, it was not until Air Force Brigadier General Buster Glosson, the director of campaign plans, entered the center on a routine check of current operations that someone thought to wake up Lieutenant General Charles Horner, the Joint Force Air Component Com-

Photo by TSgt Rose Reynolds, USAF. Defense Imagery DF-ST-92-06956

During exercises prior to the beginning of the war, Marines rush to load antitank missiles onto an AH-1W Cobra of Marine Light Attack Helicopter Squadron 369. The Cobras provided extensive close air support during the Battle of al-Khafji, both at the observation post battles and in the town proper.

mander. Prior to that time, although the 3d Marine Aircraft Wing had responded to Marine calls for air support with alacrity, the tactical air control center remained focused on the evening's strikes into Iraq. Once awakened, General Horner realized that this was a major Iraqi offensive, and a wonderful opportunity to strike at Iraqi forces while they were on the move and vulnerable. He refocused the Coalition air effort into Kuwait accordingly.[29]

Much of the Marine air support for al-Khafji fell on the Cobras of Marine Light Attack Helicopter Squadron 369, commanded by Lieutenant Colonel Michael M. Kurth, and Marine Light Attack Helicopter Squadron 367, commanded by Lieutenant Colonel Terry J. Frerker. Because the arrangement with Joint Forces Air Component Command left Marine helicopters totally in support of the Marine air-ground task force, the Cobras were able to respond rapidly to the Iraqi offensive. Two sections, comprising eight AH-1W Super Cobras, responded to initial calls from the air-naval gunfire liaison Marines, ensuring that the Iraqi advance into al-Khafji was not unopposed. Not long after 0100 on the 30th, a flight of four Cobras from Kurth's squadron, led by Major Michael L. Steele, engaged in a gun duel with six Iraqi armored personnel carriers on the coast road, reportedly pitting the helicopters' M197 20mm Gatling-type guns and 2.75mm

rockets against the armored personnel carriers' 73mm main guns.[30]

A flight of two AH-1Ws from Frerker's squadron, led by Major Gary D. Shaw, had an even more hair-raising experience. Launching from al-Mishab to provide air support at Observation Post 4, they found themselves circling and waiting for a forward air controller to provide them with targets. Eager to support the Marines on the ground, they overstayed their fuel limits and attempted to reach the logistics base at Kibrit, only to find themselves flying over an Iraqi armored column that fired on them. They then attempted to divert back to al-Mishab, but their navigation equipment malfunctioned and they landed instead at the al-Khafji oil refinery. This was a stroke of luck. They refueled their aircraft from the refinery's supplies as the Iraqis marched into the city. The unidentified fuel worked well and they were able to return to base.[31]

A third flight of Cobras, led by Captain Randall W. Hammond, destroyed four T-62 tanks. When nine Iraqi soldiers waved white flags and indicated they wished to surrender, they used their helicopters to "round 'em up like cattle" until Marines on the ground could secure the prisoners. Iraqi artillery fire forced the section to withdraw, but not before one Cobra destroyed a final T-62 with a wire-guided missile. The explosion caused "its turret to flip upside down and land on the open hole like a tiddly-winks," Captain Hammond later recalled.[32]

A little after noon on the 29th, the Iraqis also dispatched 15 fast patrol boats from Ras al-Qulayah, as a U.S. Marine raiding force was taking Umm al-Maradim Island. Apparently intending to land commandos at al-Khafji in support of *5th Mechanized Division*, the Iraqi boats were intercepted by Royal Air Force GR-1A Jaguars aircraft and Royal Navy HMA.8 Lynx helicopters from HMS *Brazen, Cardiff,* and *Gloucester*. Other Coalition aircraft then continued the attack, destroying or severely damaging all of the Iraqi vessels and landing forces.[33]

At Observation Post 7, Captain Kleinsmith continued to call for fire while forming a defensive perimeter with the U.S. Army Special Forces and Marine 3d Force Reconnaissance teams. An OV-10 Bronco arrived over the battlefield and worked with Captain Kleinsmith as the airborne forward air controller. He found it difficult to control air strikes because the location of friendly forces was unclear. Looking north of the border, Captain Kleinsmith directed an Intruder section and a Harrier section in a strike against Iraqi artillery positions while a flight of Cobras circled above. He thought the Cobras would prevent

his team from being overrun as Observation Post 8 had been, and he was "trusting that their sheer intimidation would keep the enemy away from his position." But as the Cobras circled overhead, the soldiers and Marines listened as Iraqi vehicles moved in the darkness around their position.[34]

Captain Kleinsmith had been kept informed as the other air-naval gunfire teams withdrew through al-Khafji. When the Cobras circling above his position were forced to return to base because of low fuel, Kleinsmith and the leaders of the other two teams at Observation Post 7 decided there was little reason to remain in place. The Special Forces team had two escape and evasion routes planned: one east to the coastal highway and then south to al-Khafji; the other traveling west to Observation Post 2 and then south across the desert. Both routes appeared to be cut off by Iraqi forces, so Captain Kleinsmith led the teams' humvees south, directly into the sabkhas. He hoped the heavier Iraqi armor would not follow them into the salt marsh.[35]

The teams departed at 0230 as Iraqi artillery fire briefly pursued them. They suffered no casualties in the withdrawal. Kleinsmith's group remained in radio contact with the OV-10, which was now free

Then-Capt Douglas R. Kleinsmith poses with his air-ground liaison team. Capt Kleinsmith is on the left, and to the right are Cpl John D. Calhoun, Cpl Steve F. Foss, and Cpl Edward E. Simons Jr. On the night of 29–30 January 1991, Kleinsmith's team was cut off from Coalition forces by the Iraqi advance. They evaded the enemy by maneuvering through the sabkhas (salt marshes) and returned to Coalition lines.

Photo courtesy of LtCol Douglas R. Kleinsmith

to call in air strikes around the observation post. Driving south it discovered "the remnants of the SANG [Saudi Arabian National Guard] screening force camps, complete with boiling tea on the fires just outside their tents." At approximately 0330, Kleinsmith ordered a halt, worried that the teams might come under friendly fire if they attempted to join up with a Saudi unit in the darkness. They remained deep in the salt marshes until daybreak.[36]

The Iraqi View of the Assault

At 1800 on 29 January, General Salah Aboud Mahmoud shifted from his main headquarters to his mobile headquarters so that he could better control the upcoming battle. Despite Coalition air attacks, the Iraqi offensive was progressing according to plan as night fell on the 29th. At 2000, the various brigades of the *5th Mechanized, 1st Mechanized,* and *3d Armored Divisions* crossed their lines of departure and began the attack. As General Salah Aboud later observed, "The troops faced some difficulties executing these missions. The territory of one mission faced the road, which was hard for all the mechanized equipments to use, and for that reason, this mechanized brigade didn't have another choice, except to occupy their targets by walking. Still, all the troops reached the targets on time. And this actually deceived the enemy."[37]

In particular, the *15th Mechanized* and *26th Mechanized Brigades* of the *5th Mechanized Division* passed through Ragawa at 2000. At this point, the Iraqi artillery began firing flares that the mechanized brigades could use to navigate through the desert. While moving into position, the Iraqis observed the withdrawal of Coalition forces from the border observation posts. Although the Iraqi mechanized forces had difficulties in the sabkhas, they reached their objectives on time. A convoy from the *22d Mechanized Brigade* met no resistance at the Saudi border stations, and its arrival along the beach completed the encirclement of al-Khafji. The *26th Mechanized Brigade*, encountering no resistance, returned to its positions in Kuwait after its role of defending the western flank of the *15th Mechanized Brigade* was complete.[38]

General Salah Aboud kept his promise, delivering the city of al-Khafji at 0200 on the 30th as a present to Saddam Hussein. The supporting attacks had all run into heavy resistance and been stopped with high loss of life, but al-Khafji was in Iraqi hands. Now the Iraqis had to decide how long they needed to hold the city in order to accomplish their objective of provoking a major ground war.

The Iraqi Army chief of staff then contacted General Salah Aboud and asked for his predictions and recommendations. The general replied that "when

Cpl Charles H. Ingraham's reconnaissance team used this building in al-Khafji throughout the battle as their observation post. Although the team was not discovered by the Iraqis, the building was hit by fire from Iraqis and Saudis during the night engagements, as well as by shrapnel from American air and artillery strikes.

Photo courtesy of Cpl Charles H. Ingraham III

the enemy discovers the size of my force, he will focus his air effort on it," but that "the time we have until morning will not be enough to pull back from al-Khafji." General Salah Aboud recommended that his troops pull back the next night, the evening of the 30–31 January, "after this great victory we achieved without any damage." He noted, "The first night was passed without any specific operations from the enemy side."[39]

Although the Iraqis occupied al-Khafji, they were not alone. The 3d Marines had a pair of reconnaissance teams in the city on 29 January; they had not left with the air-naval gunfire and special operations forces. They were in contact with their platoon commander, Captain Daniel K. Baczkowski, at 3d Marines' headquarters, who had informed the 3d Marines' commander, Colonel John Admire, of the teams' locations. Colonel Admire ordered the teams to remain in place.[40]

Corporal Lawrence M. Lentz commanded a seven-man team comprising Corporals Scott A. Uskoski and Scott A. Wagner; Lance Corporals Marcus C. Slavenas, Alan L. Cooper Jr., and Jude A. Woodarek; and Hospital Corpsman Carlos Dayrit. Corporal Charles H. Ingraham III commanded a six-man team consisting of Corporal Jeffery D. Brown; Lance Corporals Harold S. Boling, David S. McNamee, and Patrick A. Sterling; and Hospital Corpsman First Class Kevin Callahan. The teams were part of 3d Platoon, Company A, 3d Reconnaissance Battalion. Company A had been attached to 1st Reconnaissance Battalion for Operations Desert Shield and Desert Storm.[41]

The intent of the 3d Marines' staff was that these teams, hidden within the town, would provide a valuable view of the city during a counterattack. However, their presence impacted the Coalition in some negative ways as well. Captain Molofsky later explained that it impacted the "ability to conduct the counterattack, because we [were] not even sure where they [were] at." He also said, "They didn't even have restricted fire areas around them. Well, maybe they did, maybe they didn't. But that wasn't translated to us, so that when we want[ed] to do this counterattack and want[ed] to prep it with artillery, we [didn't] know where the Recon[naissance] teams [were]."[42]

The teams were not aware of these issues. They carefully prepared their observation posts, set out claymore mines in case the Iraqis discovered their position, and attempted to call artillery fire and air strikes on the Iraqi forces they observed. They were not always successful—artillery support was some-times refused because the teams did not know where Saudi or air-naval gunfire units were, and air support was still being sent primarily to the fight at Observation Post 4.[43]

30 January

By the morning of the 30th, the fierce battles of the night before had ended. It became clear that the Iraqis had halted, and while the fighting had been intense for those at the front, for the I Marine Expeditionary Force staff the Iraqi offensive left a feeling of bemusement. At the morning briefing on 30 January, General Boomer observed: "Other than our losses, I am not unhappy with last night. It proceeded as it should. . . . My only concern is that we get something out to kill [the Iraqi force] before it gets back up into Kuwait." "I believe that my feeling," he said later, "was that if they're trying that now, they're going to play right into our hands. . . . Then as it became clear that they were trying to do something of significance we began to react. I think by that point the MEF [Marine expeditionary force] staff was at the point where it could handle this kind of thing without it being some huge crisis."[44]

General Khaled had a less sanguine view of the invasion. The Saudis understood how easily Saddam could turn even a battlefield disaster into a propaganda victory. They simply could not accept the loss of Saudi territory, even for a short while. When he received the news of the attack, Khaled "felt a great deal of anxiety." This was compounded because King Fahd ibn Abdul Aziz of Saudi Arabia was often in contact with him. Recalling this time, General Khaled later wrote: "King Fahd wanted quick results, and rightly so. He wanted the enemy force expelled at once. He wished to deny Saddam the chance of showing the world that he could invade Saudi Arabia and get away with it. He telephoned me a number of times, calling for action." Faced with such pressure, General Khaled did not consider al-Khafji a minor skirmish.[45]

As dawn broke in the sabkha west of al-Khafji, Captain Kleinsmith's small caravan spotted unidentified tanks in the distance. His men mounted up and proceeded south to Saudi Arabian lines. At this point, the Special Forces and 3d Force Reconnaissance teams departed for al-Mishab, while Captain Kleinsmith and his Marines moved to the 2d Saudi Arabian National Guard Brigade headquarters, joining the main body of 1st ANGLICO.[46]

Meanwhile, other 1st ANGLICO teams were spread among the Saudi and Qatari forces that were preparing to retake the city and push the Iraqis back into Kuwait. Captain Mark S. Gentil's Supporting Arms Liaison Team 5, First Lieutenant Bruce D. McIlvried's Fire Control Team 13, and First Lieutenant Kurtis Lang's Fire Control Team 9 were assigned to the Qatari Brigade, commanded by Lieutenant Colonel Ali Saeed. Each of the fire control teams joined with one of the brigade's battalions, while the supporting arms liaison team acted as the fire support coordinator. Each battalion had a company of AMX-30 main battle tanks attached as well.[47]

Captain James Braden's Supporting Liaison Team 6 was attached to Colonel Turki al-Firmi's 2d Saudi Arabian National Guard Brigade. Captain Braden's team acted as a central clearinghouse for all supporting fire and allowed Colonel Turki to use the Marine communications net to keep track of his battalions. Fire Control Team 12, commanded by Captain John C. Bley II, was assigned to the 8th Battalion, 2d Saudi National Guard Brigade, along with Captain Mark V. Dillard's team from Supporting Arms Liaison Team 2. Dillard's team originally was assigned to a Moroccan unit south of al-Mishab but was called forward to assist in the battle.[48]

Responsible for the defense of al-Khafji and the coastal region, Saudi Major General Sultan's initial plan of action was to cut off the Iraqi forces in al-Khafji and convince them to surrender. His intention was to avoid a potentially costly battle within

Adapted from a 1991 Ministry of Defence (United Kingdom) map by Marine Corps History Division

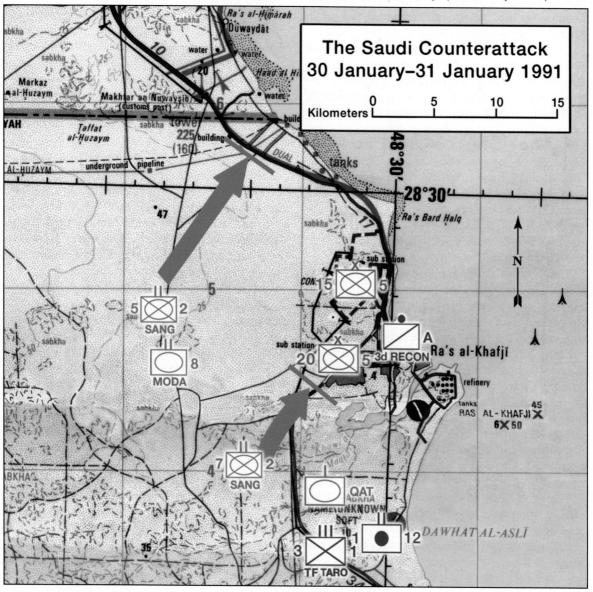

the city. To this end, he dispatched the 5th Battalion, 2d Saudi Arabian National Guard Brigade, north of al-Khafji as a blocking force, supported by a company from the 8th Ministry of Defense and Aviation Brigade, equipped with M60 tanks. He placed the Qatari Brigade, supported by the 7th Battalion, 2d Saudi Arabian National Guard Brigade, in positions to block the road south from al-Khafji.[49]

Once established just south of the city, the Qatari Brigade began to engage targets of opportunity within the city. A platoon of Iraqi T-55 tanks emerged and engaged the Qatari AMX-30s, resulting in the destruction of three T-55s and the capture of a fourth. Iraqi prisoners revealed that there was close to an enemy "brigade in the city and another brigade was to join it." In response, General Sultan bolstered the northern blocking force by committing the balance of the 8th Ministry of Defense and Aviation Brigade's armored battalion. The southern force was reinforced with the 8th Battalion, 2d Saudi Arabian National Guard, in addition to M113 armored personnel carriers equipped with antitank missile launchers from the 8th Ministry of Aviation and Defense Brigade.[50]

At 1152 on 30 January, 1st Battalion, 12th Marines—the Marine artillery battalion assigned to support the Saudi attack on al-Khafji—reported it had already expended 136 rounds of dual-purpose improved conventional munitions and 8 rounds of high explosive munitions. The Cobra attack helicopters of Marine Light Attack Helicopter Squadrons 367 continued to support the Marines along the frontier and in al-Khafji. For the same period the squadron reported one tank, seven armored personnel carriers, one jeep, and one truck destroyed.[51]

At noon, Colonel Turki al-Firmi met with Colonel Admire. Colonel Turki was in command of the Saudi force specifically tasked with retaking al-Khafji. Captain Braden, the 1st ANGLICO officer assigned to Colonel Turki's brigade, observed the meeting. Colonel Admire told Colonel Turki that Marine reconnaissance teams were still in al-Khafji and briefed him on the 3d Marine plan to remove them from the city. Captain Braden recalled that "Col Turki stated that the city was his and that he had a tasking from 'Riyadh' to rescue the Marine Recon teams. . . . Col Turki asked if the Marines lacked trust in the Saudi abilities to perform their mission of defending their sector? The question of sector defense seemed moot at this point as the Iraqis were in control of al-Khafji, but the matter of trust between Coalition partners was in question." Admire agreed and offered support.[52]

Battery C (and later Battery A), 1st Battalion, 12th Marines, provided artillery fire, and a combined antiarmor team from 3d Marines moved to the gas station four kilometers south of al-Khafji. Despite Saudi desires to fight the battle on their own, Marine air-naval gunfire liaison teams provided critical communications to the Saudis and co-

The Saudi National Guard battalions that liberated al-Khafji from the Iraqis employed Cadillac Gage V-150 Commando light armored vehicles, some of which were equipped with an M220 launcher for the BGM-71 TOW antitank missile.
Defense Imagery DF-ST-91-04523

ordinated artillery and air. In addition, U.S. Army advisors from the Office of Program Manager for Modernization of the Saudi Arabian National Guard and civilian advisors from the Vinnell Corporation fought throughout the battle alongside their assigned Saudi units.[53]

Colonel Admire said that acting as the supporting force was "one of the most difficult decisions I've ever had to make." The decision to have the Saudis lead the attack to free al-Khafji shaped the rest of the battle. Marines would observe and aid their Coalition partners, but the Saudis and Qataris did the heavy fighting from this point on.[54]

As plans were being made to liberate al-Khafji, another strange event in the battle occurred. Two U.S. Army tractor-trailer heavy equipment transporters from the 233d Transportation Company drove into the city. The drivers were lost, unaware that they were in al-Khafji and that an Iraqi offensive had occurred. One of the reconnaissance teams watched in horror as the two tractor trailers drove into town, only to be met by a hail of fire from the Iraqis. The first of the two trucks was disabled and crashed, Iraqi fire having wounded its driver and assistant driver as well as disabling the steering. The second truck performed "the fastest U-turn in history, like he was a VW bug" and fled. The Iraqis quickly overwhelmed and captured the two wounded soldiers, Specialist David Lockett and Specialist Melissa Rathbun-Nealy, whom they quickly transported back to Kuwait. Specialist Rathbun-Nealy was the first American female soldier captured since World War II. The two were not freed until after the war.[55]

Soon after the Army trucks disappeared into al-Khafji, Major Craig S. Huddleston was informed of their disappearance. On Colonel Admire's orders, 3d Battalion, 3d Marines, established an outpost, Checkpoint 67, south of the city to coordinate with the Saudis. Major Huddleston, the battalion's executive officer, was given command of the outpost. He quickly formed a patrol to enter the town and recover the two soldiers; every one of the 128 Marines at the outpost volunteered to go, but he only took about 30 Marines. Huddleston mounted the patrol in humvees, including antitank missile and heavy machine-gun vehicles, and headed for the city.[56]

Al-Khafji was still in a state of confusion. As the patrol raced into the town, they encountered some Iraqis but had no major firefights. The Marines found the disabled tractor-trailer, but not the missing soldiers despite shouts of "U.S. Marines, U.S. Marines!" There was a short engagement with Iraqi armored personnel carriers, against which Major Huddleston directed a pair of Cobras. The patrol also found a destroyed Qatari AMX-30 tank and its dead crew. Disappointed, the Marines returned to the outpost. "We wanted to get them [the missing soldiers] pretty bad," Major Huddleston later said.[57]

Journalists, who were prevented by the prevailing press system and Saudi prohibitions from observing the battle in al-Khafji, began to congregate at Checkpoint 67. Several spoke with Major Huddleston and others from the patrol, which led to a misunderstanding. The Coalition explained in press conferences that Saudi and Qatari forces were freeing al-Khafji, but the journalists who spoke with Major Huddleston mistook his brief patrol for a major Marine assault. They concluded the Marines were doing the major fighting at al-Khafji, but the Coalition was giving credit for the battle to the Saudis for political reasons. This myth was to persist; the belief that the military had lied to the press concerning al-Khafji would continue to sour military-media relations long after the Gulf War ended.[58]

Meanwhile, General Khaled arrived at the Joint Forces Command–East headquarters south of al-Khafji. He was agitated because King Fahd was pressuring him to liberate the city as quickly as possible. He also was upset about what he considered a lack of promised air support from the Marine Corps. He contacted General Horner: "I told him I wanted air support as well as strikes by B-52s to break up Iraqi concentrations and prevent reinforcements reaching al-Khafji, even if it meant diverting air assets from the air campaign against strategic targets inside Iraq. Minimize raids on strategic targets and maximize them at al-Khafji, I urged him."[59]

General Horner saw the developing battle as an opportunity to inflict maximum losses on the Iraqis, but he did not consider the Boeing B-52 Stratofortress to be the proper weapon to use in this situation. He told General Khaled the same thing he routinely told ground commanders: "Don't tell me how to do the job. Tell me what you want done."[60]

Unsatisfied, General Khaled phoned Brigadier General Ahmad al-Sudairy, Saudi Director of Air Operations, an hour after he spoke to General Horner. "Forget about the Joint Forces. If the U.S. Air Force or the Marines don't come at once, I want you to take our air assets out of the Coalition and send them all to me! I need the [Panavia] Tornados, the [Northrop] F-5s, everything you've got!" A few moments later the air assets General Horner had already designated for al-Khafji began to arrive. General Khaled was convinced his threat had worked, and as General Boomer later said, "Ultimately, it was our air support that turned the tide for them."[61]

In addition to his distress over the lack of air support, the two Marine teams in the city also presented General Khaled with a problem. "I was extremely worried that Schwarzkopf might use American troops, either U.S. Marines in an amphibious attack or a heliborne U.S. Army unit, to free *my* town in *my* sector. The shame would have been difficult to bear." Consequently, he ordered General Sultan's plan to talk the Iraqis into surrendering be abandoned and an immediate assault be launched against the city.[62]

Saudi Counterattack

Given orders from General Khaled to attack at once, General Sultan passed the order to Colonel Turki, who in turn assigned the task of assaulting al-Khafji to Lieutenant Colonel Hamid Matar's 7th Battalion, 2d Saudi Arabian National Guard Brigade, supported by two Qatari tank companies.[63]

Captain Molofsky, the 3d Marines' liaison officer, observed the Saudi preparations for battle: "Matar's battalion [was] just really lined up on the road, you know—out into the desert a little bit, into Checkpoint 67. It's a beehive. . . . And Matar's orders are to attack. And, that's it, you know—nothing else. Attack." Matar's battalion had received the order to attack at 1600, but it was not in position until 2000. Captain Molofsky recalled that Matar was "really nervous; smoking cigarettes, pacing back and forth."[64]

There was a 15-minute preparatory fire by 1st Battalion, 12th Marines, and then the 7th Battalion literally charged forward against al-Khafji. "Out of nowhere, vehicles start[ed] up and people start[ed] driving forward," remembered Captain Molofsky, who joined the 7th Battalion for the attack. The Saudi battalion drove straight up the middle of the road, but the Qatari tanks pulled to the side as the force approached al-Khafji. As the first couple of Saudi vehicles entered under the arches of the city, "The whole place lights up," Molofsky recollected. "I mean a whole lot of directed fire, straight down the road . . . just a firestorm of tracers, and tank main guns. And I notice a [Cadillac Gage] V-150 [Commando armored car] blow up, or it looked like it blew up, about 30 meters off to the side of the road."[65]

The Saudi attack was disorganized and undisciplined; they expended massive amounts of ammunition as they fired wildly into the city, as 1st ANGLICO reported afterward. At one point, Qatari

Photo courtesy of Capt Charles G. Grow
The water tower in southern al-Khafji was heavily damaged during the battle. It was a favorite target for both Iraqi and Saudi troops and was strafed at least once by U.S. Marine Cobra helicopters.

tanks fired on their Saudi allies, although quick action by Captains Dillard and Gentil ended the fire before any casualties were taken. Still, the undisciplined fire and scattered assault was suspected to have caused two Saudi deaths.[66]

Lieutenant Colonel Michael Taylor was the U.S. Army advisor to the 7th Battalion, and he aided Lieutenant Colonel Matar throughout the battle. Throughout the night Saudi and Qatari soldiers fought against the Iraqi forces, suffering fire so heavy that Taylor, a Vietnam War veteran, described it as "flabbergasting." But the Saudis and Qataris did not hesitate to return fire, as Captain Molofsky noted: "Qatari tanks came back up the road and were shooting up from behind and, at one point, the volume of fire got so heavy that we all got out of the truck and took cover in a ditch and you know the Saudis were shooting TOW [antitank] missiles up in the air. Once they started shooting, they were shooting. I mean everybody was shooting at the max rate."[67]

Despite their efforts, the 7th Battalion was not able to retake al-Khafji, nor was it able to relieve the reconnaissance teams still trapped within the city. Captain Molofsky later recalled the engagement's surreal conclusion: "We pulled back into defilade in a small depression, just south of the city, and they [the Saudis] got out of the vehicles and they put their cloaks on, built fires and brewed up coffee, and then they prayed. I think my sense then was that the team couldn't have been much different than if they were riding with [T. E.] Lawrence except that they were [using] mechanized vehicles instead of horses. Really extraordinary."[68]

North of al-Khafji

At nightfall, Lieutenant Colonel Naif's 5th Battalion, 2d Saudi Arabian National Guard Brigade, moved into position to block Iraqi movement in and out of al-Khafji from the north. This battalion was soon reinforced by a battalion of the 8th Ministry of Defense and Aviation Brigade, companies of which drifted north throughout the night. Iraqi forces attempted several times to reinforce al-Khafji, but Coalition air support was now available in copious amounts, and the air-naval gunfire teams attached to the 5th Battalion were able to call F/A-18s, AV-

8s, and A-10s down on the Iraqi forces, inflicting a large number of casualties and forcing an even larger number of Iraqi troops to surrender to the Saudis. The Saudis claimed 5 Iraqi vehicles destroyed, 6 captured, and 116 prisoners taken.[69]

The engagements were not without problems. The lack of joint training between the Saudi Arabian National Guard and Ministry of Defense and Aviation forces led the 8th Ministry of Defense and Aviation Battalion's commander to fear that the two Saudi forces might fire on each other, so in the morning he pulled back to refuel and rearm. This kept the Saudis from completely sealing al-Khafji at the end of the first night of battle, allowing a few Iraqi units to escape back into Kuwait.[70]

Coalition airpower was now focused on the al-Khafji area, taking advantage of the Iraqi offensive to strike at the forces that had previously remained hidden. E-8C Joint Surveillance Target Attack Radar System (JSTARS) aircraft were used to track Iraqi movements in Kuwait. "The new JSTARS system proved a vital asset in beating back the Iraqi attacks," an Air Force study noted. "An airborne radar that could monitor enemy vehicle traffic at night with impressive clarity, JSTARS was an indispensable element in ensuring the efficient and effective

Marines of 1st Battalion, 12th Marines, prepare an M198 155mm howitzer to fire. The battalion fired numerous missions in support of Saudi and U.S. Marine forces during the Battle of al-Khafji.

Marine Corps History Division Field History files

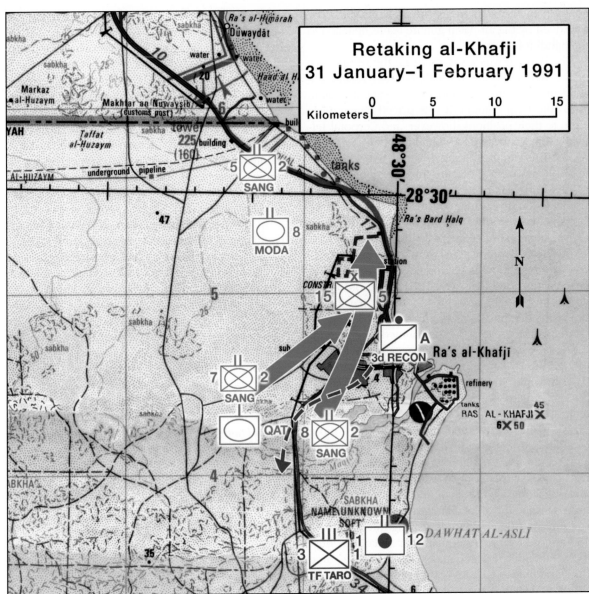

Adapted from a 1991 Ministry of Defence (United Kingdom) map by Marine Corps History Division

use of Coalition aircraft." The tactical air control center was focusing aircraft on al-Khafji and interdiction missions in southern Kuwait.[71]

But the success of the air interdiction was not without loss. A U.S. Air Force AC-130, call sign "Spirit Zero Three," remained over its targets as the sun came up despite the policy that AC-130s only be employed at night. An Iraqi surface-to-air missile struck the aircraft, killing its 14-man crew.[72]

The massive effort had an effect on the Iraqi forces. General Salah Aboud had already begun requesting permission to withdraw. Although the offensive was termed "The Mother of All Battles" by Saddam, General Salah radioed that "the mother was killing her children."[73]

31 January

Early in the morning on 31 January, Batteries A and C, 1st Battalion, 12th Marines, attached to the 3d Marines, fired an improved conventional munitions mission into al-Khafji under the control of the Marine reconnaissance teams inside the town. Corporals Charles H. Ingraham III and Lawrence M. Lentz, the reconnaissance team leaders, requested the artillery strike on a large Iraqi column between their positions at 0645. Initially clearance was denied by the 3d Marines' fire support control center, but the mission was approved at 0701. At 0705, Batteries A and C responded to the call for fire. At 0740, 1st Battalion, 12th Marines, was told by the fire support control center that all future fire missions had to be approved by the air-naval gunfire teams attached to the Saudi forces.[74]

The barrage was a success from the perspective of the Marines inside al-Khafji, because it landed a solid blow against the Iraqis and essentially eliminated the Iraqi column. It was placed dangerously close to their positions, however, and Corporal Jeffery D. Brown received a wound from the shrapnel.[75]

The fire came as a shock to the 1st ANGLICO teams maneuvering outside the city alongside the Saudis and Qataris, because Colonel Turki and Colonel Admire had agreed that all fire would be coordinated through the supporting arms liaison teams. Lieutenant Colonel William C. Grubb Jr., the 1st ANGLICO commander, went to the 3d Marines' combat operations center and fixed the fire support coordination problem, which led to the order that all fire missions be approved by the air-naval gunfire teams. Despite these attempts to avoid firing on Coalition forces, the Qataris claimed one of their AMX-30s was disabled by Marine artillery fire, although this was not confirmed.[76]

Meanwhile, the 7th Battalion, 2d Saudi Arabian National Guard Brigade, was preparing another attempt to storm al-Khafji and relieve the reconnaissance teams. This time, the attack was more carefully prepared, with artillery support from both Saudi and Marine artillery units and extensive Marine close air support coordinated by the teams working alongside the Saudi Arabian National Guard units. Despite the air and artillery support, the Iraqis still put up a fierce fight, destroying three Saudi V-150 armored cars. "Tank main gun, recoilless rifle, TOW [antitank missile], and small arms fire came thick and furious," 1st ANGLICO later reported. "The Saudis and Qataris charged through the streets firing at everything and anything and in every direction."[77]

The battle raged through the southern half of al-Khafji, while Marine AV-8B Harriers and AH-1W Super Cobras provided direct support to the Saudi and Qatari troops. Air-naval gunfire teams directed the Cobras in a strafing run against the town's water tower, and Harriers destroyed Iraqi vehicles at the major road intersection in that quarter of the city. The Marine reconnaissance teams took advantage of the confusion of this assault to withdraw safely from al-Khafji, one on foot, the other in humvees that had sat inside a courtyard, undetected by the Iraqis since the first hours of the battle.[78]

In the afternoon, the 7th Battalion withdrew to rest and resupply, and the 8th Battalion, 2d Saudi Arabian National Guard Brigade, took its place

clearing al-Khafji buildings. By this point in the battle the Saudis had lost 7 V-150 armored cars, 50 wounded, and 18 dead. The clearing operation continued throughout the night. "Saudi urban operations were different than what Americans practice," Captain Braden later noted. "Instead of room-by-room clearing, they simply occupy a block and if they take fire they target with TOWs and heavy machine guns until resistance stops and then move to the next building of street. As a result of these techniques, there were numerous pockets of Iraqis left in the city that would be killed or captured over the next few days."[79]

In the north, 5th Battalion, 2d Saudi National Guard, and its attached air-naval gunfire teams under Captain Kleinsmith and First Lieutenant Paul B. Deckert stopped Iraqi units trying to reinforce their forces in al-Khafji. At Observation Post 7, a battery of Iraqi self-propelled howitzers had taken up position, supported by infantry and armored personnel carriers. A division of four Cobras destroyed the battery under Captain Kleinsmith's direction, but their arrival coincided with the destruction by enemy fire of two Saudi armored

Operating in their doctrinal role as part of the Marine air-ground task force, AV-8B Harriers provided needed close air support during the Battle of al-Khafji.

Marine Corps History Division Field History files

Cpl Jeffery D. Brown of 3d Platoon, Company A, 3d Reconnaissance Battalion, stands in one of his team's humvees. The humvee's tires were punctured and its windshield shattered by shrapnel from a Marine artillery barrage called in on Iraqi forces near the reconnaissance teams' positions. Cpl Brown was wounded by the same artillery strike.

cars and an ambulance. Convinced that they had suffered friendly fire, the Saudis withdrew, leaving Captain Kleinsmith and his team to stabilize the line with air support. When the immediate Iraqi threats were removed, Kleinsmith's team rejoined the 5th Battalion.[80]

As the ground fight for al-Khafji drew to a close, the air effort continued to devastate the Iraqi forces.

After a slow start, Coalition air forces claimed hundreds of tanks, armored personnel carriers, and artillery tubes destroyed during the five days that al-Khafji remained the main effort. An Air Force postwar study highlighted the effect of the air attacks: "Pilots described the frantic maneuverings of surviving Iraqi vehicles as visually equivalent to the results of 'turning on the light in a cockroach-infested apart-

Marines of 3d Battalion, 3d Marines, search al-Khafji for Iraqi stragglers and examine the battle damage as depicted in the painting Cleaning up Khafji *by Sgt Charles G. Grow.*

ment.'" The report added that "perhaps the most revealing comment of all came from a member of the Iraqi *5th Mechanized Division* who had fought in the Iran-Iraq War. This veteran soldier stated that Coalition airpower imposed more damage on his brigade in half an hour than it had sustained in eight years of fighting against the Iranians."[81]

The next morning, 1 February, Saudi units advanced all the way through al-Khafji, encountering only light resistance. They cleared the city of remaining Iraqi troops, although solitary holdouts would surface to surrender over the next few days, and established a defensive position north of the city. The Battle of al-Khafji had ended.[82]

Considerations

Every battle has losses. During the Battle of al-Khafji, 25 Americans lost their lives: 11 Marines and 14 airmen. Three Marines were wounded and two soldiers were captured by the Iraqis. One LAV-25, one LAV-AT, and one AC-130 gunship were destroyed. The Saudis suffered 18 killed and 50 wounded. Ten of their armored cars and two tanks

were destroyed. After the war, the Iraqis claimed to have destroyed 4 helicopters, 30 tanks, and 58 armored personnel carriers, as well as to have captured 13 prisoners. They listed their losses as 71 dead, 148 wounded, and 702 missing, as well as 186 vehicles destroyed, but their actual losses were likely higher. In the immediate vicinity of al-Khafji alone, 1st ANGLICO reported 90 vehicles destroyed, at least 300 Iraqi soldiers killed, and 680 captured. By most accounts, the *6th Brigade, 3d Armored Division*, was badly mauled and the *15th, 20th,* and *26th Brigades* of the *5th Mechanized Division* were nearly destroyed.[83]

The Battle of al-Khafji had some immediate consequences. The deaths that occurred in the early morning hours of 30 January, when an Air Force A-10 fired a missile into a Marine LAV-25, were one of several similar events during January. As a result, General Boomer ordered an investigation to determine what measures could be taken to prevent future casualties. The investigation team's report was completed prior to the invasion of Kuwait and its recommendations implemented.

Otherwise, Marines, Saudis, and Iraqis all took differing views of the battle. Marines generally took away an increased confidence in techniques and doctrines, as well as a clearer idea of the enemy they would face. Lieutenant Colonel Myers felt that the screening forces along the border had exceeded expectations and that the battle "proved the concept, philosophically" of the light armored vehicle. Captain Braden saw al-Khafji as proof of the value and importance of the air-naval gunfire liaison company (ANGLICO), and long after the battle ended he was using al-Khafji as an example to argue against its disbandment. "Without ANGLICO, it is difficult to envision another successful Battle of al-Khafji," he wrote.[84]

Marines also gained confidence in their Saudi allies. Colonel Admire, for one, now felt there was "no doubt in the Marine Corps force's mind that when the time would come to in fact attack into Kuwait, the Saudis and the Qataris and the Coalition forces would be with us. Absolutely no doubt." Captain Molofsky agreed because "when push came to shove, without any real plan, any real direction, those Saudi soldiers obeyed their

A Qatari AMX-30 tank leads two Saudi V-150 Commando armored cars, the first of which is an antitank variant, into al-Khafji through the town arches. The arches were the focal point of each Saudi counterattack into the city.

Illustration used with permission of Jody Harmon (www.jodyharmon.com)

orders and went forward. And, they did so courageously."[85]

General Boomer saw al-Khafji as further proof that the Iraqi military was a hollow force: "We knew they weren't motivated even by the time al-Khafji occurred, and it confirmed it. We were beginning to pick up POWs who said, 'I don't want any part of this deal. I am down here getting the heck pounded out of me every day, food and water are short. Why am I here?' In essence they were saying, 'I don't want to die here, in this conflict.' We were getting enough of that so that I really came to believe that there was a significant morale problem on the other side." But for Captain Molofsky, the view at the tactical level was somewhat different: "My opinion was that if that's what it was gonna take to get started in the recovery of a small town like al-Khafji, that we were gonna be involved in a prolonged and bloody struggle."[86]

For their part, the U.S. Air Force saw the Battle of al-Khafji as proof of the importance of airpower, claiming "the Battle of Khafji was preeminently an airpower victory." Close air support and battlefield interdiction had isolated the battlefield and inflicted great destruction on the Iraqis. The result was a "devastating defeat" for the Iraqi military and "airpower was the decisive element."[87]

General Khaled bin Sultan explained that although the battle was an important victory for the Saudis, had it gone badly, "the blow to our morale would have been severe. But victory changed the mood of our soldiers to an amazing degree. They had been given a chance to prove themselves and had done so splendidly. . . . Our forces were now equal partners with our allies, ready to play a full role in any future battle."[88]

Perhaps the most surprising conclusion concerning the Battle of al-Khafji came from the Iraqis. Iraqi postwar studies present al-Khafji as a victory whose techniques and procedures should be emulated to ensure future success. The Iraqis were able to plan and launch a major offensive despite the Coalition's airpower advantage. They succeeded in capturing al-Khafji and held it for two days against an enemy force superior in technology and numbers. As General Salah Aboud concluded, "The al-Khafji conflict is on the list of the bright conflicts in Iraqi army history. . . . One of the thousands recorded in the Iraqi Army history for the new generations."[89]

In the end, everyone but the dead and wounded won the Battle of al-Khafji. Although the battle did not accomplish any of the Iraqi objectives, it presented enough of an appearance of success that Saddam was able to claim a credible propaganda victory. After the war, the Iraqis were convinced the battle had somehow influenced the Coalition's decision to end the war after evicting the Iraqis from Kuwait, but before removing Saddam Hussein from power.

The Saudis faced an invasion of their territory and defeated it. Although Coalition airpower undoubtedly played a key role in the defeat of the Iraqi offensive, it was the courageous Saudi ground troops, along with their American advisors, who actually ejected the Iraqis from Saudi soil. Al-Khafji has entered Saudi military history as a great victory.

For the Americans, al-Khafji was won almost by accident. American forces proved so superior that it did not completely register at the time that a major Iraqi offensive had occurred. As a result, U.S. Central Command planners did not expect the Iraqis to collapse as quickly as they did in the February invasion of Kuwait and Iraq.[90]

At al-Khafji, all of the Marine deaths were caused by U.S. fire, but that should not detract from their sacrifice, or from the bravery of the Marines who survived the battle through luck and training. Endorsing the final report on the Marines killed by the A-10's missile on 30 January, General Boomer stated: "The technological marvels that helped the Coalition forces defeat Iraq sometimes fail, and with disastrous results. . . . Marines, heroes in my heart, lost their lives while repelling an enemy force. They were good Marines."[91]

CHAPTER 8

The Final Preparations

Two Breaches and Shattered Amphibious Dreams

At the start of February, the Marine plan for liberating Kuwait was not popular among the Marine commanders who would have to execute it. The plan called for both Marine divisions to pass in column through one breach in the Iraqi fortifications, a difficult and time-consuming operation. After the war was underway, the Marines in the amphibious task force would land at Ash Shu'aybah and seize the port in order to establish a logistics base for the I Marine Expeditionary Force's advance. Lieutenant General Walter Boomer later recalled, "I do have to admit that the single breach wasn't brilliant. It was just pure power. I wasn't that happy with it but we spent hours around the sand table trying to think this thing through. I think at the time it was the best concept that we had."[1]

Major General William Keys, commander of the 2d Marine Division, was even less happy with the plan. It called for his division to pass through the 1st Marine Division after the breach was forced, a maneuver that had not gone well in the first rehearsals and seemed unlikely to go smoothly in combat. Moreover, the addition of the U.S. Army's Tiger Brigade, 2d Armored Division, to his command had provided him with more organic engineering equipment, which combined with additional equipment acquired from Israel convinced General Keys that he possessed the equipment required to conduct a second breach.[2]

Later General Keys recalled the dangers of the two breach plan:

It was rather radical. It called for moving the 2d [Marine] Division another 80 miles to the northwest and breaching right through one of the Iraqi oil fields. The field we picked was supposedly one of the worst, because of

The division commanders and their staff officers gather for a sand table exercise. MajGen William M. Keys (2d Marine Division) and MajGen James M. Myatt (1st Marine Division) observed the training, after which MajGen Keys advocated changing the I Marine Expeditionary Force plan from a single- to a two-division breach to avoid congestion and gain greater freedom of maneuver for his division.

Department of Defense photo (USMC) 0787 24 91

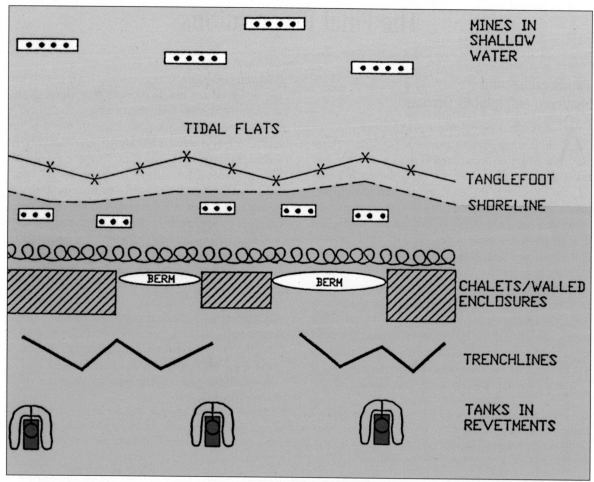

MINES IN SHALLOW WATER

TIDAL FLATS

TANGLEFOOT

SHORELINE

BERM

BERM

CHALETS/WALLED ENCLOSURES

TRENCHLINES

TANKS IN REVETMENTS

This sketch depicts the extensive beach defenses the Iraqis placed along the Kuwaiti coastline in anticipation of an amphibious landing.

heavy concentrations of hydrogen gas. But we had two or three Kuwaiti resistance fighters with us, and one—who had worked in that field—said that we could probably get through it. If things got too bad, we could always use our gas masks. They were not the most effective filtering devices for hydrogen, but they would do in a crunch.[3]

General Boomer visited 2d Marine Division on 1 February and was briefed on the suggested plan change. By coincidence, Brigadier General Charles Krulak visited the headquarters while he was touring nearby Direct Support Command units, and he attended the short talk. General Boomer and General Keys had worked together before, and General Boomer trusted Keys's judgment. Boomer later recalled: "There [was] no time left for discussion. I think my exact words were, 'Bill, you sure you can do the breach?' He said, 'I can do the breach.' I said, 'Fine, we'll change the plan.'"[4]

General Krulak was consulted on the feasibility of creating another logistics base the size of Kibrit on such short notice. He told General Boomer he could do so, but needed to start as soon as possible. Boomer ordered the two commands to begin planning for the second breach but put off making the final decision for a few more days.[5]

General Boomer later explained why he decided to make such a major change to the plan so close to the start of the ground war:

There was considerable risk in changing the plan late, but I felt the risk was worth taking, or I wouldn't have taken it. I thought we had a much stronger plan with a two division attack than we did with a one division attack with the other division following in trace. We could move much faster, we had that much more ground covered, we were going to kill that many more Iraqis. I had to have faith that we could get the equipment moved. I think that comes from more than just faith; I think that's where experience comes into play. As I weighed that in my head, I thought this is an almost impossible job, but I really believe these Marines can do it, that Krulak and his guys can do this.[6]

The day after General Keys asked for the two division breach, on 2 February, General Boomer flew out to the USS *Blue Ridge* (LCC 19) for a conference with General Norman Schwarzkopf and Vice Admiral Stanley Arthur concerning amphibious operations, especially the planned landing at Ash Shu'aybah. At the conference, it was clear the Navy was not ready to conduct any large amphibious operations, in large part because of the large number of mines the Iraqis had deployed to Kuwaiti waters. General Schwarzkopf was not enthusiastic either, since he was informed during the meeting that the amphibious operation and subsequent coastal fighting would probably involve massive destruction to Kuwait's most densely populated areas. He remarked that he was "not going to destroy Kuwait in order to save it." Asked if he required the landing, General Boomer said no, with the caveat that the amphibious deception and mine clearing continue and that the amphibious forces continue planning so the option would remain available if needed.[7]

One final piece of the Marine portion of Operation Desert Storm was still needed. The shift of the Marine assault west left a large gap in the line between the 1st Marine Division and the Saudi Arabians of Joint Forces Command–East directly across from the al-Wafrah oil field. General Boomer covered this gap prior to the liberation with Task Force Troy, a deception operation described later in this chapter. In addition he requested on 5 February that one of the Marine brigades afloat come ashore after the ground war began and fall under his operational command in order to serve as a reserve and to block that gap in the unlikely event that the Iraqis managed to identify and exploit it. Originally this mission was given to 4th Marine Expeditionary Brigade, but that unit was tasked with various amphibious raids and deceptions (most of which did not get approved in the end), so Brigadier General Peter Rowe's 5th Marine Expeditionary Brigade received the mission instead.[8]

On 6 February, General Boomer gave the final approval of the two division breach plan, ordering General Krulak to begin constructing the new combat service support area that would be needed to support the attack. At his daily staff briefing, General Boomer closed with the following remarks:

We had a good meeting today. We wrapped up our plan. I think we will probably want to

CH-46 Sea Knights operating at the I Marine Expeditionary Force forward command post at Khanjar combat service support area in February 1991. The construction of the logistics base, expeditionary airfield, and command post in less than a month allowed Gen Boomer to launch both Marine divisions at the Iraqi defenses simultaneously.

Photo courtesy of Capt Paul E. Bowen

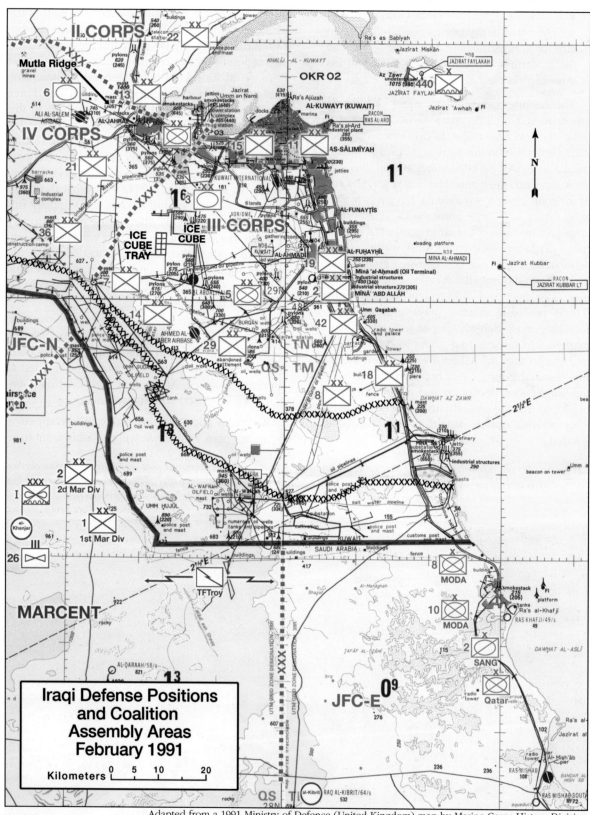

Iraqi Defense Positions
and Coalition
Assembly Areas
February 1991

Kilometers   0   5   10   20

Adapted from a 1991 Ministry of Defence (United Kingdom) map by Marine Corps History Division

The Terminator by Sgt Charles G. Grow. An LVS (Logistics Vehicle System) pulling a trailer with a D7 bulldozer aboard. Marine logistics and engineer units, as well as Navy construction units, worked around the clock to prepare for the liberation of Kuwait.

have one more MAPEX [map exercise] to decision point it and so forth, go through it in detail. Two-division breach, one breach just to the west of the [al-]Wafrah oil field, the other up a little higher. 1st Div [1st Marine Division] on the right, 2d Div [2d Marine Division] on the left. Relatively uncomplicated. Should go well. Long pole in the tent remains logistics, as has been the case for every force in this theater. Interestingly enough, Gen [James] Brabham's Saudi Motors* will help us carry the day. We are on the right track, totally confident we will accomplish that mission.[9]

The "Miracle Well" of Khanjar

On 3 February, Brigadier General Krulak sent a team headed by Colonel Gary S. McKissock 30 kilometers northwest of al-Qaarah, Saudi Arabia, to an area labeled "gravel plain" on the Marine maps, to scout

---

*"Saudi Motors" was the nickname given to the many civilian commercial vehicles provided by the Saudis to help move supplies to the forward staging areas.

for possible locations for the new combat service support area. The team returned with three possible locations; Brigadier General Krulak selected a location closest to the border yet outside Iraqi artillery range. It was designated Combat Service Support Area 2 and named "Khanjar" after the daggers worn by Saudi Arabian men. General Krulak ordered plans and preparations made so that when the decision was finalized just before noon on 6 February, at a Marine commanders' conference at Ras al-Safaniyah on the Persian Gulf, Krulak's units were able to set out immediately to begin construction.[10]

Over the next two weeks, Marines of the 7th Engineer Support Battalion and 8th Engineer Support Battalion constructed a second massive logistics base in the middle of a near featureless desert at Khanjar. They built 151 ammunition cells, berms, roads, working spaces, billeting areas, water and bulk fuel storage areas, a field hospital, an airstrip for C-130 Hercules aircraft, and 24 miles of blast wall. The entire Khanjar complex extended over 11,280 acres. Set even farther from Ras al-Mishab than Kibrit's Combat Service Support Area 1, Khan-

A crewman passes a 155mm projectile into a Battery R, 5th Battalion, 11th Marines, M-109A1 self-propelled howitzer during training before the war. This battery participated in several artillery raids after Operation Desert Storm began.

jar was designed to hold enough food, fuel, ammunition, and water for the two divisions to fight for 15 days.[11]

Khanjar's most glaring weakness was the lack of water, and Navy Commander John R. Doyle's Naval Mobil Construction Battalion 40 began digging wells on 10 February without any success. On 14 February, Captain Peter M. Ramey discovered a pipe and valve above the ground northwest of Khanjar; it produced water that was very hard on filters but useable nonetheless. Called "the miracle well" by General Krulak, it produced 100,000 gallons of water a day.

Next to Khanjar, an expeditionary airfield was built for the helicopter squadrons of Marine Aircraft Group 26. Operations from the airfield, named "Lonesome Dove," began on 20 February and were delayed in part to reduce the maintenance required by operating from the high sand environment of the new field. In addition to 9,000 feet of matting for the helicopters, a helicopter tactical air command center was established at Lonesome Dove to coordinate operations in the forthcoming offensive.[12]

Much later, General Krulak described the accom-

plishments of the Khanjar logistics complex in the following way: "When you look at Kibrit and how massive Kibrit was and then compare it to Khanjar, Khanjar was far bigger. Khanjar had a field hospital with 14 operating rooms. It was the third largest hospital in the Navy hospital system: Bethesda, San Diego, Khanjar. It had an airstrip. The forward ammunition supply point itself covered almost 800 acres. Now, think about that. That's just the ammo dump. The entire complex was over 11,000 acres. It was monstrous."[13]

Equally remarkable was the effort to shift supplies from Kibrit to Khanjar, and to keep both supplied throughout the campaign. Lieutenant Colonel Larry D. Waters's 6th Motor Transport Battalion formed and operated the required line haul capability, establishing a convoy of civilian and military trucks that was soon dubbed the "Baghdad Express." Brigadier General James Brabham elaborated on the difficulties confronted by this convoy: "They faced the challenge of operating leased, aged 18-wheel commercial trucks from various manufacturers. The principal operators of many of these vehicles were expatriate laborers from many different countries. Every truck that was sent north to supply Kibrit and Khanjar was also manned by at least one military member of the battalion. In order to supply Khanjar with the stated requirement, approximately 100 truckloads per day were dispatched north by the [6th Motor Transport] Battalion. The length of the trip required establishment of transfer sites to replace drivers and rest them for the next leg of the trip. The trucks rolled 24 hours a day. It was a magnificent effort that provided the foundation of supply support for the [I Marine Expeditionary] Force."[14]

Artillery Raids, Skirmishes, and Patrols

In the wake of the Battle of al-Khafji, raids and skirmishes along the Kuwaiti–Saudi Arabian border increased in number and intensity in a crescendo leading up to the anticipated liberation of Kuwait. The artillery raids served the same purposes they did prior to al-Khafji—they confused and bewildered the Iraqis concerning the breaching points, and they reduced the Iraqi artillery, still considered Iraq's most dangerous conventional asset despite its poor showing during Khafji. Raids by reconnaissance and light armored infantry units were focused more on acquiring prisoners. All of these raids took place well within the fire support coordination line, inside airspace controlled by I Marine Expeditionary Force. Unfortunately, this did not prevent friendly fire incidents between Coalition aircraft and Marines on the ground.[15]

From 30 January to 1 February, elements of Task Force Shepherd and 5th Battalion, 11th Marines, near Observation Post 6 conducted various artillery missions. On the evening of 30 January, they closed a gap in the berm by firing field artillery scatterable mines. The next night, an artillery barrage in support of Task Force Shepherd was credited with destroying two or three Iraqi tanks.[16]

The next raid, on the evening of 1–2 February, was aimed at Iraqi electronic warfare units at the Umm Gudair oil field. It was conducted by S Battery of the 5th Battalion, 11th Marines, which was equipped with the M109A3 155mm self-propelled howitzer, and Battery T, equipped with the M110A2 8-inch self-propelled howitzer, with Task Force Shepherd again providing security. Lieutenant Colonel James L. Sachtleben, 5th Battalion's commander, later commented:

I was a little concerned about the M110A2 as a raiding piece. Its slower rate of fire and longer emplacement times meant the battery

would be in position longer and thus at a greater risk from counterfire. However, the larger payload of the 8-inch as compared to the 155mm DPICM [dual-purpose improved conventional munitions] meant the battery could fire fewer rounds and achieve equal or greater effects. Also, by this time, we [had] started to question the Iraqi counterfire capability. We had taken mortar rounds on the first raid, but there was no evidence the Iraqis could find us with anything other than forward observers in frontline infantry units who could spot our muzzle flashes. We trusted the EA-6Bs to handle the Iraqi ground surveillance and counterbattery radars, and they obviously did. But why were the Iraqis so ineffective with the sound-ranging systems that were supposed to be so good? We weren't sure, but our confidence was growing. We decided to fight the urge to stay and shoot all night and continued to "shoot and scoot." The real ground war was still days away, and we couldn't afford to risk assets needed later.[17]

Unfortunately, as the raid force retired south it was mistaken for an Iraqi column by a Marine Corps A-6E Intruder, call sign "Blaze 65." The Intruder's crew believed they were still flying over Iraq and bombed the artillery convoy several times. Lance Corporal Eliseo C. Felix was killed, and three Marines—Staff Sergeant Michael V. Almanza and Corporals Michael D. Sanders and Rick A. Ramirez—were wounded. One of Battery S's M109A3 howitzers was damaged as well.[18]

On 4 February, 5th Battalion, 11th Marines, and Task Force Shepherd conducted another artillery raid; executed without any American casualties, this raid targeted Iraqi multiple rocket launcher batteries. The Iraqis responded with counterbattery fire and were in turn struck by F-18 Hornets flying close air support for the raid.[19]

From 3 February to 9 February, American battleships fired their 16-inch guns in support of U.S. Marines ashore as the USS *Missouri* (BB 63) and USS *Wisconsin* (BB 64) moved inshore to fire naval gunfire missions into Kuwait. Starting with the *Missouri*, the battleships rotated the fire support duties, and *Wisconsin* began firing on 6 February. Spotting was conducted by OV-10s, Marine fire control teams, and the battleships' own unmanned aerial vehicles. The massive shells struck Iraqi artillery batteries, bunkers, communications sites, patrol boats, missile batteries, and radar sites. This continual bombardment by naval gunfire destroyed Iraqi forces that threatened the Marine and Saudi lines, but it also reinforced the threat of an amphibious attack on Kuwait.[20]

The month of February saw a small but steady stream of Iraqi soldiers crossing the border to surrender. They were usually taken into custody by Marines in the light armored infantry and reconnaissance teams that patrolled the border. The night of 6 February provides a typical example, as described the next morning in the daily briefing General Boomer received: "Last night LAVs [light armored vehicles] operating in OP-6 [Observation Post 6] saw some activity. They had some loudspeaker teams with them—they have been attached as part of that task force up there. They ran the preprogrammed surrender tape that was pre-recorded, and two people came forward across the berm and said they were hungry and wanted to surrender, and so they took their arms away from them and gave them MREs [meals, ready-to-eat]." The Marines transported these prisoners to the rear, conducted short interrogations, and eventually handed them over to U.S. Army control. The relatively small numbers of prisoners in this period were far easier to handle than

the masses that would come later, but they indicated the poor morale of the Iraqi Army in Kuwait.[21]

On the evenings of 8 and 9 February, Task Force Shepherd and 5th Battalion, 11th Marines, with supporting Marine Corps air, conducted two more successful artillery raids along the border. They believed that the raids "destroyed numerous vehicles in target area," but it is difficult to determine how successful they were because the Iraqis deployed many decoys in Kuwait.[22]

From 10 to 12 February, Captain Rory E. Talkington's Company A, 1st Reconnaissance Battalion, conducted a raid on Markaz as Sur. The location was unoccupied but the raid force captured equipment, documents, and ordnance from the facility.[23]

On the evening of 11 February, elements of 3d Battalion, 12th Marines, and 5th Battalion, 11th Marines, supported by Task Force Shepherd, conducted an "illumination" raid. Illumination rounds were fired over suspected Iraqi antiaircraft artillery sites, hoping to goad them into opening fire, thus revealing them to waiting F/A-18 Hornets. In this case, the Iraqis did not take the bait, and the antiaircraft artillery remained silent.[24]

Not to be left out, 2d Marine Division's 3d Battalion, 10th Marines, conducted an artillery raid on the

A Pioneer remotely piloted vehicle (RPV) is catapulted from a launching rail set up atop an M-814 5-ton cargo truck. The RPV was first used by the Marines extensively during the Gulf War.

Defense Imagery DN-SC-91-05049

F/A-18 Hornets of Marine Fighter Attack Squadron 451 and Marine Fighter Attack Squadron 333 line an airfield in Saudi Arabia. Both squadrons were active in Operation Desert Storm, conducting strikes against targets in Iraq and Kuwait.

morning of 12 February, targeting two suspected Iraqi command posts and two artillery positions. After this raid, the focus shifted from artillery ambushes and prisoner snatches to concentrated preparation of the battlefield as the divisions readied themselves to breach the vaunted Saddam Line.[25]

Marine Air Prepares the Battlefield

The Battle of al-Khafji had presented Marine air with a cornucopia of targets that lasted for several days after al-Khafji itself was liberated as Iraqi forces struggled to return to Kuwait and relative safety. The impact of the air assault on Iraqi morale is vividly illustrated in the 1 February diary of the unknown Iraqi soldier: "I haven't found enough time to write. So much, so much passes away. The winds of war pass, years of our lives pass; the lives of young people have gone for no return. Iraq attacked al-Khafji (Saudi land) and the fighting is still going on. They are bombing our sites using planes and machine guns. There is no peace or liveliness in this world. I am dead. We were born dead."[26]

As despairing as that entry sounds, three days later the same young Iraqi conscript wrote an entry indicating that the news of American bombing in Iraq could counter the drop in morale caused by the Kuwait bombardment. After admitting to listening to the Voice of America and the British Broad-

casting Corporation on his radio despite his belief that they were designed to undermine his morale, the diarist snarled, "I hate those polytheists. I wish I could drink their blood those infidels. My hatred increased since they bombed civilians and buildings where my family is living nearby. Because I know nothing of my family my grudge against them is bigger. I wish they started their ground war, whatever the consequences might be. Anyway, I am waiting for this hour to happen every day. Whether I like it or not it is bound to happen so we'll see. God supports the oppressed."[27]

The diary was not discovered until after the war ended, of course, and while there were numerous indications through intercepted communications and prisoner of war interrogations that Iraqi morale was extremely low, it was difficult for Marine commanders to judge the effectiveness of the bombing campaign, largely because the Corps lacked dedicated reconnaissance aircraft. Ironically, since the Marine Corps' retired the last of its McDonnell Douglas RF-4B Phantom photo and radar reconnaissance aircraft in August 1990, it was forced to depend on Air Force, Navy, and other assets instead, and these rarely produced the required bomb damage assessment photos quickly enough for the Marines trying to determine if follow-up attacks were needed.

Colonel Manfred Rietsch commented on how the lack of reconnaissance impacted the 3d Marine Aircraft Wing's efficiency during the war:

Old imagery, poor quality—we were lucky to get even that. Getting up to date imagery or something of good quality was the exception—I mean the big exception—because it only happened a few times. We were asked to go attack targets where all we had was a LAT/LONG [latitude/longitude]—pull something off a map. The way the system should work—all that stuff should be fed to you. It didn't work that way. One of two things happened. Either the higher headquarters [had] up-to date imagery which identified the location of a valuable target and we didn't receive the same imageries, so therefore we couldn't tell what the target was, or else they based a mission on outdated imagery and so when we went to that place the thing that had been there and was the designated target was no longer there. Consequently, we ended up [flying] many, many sorties where we went where we couldn't identify a target that they thought might have been there or the target had moved and the people who made the decision to send us to the inset target were based on that two week old, three week old, two month old imagery of a tank battalion, for example, that very well might have clanked away and gone somewhere else.[28]

Marines attempted to fill this gap with their own Pioneer remotely piloted vehicles and OV-10 Bronco observation aircraft, but neither was a satis-

Air Interdiction (AI): missions to delay, divert, disrupt, or destroy the enemy's military potential beyond the fire support coordination line (FSCL). Close Air Support (CAS): missions requested by a ground commander for support of, and close to, friendly ground forces. Offensive Counter Air (OCA): missions to destroy or neutralize enemy air power. In the Gulf War these included, for Marines, air-to-surface attacks on enemy airfields and attacks to destroy or disrupt enemy surface-to-air defenses or integrated air defense systems (IADS). A sortie is an individual aircraft mission from take off to landing.

Data culled from *A Statistical Compendium and Chronology—Gulf War Air Power Survey*, vol. 5 (Washington, DC: U.S. Government Printing Office, 1993), pp. 260–268

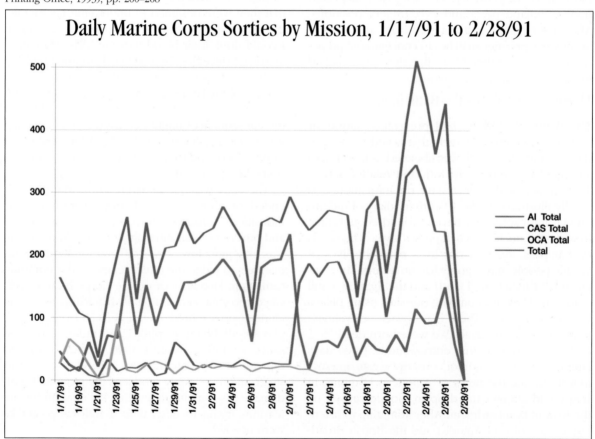

Daily Marine Corps Sorties by Mission, 1/17/91 to 2/28/91

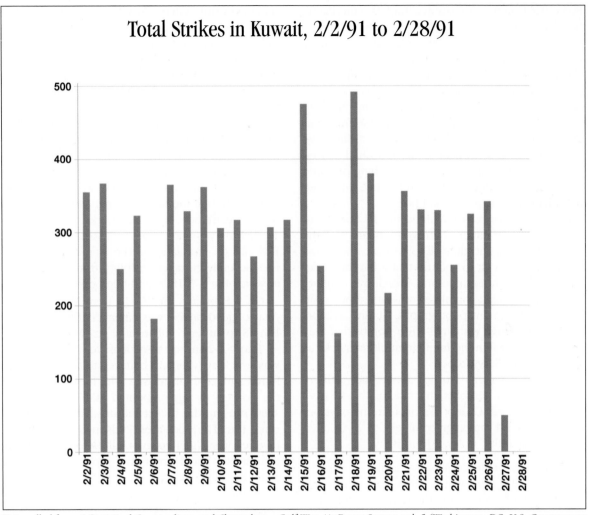

Total Strikes in Kuwait, 2/2/91 to 2/28/91

Data culled from *A Statistical Compendium and Chronology—Gulf War Air Power Survey*, vol. 5 (Washington, DC: U.S. Government Printing Office, 1993), pp. 466–467

This chart shows the number of strikes by Coalition aircraft carried out each day against Iraqi forces in Kill Boxes AF6, AG6, AH6, AF5, AG5, AH5, AG4, and AH4. These kill boxes contained the Iraqi forces most likely to engage Marine ground forces. A strike is defined as a weapon employed by a single aircraft against a target. An aircraft often made multiple strikes on each sortie. A map of the kill boxes over Kuwait and southern Iraq appears in chapter 5.

factory replacement for the RF-4B. Eventually, the lack was partially made up by fast-moving forward air controllers in two-seat F/A-18D Hornets from Marine All-Weather Fighter Attack Squadron 121, which ended its initial operational workup early and deployed to the Gulf. The problem was never fully solved, however, and fortunately the conditions of the Gulf War prevented the issue from becoming critical.[29]

The string of tragic and deadly accidents and friendly fire incidents continued in the first few days of February. On the morning of 2 February, as described above, a Marine A-6E killed one Marine and wounded three others. That evening, at 1840 local time, Marine Attack Helicopter Squadron 775 lost two of its pilots, Major Eugene T. McCarthy and Captain Jonathan R. Edwards, when the Bell AH-1J Sea Cobra they were flying crashed in the Saudi Arabian desert while escorting an emergency medical evacuation mission. The next night, 3 February, one of Marine Light Attack Helicopter Squadron 369's UH-1Ns crashed, killing the entire crew: Captains David R. Herr Jr. and James K. Thorp, and Corporals Kurt H. Benz and Albert G. Haddad Jr.[30]

Throughout February, the percentage of missions flown directly in support of General Boomer's forces increased, and he was able to establish targeting priorities within his area of operations according to Marine Corps doctrine rather than being forced to watch his targets go untargeted by Joint

Force Air Command missions. Targets were classified by category. Category One was nuclear, biological, and chemical targets; in Kuwait these were primarily artillery sites capable of firing chemical shells. Category Two was indirect fire weapons, artillery, and rockets. Category Three was command posts, and Category Four was armor, mechanized infantry, and infantry units. As the 3d Marine Aircraft Wing's Gulf War history noted, "This gave some guidance to a flight leader who had arrived at his assigned target only to find nothing but sand at that grid coordinate. He then became an armed reconnaissance in a large kill box."[31]

The main concern remained the *III Corps'* numerous artillery batteries. Towed artillery was the most numerous and difficult to destroy, and it was even more difficult to confirm that it had been destroyed since inoperable and irreparable artillery tubes often looked completely unscathed on bomb damage assessment photographs. Marine aviators met the challenge with area-effect bombs that they hoped would catch the Iraqi ammunition stocks as well as the artillery proper.

General Boomer's worries about Iraqi artillery were poignantly described in a briefing that he gave to Marine Aircraft Group 13's pilots in the days before the ground campaign commenced, as recalled by its commander, Colonel John Bioty:

> General Boomer led it off by saying, "I want to tell you a story which is not really a story, because it is true, but in the form of a story. I woke up at two or three o'clock in the morning . . . shaking[,] soaking wet . . . from a terrible bad dream where two divisions on line [were] attempting to go through two breaches . . . [were] being bogged down in the minefields and extensive obstacle belts . . . and in the middle of all that somewhere between eleven hundred and fourteen hundred artillery tubes were raining a fiery death and destruction." Then he said, "My Marines are dying." He put his hands behind his back . . . walked back and forth on the stage in silence, which seemed to be [an] eternity, and he turns around and says, "Go get the artillery!" It was about 8:30, 9:00 at night. I had guys who wanted to go man airplanes and go get artillery![32]

Throughout February, the number of strikes by Coalition aircraft in the Marine area of operations hovered around 300 per day, spiking near 500 on occasion (the drop below 200 on 17 February was due to poor weather over Kuwait). Prior to al-Khafji, the number of strikes in the Kuwaiti zone never reached 200 in one day; hence, it is fair to say the Iraqi forces in Kuwait received far more attention from Coalition airpower in February than they had in January.

Many Marine sorties over Kuwait were controlled by F/A-18Ds acting as forward air controllers. These two-seat Hornets would linger over Kuwait in 30-minute shifts at high altitudes and search for targets on the Marine targeting list. They were escorted by a single-seat Hornet armed with antiradar missiles and sometimes additional bombs. When a flight entered their zone, the F/A-18Ds would direct the strike aircraft at the targets as needed. This system worked extremely well, but it was degraded after 17 February, when the Iraqis started burning Kuwait's oil installations. The smoke from the oil fires severely curtailed visibility from the altitudes at which the F/A-18Ds had been operating.[33]

On 9 February, an F/A-18 from Marine Fighter Attack Squadron 451 was damaged, the first Marine F/A-18 to suffer combat damage. While attacking an Iraqi SA-2 surface-to-air missile site, the Hornet was struck by what was believed to be an SA-16 infrared surface-to-air missile. The missile hit one of the Hornet's fuselage-mounted AIM-7 Sparrow missiles, causing the rocket motor of the Sparrow to catch fire. The pilot then jettisoned the damaged missile over the Persian Gulf before landing at Shaikh Isa. The Hornet was repaired and flying again the next day.[34]

A more serious incident occurred that afternoon, when Captain Russell A. C. Sanborn's AV-8B Harrier II was shot down by an infrared surface-to-air missile. Part of Marine Attack Squadron 231, Sanborn was attacking Iraqi positions as directed by an F/A-18D forward air controller when he was hit. His parachute was spotted by the forward air controller, and Sanborn was taken prisoner by the Iraqis.[35]

Captain Sanborn was the fourth Marine aviator captured to date by the Iraqis. Like the others, he was badly mistreated, beaten, refused medical care, and otherwise harassed until his release after the war had ended.[36]

Lieutenant Colonel William R. Jones, Sanborn's squadron commander, later recalled:

> He was a very popular, respected officer. He worked in Maintenance at the time that I recall. His call sign was "Bart" as in Bart Simpson [of the cartoon series *The Simpsons*] on TV. . . . I was preflighting an airplane; he'd been only shot down like three or four days. On the side of an AV-8 by the exhaust nozzle

it's always kind of dark and greasy from the exhaust, and one of the plane captains had written with his finger, "Bring home the Bartman," on the side of that. . . . It really got to some of the officers who were real close to him. . . . I did write a letter—I didn't keep a copy of it—to both Linda as well as Russell's parents trying to be as upbeat as I could without claiming false hope. I just said that I thought he'd be ok. That's the only one that we had, the only aircraft we lost.[37]

On 12 February, a Marine Attack Squadron 542 Harrier was damaged by antiaircraft artillery fire, but it returned to its field safely. The same day, 3d Marine Aircraft Wing aircraft struck and destroyed two Iraqi airliners at Kuwait International Airport that were believed to be transportation for a high-level meeting that took place in Kuwait.[38]

Also on 12 February, General Schwarzkopf told the Joint Forces Air Commander that "effective immediately, the emphasis of combat operations must shift to preparing the battlefield for a ground offensive." A tragedy in Baghdad on the night of 13–14 February also contributed to the increase in strikes against Kuwait proper. On that night, two U.S. Air Force F-117s struck the al-Firdos command and control bunker in Baghdad. Unbeknownst to American targeteers, hundreds of Iraqi civilians had been permitted to shelter in the military bunker; many of them were killed or wounded in the attack. The tragedy was a public relations black eye for the Coalition, and strikes against downtown Baghdad were reduced thereafter.[39]

As the air strikes against Iraqi forces in Kuwait intensified, Iraq's Scud campaign shifted to targets inside Saudi Arabia. A catastrophe was avoided by luck on 16 February when a Scud fired on al-Jubayl landed within a few hundred yards of the pier, which was loaded with a mountain of ammunition. Eight vessels were docked at the pier, including the USS *Tarawa*, a Polish hospital ship, and the aviation logistics support ships SS *Wright* (T-AVB 3) and SS *Curtiss* (T-AVB 4).[40]

On 20 February, just four days before the ground war began, General Charles Horner approved "armed reconnaissance" missions on the air tasking order rather than limiting that document to specific targets approved by Joint Forces Air Command. This adjustment allowed the Marines to finally bypass the Air Force targeting office and follow the doctrine in which Marine ground commanders controlled which targets Marine air would strike based on the priorities of the ground commanders. From this point forward, the Marine air-ground task force

Marines load AGM-88A high-speed antiradiation missiles under the wings of an F/A-18A Hornet of Marine Fighter Attack Squadron 451 during Operation Desert Storm.

Photo by Sgt Jeff Wright. Defense Imagery DA-ST- 92-07699

Photo courtesy of Capt Paul E. Bowen

This reinforced concrete aircraft bunker at al-Jaber Air Base in southern Kuwait shows the sort of damage inflicted by the air campaign prior to the ground offensive. The airfield was a major Iraqi administrative/command and control center and one of the Marines' first objectives after the penetration of the two obstacle belts.

was functioning doctrinally without interference from higher, joint headquarters.

The shift coincided with a significant increase in the 3d Marine Aircraft Wing's already considerable aggressiveness in attacking targets in front of the divisions. Four Marine aircraft were damaged while attacking targets in Kuwait on 21 February. An A-6E Intruder of Marine Attack Squadron 224 was struck by Iraqi antiaircraft artillery fire, and two F/A-18s of Marine Fighter Attack Squadrons 314 and 333 were struck by Iraqi infrared surface-to-air missiles. All three aircraft returned safely to their respective airfields; the A-6E pilot was not even aware he had been hit until after landing. The fourth aircraft was an F/A-18D from Marine All-Weather Fighter Attack Squadron 121, the first Marine F/A-18D hit by Iraqi fire. Flying below 5,000 feet, the Hornet was struck in the right engine exhaust by an infrared surface-to-air missile. The weapon systems operator, Captain John M. Scanlan, later said, "It felt like hitting an unexpected pothole in the road." The pilot shut the engine down as a precaution, and the aircraft returned safely to Shaikh Isa on the remaining engine.[41]

The final day of air operations before the assault

on the Saddam Line was a tragic day for the air campaign. Captain James N. Wilburn III of Marine Attack Squadron 542 was bombing targets in central Kuwait under the direction of an F/A-18D when his AV-8B was struck by an infrared surface-to-air missile and shot down. Captain Wilburn's body was later recovered; he was the first 3d Marine Aircraft Wing pilot killed by enemy action during the Gulf War.[42]

Two more close calls had happy endings. A Harrier from Marine Attack Squadron 311 was damaged by Iraqi antiaircraft artillery, and a Hornet from Marine Fighter Attack Squadron 451 was hit by an infrared surface-to-air missile, but both aircraft and aircrews survived.[43]

Despite its difficulties and tragedies, the Marine air assault on the Iraqi forces in Kuwait on the eve of the ground campaign was a considerable success, as viewed by those in the best position to judge it. Major "Imad B." was the commander of the *159th Field Artillery Battalion, 7th Infantry Division*, one of the *III Corps* units placed directly in the way of the main Marine advance into Kuwait. He was captured during the campaign and questioned about his view of the conflict on 2 March:

Q: How many of your soldiers were killed by the air war?

A: To be honest, for the amount of ordinance that was dropped, not very many. Only one soldier was killed and two were wounded. The soldier that was killed did not die as a result of a direct hit but because the vibrations of the bomb caused a bunker to cave in on top of him.

Q: So, then you feel that the aerial bombardment was ineffective?

A: Oh no, just the opposite, it was extremely effective. The planes hit only vehicles and equipment. Even my personal vehicle, a "Waz," was hit. They hit everything. I explained to my soldiers they should not fear the Americans. If the Americans wanted to kill us, I said, we would already be dead. The Americans just wanted to take away our ability to fight.[44]

When considering prisoner interrogations, the reader must keep in mind that the prisoner of war has great incentive to tell the questioner what they think he or she wishes to hear, even when the interrogation is conducted in a friendly manner without any overt or subjective coercion. But this artillery officer's view was matched by numerous Iraqi reports of the air campaign in internal discussions conducted after the war and captured following Operation Iraqi Freedom in 2003. To provide one specific example, an officer of the *IV Corps* recalled that "the enemy never stopped bothering us day and night by all types of aircraft . . . high speed jets, slow flying jets, precision bombers, and [other] combat jets. The weapons that really frustrated us and harmed us were the slow-flying aircraft and the Marine types. Sometimes they spent the whole day suspended over our heads to the extent that our ears had gotten used to their buzzing sounds."[45]

Harriers Afloat

On 20 February 1991, the amphibious assault ship USS *Nassau* launched four AV-8B Harriers of Marine Attack Squadron 331, call sign "Magic," just before dawn. This flight was the first combat strike by

Air Boss by Col H. Avery Chenoweth. This painting captures the drama of flight operations on board the USS Nassau. *The Navy "air boss" looks on as a Marine air controller talks an AV-8B Harrier onto the flight deck. The "Bumblebees" of Marine Attack Squadron 331 launched the first ever fixed-wing combat strikes from the deck of an amphibious assault ship on 20 February 1991.*

Marine Corps Art Collection

fixed-wing aircraft from the flight deck of an amphibious assault ship and was directed at Iraqi antiaircraft batteries and surface-to-air missile sites at Az Zwar on the western end of Faylakah Island. Bad weather diverted the flight, however, and they instead hit targets near Iraq's Umm Qasr Naval Base on the Iraq-Kuwait border. The strike was successful, despite Iraqi opposition, including at least one surface-to-air missile launched at the four Harriers.[46]

The *Nassau* carried the 19 Harriers of Marine Attack Squadron 331, nicknamed the "Bumblebees," rather than its normal mix of Harriers and helicopters in order to provide dedicated fixed-wing air support for the Marine forces floating in the Gulf as an amphibious threat during Operation Desert Storm. This use of the *Nassau* was not without controversy, as the relatively short range of the Harriers required the *Nassau* to move closer to shore, where mines might have been a danger. In addition, the *Nassau*'s munitions storage was limited to approximately three days of strikes.

Despite these issues, the *Nassau* and Marine Attack Squadron 331 launched 242 combat strikes and expended 300 tons of ordnance against Iraqi targets from 20 and 27 February 1991. The strikes hit Iraqi defensive positions, antiaircraft batteries, artillery, and armor throughout Kuwait despite bad weather and thick clouds of smoke from oil wells the Iraqis had set on fire. On 26 February, the Iraqi retreat shifted the squadron's targets to the fleeing Iraqi columns, especially around al-Jahrah in Kuwait.

On 27 February, while engaged in strikes against these Iraqi convoys, Captain Reginald C. Underwood was killed when his AV-8B was struck by a surface-to-air missile. Captain Underwood's aircraft was the only one of the "Bumblebees" lost to enemy action during this first combat deployment of Harriers on board a U.S. Navy amphibious assault ship.

Fratricide Issues

On 3 February, General Boomer ordered the formation of a "tiger team" to investigate the multiple instances of Marines being fired on and sometimes killed or wounded by other American forces in the first weeks of the war. Marines were acutely aware that all of the Marines killed in the Battle of al-Khafji were killed by American forces. Sergeant Gregory J. "Greg" Michaels of Company A, 1st Light Armored Infantry Battalion, spoke for many Marines when he said, "For the rest of Desert Storm, I didn't worry so much about the enemy: I worried about the friendlies. I worried about buzzing aircraft intending

to drop their bombs, and I worried about itchy fingers on triggers, combatants eager to be involved in the shoot-out."[47]

The seven members of the tiger team* investigated five instances of fratricide and submitted their report on 10 February. According to the report, the incidents were caused by three issues: "(1) a lack of situation awareness by commanders, aircrew, and controllers, (2) the lack of a battlefield system for identification of friend and foe (IFF), and (3) the lack of visually defined cues on the night battlefield by which pilots could orient themselves." The team made numerous recommendations for reducing the risk of air-to-ground fratricide incidents, concluding that if followed, its recommendations "were made on the basis of their being simple, practical, and timely, using resources already available. Many only require a higher degree of discipline and rigor. All are made with a view to not only preventing fratricide incidents now, but on a battlefield that will be fast moving and constantly changing. Finally, the efficacy of close air support will actually improve."[48]

Nearly all of the team's recommendations were put into practice, and additional measures were taken as well (stationing Marine liaison officers on board the Air Force airborne command and control centers was one of the more successful measures). Despite these efforts, there were several more fratricide incidents after the team's report; unfortunately, the modern battlefield's complexity made such events nearly inevitable.

Feints and Deceptions

Many observers at the time believed the Marines were planning to advance into the teeth of formidable Iraqi defenses. Events later proved this was not quite the case, but serious efforts were made prior to the offensive to convince the Iraqis that resistance was futile while also confusing them as to the location, direction, and intention of the upcoming assault.

Convincing the Iraqis to quit was the mission of the psychological warfare campaign. This was a theaterwide campaign that used radio broadcasts, propaganda leaflets, and loudspeaker broadcasts along the border to encourage Iraqi soldiers that

---

*The team's members were Col Gene D. Hendrickson (infantry, logistics), Col Charles J. Quilter II (I MEF historian, aviator), Mr. Carroll D. Childers (civilian science advisor), LtCol Duncan H. Burgess (artillery, air observer), LtCol Robert S. Cohen (infantry), LtCol John F. Goodman (aviator), and Maj Robert T. McCarty (logistics).

This propaganda leaflet dramatically illustrated the threat of a Marine amphibious landing to Iraqi forces in Kuwait.

These propaganda leaflets were dropped on Iraqi units before and after B-52 raids. The front of the leaflet is the top image, and the blue text was printed on the back; these leaflets were dropped the day before the attack. The same leaflet was dropped the day after the attack, but the green text (bottom image) replaced the blue text on the back.

they should surrender to the Coalition. One of the more interesting leaflet operations was combined with B-52 Stratofortress raids. The day before a raid was to take place, leaflets specific to the division being targeted were dropped. They were illustrated with a B-52 dropping bombs on one side and this text in Arabic on the other:

> The [Iraqi] 7th Infantry Division will be bombed tomorrow. The bombing will be heavy. If you want to save yourself leave your location and do not allow anyone to stop you. Save yourself and head toward the Saudi border. You will be welcomed as a brother.

The raid was then conducted on the division named, and the day following the B-52 raid, leaflets with the following message in Arabic were dropped on the division:

> We have already informed you of our promise to bomb the 7th Inf. Div. We kept our promise and bombed them yesterday. Beware. We will repeat this tomorrow. . . . Now the choice is yours. Either stay and face death or accept the invitation of the joint forces to protect your lives.

Other leaflet drops were made along the Kuwaiti coast, reinforcing the idea that an amphibious operation was coming; one particularly striking example depicted a Marine as a wave coming from the

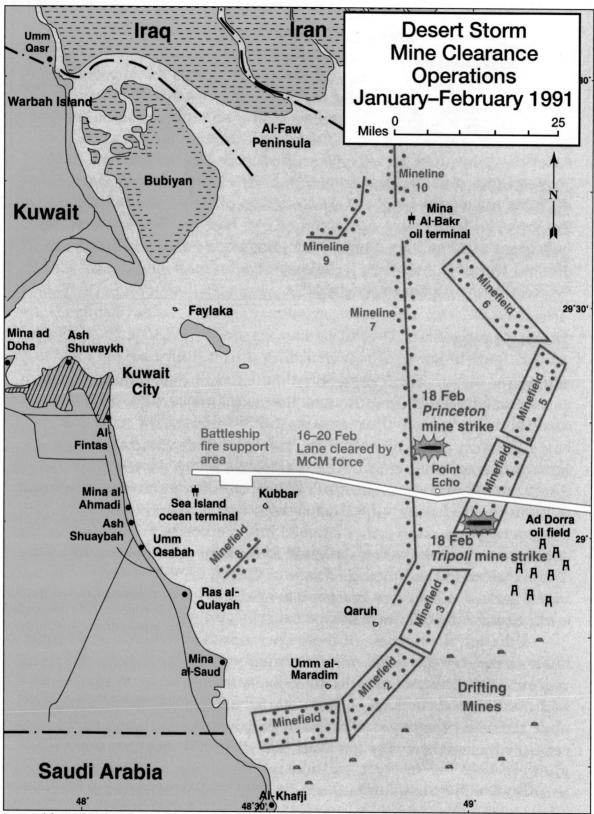

**Desert Storm
Mine Clearance
Operations
January–February 1991**

Miles 0 _____ 25

N

Iraq

Iran

Umm
Qasr

Warbah Island

Al-Faw
Peninsula

Bubiyan

Kuwait

Mineline
10

Mina
Al-Bakr
oil terminal

Mineline
9

Minefield
6

29°30'

Faylaka

Mineline
7

Minefield
5

Mina ad
Doha

Ash
Shuwaykh

Kuwait
City

18 Feb
Princeton
mine strike

Al
Fintas

Battleship
fire support
area

16–20 Feb
Lane cleared by
MCM force

Minefield
4

Mina al
Ahmadi

Kubbar

Point
Echo

Ad Dorra
oil field

29°

Sea Island
ocean terminal

18 Feb
Tripoli mine strike

Ash
Shuaybah

Umm
Qsabah

Minefield
8

Ras al-
Qulayah

Qaruh

Minefield
3

Mina
al-Saud

Umm al-
Maradim

Minefield
2

Drifting
Mines

Minefield
1

Saudi Arabia

48°

48°30'

Al-Khafji

49°

Reprinted from Edward J. Marolda and Robert J. Schneller Jr., *Shield and Sword: The United States Navy and the Persian Gulf War*
(Washington, DC: Naval Historical Center, Department of the Navy, 1998), p. 248

sea with a bloody K-Bar fighting knife, supported by air and sea forces. The importance General Boomer placed on these efforts can be seen in a comment during the daily I Marine Expeditionary Force staff briefing on 11 February: "And in special staff status reports, sir, we have the following from your psyops [psychological operations] officer. The 1.5 million leaflets that you requested were dropped in southern Kuwait yesterday; 100 percent of the public address systems are on the border doing operations in one or other of the divisions, and have been for the past three days, and the Kuwaiti linguists have now been distributed down to the divisions, sir."[49]

Although General Schwarzkopf had vetoed a major amphibious invasion, an amphibious feint remained an important part of the Coalition's plan, in order to draw attention away from both the Marine thrust into central Kuwait and the Army's wide, sweeping flanking movement to the west. As noted above, the American battleships conducted naval gunfire support missions along the coast throughout February, and Coalition minelayers began clearing lanes through the Iraqi minefields on 16 February.[50]

The U.S. Navy's fear of Iraqi mines and lack of confidence in its ability to fully clear the minefields proved well founded. On 17 February, USS *Tripoli* was disabled after it hit a mine. *Tripoli* had been pressed into service as the platform for the Sikorsky MH-53E Sea Dragon helicopters of the Navy's Helicopter Mine Countermeasures Squadron 14 during minesweeping operations and was ironically engaged in this service when it struck a mine. Later the same day, USS *Princeton* (CG 59) was also struck by a mine. Fortunately, neither vessel suffered fatalities from the mine attacks.[51]

After the war, the commander of the Iraqi Navy declared that "these [Iraqi] mines proved [their] lethality and effectiveness. . . . They caused havoc within the enemy force." He continued, "During the epic Mother of All Battles, this weapon [mines] was utilized effectively and successfully to disrupt the allies' plans in launching any operation from the sea." His view was shared by the U.S. Navy Central Command commander, Vice Admiral Stanley Arthur, who later stated, "Iraq successfully delayed and might have prevented an amphibious assault on Kuwait's assailable flank, protected a large part of its force from the effects of naval gunfire, and severely hampered surface operations in the northern Arabian Gulf, all through the use of naval mines."[52]

As the Navy's minesweeping operations began on 18 February, General Boomer gave control of 2d Marine Division's former area along the border in front of the al-Wafrah Forest to Task Force Troy, a battalion-sized deception force commanded by the 1st Marine Division's assistant commander, Brigadier General Thomas Draude. After the war, General Draude described Task Force Troy's mission:

> [The 2d Marine Division originally was] located to the east of us, so one of the first aspects for Task Force Troy was to replicate the 2d Marine Division over to the east of our location to make the bad guys think that they're still there as the division pulls out behind us and gets over to the west of us in preparation for the breach.
>
> So I had the Seabees, God bless them, and made some dummy artillery pieces, tanks, and so forth. And as the units of 2d Division came out at night, that's when the dummy pieces go in so that the trails would be there, all the things that would be associated with that particular kind of unit. We also had helicopters. I asked them, whenever they're flying anywhere in the vicinity of where the 2d Division had been located, just drop down, as if making a liaison, making a pick up and so that from the other side of the border, you're watching all the stuff that used to happen with the 2d Division, and now it seems the same kind of business as usual. We really felt good that we were able to pull that off and again to replicate the division of over 20,000 with only 200.[53]

In addition to decoys and helicopter operations, Task Force Troy attempted to replicate the noise that a Marine division could be expected to make. An Army psychological warfare unit supplied tapes of M-60 Patton tanks that were played along the border. According to General Draude, these recordings had a dramatic effect: "The first night that those tank noises ran, these guys [Iraqis] went ballistic—'Tank attack! Tank attack! Pull over.' You know, of course, nothing happened. Second night—'Tank attack! Tank attack!' After about two weeks of tank noises—ho hum. And then one night they heard tank noises, but they weren't recordings."[54]

Task Force Troy's deception campaign was augmented by artillery raids along the border as well. On the night of 19 February, Battery E, 2d Battalion, 12th Marines, fired over 100 rounds on bunkers and an observation tower near Observation Post 3. Fog led to a delay so that the raid did not occur until just after 0600, but the raid was considered very success-

Fire Mission *by Sgt Charles G. Grow. An M198 155mm howitzer of Battery E, 2d Battalion, 12th Marines, fires against Iraqi forces in late February 1991.*

ful, as there were numerous secondary explosions on the target compound. Battery E conducted a second raid later in the day on 20 February, destroying two more sets of buildings with 70 high-explosive rounds between 1600 and 1700.[55]

On 22 February, the last of the combined artillery/air raids was conducted by Battery E and Task Force Troy. Over 100 rounds were fired on four targets, destroying vehicles and buildings.[56]

These deceptions appear to have had some impact, but at least some in the Iraqi high command were skeptical. A "foreign source" passed information to the Iraqi Directorate of General Military Intelligence that an amphibious landing would occur north of Kuwait City, supported by an American armor feint through the Wadi al-Batin (at the Iraq-Kuwait-Saudi border). If the amphibious landing failed, "A direct assault by infantry into the teeth of the Iraqi defense south of Kuwait City near al-Wafra[h] would occur." Despite this information, and despite the evidence Iraq had of American plans for an amphibious operation, Lieutenant General Sabir Abd al-Aziz (director of Iraq's military intelligence) was not con-

vinced. He felt the Coalition would not risk the heavy casualties an amphibious operation would entail.[57]

It is not clear that these doubts were ever communicated to the Iraqi *III* and *IV Corps* commanders. Many of the *III Corps* divisions remained in defensive positions dug in along the coast, and sand tables captured in Kuwait after the war showed how extensively the Iraqis planned to defend against an amphibious assault. But even if they had seen through the deception efforts, the Coalition air campaign would have made shifting forces on a large scale nearly impossible.

The Battles of 19–23 February

From 19 to 23 February, the 1st and 2d Marine Divisions moved up to the berm along the Kuwaiti-Saudi border and cut through it, and then they moved into Kuwait and prepared for the offensive against Iraqi forces there. First Marine Division's Task Force Taro, commanded by Colonel John Admire and built around his 3d Marines, took up positions on the eastern flank of the division's breach to protect the flank of the division during the infil-

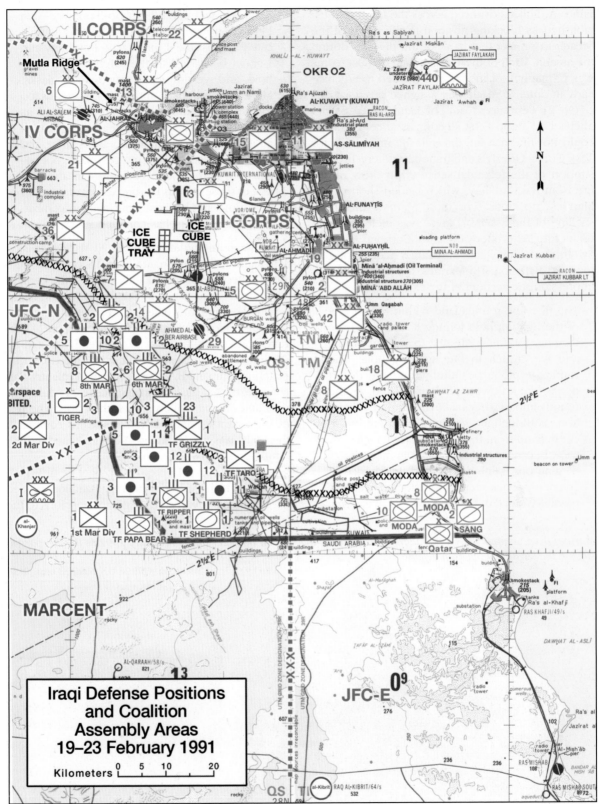

Iraqi Defense Positions
and Coalition
Assembly Areas
19–23 February 1991

Kilometers 0 5 10 20

Adapted from a 1991 Ministry of Defence (United Kingdom) map by Marine Corps History Division

tration. Task Force Grizzly, commanded by Colonel James A. Fulks, advanced across the berm and established its blocking position to the north of the breach to protect that flank of the division during the assault. Each of these regimental combat teams was primarily foot mobile and needed to advance early in order to reach their assigned positions.

On 21 February, teams of Lieutenant Colonel Michael L. Rapp's 1st Reconnaissance Battalion could not find a route through the minefields for Task Force Grizzly's infiltration. Artillery fired in support of the reconnaissance effort drew return fire from Iraqi artillery, which landed short of the Marines' positions. For most Marines this Iraqi shelling of the assembly areas was their first time under fire. Years afterward Lance Corporal Anthony Swofford of Surveillance and Target Acquisition Platoon, 2d Battalion, 7th Marines, published a florid, impressionistic account of the experience:

> The first few rounds land within fifteen feet of the fighting hole Johnny Rotten and I are digging. Johnny is the first to yell *Incoming,* and we crouch in our half-dug hole. The rounds explode beautifully, and the desert opens like a flower, a flower of sand. As the rounds impact, they make a sound of exhalation, as though air is being forced out of the earth. Sand from the explosion rains into our hole. Because we'd been deep in the labor of digging our fighting hole, and the chance of an enemy attack seemed remote and even impossible, our flak jackets, helmets, weapons,

and gas masks are stacked in an orderly fashion a few feet behind our position. . . . Then I crawl on my belly to our gear, and as delicately as possible, I throw it all to Johnny and I crawl backward to the safety of our half-hole, and we don and clear our gas masks. More rounds impact, and these explosions too look quite beautiful and make it sound as though the earth is being beaten, as though air is being forced out of the earth's lungs, and I begin to weep inside my gas mask, not because of fear, though certainly I'm afraid of one of those rounds landing closer or even on top of me, but because I'm finally in combat, my combat action has commenced.[58]

At the more northerly breach, 2d Marine Division sent teams from Lieutenant Colonel Scott W. McKenzie's 2d Reconnaissance Battalion across the berm to scout its breaches as well. For four days, the teams reported on Iraqi movements and scouted minefields without incident, but early in the morning on 20 February, one of the teams was apparently spotted by the Iraqis and threatened by a mechanized infantry platoon. Company B, 2d Light Armored Infantry Battalion, extracted the reconnaissance team while Harriers and Marine artillery struck the Iraqis. The rest of Lieutenant Colonel McKenzie's teams completed their missions, under trying conditions, and all had returned safely by 22 February.[59]

On 21 February, Lieutenant Colonel Keith T. Holcomb's 2d Light Armored Infantry Battalion crossed the berm and began attacking Iraqi positions to the

Marines from Company E, 2d Battalion, 10th Marines, dig in their howitzer on 23 February 1991 as they prepare to support the assault on the Iraqi defenses.

Photo by GySgt C. Archuleta. Official U.S. Marine Corps photo

north of 2d Marine Division's intended breach site. Within an hour the battalion began taking Iraqi artillery and mortar fire. Two Marines from a 3d Marine Aircraft Wing low-altitude air-defense team attached to the battalion proved to be some of the luckiest Marines in the Persian Gulf when their humvee was destroyed by a direct hit from an Iraqi mortar. The official monograph on the 2d Marine Division in the Gulf War documented this incident: "The round impacted in the rear of the vehicle, the force of the explosion pushing the occupants, Lance Corporal Robert M. Grady and Lance Corporal William B. Noland, across the hood, from which they rolled onto the sand. Although the vehicle was destroyed, both Marines were unhurt, emerging from the wreck literally without a scratch. Apparently their personal gear and other equipment, piled behind them, absorbed the effects of the blast. After returning to the division CP [command post] and briefing [Major] General [William] Keys, their only request was for another vehicle so they could return to the fight."[60]

For two days, the battalion aggressively moved in front of the Iraqi positions. Their success in convincing the Iraqis they were about to undergo a major attack can be seen in comments made after the war by Iraqi commanders:

On the 21st a group of enemy tanks . . . an estimated size of one battalion moved toward our covering troops in front of the battalion at the al-Manaqish region [center of Kuwait border] and attacked the covering troops using their [Coalition] artillery supported by missiles [and] armored vehicles . . . clashing with our troops . . . leading to heavy maneuvering and concluding [with] some of the enemy tanks and [armored vehicles] withdrawing. [At] 1500 [hours] the vehicles returned for the second time and tried to attack two different locations. . . . [The] enemy was unable to remove the covering troops because of our missiles [free rocket over ground and multiple rocket launcher] and our reserve armor retaliation. . . . The enemy was unable to defeat the covering troops and the [*7th Infantry Division*]. . . . The army commander called to present his appreciation to the soldiers for their resistance, and he gave a [commemorative] gun to each soldier.[61]

Captain Kenneth W. Amidon, commander of Company C, 2d Light Armored Infantry Battalion, was awarded the Silver Star for his conduct and leadership during these actions. As described in his award citation, Captain Amidon "aggressively and skillfully maneuvered his Company through heavy artillery, mortar, rocket, and tank fire to seize an enemy battalion position and secure a lodgment in face of an enemy brigade. Over the next two days, his calm, fearless leadership, and expert employment of forces and supporting arms enabled the Marines of his company to hold their critical flank position despite sustained, heavy indirect fire and repeated attempts by numerically superior tank and infantry forces to dislodge them. On G-l [23 February], concerned that the deception was losing its effect, Captain Amidon launched a determined and well-coordinated assault to gain a commanding view of the enemy's defenses. Despite incoming artillery, mortar, tank, and antitank fires, he moved to and occupied a highly exposed position for over four hours to coordinate combined arms attacks on the targets he uncovered."[62]

The success of Captain Amidon and his fellow light armored infantry company commanders was in large part due to the support they received from the 3d Marine Aircraft Wing, despite the poor visibility and hazardous flying conditions created by the smoke from the many oil fires Iraq had set in Kuwait. The Iraqi antiaircraft defenses were far from supine as well, as Captain Troy A. Ward and First Lieutenant Kevin G. Mechler of Marine Observation Squadron 2 discovered during the eight hours they flew in support of the battalion in an OV-10 Bronco. Both Captain Troy and Lieutenant Mechler received the Distinguished Flying Cross because they

conducted two flights totaling 8.1 hours. . . . During the first flight, [they] simultaneously supported two companies from 2d Light Armored Infantry Battalion by engaging revetted enemy tanks and troops in trenches with close air support and adjusting artillery fire. During the process of controlling a section of Marine AV-8B Harriers, [they] successfully avoided two SA-6 surface-to-air missiles. [They] remained in the battle and despite the constant threat of antiaircraft artillery and surface to air missiles, controlled a section of F/A-18 Hornets on an enemy trench line which resulted in the destruction of an Iraqi tank. On another flight later that evening, using the forward looking infrared radar, [they] located twelve vehicles despite severe smoke from fire trenches and burning oil wells.[63]

Marine Corps Art Collection
Harriers Fire the Trenches by Col H. Avery Chenoweth.
AV-8B Harriers from Marine Aircraft Group 13 drop na-
palm to "fire" oil-filled trenches in Kuwait.

Shortly after midnight on 22 February, Task Force Grizzly advanced to the first minefield and moved into hidden positions in front of the Iraqi lines. Throughout the day they engaged the Iraqis with 81mm mortars, MK19 grenade launchers, machine guns, antitank missiles, artillery, and air strikes. The Iraqi return fire was ineffectual, and Colonel Fulks, the task force commander, withdrew his Marines to less-exposed positions in the afternoon. Unfortunately, a poorly coordinated friendly air strike prevented another attempt to discover a lane for the task force through the minefields.[64]

Iraqi commanders continued to believe that the light armored infantry attacks, reconnaissance excursions, and infantry probes along the berm were major Marine assaults that they were fending off. On 22 February, for instance, the Iraqis believed that

the enemy managed to move forward toward the *26th [Infantry] Division* using heavy forces. The enemy tried to [defeat the division], but the enemy was forced to withdraw behind the border [with Saudi Arabia]. . . .

Then the enemy returned with heavy armor toward the *14th [Infantry] Division*. . . . At 1300 the enemy was forced to stop one kilometer in front of the [Iraqi] covering troops. On the same day, the enemy troops, using armor, managed to go forward toward the covering troops for the *29th [Infantry] Division*. The enemy was forced to step backward after we launched twelve missiles. These missiles were successful in forcing half the enemy unit to withdraw and the other half to stop. The enemy's attacks and air raids became rapid on this day.[65]

Concerning Iraqi reports that the Coalition offensive had already begun, General Boomer told General Schwarzkopf "that was our 2d LAI Bn [2d Light Armored Infantry Battalion]. If they think that's the war, they better pray it never starts. We will see." The intensity and success of the light armored infantry is vividly illustrated in the report General Boomer was given on 22 February at the daily briefing:

Highlight of the day was in the 2d Div [2d Marine Division] sector, where besides scaring the s——t out of Saddam Hussein, 2d LAI [2d Light Armored Infantry Battalion] aggressively engaged, all morning, a series of enemy positions along this general line here. Aggressive prosecution of tanks throughout the morning led to engaging tanks at 0910 with direct fire weapons, engaging tanks with arty [artillery] and air at 0930. The bottom line—and this engagement petered out right around noon, but the bottom line on the engagement is over the course of the 24 hours of operations, some 87 confirmed EPWs [enemy prisoners of war], with more inbound that the Div[ision] did not wish to take credit for until they finished counting, but they are confident the total will be over 100. Seven T-62s destroyed by fire with TOWs [antitank missiles], 11 T-62s destroyed with air, 15 vehicles destroyed by direct and indirect fire, and 80 to 90 dead Iraqis counted in the trench lines that were cleared by 2d LAI.[66]

On 23 February, Task Force Taro infiltrated to its line of departure on 1st Marine Division's southeastern flank. The task force was led by 2d Battalion, 3d Marines, which suffered a tragedy during the march when a grenade accidently exploded, killing one Marine, Private First Class Adam T. Hoage, and wounding another. Private First Class Hoage "dismounted from a transport truck. One of his grenades caught on the vehicle and the safety pin came out. Knowing what happened and the hopelessness of his situation, PFC Hoage stepped away from his group. The resulting explosion killed him and wounded another Marine." The movement was slowed while the casualties were evacuated, and then the battalion continued its mission.[67]

On the northwestern flank, Task Force Grizzly also advanced to its flanking position. Throughout 23 February, Task Force Grizzly cleared several Iraqi bunkers and destroyed some Iraqi tanks as it searched for an infiltration route, preparing its way as it advanced into Kuwait with numerous artillery barrages and air strikes. Members of the defending *29th Infantry Division* began to surrender to Task Force Grizzly, and that afternoon this provided the break that led to the required infiltration route when Marines searching for the way observed the routes taken by the surrendering Iraqis.[68]

The Iraqis continued firing sporadic artillery strikes against Task Force Grizzly, but these were ineffective. The Marines' own artillery missions were more successful, and Iraqi soldiers continued to surrender as the Marines prepped to breach the first minefield. By midnight, Task Force Grizzly had done just that, breaching the virtually undefended first minefield and occupying its assigned blocking position on the division's left flank.[69]

Colonel Charles J. Quilter II described the advance:

Fulks now ordered the commander of 3rd Battalion, 7th Marines, Lieutenant Colonel [Timothy J.] Hannigan, to infiltrate the mine belt by force on the night before G-Day. Hannigan's first problem was resolved by Iraqis who began walking through the minefield to surrender. The new enemy prisoners of war now obligingly marked the lane with chemical lights provided by the Marines. Then to the dismay of Fulks and Hannigan, a second unreported mine belt was discovered. This had evidently been emplaced to discourage retreating by the Iraqi defenders.

This second difficulty was resolved in traditional Marine fashion: Staff Sergeant [Charles T.] Restifo of the Engineer Platoon took his bayonet and probed for mines quietly in the darkness, marking a footpath as he went. Two companies passed through the second minefield by 0200 of G-Day [24 February] via Restifo's path, which was soon enlarged to allow passage of the artillery of 5th Battalion, 11th Marines.[70]

Staff Sergeant Restifo was awarded the Silver Star for his work in preparing the breach. According to Restifo's official award citation, "In broad daylight,

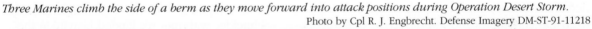

Three Marines climb the side of a berm as they move forward into attack positions during Operation Desert Storm.
Photo by Cpl R. J. Engbrecht. Defense Imagery DM-ST-91-11218

On 23 February 1991, Iraqi artillery shells the positions of 2d Platoon, Company A, 1st Reconnaissance Battalion, near Observation Post 4. The shelling was ineffective.

with enemy positions less than 100 meters away, he identified two enemy soldiers attempting to surrender. Completely disregarding his own safety, Staff Sergeant Restifo, with two other Marines, ran across the uncleared minefield and captured the enemy soldiers. Unnerved by this bold act, an entire enemy company defending the minefield surrendered. He bravely supervised the detonation of 15 to 20 anti-tank mines and completed the clearing of three lanes through the minefield."[71]

Another of the remarkable actions taken by a Marine during the liberation occurred in these minefields, when Corporal Gregory R. Stricklin, Company G, 2d Battalion, 7th Marines, found himself in an unmarked section of the minefields. Corporal Stricklin believed the antitank mines were rigged to go off with the weight of a tank, and he was far less than that. He then "without hesitation, personally pulled a 300 pound ammunition cart through an unmarked minefield along a very narrow path. He negotiated the route, heavily laden with anti-tank and anti-personnel mines, by using the anti-tank mines as stepping stones. Returning to his section, Corporal Stricklin guided a second cart through the minefield."[72]

As the artillery of the 1st Marine Division established itself in its firing positions prior to the ground assault on the evening of 23 February, Captain Phillip Thompson of 1st Battalion, 12th Marines, was an eyewitness to another tragic case of Marines killing other Marines:

That's when I heard a shriek overhead, like the sound of a huge bedsheet being ripped, followed by the "tremendous explosion." At the same time, an enormous concussion slammed into the canvas, slapping my legs and nearly knocking me off balance. Without thinking, I dove outside toward my shallow hole, dragging [Private First Class Kyle] Schneider with me. We landed heavily in the bottom, confused and frightened. When I looked up, I saw a huge ball of fire about 50 yards behind my vehicle. Our Q-36 counter battery radar was completely engulfed in flames, along with the humvee next to it.

I swiveled my head around, thinking for some reason that we must be under attack from tanks. The thought didn't make sense, but it's all my mind would register. It sounded just like tank fire. I heard Marines screaming near the burning radar and saw silhouettes dashing around the flames.[73]

What Thompson heard was not tank fire. A Marine EA-6B Prowler had launched an AGM-88 missile at an Iraqi antiaircraft radar unit when the Iraqi radar was turned off. The already fired missile apparently honed in on the Marines' Q-36 AN/TPO counterbattery radar instead and destroyed it. Corporal Timothy W. Collins was wounded, and Corporal Aaron A. Pack was killed in the incident.[74]

In Kuwait, Iraqi forces intensified the "Tariq

This Q-36 counterbattery radar was mistakenly hit by an AGM-88 HARM missile fired by a Marine EA-6B Prowler on 23 February 1991. Cpl Aaron A. Pack lost his life, and Cpl Timothy W. Collins was wounded in the incident.

G-1, Task Force "Ripper" CP Group *by Col H. Avery Chenoweth. On 23 February 1991, the day before the Coalition offensive, the command element of Task Force Ripper makes final preparations for the assault.*

General Boomer's Message

On 23 February, Lieutenant General Walter Boomer sent the following message to all members of the I Marine Expeditionary Force:

Message to members of
I Marine Expeditionary Force, 23 Feb 91
Lieutenant General Walter E. Boomer, USMC

After months of preparation, we are on the eve of the liberation of Kuwait, a small, peaceful country that was brutally attacked and subsequently pillaged by Iraq. Now we will attack into Kuwait, not to conquer, but to drive out the invaders and restore the country to its citizens. In so doing, you not only return a nation to its people, but you will destroy the war machine of a ruthless dictator, who fully intended to control this part of the world, thereby endangering many other nations, including our own.

We will succeed in our mission because we are well-trained and well equipped; because we are U.S. Marines, Sailors, Soldiers, and Airmen; and because our cause is just. Your children and grandchildren will read about your victory in the years to come and appreciate your sacrifice and courage. America will watch her sons and daughters and draw strength from your success.

May the spirit of your Marine forefathers ride with you and may God give you the strength to accomplish your mission.

Semper Fi,
Boomer

Project," their plan to use oil fires as a weapon and shield against the Coalition forces. The sky above Kuwait was darkened by over 140 burning oil wells as well as blazing oil-filled trenches along the Saddam Line. The commander of the *III Corps* reported that the entire *29th Infantry Division* had been captured by the allies and requested permission from Baghdad to withdraw. The Iraqi chief of staff, Lieutenant General Husayn Rashid Muhammad, denied the request.[75]

The Marines of the I Marine Expeditionary Force were poised to begin the liberation of Kuwait as ordered as 23 February came to a close. They were perched on the edges of the Iraqi defenses and had already established dominance on the battlefield.

Breaking the Saddam Line

24 February

On 24 February, the Coalition launched a ground offensive to free Kuwait and destroy the Iraqi Army and the *Republican Guard*. The Coalition forces were organized into five major maneuver commands. On the far western flank was the XVIII Airborne Corps, commanded by Lieutenant General Gary Luck, USA, and consisting of the 82d Airborne Division, the 101st Airborne Division (Air Assault), the 24th Infantry Division (Mechanized), and the French 6th Light Armored Division. Deployed next was the VII Corps, commanded by Lieutenant General Frederick M. Franks Jr., USA, and containing the 1st Infantry Division (Mechanized), the 1st Cavalry Division (Armored), the 1st and 3d Armored Divisions, and the British 1st Armored Division. Next, opposite western Kuwait, was Joint Forces Command–North, made up of divisions from Egypt, Syria, and Saudi Arabia. Then came I Marine Expeditionary Force, and finally on the coast was Joint Forces Command–East.[1]

The XVIII Airborne Corps began the offensive when the French 6th Light Armored Division dashed across the border at 0100 to seize As Salam, Iraq, while the 101st Airborne Division (Air Assault) moved toward an-Nasiriyah, establishing a screen to the north of the major Coalition operations. Late in the day, the VII Corps began its own advance against the Iraqi forces in southeastern Iraq while its British 1st Armored Division began an assault on the Iraqi minefields on the Wadi al-Batin, the avenue of approach on the Iraqi-Kuwaiti border that the Iraqis expected the allies to follow.[2]

Breaching the Line with the 1st Marine Division

Beginning on the evening of 23 February, Colonel James Fulks's Task Force Grizzly* infiltrated the first

---

*1st Marine Division's regimental combat teams were very heterogeneous due to the hurried, ad hoc nature of the deployment during Operation Desert Shield. To increase unit identity, they were designated task forces and assigned names rather than being known by regiment. Task Force Grizzly was typical of these task forces. It was commanded by Col Fulks, whose 4th Marines provided the regimental command group. None of 4th Marines' battalions were in the task force, however. Instead, the three infantry battalions were 2d and 3d Battalions, 7th Marines, and the 1st Battalion, 25th Marines.

Iraqi minefield on foot, beginning a long, slow foot march to its position flanking the main division breach. This slow advance on foot was taxing for the Marines who conducted it throughout the night. Sergeant Charles G. Grow, a combat artist attached to 3d Battalion, 7th Marines, later described the event: "We marched through the cold, damp evening. When we'd stop we were like frothy horses and the chill night air would have its way with us. After donning our chem[ical] gear we marched 'til sweaty in the warmth of the day. Now as evening sets in we'll shiver again and await our next mission."[3]

More than discomfort, the Marines found once again that they were in more danger from each other than they were from their Iraqi foes. Just after dawn on 24 February, Task Force Grizzly engaged a small group of Iraqi armored columns that fled the scene. Shortly afterward, Task Force Ripper, preparing to breach the minefields to the south and having just seen Iraqi vehicles depart the area, opened fired on the logistics vehicles of Task Force Grizzly's 3d Battalion, 7th Marines, which was leading the task force's advance.[4]

Lance Corporal Anthony Swofford of Surveillance and Target Acquisition Platoon, 2d Battalion, 7th Marines, observed the incident: "Rounds pass directly over our heads while I retrieve my spotter's scope from my ruck[sack]. As they pass over, it's as though all sound and time and space in their path are sucked into the rounds. A five-ton truck blows one hundred yards behind us. Its water buffalo also blows, into a large bloom of five hundred gallons of water. And another five-ton takes a hit."[5]

Writing years later, Swofford described the feelings engendered in the Marines being fired on by fellow Marines, as another Marine tries to stop the shelling by using the radio:

> And Johnny continues to scream at the man, and I hear in his voice astonishment and rage, because of all the things that Johnny believes in, the superiority of the sniper and the importance of the small unit, first he believes in the Marine Corps and that the Marine Corps takes care of its own, as in doesn't kill its own, and even though he knows different, just like the rest of us he's never experienced the horribly sublime reality of Marine Corps tanks shooting at you and hitting

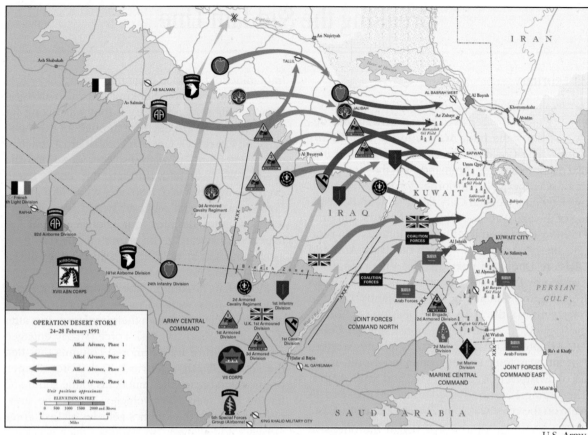

OPERATION DESERT STORM
24–28 February 1991

Allied Advance, Phase 1
Allied Advance, Phase 2
Allied Advance, Phase 3
Allied Advance, Phase 4

Unit positions approximate
ELEVATION IN FEET
0   500 1000 1500 2000 and Above

0   40
Miles

U.S. Army

your very own supply convoy, and strangely enough, hearing the loud, screeching friendly fire rounds rip overhead, the rounds pulling all time and space with them, is more mysterious and thrilling and terrifying than taking the fire from the enemy, because the enemy fire made sense but the friendly fire makes no sense.[6]

Swofford goes on to say that "word is that only two men died and six were injured at the hands of the trigger-happy and blind tankers. I don't believe this, because the damage is extreme." In fact one Marine, Lance Corporal Christian J. Porter, was killed and three Marines were wounded in the attack. Sergeant Gordon T. Gregory was awarded the Silver Star for "exposing himself numerous times to tank and artillery fire while moving his Marines into defilade positions" during the attack.[7]

Task Force Grizzly continued its advance after the tragic incident and reached its assigned blocking position, Hill 191, at 0730. The position was occupied, and the task force spent the rest of the day taking a "steady stream" of Iraqi prisoners and sending artillery barrages against various Iraqi units. Some Iraqi mortar fire came in (and was met by artillery fire), but the task force primarily rested and

prepared to take al-Jaber Air Base the next day, as planned.[8]

Task Force Taro,* commanded by Colonel John Admire, encountered extremely light resistance during its infiltration of the Iraqi minefields. Taro called in four artillery strikes on various small Iraqi forces the first day and took many prisoners, but otherwise the advance was "anticlimactic." In addition, Taro's attached engineer units constructed an additional lane through the minefield breach to reduce congestion and speed the prisoners' movement to the rear.[9]

At 0400 on 24 February, while Task Forces Grizzly and Taro were conducting the infiltrations on the left and right flanks of the division, Major General James Myatt, the 1st Marine Division commander, ordered Colonel Carlton Fulford's Task Force Ripper** to begin the division assault. Lieutenant Colonel Charles H. Cureton witnessed the

---

*Task Force Taro was the only homogenous unit of the 1st Marine Division task forces; it consisted of the 3d Marines' 1st, 2d, and 3d Battalions.

**Task Force Ripper was built around Col Fulford's 7th Marines. Its battalions included 1st Battalion, 7th Marines; 1st Battalion, 5th Marines; 1st Combat Engineer Battalion; and the 3d Tank Battalion. As one of the two "mechanized" task forces, its infantry battalions were mounted in assault amphibious vehicles.

breaching operations and later described them in detail.

Each obstacle clearing detachment used similar equipment and techniques. On order from the officer commanding the detachment, an M60A1 tank equipped with a track-width mine plow (TWMP) moved to the edge of the minefield and fired a MK58 single-shot line charge (MCLC) from a trailer towed behind the tank. Attempts to remotely detonate this type of line charge invariably failed and a combat engineer then left the comparative safety of an accompanying AAV [amphibious assault vehicle] and manually primed the charge. When subsequently detonated, the resulting blast normally cleared a path some distance into the minefield. The combat engineer repeated the process until they reached the other side. In some instances, the MK58 single-shot line charge failed completely and an AAV with the newer MK154 three-shot line charge came forward. This happened with "Team Tank," 1st Battalion, 7th Marines. The AAV simply moved behind the tank, fired the line charge over the tank, then detonated the charge either remotely or manually—normally the latter as both the MK58 and MK154 remote detonating systems proved unreliable. Once through a lane with the line charge the track-width mine plow-equipped tank plunged forward to clear and thus proof the lanes against loose or deeply buried mines.[10]

Although there was some malfunctioning mine clearing equipment, the process went essentially according to plan, and all but one of the four initial lanes were quickly cleared. The fourth took somewhat longer because a mine disabled an assault amphibious vehicle engaged in clearing the minefield. After clearing the minefields, Lieutenant Colonel James N. Mattis's 1st Battalion, 7th Marines, shifted to the eastern flank, while Lieutenant Colonel Christopher Cortez's 1st Battalion, 5th Marines, shifted to the western flank and Lieutenant Colonel Alphonso B. Diggs Jr.'s 3d Tank Battalion led the

Night Firefight *by Sgt Charles G. Grow. Marines of Company E, 2d Battalion, 7th Marines (part of Task Force Grizzly), engage in a firefight with Iraqi defenders on 24 February 1991.*

Marine Corps Art Collection

An Iraqi minefield with an unexploded line charge. The Iraqis did not maintain the minefields very well after they were laid, and the wind uncovered many mines.

way up the center. The advance continued fairly easily; many Iraqis were surrendering to the advancing Marines of Task Force Ripper until shortly before 0900 when Iraqi artillery began to fall upon surrendering Iraqi soldiers. General Thomas Draude later recalled hearing this described on the radio: "I'll never forget this voice, the Marine's voice; it was just outraged and shocked, 'I can't believe they're doing this. What kind of officers are these? They fire on their own troops.' I guess that gave us further reinforcement, 'God these guys are really desperate, if that's what they've got to do in order to hold people in position.' I think that along with the fact that things were going well, that meant maybe things are going to go too well." The Iraqi artillery spotter's position was located in a tower, and an AH-1W helicopter destroyed it with a missile shot, after which Iraqi artillery fire became noticeably less effective.[11]

Shortly before noon, Task Force Ripper began its assault on the second band of minefields, led by Lieutenant Colonel Mattis's battalion, which had rejoined the center after Task Force Papa Bear moved to the eastern flank of the advancing mechanized forces. Unlike the first obstacle belt, the Iraqis tried to oppose this breach. While some Iraqi units continued to fight, other Iraqis attempted to surrender

in ever increasing numbers. Gunnery Sergeant Paul S. Cochran of the 3d Tank Battalion noted in his journal that "POWs [prisoners of war] started appearing from everywhere. A total of approx[imately] 300 to 350 were credited to 2nd Plt [platoon], because the[y] surrendered to our t[an]ks in our sector. POWs were blowing us kisses, waving American flags and ask[ing] for food and water." The combination of determined defenders and masses of surrendering soldiers created a great deal of confusion.[12]

Task Force Ripper's combat engineers had three lanes open through the second obstacle belt by 1215, and Mattis's battalion and Diggs's 3d Tank Battalion started passing through to begin their assault on the Iraqi fortifications. Mattis attempted to control the burgeoning numbers of prisoners by establishing a temporary holding point, but Lieutenant Colonel Cureton later noted that "the effort proved futile. Within minutes the situation worsened. The loss of one lane forced the diversion of traffic to the single open lane, [lane] 3. Then, as the mechanized columns converged, the absence of the division breach control party, which had not yet been able to get to the second obstacle belt, compounded an already difficult situation. Because there was no one there controlling traffic the lane became a jumble of prisoners with their Marine guards going in one

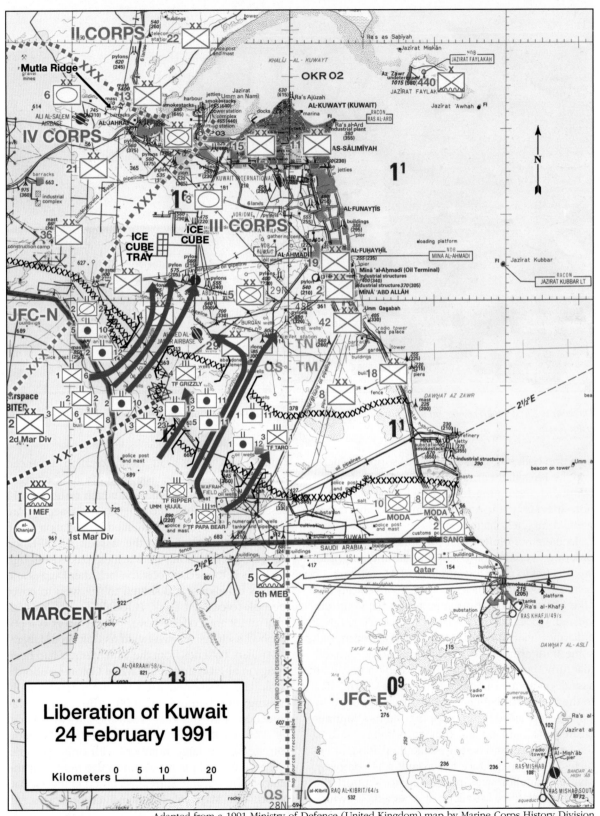

Liberation of Kuwait
24 February 1991

Kilometers   0   5   10   20

Adapted from a 1991 Ministry of Defence (United Kingdom) map by Marine Corps History Division

Photo by TSgt Perry Heimer, USAF. Defense Imagery DF-ST-92-08042

Darkening the sky with smoke, oil wells burn out of control over the al-Wafrah Forest after being set ablaze by retreating Iraqi forces.

direction colliding with the press of supply vehicles and the LAVs [light armored vehicles] of Task Force Shepherd attempting to go in the opposite direction. Inevitably, the lane got congested and movement completely halted."[13]

Lieutenant Colonel Mattis uncluttered the lane by ordering his men not to stop for surrendering Iraqi soldiers but to press forward instead. He ordered the battalion logistics vehicles to stage their vehicles and take charge of the prisoners as the battalion advanced. Once through the lanes, he sent a combined antiarmor team forward. After a brief skirmish with some Iraqi armor, and after clearing some bunkers that turned out to be empty, the battalion began an assault on an area known as the "Emir's Farm" due to the trees and buildings in the area. Supported by Cobras and artillery fire support, Mattis's Marines cleared the bunkers and fighting positions around the Emir's Farm and destroyed the Iraqi armored vehicles in the area. Once the assault was complete, Mattis's battalion was positioned to support the planned task force assault on al-Jaber airfield, which had been designated "MEF Objective A."[14]

While 1st Battalion, 7th Marines, assaulted the

Emir's Farm, Diggs's 3d Tank Battalion advanced along the center of the task force's front. It engaged in a series of small skirmishes, which resulted in 11 destroyed Iraqi tanks and over 100 prisoners before Diggs halted the unit and oriented his battalion to the west in preparation for the assault on al-Jaber. Cortez's 1st Battalion, 5th Marines, passed through the lanes in the second obstacle belt after Diggs's and Mattis's battalions, and shifted to the west to cover the task force's left flank. It fought a skirmish with Iraqi armor and collected over 500 prisoners as it positioned itself for the westward assault on al-Jaber.[15]

Artillery batteries from the 11th Marines had been firing on al-Jaber for hours while Colonel Fulford's command positioned itself for the assault, finally ceasing the barrage at 1600. The assault was launched at 1630 and by 1800 the airfield was cut off. The attack was extremely successful—the Iraqis surrendered in large numbers with only sporadic, ineffectual attempts to continue the fight. But the atmosphere became surreal, as noted in the 1st Battalion, 7th Marines' command chronology: "All hands were awestruck by the ominous pall of smoke emanating from over 50 wellhead fires in the

Photo by SSgt J. R. Ruark. Defense Imagery DM-ST-92-00047

One of 3d Tank Battalion's M60A1 main battle tanks fitted with reactive armor. This battalion provided the armored punch to Task Force Ripper.

al-Burqan Oilfield. Commanders whose senses were sharply focused found that the rumbling from the burning [wellheads] played tricks on their hearing, sounding almost like columns of armored vehicles approaching our right flank."[16]

It was clear that no organized Iraqi force remained at al-Jaber, and Task Force Ripper reoriented itself to the northeast in preparation for the second day's advance, settling into position for a very dark night beneath a sky filled with black smoke. Small engagements with isolated Iraqi soldiers and tanks continued through the night. Second Lieutenant James D. Gonsalves of Company C, 3d Tank Battalion, later described one such event, which was fairly typical of all of the Marines armored encounters on the first day:

> We had pulled up to our 2nd day's objective and were awaiting further orders. The smoke clouds from the burning oil wells were closing in fast, reducing visibility to less than 1,500 meters. All of a sudden my loader, Lance Corporal Rodrigues, yelled: "We got a T-62 out there—Look!" "Gunner! SABOT! Tank! Range 1100 meters!"* The first explosion was small but then its ammo started cooking off. I counted 14 secondary explosions.[17]

Task Force Shepherd,* commanded by Lieutenant Colonel Clifford Myers, started the liberation of Kuwait with only two of its four line companies. Company C was attached to Task Force Taro, and Company D was attached to Task Force Ripper. Myers's task force passed through the first obstacle belt without opposition, and Company C returned to it due to Task Force Taro's own lack of opposition. Task Force Shepherd was stymied by the traffic jam that developed at the second obstacle belt's cleared lanes, but it bypassed that by driving through the minefield in the recent tracks of Iraqi vehicles.[18]

Task Force Shepherd's command chronology narrative describes its advance after the second obstacle belt to a screen position northwest of Task Force Ripper:

> En route to its proposed screening position, Task Force Shepherd, now consisting of Companies A, B, and C, skirts the western boundary of the al-Burqan Oil Fields, and due to the hundreds of burning oil wells, encounters a surrealistic battlefield where visibility at 1500 was down to 50 to 100 meters. As Shepherd continued to lead the [1st Marine] Division's advance into Kuwait, progress was slowed by

---

*2dLt Gonsalves is describing the commands given in order to bring the tank's main gun to fire on the enemy. "Gunner" alerts the gunner that a command is being given. "SABOT" is the type of ammunition to be used, an antitank round.

*LtCol Myers's Task Force Shepherd was built around the 1st Light Armored Infantry Battalion headquarters company with its line companies drawn from both the 1st and 3d Light Armored Infantry Battalions.

Photo by Sgt Roberts. Marine Corps History Division Reference Branch photo files
Marine light armored vehicles pass through lanes cleaned in the Iraqi minefields on 24 February 1991.

not only the poor visibility, but by the multitude of surrendering Iraqi soldiers. Literally thousands of Iraqis emerged, at times begging for food. The surrendering Iraqis were told to continue to march south with their hands in the air. . . . Any abandoned Iraqi vehicles were either destroyed in place or bypassed. Though the advance was extremely slow at times, Task Force Shepherd effectively established the screen line.[19]

Colonel Richard W. Hodory's Task Force Papa Bear* began the first day of the assault as the division reserve, supporting Task Force Ripper's main attack and conducting breaches of the two Iraqi obstacle belts. At 0900, Hodory's engineers began to clear the first obstacle belt, which was unopposed, and within an hour the task force's first troops had passed through the obstacle belt and were proceeding to the second belt. Preparations for the second obstacle belt began, and by 1200, despite sporadic Iraqi artillery fire, Task Force Papa Bear was prepared to breach the second obstacle

belt and prepare a safe landing zone for helicopterborne Task Force X-Ray.[20]

Shortly after 1500, Colonel Hodory ordered 3d Battalion, 9th Marines, to assault the second minefield and obstacle belt, as well as trenches occupied by the Iraqi *22d Brigade, 5th Mechanized Division.* The Iraqis vigorously opposed the assault with armor, artillery, and mortars. During the breaching operation, Lance Corporal Kasey A. Krock

distinguished himself by twice braving enemy direct and in-direct fire in order to successfully complete his mission. When a line charge fired from his MK 154 [mine clearance launcher] failed to detonate, he quickly gathered together the required equipment and proceeded outside to manually detonate the defective charge. After successfully doing so Lance Corporal Krock re-entered the MK 154. The second line charge shot into the breach also malfunctioned and again Lance Corporal Krock instantly exited the vehicle to manually prime it. This time, however, as the line charge did not lie exactly in line as the previous shot, he had to navigate through over 20 meters of live minefield in order to successfully prime the charge. After the detonation of the second line charge, the breach was complete and the assault element was able to

_____

*Task Force Papa Bear was built around Col Hodory's 1st Marines. Its battalions included 1st Battalion, 1st Marines; 3d Battalion, 9th Marines; and the 1st Tank Battalion. As one of the two "mechanized" task forces, its infantry battalions were mounted in amphibious assault vehicles.

successfully assault through the lane and defeat the defenders.

For his actions, Lance Corporal Krock received the Silver Star.[21]

When 10 Marines clearing bunkers and rounding up prisoners were wounded by Iraqi mortar rounds, Hospitalman Anthony M. Martin, a U.S. Navy corpsman serving with the 3d Battalion, 9th Marines, carried three Marines to safety through heavy mortar fire and came to the aid of six others. Like Lance Corporal Krock, Hospitalman Martin received the Silver Star for his actions.

Lieutenant Colonel Michael H. Smith's 3d Battalion, 9th Marines, continued advancing while the casualties were evacuated to the battalion aid station. Marine Harriers and Cobras supported the battalion's advance as it cleared the Iraqi positions that had opposed its advance, and hundreds of Iraqi soldiers began surrendering to the battalion. In two separate incidents, M60 tanks were damaged by mines, temporarily closing lanes, but Lieutenant Colonel Michael M. Kephart's 1st Tank Battalion passed through the lanes, followed by Lieutenant Colonel Michael O. Fallon's 1st Battalion, 1st Marines. Minor engagements with Iraqi tanks and armored personnel carriers were easily defeated by the task force or the omnipresent Cobras of 3d Marine Aircraft Wing, and hundreds of Iraqi soldiers continued to surrender. All three battalions of Task Force Papa Bear took up positions for the night on the edge of the al-Burqan oil field.[22]

Field historian Lieutenant Colonel Cureton provided a vivid description of the situation as night closed on the 1st Marine Division:

> The assault battalions spent the next few hours sweeping their areas and making final dispositions in a landscape littered with enemy bunkers, revetted positions, and wrecked tanks, personnel carriers, and vehicles of all types. Behind the task force, between the two obstacle belts, moved support units of the 1st Marine Division as they took up night defensive positions in the gathering darkness. To the north the burning wells belched great columns of flame and smoke. The entire al-Burqan Oilfield seemed to be on fire and no one knew what enemy force might be lurking there, if indeed any Iraqis remained in the oilfield at all. Light from burning wells overpowered thermal sights and smoke obscured the area.[23]

The 1st Marine Division's extensive training paid off during the assault on the Iraqi minefields and obstacles.
Marine Corps History Division Reference Branch photo files

An M270 Multiple Launch Rocket System and an M88 armored recovery vehicle of the Tiger Brigade in Kuwait.

Breaching the Line with the 2d Marine Division

Major General William M. Keys's 2d Marine Division and the U.S. Army's attached 1st (Tiger) Brigade, 2d Armored Division, began their advance into Kuwait with an extensive bombardment of Iraqi artillery by the 10th Marines and the multiple rocket launchers of the Army's Battery A, 92d Field Artillery.[*] At 0530, Colonel Lawrence H. Livingston's 6th Marines,[**] reinforced for the breach by the 1st Battalion, 8th Marines, began its assault by advancing rapidly to the two minefields and wire obstacles that 2d Marine Division faced.[24]

Attached to the regiment was Task Force Breach Alpha,[***] which began clearing the minefields at 0600. The process was just as difficult and fraught with malfunction as it was earlier in the morning for 1st Marine Division, and the engineers performing the dangerous work took similar risks to secure the breaches.

During the breaching process, one of the division's XM93 Fox chemical reconnaissance vehicles reported a possible chemical weapon, and all of the Marines in the two divisions went to the highest mission-oriented protective posture. The heavy, charcoal-lined suits would be worn for most of the rest of the liberation of Kuwait by the Marines of both divisions; fortunately for the Marines, the weather remained cool. There is no documentary evidence that any Iraqi chemical weapons were used in Kuwait.[25]

Direct Support Command's 8th Support Engineer Battalion supported the division's breaching efforts by attaching a company to Task Force Breach Alpha. Staff Sergeant Daniel A. Kur of that company was awarded the Silver Star because he

> gallantly led his team in the removal of enemy mines, while under intermittent mortar fire and wearing chemical protective over garments[.] Staff Sergeant Kur courageously extracted enemy mines by hand, carried the mines out of the minefield, and guided traffic to keep the assault force moving. Without regard for his personal safety, he bravely guided an armored D7-G dozer through the minefield during conditions of reduced visibility. When the dozer was hit and disabled by an Iraqi anti-tank mine, Staff Sergeant Kur was knocked to the ground. Immediately, he shook off the blast, checked the operator's condition, and continued clearing the land of' mines.[26]

Such actions were not unique among the engineers clearing lanes through the minefields while suffering Iraqi mortar and artillery fire. Gunnery Sergeant Mart J. Culp, the noncommissioned officer in charge of a demolitions team, was kept busy with unexploded mines all morning. As the recommendation to award Culp a Bronze Star recounts, "Time and again he entered the minefields, supervising

---

[*]Battery A, 92d Field Artillery, was a multiple-launch rocket-system battery attached to the Tiger Brigade, 2d Armored Division, commanded by Col John Sylvester. The Tiger Brigade fought under the operational control of 2d Marine Division, as explained in chapter 4.

[**]6th Marines comprised 1st Battalion, 6th Marines; 3d Battalion, 6th Marines; and 2d Battalion, 2d Marines.

[***]Task Force Breach Alpha comprised Company B, 2d Combat Engineer Battalion; Company D, 4th Combat Engineer Battalion; Provisional General Support Company, 4th Assault Amphibian Battalion; and Detachment, 4th Tank Battalion.

the setting of demolitions charges and personally activating the fuzes."[27]

The lanes cleared through the minefields were identified by color (red, blue, or green) and by number. In the green lanes, Lieutenant Colonel Bruce A. Gombar's 1st Battalion, 8th Marines, saw some of the heaviest fighting experienced during 2d Marine Division's breach. Several vehicles were disabled by mines, and many of the line charges intended to clear the fields failed to explode. Two demolition team Marines, Corporal George J. Morgan and Lance Corporal Gerald Randolph, entered the minefields to fix this: "They set new fuses to unexploded line charges, ignited them, and raced back through the minefields with only seconds to spare before the charges exploded." Lieutenant Colonel John D. Winchester, commanding officer of the 2d Combat Engineer Battalion, believed that the minefield at the green lanes was laid more competently than the fields through which the red and blue lanes passed.[28]

Once through the first minefield, Gombar's battalion fought against small, scattered groups of Iraqi soldiers. Corporal Robert L. Novak, a squad leader for Combined Anti-Armor Team II, Weapons Company, 1st Battalion, 8th Marines, showed how effi-

cient the Marines were in quickly overwhelming Iraqi opposition. As documented in his Silver Star citation, Novak was part of "the lead element of the battalion as it continued its attack north of the initial Iraqi defensive belt. As lead elements of the platoon encountered small-arms fire, Corporal Novak, acting through his own initiative, directed his squad into firing positions and personally acquired targets. Within minutes, he destroyed an enemy tank, two armored personnel carriers, and a towed artillery piece that was in the process of displacing."[29]

Lieutenant Colonel Dennis P. Mroczkowski, the field historian attached to the 2d Marine Division, later described one of the small firefights the battalion engaged in as it cleared the obstacle belt:

Company A had the mission of guarding the battalion's flank in this area; accordingly, the 3d Platoon was ordered to secure a building, surrounded by a chain-link fence, located 800 meters to the east. The platoon was mounted in assault amphibious vehicles. As they came within 300 meters of the building, Iraqi soldiers inside it opened fire with rocket-propelled grenades. The platoon dismounted, and under cover of the vehicles' .50-caliber

An M60A1 main battle tank equipped with reactive armor and mine-clearing rollers and plows stands by at the head of a column of AAV-7 amphibious assault vehicles as the 2d Marine Division prepares to enter Kuwait.

Photo by SSgt Masters. Defense Imagery DM-ST-91-11590

Defense Imagery DM-ST-91-11583

Marine artillerymen from the 2d Marine Division fire their M198 155mm howitzer in support of the opening of the ground offensive to free Kuwait during Operation Desert Storm.

machineguns, attacked through volleys of grenades. Within 100 meters of the building, the platoon was pinned down by automatic weapons fire. The 3d Squad was ordered to attack the building while the rest of the platoon laid down covering fires. In open view of the Iraqis and under fire, Sergeant William J. Warren, leader of the 3d Squad, stood up and moved among his fire teams, giving orders and encouraging his men. He maneuvered his teams to within 20 meters of the building, and then led an assault through a hole in the fence. As the squad entered the building, the shaken Iraqi troops fled from it, seeking escape across the desert.[30]

Soon all of the assault battalions were facing similar skirmishes as the obstacle belt was pierced. Lieutenant Colonel Mroczkowski noted that

these early actions set the precedent for the next three days of the war. As elements of the division moved forward or approached objectives, they would encounter enemy resistance. But through rapid fire and maneuver,

the Iraqis were overwhelmed. By outflanking them constantly, destroying their heavy weapons with air and artillery fire, the division gave the Iraqis the choice of surrendering or dying where they stood. Thousands of them chose the former.[31]

All of 6th Marines' battalions proceeded through their objectives throughout the morning. By noon, they had advanced far enough for the division's armored and mechanized forces to begin moving through the breach. The 2d Tank Battalion had passed through by 1250; by 1600, the Tiger Brigade was passing through the lanes in force. The division halted its forward movement with the arrival of sunset. Most of Major General Keys's combat power had advanced through the minefields and was securing the breach head. On the left, Colonel John Sylvester's Tiger Brigade was preparing for the next northward advance. The 6th Marines held the center, and Lieutenant Colonel Cesare Cardi's 2d Tank Battalion held the left, which rested on the isolated, reportedly abandoned but not yet cleared al-Jaber Air Base, also known as "MEF Objective A." It was 1st Marine Division's task to seize and clear al-Jaber, so

Major General Keys contacted 1st Marine Division's Task Force Grizzly to ensure the flank was secure and merely screened that flank with a company-sized, humvee-mounted task force.[32]

The day's fighting cost the 2d Marine Division 14 casualties. Two of these casualties were deaths: Corporal Phillip J. Jones, 3d Battalion, 10th Marines, was killed when the breech mechanism of a howitzer misfired; the other death was a soldier from the Tiger Brigade. The 8th Tank Battalion's command chronology described the soldier's death in the following way: "Shortly after nightfall, a U.S. Army HMMWV [humvee] with three soldiers in it wandered into a nearby minefield and ran into an anti-personnel mine. . . . One soldier, the driver, was fatally injured and died shortly after the mine detonation. The gunner was injured and was medevaced [medically evacuated] from the battalion's Alpha Command area. The lieutenant, riding in the front seat, had minor injuries. . . . The death of the soldier weighed heavily on the battalion personnel involved in the rescue." Twelve Marines and soldiers were wounded during the day's advance.

Many Iraqis had been killed, but far more had surrendered, and the division had achieved all of its objectives for the first day of fighting.[33]

With Joint Forces Command–East and the Marines Afloat

As the Marines of the I Marine Expeditionary Force advanced through the defenses at the center of the Saudi-Kuwait border, Marines of 1st ANGLICO, 2d ANGLICO, and force reconnaissance supported the Saudi Arabian forces of Joint Forces Command–East as they advanced into Kuwait along the coastal highway.

Joint Forces Command–East, commanded by Major General Sultan 'Adi al-Mutairi, was organized into four task forces; three of these (Abu Bakr, Othman, and Omar) were named after the first three caliphs. The fourth, Tariq, was named for the Muslim conqueror of Spain. Abu Bakr Task Force comprised the 2d Saudi Arabian National Guard Brigade and an attached Qatari armored battalion. Othman Task Force was built around the 8th Mechanized Brigade of the Ministry of Defense and Aviation,

The battleship USS Wisconsin *(BB 64) fires a round from one of its 16-inch guns at Iraqi targets in Kuwait. In the first days of the ground war, the battleships—directed by Marine ANGLICO teams—often fired in support of the Saudi troops advancing along the coastal highway.*

Defense Imagery DN-SC-92-08659

Photo by GySgt C. Archuleta. Marine Corps History Division Reference Branch photo files
Cobra helicopters escort vehicles of 2d Battalion, 10th Marines, through a minefield breech. Cobra pilots closely supported the Marines on the ground during the advance through the Iraqi minefields.

with Bahraini and Kuwaiti infantry companies attached. Omar Task Force was built around the 10th Mechanized Brigade of the Ministry of Defense and Aviation and included an Omani infantry battalion. Tariq Task Force comprised two battalions of Saudi Arabian marines as well as Moroccan and Senegalese infantry battalions.[34]

The Saudi forces met no significant resistance, but they received extensive support from the two U.S. battleships firing at targets along the coast. Admiral Stanley Arthur used the battleships to continue the amphibious feint because they were strongly associated with an amphibious assault. After the war he remarked, "All I had to do was start moving the battleships . . . and then line General Jenkins and his fine Marines and our amphibs [amphibious ships] up behind them, and there was no doubt in anybody's mind that we were coming."[35]

Most of the battleships' 16-inch naval gunfire was directed at preplanned targets, but some spectacular direct support was also provided. On the first day, this came to the aid of the Joint Forces Command–East troops and Captain Douglas Kleinsmith of the 1st ANGLICO:

The Saudi battalion commander, a colonel, looked at him [Kleinsmith] incredulously. "You can call in the battleships?" he asked. "Yea[h]," answered Captain Kleinsmith, "That's why we're here." Kleinsmith contacted *Wisconsin* and the battleship opened fire. The captain heard the muted roar of her 16-inch

guns through his radio. The 43 seconds required for the first shell to reach its target seemed an eternity. Kleinsmith was beginning to wonder if he had transmitted the wrong coordinates when projectiles began to fall precisely where he wanted them. The Saudi marines stared in amazement as the 2,700 pound shells lifted whole houses into the air. "You can do this anytime?" asked the Saudi battalion commander. Kleinsmith replied in the affirmative. "Ah," exclaimed the colonel, "we can win now."[36]

The battleship support was somewhat irrelevant, however, because the Saudi advance encountered almost no resistance on the first day as it advanced into Kuwait and captured thousands of Iraqi prisoners.

Also on 24 February, the 5th Marine Expeditionary Brigade began moving ashore in order to fill the gap between the I Marine Expeditionary Force and Joint Forces Command–East. The brigade's 3d Battalion, 1st Marines, was helilifted directly to the south of the al-Wafrah oil field on the Saudi-Kuwaiti border, where it established a blocking position. Meanwhile, the rest of Colonel Randolph A. Gangle's Regimental Landing Team 5 began landing at the port of al-Mishab.

Air Operations

On 24 February, the Marine air-ground task force concept was operating according to Marine doctrine, as the 3d Marine Aircraft Wing's Harriers, Hornets, and Hornets, and Cobras provided close air support to the 1st and 2d Marine Divisions during the assault. This support was primarily focused on the artillery. The 1st Marine Division commander, General James Myatt, explained after the war that "between 0600 and 1400 on that first day, we had 42 instances of incoming artillery. . . . We were able to use our artillery to attack 24 of the 42 targets. The remainder were attacked by Marine AV-8B aircraft within a few minutes of the artillery fire being detected. I am very proud of that air-ground coordination."[37]

Even with the close air support calls, most Marine aircraft ended up shifting north to fly battlefield air interdiction missions during the busy first day of the war, and the Iraqi air defenses were not entirely supine. At 1010 Major Robert M. Knutzen and First Lieutenant Scott M. Quinlan of Marine Fighter Attack Squadron 314 were flying their F/A-18s north after attacking targets west of Kuwait City when they were each hit by Iraqi infrared guided surface-to-air missiles. Although each jet lost one engine, both aircraft returned safely to base and were successfully repaired.[38]

Not all of the 3d Marine Aircraft Wing's operations were successful on 24 February, however. Task Force Troy was intended to land an infantry battalion on the right flank of the 1st Marine Division after it had passed through the obstacle belts. Task Force Papa Bear was to secure Landing Zone

Sandy for the assault. A "one wave" assault was planned, utilizing over 50 CH-46 and CH-53 helicopters from Marine Aircraft Group 16. The helicopters were commanded by Marine Helicopter Squadron 165's commander, Lieutenant Colonel Marvin D. "Sam" Hall. His helicopters were to carry 132 troops and 40 vehicles from the 1st Battalion, 3d Marines, commanded by Lieutenant Colonel Michael V. Maloney. Because the crews were not trained for, or the helicopters equipped for, a night assault, the task force was scheduled to launch prior to 1645.[39]

In the event, the mission was ordered at 1740, and a dust cloud rose up in the launch area, causing a CH-46 to roll over, though all on board escaped severe injury. After takeoff, the task force reached the landing zone at 1800, finding "a battlefield active with burning wells, burning enemy tanks, machine-gun and antiaircraft fire, and Marine vehicles that milled about without any apparent sense of direction." The decision was made to abort the operation, and Task Force Troy made a confused, dangerous return to the Lonesome Dove airfield. Lieutenant Colonel Michael J. Aguilar, executive officer of Marine Aircraft Group 16 would later state: "The mission was never planned to be run as a night NVG [night-vision goggle] assault. The requirements to execute had not been met. In fact the aircrews were not qualified to do a night NVG assault. Only because of individual aviator skills did we avoid mul-

An F/A-18 Hornet of Marine Fighter Attack Squadron 314 during the Gulf War.
Marine Corps History Division Reference Branch photo files

tiple mid-air collisions, and I am not exaggerating that at all. Oh, there were a lot of people that came back with religion [after that mission]."[40]

In the morning on 24 February, Saddam Hussein noted at a command meeting that "the enemy continues to drown in his own blood and shame in front of our [frontline] units. . . . Despite all that took place, our faithful men were able to drive out the first surprise attack. . . . Generally, our units are in the best shape possible under this kind [of attack]. The enemy's attack has failed completely." The *III Corps* commander, Major General Salah Aboud Mahmoud, was better informed of events in Kuwait, but none of the Iraqi leaders appear to have realized how badly the first day of the Coalition attack had gone for the Iraqi forces. Even General Salah Aboud later noted that "in spite of the enemy's huge penetration to many locations . . . I made sure that the enemy's troops suffered the most casualties."[41]

25 February

On 25 February, the XVIII Airborne Corps' 24th Infantry Division advanced toward the Euphrates valley while the rest of the corps continued to screen to the north and west of the Coalition advance. The VII Corps continued its advance into southeastern Iraq as it drove across the desert toward the *Republican Guard*. As it advanced, the VII Corps de-

stroyed the divisions of the *VII Corps* charged with defending the Iraqi western flank as they were encountered.[42]

The Battle of Burqan

During the afternoon and evening of 24 February, General Salah Aboud revised his plan for a counterattack against the advancing Marines. The plan called for a pincer attack, with the *7th Infantry Division* attacking from the north into the 2d Marine Division's area of operations while the *5th Mechanized Division* attacked in the southwest, out of the al-Burqan oil field, with al-Jaber airfield as its objective. The *8th Infantry* and *3d Armored Divisions* would reestablish defensive lines behind the counterattack. The Iraqis began moving long before dawn on 25 February, slowed by extremely poor visibility in the smoke-filled night.[43]

Shortly after 0100, General Myatt was convinced from captured Iraqi maps, prisoner interviews, and radio intercepts that an Iraqi counterattack was imminent and that this attack could come "out of the fire" of the al-Burqan oil field. At this time, Task Force Shepherd was screening Task Forces Ripper and Papa Bear along the al-Burqan flank, but General Myatt's forward division headquarters was set up right next to the oil fields, with only Company C, 1st Battalion, 1st Marines, as a security force.

Marines of the 1st Marine Division board CH-46 helicopters. The blowing dust and poor visibility highlight the difficulties helicopters encountered in the desert.

Photo by LtCol Charles H. Cureton

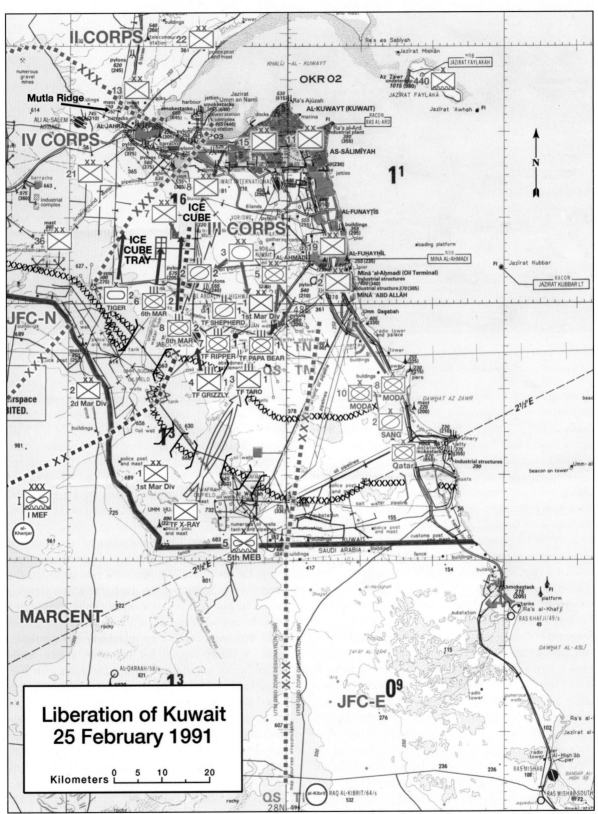

**Liberation of Kuwait
25 February 1991**

Kilometers

0   5   10   20

Adapted from a 1991 Ministry of Defence (United Kingdom) map by Marine Corps History Division

Photo courtesy of Capt Paul E. Bowen

Aerial view of a Marine force, comprising five M60A1 tanks and four AAV-7 amtracs plus HMMV support vehicles, advancing near al-Burqan oil field in Kuwait.

Company B of Task Force Shepherd was detached to reinforce the division headquarters. Captain Eddie S. Ray, Company B's commander, was disappointed and felt this new mission would leave his company out of the action on 25 February.[44]

The first Iraqi attacks came in the early dawn hours, as Task Force Shepherd's Company D and Task Force Ripper's 3d Tank Battalion engaged in an hour-long firefight with Iraqi armor and infantry. Five to 10 Iraqi tanks were destroyed before this first Iraqi assault was fended off. Staff Sergeant Joseph A. LeGarde was a section leader in the antitank company of the 3d Tank Battalion for this engagement. His Silver Star award citation describes his actions in the assault: "Early that morning, Staff Sergeant LeGarde moved his section forward of the battalion in response to a message indicating that enemy tanks were approaching. Positioning himself well forward, he identified two platoons of Iraqi tanks and one platoon of armored personnel carriers rapidly closing. Staff Sergeant LeGarde quickly directed his squads into their primary firing positions and without regard for his own safety, delivered suppressive fire from a heavy machinegun. From an exposed position, he maintained firm control over his squads and directed the identification, isolation, and destruction of five Iraqi tanks and one armored personnel carrier."[45]

While Task Force Ripper was fending off the initial thrust of the southwest pincer, the 2d Marine Division was destroying the north pincer of the Iraqi attack. This action was called the "Reveille Counterattack" by some. During the event, the armored columns of the Iraqi *7th Infantry* and *3d Armored Divisions* were met around 0620 by 1st Battalion, 8th Marines, and the attached Company B, 4th Tank Battalion.

Lance Corporal Chris A. Sweeney, then serving as an antitank missile gunner with Weapons Company, 1st Battalion, 8th Marines, was awarded the Silver Star for his actions in the fight. When the Iraqi assault began, Lance Corporal Sweeney "positioned his vehicle and within minutes destroyed two Iraqi tanks that were rapidly approaching the battalion's flank. Without regard for his own safety while under heavy small-arms and tank main gun fire, Lance Corporal Sweeney remained dangerously exposed for more than eleven seconds as he engaged and destroyed an enemy armored personnel carrier. Realizing his position had become untenable, he directed his vehicle into an abandoned enemy revetment and engaged and destroyed a third enemy tank. As the battalion continued its attack, Lance Corporal Sweeney observed several enemy tanks in hull-defilade positions in prepared revetments. Recognizing the imminent threat to the battalion, he quickly went into action destroying three enemy tanks with lightning speed."[46]

Company B, 4th Tank Battalion—a reserve unit—was equipped just before they departed for the Gulf with M1A1 Abrams main battle tanks. According to Colonel Charles Quilter, "The company [Company B] was stopped near the division boundary line about five miles north of the al-Jaber Airfield shortly before dawn at 0555 on the second day. The tankers were now surprised to hear, then see in their night vision devices, a formation of T-72s—Iraq's most formidable main battle tank—coming through a position of what turned out to be another formation of T-55 tanks that were dug into revetments. . . . In an action that lasted only a few minutes, the company destroyed or stopped 34 of 35 enemy tanks."[47]

At 0730, 1st Battalion, 1st Marines, began to move into the oil fields. Visibility was reduced to 200 meters or less, and the battalion moved forward very slowly. Then from 0750 to 0820, the 11th Marines fired massed, multibattalion artillery barrages on the suspected locations of the Iraqi *22d Brigade, 5th Mechanized Division,* and *15th Brigade, 3d Armored Division.*[48]

Meanwhile, as Task Force Papa Bear prepared for the day's actions, one of the war's more unique events occurred at its command post:

At 0800 Colonel Hodory and his staff were still briefing late arriving commanders when a T-55 tank and three Type-63 armored personnel carriers emerged from the fog and halted about 50 meters from where Colonel Hodory stood. The tank sat motionless with its gun perfectly sighted on Hodory's command vehicles. It never fired. Instead, the brigade commander came forward and surrendered to the astonished Marines. When questioned, he revealed that his force made up part of the *22d Brigade, 5th Mechanized Division* assigned to attack the American right flank. When questioned further, he explained that he no longer wished to fight nor did the group accompanying him. However, he could not speak for those behind him in the fog.[49]

The Iraqi colonel's brigade started attacking the command post even as Colonel Hodory was accepting the colonel's surrender. The task force operations officer, Major John H. Turner, recalled that "we had main gun rounds, machine gun tracers and even 5.56mm fire (from India 3/9 [3d Battalion, 9th Marines]) coming through the CP [command post]. I remember hitting the deck for the first time during the war and I saw tracers going through the CP from east to west at knee height." The headquarters

A Marine Corps M1A1 Abrams main battle tank equipped with a mine-clearing plow passes a truck in an abandoned Iraqi position. Marine tankers were very successful with the Abrams in the first Marine Corps combat service of the new tank.

Photo by SSgt Masters. Defense Imagery DM-ST-91-11623

Photo by LtCol Charles H. Cureton

Task Force Papa Bear's armored vehicles on 23 February, staging for the ground assault. During the Battle of Burqan, this task force's M60A1 tanks smashed an Iraqi armored brigade's counterattack.

Photo by LtCol Charles H. Cureton

An M60A1 of Task Force Papa Bear sits before a burning oil well. This photograph was taken in the afternoon, at approximately 1500.

element fought off the Iraqi attack. Two Marines, Corporal Bryan K. Zickefoose and Lance Corporal Michael S. Kilpatrick, both with 3d Battalion, 9th Marines, were instrumental in driving off this Iraqi counterattack. To achieve this, they employed AT-4 antitank rockets to destroy an Iraqi armored personnel carrier, and both were awarded the Silver Star for their actions.[50]

Informed by Colonel Hodory of the Iraqi counterattack, Task Force Papa Bear's 1st Tank Battalion—with Company I of the 3d Battalion, 9th Marines, attached—engaged the Iraqi brigade in a

classic armored clash and destroyed at least 18 Iraqi armored vehicles. This engagement continued for the next three hours.[51]

Inside the oil field, the 1st Battalion, 1st Marines, encountered the *15th Mechanized Infantry Brigade, 3d Armored Division*, at 0915. During the ensuing struggle, the battalion captured large numbers of Iraqi prisoners and destroyed multiple Iraqi armored vehicles.[52]

Despite events on the ground, the senior Iraqi commanders felt these initial attacks were successful. After the war, General Salah Aboud Mahmoud

Photo by Sgt Roberts. Marine Corps History Division Reference Branch photo files

Marine Cobra attack helicopters fly above light armored vehicles. Cobras and light armored vehicles worked together closely during the Battle of Burqan, driving off three different Iraqi attacks on the division headquarters.

recalled, "This action caused the enemy to withdraw from [the] battleground as our tanks were firing at the enemy tanks across the minefield while it was advancing to stop whatever was left of the penetration."[53]

At 0930, the first of the day's multiple Iraqi attacks on the 1st Marine Division's forward headquarters began:

The first hint that something was amiss occurred soon after Company B arrived. Commanded by Captain Eddie S. Ray, the company had just gotten into position when one of its LAVs suddenly fired into the fog. That caught everyone's attention. There had been no radio communication and a quick check showed the firing to have been the result of an accidental discharge. However, no sooner did the company commander complete his investigation than 100 Iraqi soldiers appeared wanting to surrender. Spooked by the 25mm gun fire, their arrival at a location already swept the previous day raised questions about what might be developing further out in the fog and smoke. At first, Marines around the command post could only hear the low sound and rumble of moving

tanks and vehicles. Then, the smoke and fog suddenly lifted to reveal an attacking force consisting of five T-55s, 33 armored personnel carriers, and some dismounted infantry.[54]

This attack led Second Lieutenant Thomas O. O'Connor, a platoon commander with Company C, 1st Battalion, 1st Marines, to sweep a tree line to establish security when "the five man team led by Second Lieutenant O'Connor came under an Iraqi mechanized attack, supported by dismounted infantry. Leading his team forward in the face of a numerically superior enemy, Second Lieutenant O'Connor positioned them in an unoccupied enemy bunker, where they were pinned down by accurate mortar, rocket-propelled grenades, heavy machinegun and 73mm fire. Sensing the grave situation facing his team and with total disregard for his own welfare, Second Lieutenant O'Connor maneuvered through intense enemy fire to a position on the enemy's flank, firing light antiarmor weapons and AT-4 Rockets . . . at the lead enemy elements, thus drawing fire onto himself and relieving his team."[55]

After an hour of fierce fighting, this first attack on the division command post was driven off.

Meanwhile, Task Force Papa Bear was continuing its destruction of the *22d Brigade, 5th Mechanized Division*. As the smoke began to clear, 3d Marine Aircraft Wing Cobras were able to make a more direct contribution to the fight. Corporal Bryan R. Freeman of the 1st Tank Battalion was awarded the Silver Star for his efforts in finding and designating targets for the Cobras.[56]

Only 15 minutes after the first attack had been repulsed, the Iraqis attacking the division command post had reorganized and launched a second attack. Captain Eddie Ray's Company B of Task Force Shepherd and Company C, 1st Battalion, 1st Marines, responded with a heavy dose of firepower that again drove the Iraqis away.[57]

In the meantime, the division's artillery was shifting to prepare for the next part of the offensive and was encountering its own Iraqi forces.

In the late morning as Battery A, 1st Battalion, 11th Marines, and the battalion command post moved to a new firing position, they came under automatic weapons fire from a group of Iraqi vehicles positioned to the northeast of them. The battery commander immediately ordered one gun into a hasty firing position to engage the enemy force with direct fire. It destroyed one vehicle and dispersed the remainder. An hour later, Sergeant Shawn Toney of Battery H, 3d Battalion, 14th Marines (a re-

The dark, overcast sky and burning oil wells beyond this Marine humvee illustrate the surreal conditions Marines faced during the Battle of Burqan on the morning of 25 February.

Photo by LtCol Charles H. Cureton

Photo courtesy of MGySgt Gregory L. Gillispie

Marines of 2d Platoon, Company A, 1st Reconnaissance Battalion, examine a captured Iraqi T-62 at al-Jaber airfield on 25 February 1991.

serve unit from Richmond, Virginia, attached to the 1st Battalion, 11th Marines), spotted two enemy multiple rocket launchers preparing to fire on Marine positions. He thought they were tanks but his gun commander, Sergeant Thomas Stark, IV, looked closer and confirmed that they were rocket launchers. After quickly swinging their guns on the vehicles and taking direct aim at point-blank range, the artillerymen put both launchers out of action with a combination of automatic weapons and direct fire from their M198 155mm howitzers.[58]

By 1100, 1st Tank Battalion controlled the battlefield. Remnants of the Iraqi force soon surrendered or withdrew north through the burning wells. In a fight lasting three hours, the battalion had successfully stopped an attack by two Iraqi Brigades (the *501st Brigade, 8th Infantry Division,* and the *22d Brigade, 5th Mechanized Division*). Fifty Iraqi tanks were disabled, 25 armored personnel carriers were destroyed, and 300 prisoners taken. There were no Marine casualties.

The third and final Iraqi attack was also launched against the 1st Marine Division headquarters. During this assault, "General Draude raised the side of the headquarters tent to provide command element staff with a panoramic view of the battlefield as Iraqi tanks and personnel carriers came under fire." This attack was again repulsed by the command post's security force, and in this final attack Iraqi losses were at least 2 tanks, 27 armored personnel carriers, and 300-plus captured soldiers. Captain

Ray was awarded the Navy Cross for his aggressive, skillful defense of the division headquarters,* one of only two awarded to Marines in the Gulf War.[59]

General Salah Aboud recalled that the Americans needed a heavy air raid just to "retain their positions." He believed it was "a heavy battle . . . [with] both sides suffering many casualties including armored vehicles and tanks."[60]

As Task Forces Papa Bear and Ripper reoriented themselves to continue the offensive after the Iraqi counterattack, Task Force X-Ray, whose helicopter insertion was postponed from the previous day, launched and inserted without incident. Task Force X-Ray landed just south of the second obstacle, and its ground element was then attached to Task Force Papa Bear. By 1830, Task Force X-Ray had moved through the second obstacle belt and was in its blocking position guarding the division's right flank.

At 1600, 1st Battalion, 1st Marines, reached its designated limit of advance, having destroyed 43 Iraqi vehicles and captured over 500 Iraqi soldiers during its advance. Three Marines of the battalion were wounded in the surreal fighting inside the burning oil fields. The Battle of Burqan was over, and the 1st Marine Division was prepared to continue the advance to Kuwait City.

Task Force Grizzly had been given the task of clearing al-Jaber airfield, but the darkness and various logistical issues slowed its passage through the second obstacle belt and its relief of 1st Battalion, 7th Marines. By 1600, however, the task force was prepared to begin its assault on the airfield, and at 1722, artillery barrages were launched against the airfield's defenses. The Iraqi *449th Artillery Brigade* replied with one of the most accurate Iraqi artillery barrages of the war, in which 12 Marines were wounded and Lance Corporal Brian L. Lane from 3d Battalion, 7th Marines, was killed. Despite this setback Task Force Grizzly pressed the attack into the airfield, encountered minimal resistance inside the perimeter wire, and by 2100 had cleared most of the field, with just a few buildings remaining.[61]

The Iraqi counterattack had impacted the 1st Marine division's plans:

> Instead of bypassing the al-Burqan Oilfield as originally decided—scientists said the burning wells produced toxins that made the area uninhabitable, thus it was seen as a barrier—the Iraqi attack proved that a large unit could operate and survive there. General Myatt had to

Marine Corps History Division Reference Branch photo files
An amtrac from the 2d Assault Amphibian Battalion attached to 2d Battalion, 4th Marines, advances through Kuwait with the 2d Marine Division.

adjust the advance of the division's right flank to encompass the oilfield.[62]

The division ended the day prepared to advance on a broad front against Kuwait International Airport, but poor visibility and blowing smoke prevented air support for a night attack and reduced the ground forces' visibility considerably as well. The division settled in to wait for the dawn.

Taking the Ice Cube Tray

After destroying the north pincer of the Iraqi counterattack in the morning, General Keys's 2d Marine Division continued the process of preparing for its northward advance. He placed his three maneuver elements on line, with the Tiger Brigade on the left (with an unguarded flank, since the Egyptian, Syrian, and Saudi Arabia forces of Joint Forces Command–North advanced very slowly), the 6th Marines in the center, and the 8th Marines on the right. The 2d Light Armored Battalion screened the right flank between the two divisions.

At 1315, 2d Marine Division started its attack north toward the "Ice Cube Tray" and the "Ice Cube" (built-up areas named after the way they appeared on maps). The Marines and soldiers of the division fought skirmishes all the way north:

> A platoon of tanks from Company C, 8th Tank Battalion was attached to Company C, 1st Battalion, 6th Marines. This platoon's experiences were representative of the actions across the division's front on this day. Commanded by Chief Warrant Officer-2 Charles D. Paxton, the tanks encountered several Iraqi tanks and armored personnel carriers soon after crossing the line. The platoon quickly destroyed seven

---

*See appendix D for the complete citation.

tanks and four of the APCs [armored personnel carriers], all the while continuing the momentum of the attack. When smoke and fog reduced visibility to only 200 meters, enemy targets had to be engaged at close range. Nevertheless, Chief Warrant Officer Paxton continued to press his platoon forward, destroying another six tanks and two ZSU 23-4 antiaircraft guns before consolidating his own defense for the night.[63]

By sunset, or what passed for sunset in the oil-smoke-filled, burning Kuwaiti oil fields, 2d Marine Division had reached Phase Line Horse and was prepared for its planned assault on the Mutla Ridge and al-Jahwarh the next day. As with the 1st Marine Division, the 2d Marine Division faced a very, very dark night. Many Iraqis continued to surrender en masse to the Marines, but there were some unexpected firefights. Corporal Robert Novak found himself in such a fight, much like that he faced the previous day. His platoon was "screening forward of the battalion when it encountered, at close range, six enemy armored personnel carriers. He directed his squad to firing positions and then began employing his own weapon, quickly destroying three enemy armored personnel carriers." He was awarded the Silver Star

for his continual calm leadership and actions under fire.[64]

As the 1st and 2d Marine Divisions fought through the Iraqi defenses on 25 February, Lieutenant General Walter Boomer left the I Marine Expeditionary Force (Forward) headquarters in a mobile command post built around two command-variant light armored vehicles and comprised of 48 Marines and one news reporter, Molly Moore of the *Washington Post*. After passing through the lanes in the minefields, General Boomer's mobile command post linked up with 2d Marine Division. Boomer's convoy had a scare shortly after 2200 that evening, southwest of the Ice Cube Tray, when it was suddenly surrounded by Iraqi soldiers trying to surrender.[65]

Molly Moore later described the scene: "On the second night of the war, the command convoy was suddenly surrounded by armed Iraqis. Confused radiomen screamed warnings about 'dismounted infantry!' Some Iraqis appeared ready to surrender; others remained prone behind sand berms with rifles pointed toward the convoy. It turned out that the Iraqis were indeed surrendering, but the convoy was immobilized for three hours while the Marines rounded them up."[66]

General Boomer's convoy continued on through the night, but it was a nerve-wracking advance:

Gen Boomer's mobile I Marine Expeditionary Force command post near Khanjar, Saudi Arabia.

Photo courtesy of Capt Paul E. Bowen

Photo by Sgt Charles G. Grow. Defense Imagery DM-SD-00-01223

A Marine Corps OV-10A Bronco at King Abdul Aziz airfield, with AV-8B Harriers in the background. Two Broncos were shot down during the Gulf War.

When the convoy finally began to move again, the inky darkness created by the thick layers of oily smoke forced traffic directors carrying faint red flashlights to physically walk the hulking armored vehicles and trucks through fields of mines and unexploded bombs.

The movements became so treacherous that the convoy finally pulled into a small campsite that had been cleared of explosives. As armed Humvees formed a safety circle around a small patch of sand, their drivers warned us not to step beyond the ring because of the mine dangers, Marines began setting up a makeshift radio command center. Forbidden to use any light except dim red filters because of fear of discovery by enemy troops, the young Marines worked by feel in virtual blindness.[67]

Air Operations

In the predawn hours of 25 February, 13th Marine Expeditionary Unit (Special Operations Capable) conducted a helicopter feint in the Ash Shu'aybah area, attempting to convince the Iraqis that an amphibious landing was occurring there. The flight included six CH-46Es, two AH-lWs, one CH-53E, and one UH-1N; the helicopters flew in low and deliberately "popped up" to be detected by Iraqi radar at 0449 before returning safely to USS *Okinawa*. Combined with the battleships' naval gunfire, the operation appeared to be a success.[68]

Hampered by the weather and the smoke from the burning oil fields, the 3d Marine Aircraft Wing nonetheless pushed its support of the Marines on the ground, delivering close air support when called on. Two aircraft were lost during this push to support the ground troops. One of these was a downed AV-8B piloted by Captain John S. Walsh of Marine Attack Squadron 542. One of two Harriers attacking a column of Iraqi tanks, Captain Walsh was struck by a heat-seeking surface-to-air missile in his right rear jet nozzle. "It was a big bang. All my warning lights came on, and the airplane began burning pretty good," he recalled later. Walsh flew to al-Jaber Air Base to try an emergency landing, but his controls froze and the aircraft rolled. He ejected successfully and was recovered by Task Force Ripper, and he was even able to rejoin his squadron that evening.[69]

The other aircraft loss was less fortunate. Major Joseph J. Small III and Captain David M. Spellacy of Marine Observation Squadron 1 were flying an OV-10A Bronco when it was struck by an infrared surface-to-air missile. Captain Spellacy was killed, and Major Small was captured. The Iraqis believed this was a major intelligence coup; General Salah Aboud later recalled that "we downed an enemy helicopter that had two pilots. One of them died inside the chopper and the other one was brought [to us] at the airport. The surviving pilot was carrying on him the [American] plan of the attack." Major Small was beaten by the Iraqis and sent to Baghdad. The "plan of attack" was apparently the aircraft's flight map. Major Small later recalled that "the biggest grandest lie I think I've ever told in my entire life" was the source for the Iraqi belief that they had acquired the American battle plan.[70]

With the Joint Forces Command–East

As the Marines of I Marine Expeditionary Force fought the Battle of Burqan inland, the Marines from the air-naval gunfire liaison companies continued to fight alongside the Saudi Arabians and other Coalition Muslim partners with Joint Forces Command–East. Most of the Iraqi forces surrendered quickly along the coast, but there were still pockets of resistance, and the minefields that the Iraqis laid remained a danger whether the defenders fired or not. In one instance, the minefields and a rare active Iraqi defense demonstrated what might have been if the entire Saddam Line had been held by determined defenders.

Captain David W. Landersman was a fire control officer with a supporting arms liaison team attached to the Saudi Arabian 10th Mechanized Brigade. On 25 February, during the brigade's advance, Landersman was with the brigade's artillery battalion when he discovered that "[the Saudi officers] had placed an entire artillery battalion on line, in the most beautiful parade sequence you could possibly imagine, 1,500 meters from the objective, in the middle of a minefield." The Iraqis began to fire on the battalion with direct and indirect fire, but Landersman "took command and began removal of all personnel and equipment to a new position. Without regard for his own safety, Captain Landersman repeatedly exposed himself to enemy fire, coolly reorganized the battalion and moved them out of the minefield. As this process was complete, the trail elements came under attack by several Iraqi tanks. Captain Landersman realizing the gravity of the situation, again exposed himself by boarding an abandoned howitzer and fired on the attackers. He personally destroyed the lead tank, disabled at least one other, and forced the enemy to withdraw."[71]

Captain Landersman was awarded the Silver Star for his actions in the minefield, but that was not his most personal fight that day. That fight came later when he and his team were forced to clear some Iraqi trenches, after the minefield incident:

I caught something out of the corner of my eye, so I look back in the trench and there is to my left, 10 meters, maybe, down at the end of the trench, this Iraqi first lieutenant with an AK-47 [assault rifle] at low port. . . . I thought, if I just get my hand on my 9-millimeter pistol, I'm going to own this guy. And just about the time my hand reached, he came up to a high port. So we had a very short exchange. I started shooting and then two Iraqi soldiers sort of stick their heads up, and I'm shooting, and I'm going, two in the chest, one in the head, two in the chest, one in the head, and the guy's not moving. I'm just like, why did we go to 9 millimeter? That's exactly what I said. And I saw one guy stand up and I rolled to one side of the trench and I shot, and he went immediately down. And then the other guy is standing there and he kind of shot across the side of the trench. . . . This guy shot across in front of me and I rolled over, shot him. I got two shots out before he went down and then I went back and I thought, "I'm about ready to go black." My slide locks, I pull out the magazine, put another magazine in and keep shooting, and I'm starting to walk forward. And it's at that point where [my staff sergeant] reaches across and touches me on the shoulder and said, "Jesus, Skipper, I think you got him."[72]

After a long day of fighting, it was obvious even to the Iraqi high command that Iraq's defense of Kuwait had failed:

By the afternoon of the 25th, remnants of the *III Corps* fell back into Kuwait City and, according to its commander, "organized a plan to fight from the city's border and from inside the city in cooperation with the Gulf Operations Command." At this point in the battle for Kuwait, the *III Corps* commander reported to Baghdad that the *7th, 14th,* and *29th [Infantry] Divisions* were combat ineffective. He ordered his remaining divisions to re-establish a defensive line close to Kuwait City. However, before any significant movement occurred, the *III Corps* commander received a broken message that Saddam had ordered all remaining units to withdraw toward al-Basra "to cover the border [area] so we can distribute our divisions within the [Iraqi] cities."[73]

CHAPTER 10

Liberating Kuwait

26 February

On the far right of the Coalition forces, the XVIII Airborne Corps pushed forward to the Euphrates valley, led by the U.S. Army's 24th Infantry Division (Mechanized). The 24th Division fought against the heaviest resistance it faced during the war but overcame the Iraqis. Farther east, the VII Corps completed the destruction of the Iraqi *VII Corps*, capturing its headquarters and massive logistics bases. In the afternoon, the U.S. Army's 2d Armored Cavalry Regiment, at the tip of the VII Corps' advance, contacted the *12th Armored Division* and the *Republican Guard's Tawakalna Division*. In a four-hour engagement later named the Battle of 73 Easting, the cavalry regiment destroyed the units facing it. To the south, the British 1st Armored Division began a series of running battles against the *48th Infantry* and *52d Armored Divisions* as they advanced up the Wadi al-Batin.[1]

Surrounding Kuwait International Airport

On the morning of 26 February, the 1st Marine Division advanced northwards, with Task Force Ripper on the left, Task Force Papa Bear in the center, and Task Force Shepherd passing through the oil fields on the division's right. The 11th Marines' artillery battalions followed the mechanized task forces in trace, prepared to provide artillery support as required. Task Force Grizzly continued clearing al-Jaber, a process slowed by the numerous pieces of unexploded aerial ordnance found around the airfield.

Task Force Ripper advanced rapidly northward. Moving across a landscape covered in destroyed or abandoned Iraqi fighting vehicles, it was difficult to tell them apart from the crewed enemy tanks that appeared occasionally and were quickly destroyed in a small skirmish. The task force came up with an ingenious system to determine which type of vehicle was which:

> In Task Force Ripper, 3d Tank Battalion tested Iraqi vehicles with long-range machine gun fire to see if the enemy responded. If it did, a tank round or TOW [tube-launched, optically tracked, wire-guided] missile followed and dispatched the Iraqi vehicle. The infantry battalions led with their scout detachments, which used TOW thermal sights to determine whether the enemy vehicle gave a "hot" or a "cold" signature. If the Iraqi vehicle or tank had its systems turned on and registered "hot" as a result, they engaged it. The frequent firefights interrupted the rapid advance with numerous stops and starts.[2]

Lieutenant Colonel James Mattis's 1st Battalion,

Light armored vehicles from Task Force Shepherd move forward during a break in the generally poor visibility that characterized 26 February 1991. The vehicles are approaching the power lines southwest of Kuwait International Airport.
Marine Corps History Division Reference Branch photo files

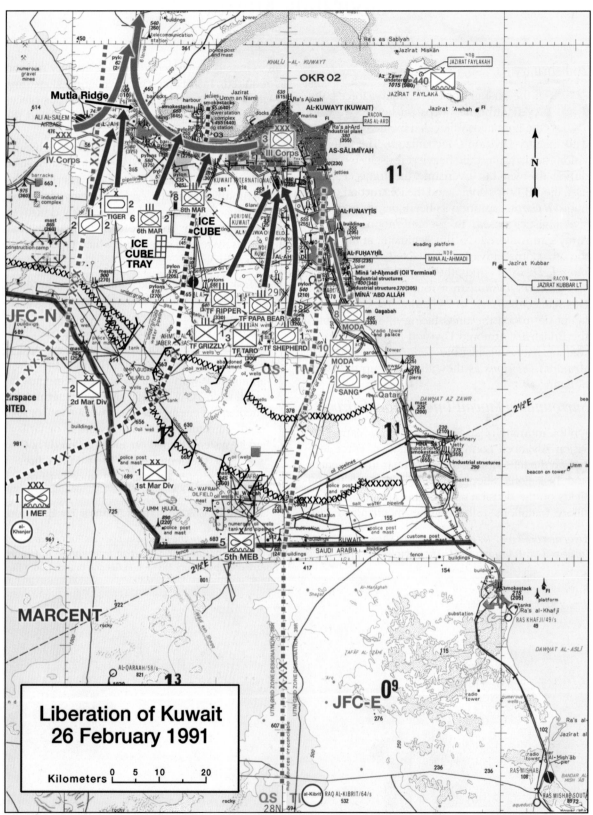

**Liberation of Kuwait
26 February 1991**

Kilometers 0 5 10 20

Adapted from a 1991 Ministry of Defence (United Kingdom) map by Marine Corps History Division

Marine Corps Art Collection

"Ripper" in MOPP-4 *by Col H. Avery Chenoweth. This painting highlights the encumbering nature of the chemical protective suits worn by Marines in response to the gas alert. There were four levels of mission-oriented protective posture or "MOPP"; MOPP-4 was the highest.*

7th Marines, found its way blocked by a pair of large quarries that did not appear on the maps. They turned out to house small bands of Iraqi soldiers who continued to fight, slowing the battalion as it tried to speed to the airport. The battalion slowed even more when a false gas warning sent the Marines scrambling for their gas masks and chemical protection suits:

> Upon reaching the LOA [line of advance] the Battalion stopped to await further orders from Task Force Ripper. Sporadic small arms fire was taken by CAAT 2 [combined antiarmor team 2] from a small built up area 600 meters northwest of the Battalion. The "Chicken Force," as one Marine called it, was immediately engaged with .50[-]cal[iber machine guns], MK-19 [grenade launchers] and LAAWs [light antiarmor weapons]. Additionally, 60mm and 81mm mortars as well as "danger close" artillery fires were brought to bear on the enemy. The sporadic enemy small arms fire

ceased. Moments after the indirect fires stopped, darkness once again engulfed the day as clouds of black smoke rolled over the Battalion around 1510. "Gas, Gas, Gas" was called over Battalion TAC I seconds after Task Force Ripper reported gas at their position. [The] 1/7 Marines calmly donned and cleared their masks while the NBC [nuclear, chemical, biological] Officer, Chief Warrant Officer Larry Snyder, once again went to work and tested our area for contamination. After negative readings were observed, the "all clear" call was given by Lieutenant Colonel Mattis, and the Battalion prepared to continue its attack.[3]

The sporadic Iraqi resistance and the terrain slowed the battalion's advance but did not halt it, and Mattis's unit cleared the quarries and had positioned itself to take the airfield on order by the end of the day.[4]

Task Force Papa Bear began an hour later than Task Force Ripper but passed through a similar landscape of destroyed and abandoned Iraqi armor interspersed with crowds of surrendering Iraqi soldiers and pockets of Iraqi resistance. Task Force Papa Bear responded to the problem of stationary Iraqi armor that may or may not be playing possum much as Task Force Ripper did, although 1st Tank Battalion did use thermite grenades on some abandoned Iraqi tanks.[5]

By 1300, both mechanized task forces were preparing to march north, but they expected the second half of the advance to be more vigorously defended then the first half. Major General James Myatt met with the task force commanders to issue new orders, and by 1600 the task forces were on the move again.

Task Force Ripper ran into problems very quickly when Mattis's battalion encountered three bands of wire obstacles and minefields. A hasty breech had to be accomplished, which was made more difficult by the increasing smoke and a rising sandstorm. Eventually the position was forced, and the task force assumed a blocking position to the northwest of the airport. Visibility was so poor that Kuwait City, on the other side of the highway, was not visible to the Marines of Task Force Ripper.

Task Force Papa Bear's assault on the right ran into similar issues. Skirting the northern portion of al-Burqan oil field, the task force traveled in two columns. The near-zero visibility and sandstorm hindered the task force's advance and "slowed its movement to a crawl around the wells, pipelines,

Photo by LtCol Charles H. Cureton

Task Force Papa Bear on the morning of 26 February, preparing for a third day of battle.

Photo by LCpl R. Price. Defense Imagery DM-SN-93-02272

AAV-7 amphibious assault vehicles of the 1st Marine Division advance toward Kuwait City on 26 February 1991. An AH-1 Sea Cobra helicopter can be seen flying in the background.

and the occasional oil lakes." After passing the field and breeching two wire obstacle belts, the task force found itself facing a defensive position before the airfield. The Iraqi *20th Infantry Regiment, 3d Armored Division*, had a complex of bunkers, armored personnel carriers, and tanks, but like most Iraqi soldiers during the advance, the majority of the defenders chose to surrender. At 2300, the task force had cut through the perimeter fence of the

airport and established a small toehold in the airfield's perimeter.[6]

By 2100, the 1st Tank Battalion was in its position for the evening, on the airfield's perimeter road on the right flank of the task force. Meanwhile, Task Force Papa Bear's engineering detachment was establishing a night position about half a mile south of the road. A shift in the wind cleared visibility considerably, and shortly before 2200, Iraqis on the

Last Tank Battle, Kuwait Airport *by Col H. Avery Chenoweth. The 1st Marine Division's firefight outside the airport on the night of 26 February presented a surreal, flaming landscape and involved some of the last armored actions fought by Marines in the Gulf War.*

airport highway to the north opened fire with rocket-propelled grenades, mortars, and machine guns on the combat engineers' positions. The combat engineers and their attached tanks and amphibious assault vehicles quickly fired back. During the firefight, one of the assault amphibians pivoted to bring its weapons to bear. Lance Corporal John E. Waldron of Company A, 7th Engineer Support Battalion, was too close to the assault amphibian and was caught in the tracks; he died instantly. Captain John M. Allison, the combat engineer detachment's deputy commander, was shot in the face during the firefight.[7]

Lieutenant Colonel Charles Cureton, 1st Marine Division's field historian, was present for this fight and later wrote a detailed description of the event. It was much like the scattered firefights that took place across the division on the night of 26–27 February:

Once Captain Allison finished placing the ve-hicles, the engineer task force commander, Major Joseph I. Musca, held a leader's brief in his AAV [amphibious assault vehicle] to establish radio procedures, the watch schedule, the enemy situation, and other relevant items. When the meeting ended 20 minutes later Major Musca discovered that a sudden shift in wind direction not only improved visibility, but also enabled the flames from nearby wells to illuminate every vehicle in the task force, except for the three tanks.

Allison felt good about being able to see again, but the unit's exposed situation troubled him as he walked the perimeter a few minutes later, checking positions. Tempering uneasiness with the knowledge that fighting was virtually over, he cut across the circle of AAVs. Suddenly, a series of explosions from mortar fire, instantly followed by RPG [rocket propelled grenade] and heavy machine-gun fire, poured in on him. The next few minutes passed in a blur. He noticed that the enemy fire was coming from the airport highway to the north, while it was the AAVs and tank nearest the Iraqis returning fire. As an AAV next to Captain Allison pivoted to bring its gun to bear he saw a combat engineer get caught under its tracks. Fearing that the Marine was dead, Captain Allison ran to get assistance. He had gone only a few feet when a sledgehammer blow across his face knocked him down. Dazed and bleeding from a machine gun round through the face, Allison crawled to the dubious shelter of one of the obstacle clearing detachment AAVs. There, he removed his bulky chemical suit and ran to the command vehicle where he hoped to get medical attention for the combat engineer, and now for himself.

Inside the command AAV, Major Musca had already started coordinating return fire. Concerned over the proximity of adjacent Marine units, Musca held his tanks in checkfire. Sitting in darkness, the three M60A1s had been ignored by the attackers and their commanders used their night sights to track Iraqi movement and acquire targets. Of the three, Musca cleared only "Phambo 07" to fire. In almost the same moment that Captain Allison was wounded, Corporal Duchoa Pham, the tank commander, destroyed an armored personnel

carrier with two well-aimed shots. Corporal Pham explained, "I meant to hit the target with HE [high explosive] but was so excited that I forgot [and fired SABOT (an antitank round)]. The first round went right through the vehicle without damaging it. The second round must have hit something sensitive because the whole vehicle exploded with a flash."[8]

The firefight continued in intensity as these Iraqis put up a tougher fight than most, continuing the firefight even after one of their armored personnel carriers was destroyed. The survivors finally fled after another 15 minutes of intense fire.[9]

Task Force Shepherd advanced through the east side of the al-Burqan oil fields, destroying Iraqi forces sporadically along the way but encountering relatively light resistance. By 1700, the light armored infantry had passed by the east side of the airport and established itself near the Kuwaiti racetrack. By 1830, it had established contact with Kuwaiti resistance fighters who reported the city largely empty of Iraqi troops. At 2230, Major General Myatt ordered Task Force Shepherd to take Kuwait International Airport. By 2300, the light armored vehicles of the light armored infantry were advancing on the airport from the east.[10]

Task Force Taro encountered the same lack of visibility, difficult terrain, and large number of surrendering Iraqis as the other Marine task forces.

In Flank Threat by Col H. Avery Chenoweth, Marines have sprung into action from a light armored vehicle to secure the flank as enemy are spotted. The terrain is littered with knocked-out enemy vehicles.

Marine Corps Art Collection

Photo by SSgt J. L. Roberts. Defense Imagery 0338-18-9

M1A1 Abrams tanks of the 2d Marine Division sit menacingly in the desert. With the Army's Tiger Brigade and a Marine armored battalion attached to each of its two regimental combat teams, it was one of the most armored divisions in Marine Corps history.

Colonel John Admire later explained, "We had procured sufficient transport, especially by aggressively ferrying our units forward unit by unit, that we continued our attack and advance without interruption. . . . General Myatt personally radioed me and ordered us to halt for the evening while the division repositioned units for the final assault into Kuwait City the next day. We halted on the general's orders, however, [and] immediately began preparations throughout the night for continuing the attack the next morning."[11]

Mutla Ridge

Major General Keys recognized that the Iraqis were now trying to flee Kuwait rather than trying to defend it, and he resolved to take advantage of the flight to destroy all the Iraqi military power that his division could as the Iraqis left the relative safety of bunkers and revetments. The 6th Marines advanced to the main highway interchange out of Kuwait City and established a blocking position, fighting some small skirmishes along the way. The 8th Marines was ordered to take an Iraqi barracks to the northeast and defend against any Iraqi counterattack out of Kuwait City.

In August, Iraqi *Republican Guard* tanks had raced to take Mutla Ridge to the west of the capital and seal the fate of Kuwait. Now the U.S. Army's 1st (Tiger) Brigade, 2d Armored Division, was racing to the same position from the opposite direction in order to seal the fate of the Iraqi army. A U.S. Army history of the Gulf War notes, "By occupying

the ridge, the brigade could seal a major crossroads and slam the door on Iraqi columns escaping north to Baghdad."[12]

The brigade began its race for Mutla Ridge at 1200 with the 3d Battalion, 67th Armor, in the lead, destroying Iraqi armor and fighting positions along the way. Shortly after the war, Colonel John Sylvester described the Tiger Brigade's attack on Mutla Ridge to a field historian:

At noon we did attack, and at that point I did not concern myself with maintaining a good length with the 6th [Marine] Regiment on my flank. I trusted the boundary and I went as fast as I could go to get them up there. And that attack, in time, turned into, on occasion, 45 and 50 mile an hour tank assaults across the desert. My two lead battalions breached the initial points on their initial objectives simultaneously, and there was an awful lot of armor at that point fleeing Kuwait City. There were many, many kills of tanks and BTRs [Russian armored personnel carriers] and other types of personnel carriers that were moving around the six-ring road and on various roads, the al-Salami Road that went past Ali al-Salem airfield. There was an awful lot of equipment moving. As they moved in they were rapidly killing everything that they could see.

And my instructions at that time changed. I told them to kill every mechanical piece of equipment that they saw—whether it was a tank, a truck, a howitzer, or a bicycle—to take it out with direct fire. All enemy dismounted soldiers, unless they were engaging, were to be bypassed and waived on to the rear and to go as fast as they could move. And there were literally thousands of enemy soldiers marching to the rear, running to the rear and attempting to stop vehicles. And we didn't stop. We just waived them on. And I'm sure they were bewildered by all of that. . . . But of course they were a dispirited enemy. They were broken. They had no further intent to fight.[13]

As the brigade neared its objective, it came upon a final position that had to be taken: the al-Mutla police post. Colonel Sylvester described the fight for the police station:

That particular battalion then accomplished the hardest physical fight of this conflict. The police post itself was manned, the building was manned with about 40 soldiers, all determined to hold the building. The high ground immediately to the north and east was dominated by enemy infantry and armor. There was a lot of enemy armor that had caused a bypass around the great huge traffic jam that was caused by the Air Force bombing, on what we called "Death Road" up there where

there were in fact three or four thousand dead, dying vehicles, and many, many hundreds of dead and wounded Iraqis. And that was indeed a scene from hell, particularly at night. They were moving vehicles in there. As the tanks engaged and killed them, of course they flared and burned. There were a number of burning vehicles already. The building was immediately behind a number of burning vehicles. The building had to be cleared by dismounted troops. They had to move in and around the burning and exploding vehicles. And there was an awful lot of very heroic stuff going on by some soldiers in that particular operation. They had to control that high ground.[14]

Lieutenant Colonel Dennis Mroczkowski, the 2d Marine Division's field historian, recounted the results of the attack: "At this time, Company C crossed the road to clear the police station. The fighting here had to be done room by room; when it was over, 40 Iraqis had been killed or made prisoner. But it was here that the Tiger Brigade suffered its own second loss. While assisting in positioning the command post, the battalion's master gunner, Sergeant First Class Harold R. Witzke, was shot by a sniper and died while awaiting evacuation."[15]

After two days of creeping through minefields,

A pair of Tiger Brigade M1A1 Abrams main battle tanks and an M2 Bradley infantry fighting vehicle near al-Jahra after the Operation Desert Storm cease-fire.

Photo by SSgt J. R. Ruark. Defense Imagery DM-SC-93-05269

Photo by PO1 Olson, USN. Defense Imagery DN-ST-91-06878

A Super Cobra from Marine Light Attack Helicopter Squadron 269 lands on the flight deck of the amphibious assault ship USS Nassau. *The squadron flew many missions during Operation Desert Storm, culminating with providing close air support to the Marine offensive in Kuwait.*

oil fields, obstacle belts, and crowds of Iraqi soldiers trying to surrender, the brigade had finally gotten the opportunity to advance at speed against the enemy. Holding Mutla Ridge, the highest point in Kuwait, they dominated the routes out of Kuwait and could fire on Iraqi military forces withdrawing from the city. The result did not disappoint, as the official Army history recounts: "They could see hundreds of burning and exploding vehicles, including civilian automobiles, buses, and trucks. Hundreds more raced west out of Kuwait City to unknowingly join the deadly traffic jam. Here and there, knots of drivers, Iraqi soldiers, and refugees fled into the desert because of the inferno of bombs, rockets, and tank fire. These lucky ones managed to escape and join the ranks of the growing army of prisoners."[16]

Late on the night of 26–27 February, at the I Marine Expeditionary Force mobile command post, located with the 2d Marine Division, a humorous incident ended the day of battle and was later recounted by Molly Moore: "[Lieutenant General Walter] Boomer was awakened by a frustrated voice outside his tent: "It's the [expletive] president. He's trying to reach the [expletive] CG [commanding general] and we can't get a [expletive] connection!" "As smart as these kids are," Boomer said later,

"sometimes you'd think they know only one word."[17]

Air Operations

On 25 February, General Boomer asked Admiral Stanley Arthur to transfer the amphibious landing force's AH-1W Super Cobra attack helicopters to 3d Marine Aircraft Wing. The smoky, night-like conditions of the battlefield made this difficult, but the AH-1W's AGM-114 Hellfire air-to-surface missiles and laser range-finders were perfect for this environment. Marine Light Attack Helicopter Squadron 269 transferred six Super Cobras ashore. They flew 22 combat missions from the Lonesome Dove expeditionary airfield.[18]

The smoke made close air support missions extremely difficult as the Marine divisions marched on Kuwait International Airport and Mutla Ridge, respectively. As a result, Marine air concentrated on the highways leading out of Kuwait, which were clear of the smoke and choked with targets. Misnamed the "Highway of Death" (there was much equipment destruction, but relatively little loss of Iraqi life on the road), these roads were filled with the Iraqi military forces fleeing Kuwait, many of whom were taking their loot with them.[19]

Colonel Sylvester of the Tiger Brigade, which

A Marine Corps Cobra helicopter in flight during the Gulf War.

prevented the remaining Iraqis in Kuwait City from passing down the highway on 26 February, described what was discovered there:

> Vehicles kept coming into it, and it became like a stopped up sink—things kept piling up and piling up and piling up. And ultimately there were literally thousands of vehicles in there, fully half of which were enemy combat vehicles and half of which were looted and stolen. Everything from school buses to ambulances, to brand new automobiles. Every single vehicle stuffed with the loot of the city. Jewelry and furniture and clothes and people's personal belongings, and you name it and it was there. Along with, in every vehicle that I saw, military paraphernalia. And all the vehicles were hot-wired. Even the ambulances were full of loot and booty. And it was very obvious that what was stopped at that particular point was the literal theft of the city.[20]

Despite the difficulties, Marine aviators made heroic efforts to provide air support to the Marines on the ground. Commanding Marine Light Attack Helicopter Squadron 369, Lieutenant Colonel Michael M. Kurth was awarded the Navy Cross for his efforts on 26 February.* He led four of his squadron's Cobras north to the recently captured al-Jaber airfield, where they landed and awaited his solo scouting mission:

> Soon the smoke became so dense, [Kurth] was forced to fly only a few feet off the ground in

order to see, occasionally flying UNDER power lines, until he located 1st Battalion, 5th Marines, and then shortly, 3d Tank Battalion and 1st Battalion, 7th Marines. He then returned to his informal landing zone, wheedled fuel out of some nearby Marine tanker trucks, and then led his wingman back through the obscuration where they delivered Hellfire missiles, rockets, and 20mm rounds against tanks, armored vehicles, and bunkers.[21]

Lieutenant Colonel Kurth flew for 10 hours on 26 February, repeating this process over and over again, ensuring that the Marines on the ground had the required air support.[22]

Another aerial operation took place on 26 February, when the air component of the 4th Marine Expeditionary Brigade, Marine Aircraft Group 40, launched an aerial feint. Similar in concept to the feint launched on 25 February but larger in size, this operation was directed at Bubiyan Island. The Marines sent 10 CH-46s, 4 CH-53s, and 3 AH-1s on the mission. Flying low over the ocean in extremely poor flying conditions, the entire flight was made using night-vision goggles. Just before dawn the helicopters rose suddenly in the air to simulate a helicopter assault and fired tracers from their .50-caliber machine guns to attract Iraqi attention. The Iraqis responded with a heavy volume of antiaircraft fire, much of it tracers as well, and with a large number of flares. Thus illuminated, they were attacked by a flight of Navy A-6E Intruders flying as part of the mission.[23]

At the same time, Marine Light Attack Helicopter Squadron 269 attacked Az Zwar on Faylakah Island with a flight of six UH-1Ns. The six Hueys strafed

---

*See appendix D for the complete citation.

Marine Corps History Division Reference Branch photo files

Marines guard Iraqi prisoners of war during the Gulf War. The sheer number of surrendering Iraqi soldiers presented tactical and logistical challenges to the Marines, but they were a strong indication of how unpopular the war was with the Iraqi people.

the target with rockets and machine guns before returning to their base, the USS *Nassau*.[24]

Iraqi Prisoners of War

The thousands of Iraqi soldiers the Marines had taken prisoner in the first two days of fighting continued to be a problem. These prisoners of war had to be provided with food and water, searched for weapons, interrogated, and transported to the rear areas safely. Central Command had planned for the prisoners to be given to the Army for processing, but the numbers were far higher than expected, and the process became a large strain on the logistics system that the Direct Support Command was using to pump food, water, fuel, and ammunition through the lanes cut in the obstacles and minefields to the two Marine divisions.

On 26 February, 5th Marine Expeditionary Brigade's 3d Battalion, 1st Marines, was attached to 2d Marine Division to aid in processing the thousands of prisoners the division had taken during the northward advance. The battalion was helilifted to the area known as the Ice Cube Tray and spent the next two days processing the starving, thirsty Iraqi prisoners.[25]

The Direct Service Command trucked the prisoners out of Kuwait to temporary holding pens; a temporary holding pen was constructed at Khanjar, the combat service support area, when the overcrowding problem became apparent. Drivers and transportation were then scrounged up by the Direct Service Command's assistant chief of staff for operations, Lieutenant Colonel John A. O'Donovan, who gathered volunteers from the support troops, including women Marines, to act as drivers and guards. Small convoys then began driving north to the minefields and returning with loads of Iraqi prisoners. By the end of

the day on 26 February, Khanjar's newly constructed prisoner compound held 6,000 prisoners transported from the 2d Marine Division's area of operations.

Another 8,000 prisoners were transported to the pens constructed at Kibrit, although the sheer numbers had begun to overwhelm the resources there. To make matters worse, high winds blew over the mess tent, interrupting food distribution and sparking a near riot among the prisoners. In addition, the Iraqis ignored the latrines and slit trenches built for them and instead relieved themselves along the fence line. Despite these problems, the Marines persevered, calming the prisoners and transporting them southward as quickly as possible to the Army's facilities.[26]

Entering Kuwait City

The Joint Forces Command–East broke through the Iraqi defenses in the late afternoon and rushed forward to Kuwait City, along with the Force Reconnaissance teams attached to them. Colonel Charles Quilter, the I Marine Expeditionary Force field historian, noted that "the way to the American Embassy seemed clear, and in accordance with the combined operations plan, one team, under First Lieutenant Brian G. Knowles, made a dash for it in conjunction with Saudi teams headed for their own embassy nearby. At last light, the team entered the compound where Knowles found a tattered American flag still flying."[27]

Edward J. Marolda and Robert J. Schneller Jr., historians writing for the Naval Historical Center after the war, describe Lieutenant Knowles's action as dereliction of duty. Quoting the 1st Surveillance, Reconnaissance, and Intelligence Group's after action report, they state, "Force Recon Team Piglet 2-1 ordered to assume fire support responsibilities for 2/8.

They abandon their posts and begin a series of grandstand plays to race for the embassy. Fortunately none are killed by friendly fire." It is unclear if the "2/8" unit referred to in the report is a Marine or Saudi Arabian battalion. The sources are unclear on whether or not Knowles was justified in taking the embassy, but it is clear that a Special Operations Central Command SEAL and Army Special Forces team had originally been given the mission of securing the embassy. Although the Marines had already secured the embassy, the special operations teams proceeded to conduct the mission as if it were an unsecured location.[28]

Asked about the controversy 20 years after the fact, General Boomer said, "There actually was a Marine reconnaissance lieutenant who sort of on his own went up and took the embassy, and I was prepared to chew his a——s out when I finally got my hands on him, but I couldn't bring myself to do it. I couldn't. What are you going to say? Here's this lieutenant that's come up the coast and the embassy is a special place. So, he took charge and occupied it. He didn't have to fight for it."[29]

27 February

On 27 February, the XVIII Airborne Corps turned east, crossing the Euphrates River valley and advancing to the Tigris River. Led by the 24th Infantry Division, the corps advanced on the Iraqi city of Basrah, destroying hundreds of Iraqi tanks and armored personnel carriers along its advance and capturing two Iraqi military airfields. The VII Corps continued its advance east toward Safwan and Umm Qasr and against the *Republican Guard*. The VII Corps destroyed the *Guard's Tawakalna, Medina*, and *Adnan Divisions* as well as the *12th* and *10th Armored Divisions*. The British 1st Armored Division completed the destruction of the *52d Armored Division*.[30]

Taking Kuwait International Airport

Task Force Shepherd arrived at the airport over three hours after departing and began its assault at 0430. There was some minor resistance, and many mines were discovered. Since the Iraqis were clearly defeated, the task force commander elected to wait until morning to continue the advance. At 0615, at the break of dawn, Task Force Shepherd resumed its attack. It was joined at 0800 by Task Force Taro's 2d Battalion, 3d Marines, which helped clear the airfield building and captured 80 Iraqis lurking about the airfield.

Marines of Task Force Shepherd roll into Kuwait International Airport in light armored vehicles after the defeat of Iraqi forces. At right is a CH-53 Sea Stallion helicopter.

Photo by TSgt David McLeod, USAF. Defense Imagery DF-ST-92-08209

Kuwait International Airport by LtCol Keith A. McConnell. A commercial airliner destroyed by a Marine airstrike earlier in the war sits near the control tower of Kuwait International Airport. The smoke from the burning oilfields can be seen in the background.

With the morning, the Marines surrounding the airport gradually realized that offensive operations were ending and only mopping up remained. The 1st Battalion, 7th Marines' command chronology describes the sunrise:

As the sun rose Kuwait City stood amazingly in front of the battalion. Because of restricted visibility the day prior, many of the Marines didn't fully comprehend just how close we were. . . . Blowing horns and random shots could be heard throughout our position as jubilant Kuwaitis waved Kuwaiti, British, and American flags in celebration of their liberation. Great pride was written across the faces of our sailors and Marines. Remarkably we made it with no deaths and only minor injuries. . . . [Our battalion] found itself in a strange position as several EPWs [enemy prisoners of war] turned themselves in to us so they would not be killed by Kuwaiti Resistance Forces. We were now protecting the Iraqis.

Some, however, did not want our protec-
tion. As Company A 1/7 [1st Battalion, 7th Marines], our detached infantry company with Tiger 3, was conducting a sweep in zone, they came across four wounded Iraqis. While Cpl Kerry Lee was searching one of them, the Iraqi lunged at Cpl Lee and was instantly killed by the Marine standing cover for him.[31]

Major General Myatt established his command post at the airport at 0900, and the 1st Marine Division spent the rest of the day securing its areas from loose ordnance and policing up Iraqi stragglers. It awaited word of what would happen next: an advance on Baghdad or a cease-fire.

While the 1st Marine Division was securing the airport, the 2d Marine Division was finally making contact with the Egyptian and Syrian forces of Joint Forces Command–North. In the dawn hours, these Coalition forces passed north of the division and moved into Kuwait City to secure it.

The 2d Marine Division spent the day securing its positions as well, but the sweeps took on a more tragic note when a massive secondary explosion occurred in an Iraqi tank being destroyed by combat engineers. The explosions wounded one Marine and took the life of Sergeant James D. Hawthorne of the 2d Tank Battalion as he assisted the engineers.[32]

Molly Moore, a reporter for the *Washington Post* who traveled with the I Marine Expeditionary Force, described some of the 2d Marine Division's captures: "In contrast to the Iraqi front lines, the bunkers of troops stationed farther north and nearer Kuwait City were stuffed amply with sacks of potatoes and rice and other foodstuffs. One Marine said he entered an Iraqi bunker and saw a plump roast in a pan near a stove, indicating the cook fled minutes before he planned to start dinner. In some areas, entire prefabricated houses had been buried, complete with indoor toilets, showers, kitchens, and potted plants."[33]

Air Operations

Early on 27 February, an AV-8B from Marine Attack Squadron 331, flying from the USS *Nassau*, was the last Marine aircraft downed by hostile fire in the Gulf War. Captain Reginald C. "Woody" Underwood's aircraft was hit by an infrared surface-to-air missile as he flew an air interdiction mission against Iraqi forces retreating north along the so-called Highway of Death. Captain Underwood did not survive the crash, but his body was later recovered.[34]

In an article written after the war, Major Ben D. Hancock, a pilot who witnessed the event, described how Captain Underwood was lost:

We were at 8,000 feet, doing over 480 knots, and I started a hard left turn away from the highway as I strained to keep my eyes on the target. We rolled out heading southeast, and I was about to roll in when Mystic yelled "Break! Break! Flares!" It was every man for himself as there was no time to ask questions. I strained under the G forces and looked around frantically as multiple SAMs [surface-to-air missiles] were in the air. At least two were streaking toward Woody [Captain Underwood] and one hit him in the left exhaust nozzle of his jet engine, right below the wing. He yelled "I'm hit! I'm hit!" and pulled up into the clouds trailing black smoke. The missiles had been launched from our 7 o'clock and were on us in seconds. Mystic had one SAM chasing him as he disappeared from sight into the clouds. I reversed my turn and came back trying to find Woody. The heat-seeking missile chasing Mystic couldn't track him through the clouds, and he radioed to Woody to turn his jet to the southeast. Woody's last transmission was, "I can't control it!" For what seemed like

Iraqi soldiers surrendering to the 2d Light Armored Infantry Battalion of the 2d Marine Division in Kuwait.
Photo by Sgt J. L. Roberts. Marine Corps History Division Reference Branch photo files

Photo by PO1 Scott Allen, USN. Defense Imagery DN-SC-91-00632

Flight deck crewmen on board the USS Nassau *refuel two Marine Corps AV-8B Harriers as a third Harrier comes in to land. The* Nassau *ended its historic combat deployment as a "Harrier Carrier" on a tragic note when Capt Reginald C. Underwood was killed in action.*

an eternity but was probably only about 20 seconds, Peewee and I were looking northwest when we saw Woody's jet impact the ground in one huge, orange fireball. It was like watching a slow motion movie, only this was the real thing. We never saw a parachute.[35]

Throughout the day on 27 February, the Iraqi retreat along the northern highway turned from a rout to pure chaos as Air Force, Navy, and Marine attack aircraft continued the destruction they had begun along that route on 26 February. Long after the war, an A-6E pilot, Lieutenant Colonel Michael B. Parkyn, described the highway to a historian: "It's incredible, hellish, red, orange glow off the fires . . . a ribbon or road, cars and vehicles on both sides, on fire, you could see movement, people scattering. Oil well smoke created overcast, you dropped all your bombs then climbed above the clouds heading home. It was clear, cool and quiet; behind you the clouds were glowing red."[36]

After the war, the Coalition air forces received some criticism for the Highway of Death in the media. General Walter E. Boomer described it as he saw it:

We didn't talk about the "Highway of Death,"

but that was misportrayed by the media. There were a couple of pretty horrible scenes, but in the scheme of things, [they were] relatively unimportant. A couple of buses that had escaping Iraqi soldiers were hit, and they were burned. Most of them were smart enough as they saw vehicle after vehicle stopping in front of them, and the line behind them becoming miles and miles long, and our aircraft methodically picking them off, to get the hell out, and they did. They ran over into the marsh and made their way up the coast to get out of Kuwait. We were stopped at about that time, so they did escape.

I was actually on that highway when the Iraqi truck engines were still running. They were so anxious to get out; they slammed on the brakes, put it in neutral, didn't shut the engine off and ran. The event got blown up in the media and it caused undo concern about us piling on. The question that I saw raised was that, you wanted them to leave Kuwait and they were trying their best and you were killing them as they were leaving. Well, not quite right. They were escaping with

Marine Pilot Flies 719 Combat Missions

Colonel Quilter, the I Marine Expeditionary Force historian, described the record-breaking achievement of the commander of Marine Aircraft Group 11 on 27 February:

Colonel Manfred A. Rietsch, 49, is commanding officer of the Marines' larger fighter/attack unit, Marine Aircraft Group 11, which arrived at its base in Bahrain in mid-August. The colorful flyer, who retains the faint accents of his German birth and the call sign "Fokker," was already something a legend in Marine aviation, having flown 653 combat missions in Vietnam. During this war he flew another 66 missions in F/A-18 Hornets.

On the night of 26–27 February, the Iraqis began their frantic retreat from Kuwait. The A-6E Intruders of his group detected huge numbers of vehicles streaming north which they attacked, helping to bottle up the Iraqis. Rietsch now increased the surge of his sorties; MAG-11 [Marine Aircraft Group 11] flew 298 missions that day alone.

He himself took off mid-morning in a two seat F/A-I8D of Marine All-Weather Fighter Attack Squadron 121 with his Weapons System Operator, Major [William C.] Macak, on a Fast Forward Air Controller mission. Bad weather and smoke from burning oilfields were obscuring the choked escape route when the crew found a convoy of about 40 transporters carrying tanks and armored personnel carriers making their way along a parallel dirt track to the west. Sixteen of his Hornets were inbound, but now he had to stop the convoy from getting underneath a thick band of oil smoke which would hide them from visual attack.

He fired a white phosphorous rocket ahead of the lead truck. The drivers, knowing an attack was imminent, piled out of the vehicles. After a few minutes, when no attack was forthcoming, they got back into the trucks and started up. Rietsch repeated the process with the same result. After the convoy started up a last time, he strafed the lead vehicles, which began to burn. This time the Iraqis got the message. Now short on fuel, he handed over control to Major [Kenneth] Bode, who directed the Marine Hornets in an attack pilot's dream mission: halted tanks and APCs [armored personnel carriers]. Rietsch returned from his last mission. It was his 719th.[37]

---

their vehicles and their weapons. They were fair game. It wasn't the duck shoot that it was portrayed to be.[38]

As long as the fleeing Iraqis did so in their military vehicles with their weapons, they certainly remained valid targets, and the Marines of the 3d Marine Aircraft Wing, along with their Air Force and Navy comrades, continued to visit destruction upon the fleeing columns throughout 27 February.

The War of Logistics Never Ends . . .

Even as Iraqi resistance in Kuwait crumbled, the Marines of the 1st Force Service Support Group and its subordinate Direct Support Command continued to rush supplies forward to the Marines in the field and to truck Iraqi prisoners of war back to the waiting Army compounds. Although the war was winding down, driving through the gaps in the obstacle belts and north through Kuwait remained dangerous. Mines and bypassed Iraqi soldiers kept the logistics soldiers alert on their missions.

The Iraqi prisoners were docile and happy to be out of the war for the most part, but they could be unruly in some situations. One such event occurred when Lieutenant Colonel Thomas S. Woodson, commander of the 8th Motor Transport Battalion, dispatched a 70-truck Logistics Vehicle System* convoy from Khanjar in Saudi Arabia to Kuwait on 26 February to help bring prisoners out of Kuwait. The convoy had gotten lost in the night and wisely waited until dawn before continuing its mission; then it loaded approximately 2,000 Iraqi prisoners onto the beds of its vehicles and headed back to Khanjar. Along the way, the convoy met Brigadier General Charles Krulak, and he directed it to Kibrit

---

*The Logistics Vehicle System is the Marine Corps' heavy tactical vehicle system. These vehicles are eight-wheel drive and are designed modularly; each can be customized to pull a particular type of load. These trucks came into use in 1985 and can pull up to 22 tons.

Photo courtesy of BGen Granville Amos

The "Highway of Death" photographed in March 1991. This was the road to the west of Kuwait City where retreating Iraqi troops and vehicles were concentrated during their retreat.

Official U.S. Marine Corps photo

Iraqi prisoners of war being transported to holding facilities in Saudi Arabia on returning Logistics Vehicle Systems of the Direct Support Command's 8th Motor Transport Battalion.

Photo by SSgt J. R. Ruark. Defense Imagery DM-SC-93-05230

This Iraqi sand table was found in a school gymnasium in Kuwait City. The marked Iraqi positions corresponded to their defense plans and indicated how successful the Marines' amphibious deception was at distracting Iraqi attention from the Saudi-Kuwaiti frontier.

instead of Khanjar to save time. At Khanjar, Lieutenant Colonel Woodson was informed of the destination change, and he

> dispatched his battalion's executive officer, Major Robert L. Songer, to find the convoy. As Songer neared Kibrit, he noticed that the road was mysteriously covered with thousands of empty milk containers. At CSSD-91 [Combat Service Support Detachment 91], Songer found the convoy and discovered the answer to the riddle of the empty milk cartons. As the convoy carrying the Iraqis approached Kibrit, it stopped to allow the Iraqis to relieve themselves. A passing truck carrying milk cartons slowed down to look at the Iraqis who leaped onto the milk truck and raided its cargo. The convoy drivers quickly restored order and loaded the Iraqis back on the LVSs [vehicles from the Logistics Vehicle System], but not before the thirsty prisoners consumed most of the milk on the truck.[39]

Combat Service Support Detachment 91, commanded by Lieutenant Colonel Linden L. Sparrow, operated the Marines' prisoner of war holding facility at Kibrit. Reinforced by a medical detachment and a company of Marine Reserve Military Police, they handled the prisoners until they could be turned over to the U.S. Army. According to Brigadier General James Brabham, "They carried out their duties under the stress of overwhelming numbers of enemy prisoners of war, threats of enemy incursion, and an initially unknown length of time before rearward movement would reduce the numbers in the camp."[40]

The I Marine Expeditionary Force took approximately 22,308 Iraqi soldiers prisoner during the four day campaign to liberate Kuwait. All of these soldiers were fed, watered, sheltered, and provided with required medical care as they were moved out of the war zone and into Saudi Arabia. There, the Marines turned them over to U.S. Army Central Command's 800th Military Police Brigade. The last of the Marines' prisoners of war were turned over to the military police brigade on 6 March.[41]

Kuwait Liberated

The Egyptians and Syrians of Joint Forces Command–North and the Saudi Arabians of Joint Forces Command–East met in the middle of Kuwait City, near the city's water towers. Organized Iraqi resistance was over, and the people of Kuwait came out into the streets to celebrate. General Boomer led a party into the city and to the American embassy, and along the way the crowds of Kuwaitis thanked the Marines and shouted "Allahu Akbar!" (God is great). Many Kuwaitis fired firearms into the air in celebration. The Marines found the contrast with the recent desert battles jarring, contrasting the jubilant civilian population and relative greenery of the city with the harsh desert conditions.[42]

Molly Moore, the reporter with General Boomer's mobile command post, later described the scene: "The curbs were alive with gleeful young girls wearing skirts fashioned from green-white-red-and-black Kuwaiti flags, sobbing women in black robes and young men flashing victory signs and pumping clenched fists. They waved flags and tossed candy and shouted thanks. The rooftops of buildings blossomed with teenagers and children waving flags and banners. Robed women streamed out of doorways and flailed their arms through windows."[43]

The American embassy was relatively intact; it had been deserted for months but not vandalized. One of the more interesting finds was in a school near the embassy; in the school's gymnasium the Iraqis had constructed a large sand table detailing the defenses they had placed around Kuwait City, complete with toy artillery pieces, Lego blocks, and small signs identifying Iraqi units. The sand table was very clear evidence of the success of the amphibious deception in diverting Iraqi forces to the coast.[44]

The I Marine Expeditionary Force held Mutla Ridge and the Kuwait International Airport, controlling entry to and egress from Kuwait City. The sub-

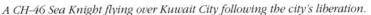

A CH-46 Sea Knight flying over Kuwait City following the city's liberation.

Photo courtesy of BGen Granville Amos

urbs of the city were ringed by Marines, and all the ground campaign's objectives had been achieved. Fighting continued in the north of Kuwait, where Marine aircraft continued attacking retreating Iraqi columns through the night, and in southern Iraq, where the Army continued to destroy divisions of the *Republican Guard*, but on 27 February the primary Marine Corps contribution to Operation Desert Storm came to a successful conclusion.

During the four-day campaign, General Boomer's forces destroyed the Iraqi *III Corps* commanded by Major General Salah Aboud Mahmoud and much of the *IV Corps* commanded by Major General Yaiyd Khalel Zaki. The I Marine Expeditionary Force estimated that it inflicted the following losses on the Iraqis: 460 tanks destroyed; 600 tanks captured; 218 armored personnel carriers destroyed; 390 armored personnel carriers captured; 432 artillery pieces destroyed; 5 free rocket over ground missile sites destroyed; and 1,510 Iraqi soldiers killed (as mentioned above, an estimated 22,308 Iraqis were captured).[45]

During the evening of 27 February, as the ground war came to a close, General Norman Schwarzkopf, commander in chief, U.S. Central Command, presented the famous "Mother of All Briefings" on live television, describing how the Coalition forces had routed the Iraqi Army. Concerning the Marine efforts in Kuwait, General Schwarzkopf stated:

> I can't say enough about the two Marine divisions. If I used words like brilliant, it would really be an underdescription of the absolutely superb job that they did in breaching the so-called impenetrable barrier. It was a classic, absolutely classic, military breaching of a very, very tough minefield, barbed wire, fire trenches-type barrier. They went through the first barrier like it was water. They went across into the second barrier line, even though they were under artillery fire at the time—they continued to open up that breach. Then they brought both divisions streaming through that breach. Absolutely superb operation, a textbook, and I think it will be studied for many, many years to come as the way to do it.[46]

CHAPTER 11

Standing Down after Victory

Cease-Fire

Most Marines first heard of the cease-fire around 0500 on 28 February, when President George H. W. Bush's announcement was broadcast on the BBC. Shortly thereafter, I Marine Expeditionary Force transmitted the following message: "Cease all offensive operations effective 280500Z 0800C. Remain in current positions and assume defensive posture. Wartime rules of engagement remain in effect. Be prepared to resume offensive operations. Forces are allowed to defend themselves." For most of the Marines, the cease-fire was not a surprise because their objectives had been taken the day before; the question was, what would happen next? Would the Marines be expected to turn north and support the Army in a drive to Baghdad, or would the war end?[1]

Colonel William Jones was the commander of Marine Attack Squadron 231 at the time. Long after the war, he described the first few days of the cease-fire and how he started working with his men on the transition from war to peace:

I talked to my officers, saying we've got to keep everybody busy. We've got to worry about postcombat coping. I've got notes that I made to myself about talking to them about how they've got to transition from what they've been doing to going back to the way that things were. By that I mean I tried to do more of a fatherly kind of discussion if you will, and that is to say, "Look, you have to reconcile a lot of things that have been going on here. I mean between your own ears you've got to reconcile this stuff. Combat is a very personal experience. But at the same time you're only one cog in this huge machine, and it really is rather mechanical and somewhere in there you have to deal with that." I said,

Damaged Iraqi Tank *by Sgt Charles G. Grow. An Iraqi tank sits destroyed in its revetment.*
Marine Corps Art Collection

"You also have to deal with the fact that you've been killing people. And the ready room or bar comeback—it was saying something flippant like, "Well I'm just really good at killing people." That won't work when your favorite aunt or niece asks you this question over a breakfast table sometime in the next two years because you will not see the question coming. Out of the blue Aunt Susie is going to say, "Did you really kill people in Kuwait?" And you better think this through because what works in a ready room or among your friends or over a beer ain't going to work with Aunt Susie. You've got to deal with it.[2]

When the cease-fire was declared, it was clear to the Marines in Kuwait that the Iraqi resistance around Kuwait City was over. Some Marines rested after three days of swift movement and hard work; others examined the fighting positions taken from the Iraqis. Captain Phillip Thompson of 1st Battalion, 12th Marines, and his unit were emplaced near Kuwait International Airport; their position had been seized from an Iraqi tank battalion. In his memoir, he described the Iraqi unit's equipment and the end of the war:

I was not impressed with the bunkers or the tanks. The tanks that were still in one piece probably couldn't have made it to the city—which we could see from our position—on their own power. The tracks were coated in rust, the insides were filthy, and none looked like they had seen a drop of grease in months. The crews never stood a chance.

While we meandered through the wreckage, somebody near the FDC [fire direction control] began shouting. We trotted back just in time to hear a Marine yell "The war's over!" A dozen lusty cheers went up. I stopped in my tracks and said a silent prayer.[3]

Many Marines with access to transportation tried to get into Kuwait City to see the liberation celebrations and the aftermath of the war. Captain Thompson took half a dozen Marines in his humvee into the city. He recalled, "We felt like conquering heroes, but we didn't know how to play the part." He also recounted how the Marines were shocked by the extent of the looting: "We drove through the looted, destroyed city blocks, viewing the Iraqis' handiwork. All the pity I had felt for the prisoners we'd taken days before now turned to utter rage. Everything had been sacked. Expensive cars lay

Kuwaiti civilians and Coalition troops celebrate the liberation of Kuwait.
Photo by CWO-2 Ed Bailey, USNR. Defense Imagery DN-SC-91-06903

Marines of Company D prepare to enter a residential area on Faylakah Island, Kuwait, on 3 March 1991. The Marines secured the island without resistance from its Iraqi garrison.

crippled on the roadside, their wheels torn off, doors missing, glass shattered. Stores had been completely emptied. I walked, in shock, past a shoe store that held nothing but a seven-foot pile of empty shoeboxes. Oddly enough—and in a revealing statement on the attackers—the bookstore next door was left largely untouched, its rows of textbooks still neatly aligned on the shelves."[4]

Other Marines tried the same thing. First Lieutenant Sean T. Coughlin of Marine Wing Support Group 37 acquired a humvee and drove with two other Marines from King Abdul Aziz Naval Base to Kuwait City and back again. The entire trip took seven hours each way, with the Marines driving past journalists and Arab forces on the roads. Inside Kuwait City they found similar scenes of destruction and jubilation.[5]

Captain Thompson recorded a vivid description of what the Marines found in Kuwait City and how it helped many of them put their labors in the desert into perspective:

> The spectacle before us was the reason we had come to this country. Huge Kuwaiti flags draped out nearly every apartment building and welcomed us in the gentle breeze. All the anger and frustration of the previous six months began melting away in the hundreds of smiles I now saw.

> "Thank you for saving our country!"

> "We love U.S. Marines!"

> "We love USA!"

> We heard it over and over. I could only smile and nod. I was afraid to speak. Somewhere along the line, someone gave me a ragged, soot-covered Kuwaiti flag, which I still have.[6]

The battlefield was littered with unexploded ordinance; mines; destroyed Iraqi vehicles; and, sadly, many Iraqi dead. The explosive ordinance disposal teams and engineers were soon busy working to defuse or safely detonate the live ordinance, while the 1st Force Service Support Group graves registration teams worked to handle the Iraqi dead properly. Information on the Iraqi dead was recorded, and the bodies were transferred to Saudi Arabian authorities, who ensured that proper Islamic burials were provided. There were fewer Iraqi dead than might be expected, as vast numbers had surrendered and even more had fled back to Iraq.[7]

Al-Wafrah Forest and Faylakah Island

Although a cease-fire had been declared, not all Iraqi units abided by it (nor were all aware of it, as Iraqi communications were sporadic). On 2 March, the *17th Brigade* of the *Republican Guard's Hammurabi Division* opened fire on the U.S. Army's 24th Infantry Division (Mechanized) just west of Basrah and was mauled in return. Along with occasional small-arms fire and poor communications between Iraqi units—some of which did not know of the cease-fire—clearing operations remained dangerous even beyond the myriad bits of unexploded ordinance and mines scattered about the battlefield.

The 5th Marine Expeditionary Brigade was given the task of clearing the bypassed regions of the al-Wafrah Forest as it transited from Kuwait back to al-Mishab to rejoin its amphibious squadron. It began to clear al-Wafrah on 1 March. The process was slow and methodical, and it began with helicopters flying over the forest, their loudspeakers announcing the cease-fire and calling on the Iraqis to surrender. During the clearing, the brigade came under sporadic fire from isolated pockets of Iraqi soldiers, and each time the Marines responded in kind and called in Cobra air strikes. One Marine was wounded by an Iraqi booby trap on the morning of 3 March, the last day of the forest clearing operation, but none of the Iraqis in the forest surrendered. On 4 March, the brigade's infantry battalions traveled south via helilift and ground

convoy, returning to the ships of Amphibious Group 3.[8]

Also on 3 March, the 13th Marine Expeditionary Unit (Special Operations Capable) cleared the other major piece of Kuwaiti territory still held by Iraqi troops, Faylakah Island. It was held by the Iraqi *440th Naval Infantry Brigade,* comprising just over 1,400 troops. On 2 March, two UH-lNs from Marine Light Helicopter Squadron 767 flew over Faylakah, broadcasting the surrender message on loudspeakers to the Iraqi troops. They were not fired on. The next morning, helicopters flying over the island saw white flags, and the Iraqis gathered in a communications compound. The Marine assault element landed at 0800 and began securing the island. Colonel John Rhodes, commander of the 13th Marine Expeditionary Unit, accepted the surrender of Brigadier General Abbud Gambar Hasen Almiki, the Iraqi commander, at a formal ceremony at 1430.[9]

The Iraqi naval troops were evacuated from the island via helicopter to the USS *Ogden*. They were searched for weapons, provided with food, and screened for medical care. Meanwhile, Marine intelligence officers examined the defenses on Faylakah, which had been bombed repeatedly during the aerial campaign. The Iraqis had suffered no serious casualties from these raids; they abandoned

Col John E. Rhodes, commanding officer of the 13th Marine Expeditionary Unit (Special Operations Capable), walks out to accept the surrender of the Iraqi 440th Naval Infantry Brigade *from BGen Abbud Gambar Hasen Almiki on Faylakah Island*.

Marine Corps History Division Reference Branch photo files

Army Gen H. Norman Schwarzkopf (at left), commander in chief of U.S. Central Command, and LtGen Khalid bin Sultan bin Abdul Aziz, commander of Joint Forces in Saudi Arabia, sit across the table from an interpreter and (from left to right) Iraqi LtGens Muhammad Abdez Rahman Al-Dagitistani, Sabin Abdel-Aziz Al Douri, and Salah Aboud Mahmoud during cease-fire talks at Safwan, Iraq.

their firing positions during each attack. On 5 March, the last of the Iraqis were transferred ashore to the Army's military police, joining the rest of the enemy prisoners of war.[10]

On 3 March, General Norman Schwarzkopf and General Khaled bin Sultan met with Sultan Hashim Ahmad, deputy chief of staff of the Iraqi Ministry of Defense, and Lieutenant General Salah Aboud Mahmoud, commander of the destroyed *III Corps*, at Safwan, Iraq, in order to formalize the cease-fire. In the short meeting they dictated the terms of cease-fire to the Iraqis, thus officially ending the major combat period of the Gulf War. During the talks, the Iraqis requested and received permission to fly helicopters over their own territory, the only concession they were granted.[11]

Leaving the Desert

The formal cease-fire agreement made it clear that the United States was not going to continue to Baghdad and started the troops in the Persian Gulf thinking about when they could return to the United States. Moving hundreds of thousands of troops and their equipment to Saudi Arabia and the Gulf's waters had taken months, and returning those troops

and supplies would take months as well. The equipment and supplies needed to be returned in good condition to avoid waste, and the territories of Saudi Arabia and Kuwait needed to be left in the condition in which they existed prior to the war, as much as possible. Additionally, although the cease-fire was signed, no formal peace agreement was reached, and Iraq remained a threat to peace and stability in the region after the war, albeit a greatly reduced one. Iraq's ability to sow discord was reduced by the conflict, but this left a power vacuum in the region that could easily be filled by nations such as Iran or Syria. It was apparent even as the cease-fire was signed that an American presence in the region would be required for the foreseeable future.

The primary consideration in the withdrawal was that the Marines maintain combat readiness while departing the area of operations, returning as "deployable air-ground task forces." Marines would generally return to the United States with the same units with which they deployed to Southwest Asia. The priority would be "first in/first out" according to units. The initial I Marine Expeditionary Force units to depart the Gulf were those that deployed with the 7th Marine Expeditionary Brigade in August; they began returning to the States on 8 March.[12]

General Walter Boomer established the basic priorities and guidelines for the retrograde movement in the first days after the cease-fire, warning his staff on 1 March that the "most dangerous part of the campaign, as it turns out, may still be ahead of us. That is moving all this stuff out without getting anybody hurt." With the threat of war apparently ended, there was a real worry that Marines would lose focus, resulting in deadly accidents. Many hazardous tasks were required for the withdrawal—ammunition needed to be properly stored, for instance, and large, dangerous equipment needed to be operated—and these jobs required focus.[13]

Additionally, there was concern about the massive pile of weapons abandoned by the Iraqis in Kuwait. Marines were not permitted to bring back firearms, grenades, or other potentially dangerous war souvenirs. As for other types of souvenirs, General Boomer instructed that "as far as I'm concerned,

what the troops find on the battlefield in terms of hats, belt buckles, that kind of thing they should be allowed to take home, and they are going to do it. They ought to have something to show their grandchildren in a few years." Field historians working for the Marine Corps History and Museums Division chose pieces of captured Iraqi equipment for later museum exhibits, and major units were permitted to bring back a limited number of trophies (such as field guns and armor) for display at their command post.[14]

Another duty that needed to be accomplished before all the Marines involved returned to the States was convening the various awards boards to recognize those Marines who had performed exceptionally well during the conflict. General Boomer had specific guidance for the awards boards: "One of the things that I saw coming out of Vietnam that continued to disgust me, and has for the last 25 years, is the fact that most of our young Marines, time and time again, got screwed while senior offi-

A pile of captured Iraqi arms in Kuwait City. The Iraqis left weapons and equipment of all descriptions littering the battlefield.

Photo by Col John Shotwell. Marine Corps History Division Reference Branch photo files

Photo by PO1 Joe Gawlowicz, USN. Defense Imagery DN-ST-92-00829

An HY-2 Silkworm antiship missile left behind by retreating Iraqi troops sits on a flatbed trailer as captured equipment and ordnance are prepared for shipment following the Gulf War.

cers got awards. I promise you that will not happen, and those of you sitting on these awards boards pay attention to the youngsters, and if I catch you downgrading what a commander has recommended for a lance corporal in terms of heroic award, I'll disband the board and start again." In the event, 2 Navy Crosses, 15 Silver Stars, 22 Distinguished Flying Crosses, and 523 Bronze Stars as well as thousands of other awards were presented to Marines for meritorious actions during the Gulf War.[15]

While the withdrawal was taking place, the Marine Corps instituted a major effort to preserve the institutional lessons learned from the Gulf War. The Marine Corps Combat Development Command deployed a large battle assessment team under Colonel Clifford L. Stanley to gather postcombat data and interviews. This data was collated, analyzed, and published through the Marine Corps Lessons Learned System; it was eventually deposited in the General Alfred M. Gray Marine Corps Research Center's Southwest Asia Archive in Quantico, Virginia.[16]

On 5 March, General Boomer reestablished the I Marine Expeditionary Force headquarters in al-Jubayl, Saudi Arabia, and reunited the separate command posts that had run the liberation. The combat replacement regiment was dissolved on 21

March, and on 26 March the first Marines from the expeditionary force's headquarters began to return to the United States. General Boomer and most of his staff departed on 16 April. On 21 April, a new Marine command was instituted for the region: Marine Forces, Southwest Asia. Major General Norman E. Ehlert, former deputy commander of U.S. Marine Forces Central Command, was the first commander of this new organization.

The Marine forces afloat, which fell under the control of U.S. Naval Forces Central Command, were already embarked for the most part and could depart Southwest Asia relatively quickly. The 13th Marine Expeditionary Force (Special Operations Capable) was the first to depart, leaving the Persian Gulf proper on 11 March. The unit sailed back to San Diego, California, making stops in the Philippines and Hawaii before arriving on 16 April. The 4th Marine Expeditionary Brigade was the next amphibious landing force to leave the Gulf, departing on 4 March. Returning to the United States in two transit groups, the brigade returned via the Suez Canal and the Mediterranean. The groups reached the States and unloaded from 17 to 19 April.[17]

When the 4th Marine Expeditionary Brigade departed the region, Brigadier General Peter Rowe's 5th Marine Expeditionary Brigade became Central Command's landing force and its strategic reserve as well. It faced two difficulties right away. First, the USS *Tripoli* was badly damaged and unavailable due to the mine it struck on 17 February. Second, USS *New Orleans* had replaced the *Tripoli* with the mine countermeasures force and was still involved in mine clearing operations, and thus unavailable. Amphibious Group 3 had lacked sufficient shipping space from the beginning, and losing both of these large amphibious vessels made reloading the brigade difficult. The brigade nonetheless began reloading after its stint ashore, and by 10 March the entire brigade, aside from those units awaiting the return of the *New Orleans*, was reembarked.[18]

On 17 March, Colonel Robert Garner's 11th Marine Expeditionary Unit (Special Operations Capable) separated from the 5th Marine Expeditionary Force and departed the Gulf. As originally intended, it comprised Battalion Landing Team 3/1, Marine Medium Helicopter Squadron (Composite) 268, and Marine Expeditionary Unit Service Support Group

11 and was embarked on Amphibious Squadron 1, commanded by Captain Michael Barker, USN. Captain Barker's squadron included the USS *New Orleans* (finally returned from mine-clearing duties), USS *Denver*, USS *Germantown*, USS *Peoria*, and USS *Mobile*. Colonel Garner and Captain Barker's force remained in the Gulf as Central Command's afloat reserve until July, training with local forces and planning contingency operations for the unrest in Ethiopia (these never came to pass, as the Ethiopian crisis stabilized).[19]

On 7 May, the 5th Marine Expeditionary Brigade and Amphibious Group 3 departed the Persian Gulf on their homeward journey. It was not a direct journey, however. In April, Cyclone Marian had devastated Bangladesh, and the brigade and amphibious group were ordered to undertake a humanitarian relief effort. On 17 May, the force arrived off Bangladesh and began relief operations. After two weeks of successful operations, their mission ended

Aircraft Losses due to Enemy Action in the 1990–91 Gulf War				
Dates: 1991	**Aircraft Type**	**Squadron**	**Cause**	**Result**
18 January	OV-10	VMO-2	surface-to-air missile	aircraft lost, pilot and observer captured
28 January	AV-8B	VMA-311	surface-to-air missile	aircraft lost, pilot captured
9 February	F/A-18	VMFA-451	surface-to-air missile	aircraft damaged
9 February	AV-8B	VMA-231	surface-to-air missile	aircraft lost, pilot captured
12 February	AV-8B	VMA-542	antiaircraft artillery	aircraft damaged
21 February	F/A-18	VMFA-314	surface-to-air missile	aircraft damaged
21 February	F/A-18	VMFA-121	surface-to-air missile	aircraft damaged
21 February	A-6E	VMA-224	antiaircraft artillery	aircraft damaged
21 February	F/A-18	VMFA-333	surface-to-air missile	aircraft damaged
23 February	F/A-18	VMFA-451	surface-to-air missile	aircraft damaged
23 February	AV-8B	VMA-542	surface-to-air missile	aircraft lost, pilot killed in action
23 February	AV-8B	VMA-311	antiaircraft artillery	aircraft damaged
24 February	F/A-18	VMFA-314	surface-to-air missile	aircraft damaged
24 February	F/A-18	VMFA-314	surface-to-air missile	aircraft damaged
25 February	OV-10	VMO-1	surface-to-air missile	aircraft lost, pilot captured, observer killed in action
25 February	AV-8B	VMA-542	surface-to-air missile	aircraft lost, pilot parachuted to friendly hands
27 February	AV-8B	VMA-331	surface-to-air missile	aircraft lost, pilot killed in action

Photo by Sgt Rodney Jones. Defense Imagery DF-ST-92-08163

LtCol Clifford M. Acree clasps his young daughter as former American POWs are greeted by their families on arrival at Andrews Air Force Base, Maryland, on 10 March 1991.

on 29 May when the ships departed Bangladesh and continued back to the United States. The brigade finally completed its deployment when it disembarked in San Diego on 29 June.[20]

As the Marines in the amphibious task forces were sailing home, the Marines who had deployed via airlift and Maritime Prepositioning Ships were reloading those squadrons and preparing to return home as well. The 1st Marine Division returned to Saudi Arabia from Kuwait on 5–6 March, and the division's first units into Saudi Arabia began redeploying home right away. By the end of March, over half of the division had returned, and the entire division was back in the United States by 24 April.[21]

The 3d Marine Aircraft Wing nearly ended the war with a tragedy when two Marine F/A-18 Hornets collided while conducting air-to-air combat training on 8 March. The pilots, both from Marine Fighter Attack Squadron 212, parachuted to safety following the collision. No Marine F/A-18s had been lost to Iraqi antiaircraft gunnery or missiles in six weeks of air combat; now two were lost in a training accident only a week after the war ended. Squadrons from the wing began returning to the United States during the spring: eight left in March,

several others in April, and the final two squadrons of the wing departed on 17 May.[22]

The 2d Marine Division remained in Kuwait, establishing a forward defense as the Kuwaiti and Coalition forces began the extensive effort required to clean and reconstruct Kuwait. The Tiger Brigade separated from the division on 23 March, and the division, minus the 8th Marines, returned to Saudi Arabia on 30 March. The 8th Marines remained in Kuwait providing an American presence until mid-May, when the last of the 2d Marine Division's troops returned to the United States.[23]

The 1st Force Service Support Group's job before leaving Southwest Asia was just as large, and just as critical, as its job had been when arriving. Three squadrons of Maritime Prepositioning Ships had to be reloaded, and reloaded so that their stores and equipment would be in excellent shape if they were called on for another emergency. Large amounts of unused stores and equipment had to be safely and economically returned to the United States. For example, when the conflict ended, over 60 percent of the Marine Corps' ammunition stocks were in the Persian Gulf region. Cleaning and restoring the equipment was a major effort, and the wartime practices of some Marine units did not make it easier.

The Direct Support Command spent the first half of March searching for and retrieving Marine Corps equipment left on the battlefield. Much of this was maritime prepositioning equipment apparently abandoned by units returning to the United States. General Charles Krulak was incensed at this waste, referring to it as "the biggest disgrace of the war" and "a Marine Corps shame."[24]

On 17 March, the Direct Support Command stood down, and the 2d Force Service Support Group stood up, continuing the work of the remaining combat service support units in Southwest Asia. Throughout the rest of March, April, and May, the group continued moving supplies, cleaning equipment, and loading ships. On 23 June, General Krulak departed the region, along with the bulk of 2d Force Service Support Group. Marine Forces, Southwest Asia finally stood down on 10 October, and the last Marines deployed for the Gulf War departed the region.[25]

A Triumphant Return

Five Marines were captured by the Iraqis in the Gulf War: Lieutenant Colonel Clifford Acree, Chief Warrant Officer-4 Guy Hunter, Major Joseph Small, Cap-tain Russell Sanborn, and Captain Michael Berryman. All were aircrewmen belonging to 3d Marine Aircraft Wing squadrons. They spent varying amounts of time in Iraqi custody, but all were treated with brutality and contempt for the accepted, proper treatment of prisoners of war. The return of Coalition prisoners of war was one of General Schwarzkopf's priorities at the Safwan cease-fire talks, and the Iraqis readily agreed to it. The five Marine prisoners of war were returned to the United States and reunited with their families on 10 March.

At home, Marines who participated in Desert Shield and Desert Storm were shocked at the enthusiastic welcome they received in the States, not just from their loved ones but from the nation as a whole. There were many parades and celebrations around the country. On 8 June, East Coast Marines participated in a victory parade on the National Mall in Washington, DC, and there were numerous parades on 4 July in which the Independence Day holiday celebrations merged with gratitude for those who had returned from the Gulf. Returning as whole units, beside the Marines with whom they fought, created a very different homecoming for the Gulf War veterans than that experienced a generation earlier by veterans of the Vietnam War.

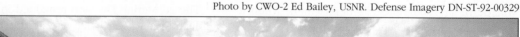

Passing before the Lincoln Memorial, a Marine waves to the crowd from his vehicle as he participates in a parade in Washington, DC, held in honor of the troops returning from the Gulf War.

Photo by CWO-2 Ed Bailey, USNR. Defense Imagery DN-ST-92-00329

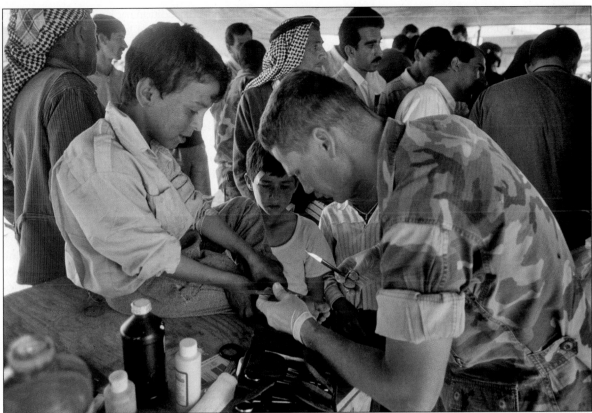

During Operation Provide Comfort, a Navy corpsman with Marine Expeditionary Unit Service Support Group 24 provides medical services to a Kurdish boy in a medical clinic in northern Iraq.

Postwar Iraq: Operations Provide Comfort, Northern Watch, and Southern Watch

Yet the end of combat operations in the Kuwaiti theater of operations did not end the armed confrontation between the United States and Saddam Hussein's Iraqi government. Marines remained involved with the ongoing confrontation over the next 12 years. Throughout the war, the Coalition had expressed the desire that Iraqis overthrow Saddam's government, encouraging the Iraqi military in particular to overthrow their president. In the aftermath of the Coalition's destruction of the Iraqi military, the government's foes attempted to do just that. On 1 March, an uprising began in Basrah that was apparently begun by soldiers who had fled from the Coalition in Kuwait, and it soon spread to most of the southern cities dominated by the Shia. On 4 March, another uprising began in the north among the Kurds, beginning in the town of Rania and soon spreading throughout Iraqi Kurdistan.[26]

In keeping with his belief that the United States had been maneuvering to destroy Iraq (or, even worse, to bring about his downfall) throughout the

1980s, Saddam Hussein believed that these uprisings were planned by America. In fact, he believed that they were the intended "next step" following the Coalition military operations that liberated Kuwait. As he told his senior military officers in April, "The entire siege that happened, the air bombardment until the land attack began, they were all methods used to create the appropriate environment for the operation [uprising] to take place."[27]

Faced with insurrection in 14 of Iraq's 18 provinces, the *Republican Guard* and the Iraqi military (which remained predominantly loyal to Saddam) responded fiercely and effectively. They had been ineffective in the face of Coalition military power, but smashing poorly armed civilian uprisings was an Iraqi military specialty in 1991. Artillery was used widely and indiscriminately to smash the rebels, and helicopters were also operated on a widespread scale. Many believed that this use was why the Iraqis had insisted on obtaining the right to fly helicopters within Iraq in the Safwan Accords. By 15 March, the Iraqi military had essentially crushed the nascent rebellion of the Shia in southern Iraq, often in full view of the U.S. Army's VII

Corps, which occupied much of this area until May 1991. The United States was reluctant to become involved, but when Iraqi military forces turned north and began to roll back Kurdish forces in late March and early April, international pressure to intervene began to grow. The pressure grew greater as it became apparent that a humanitarian disaster was imminent in the northern Iraq refugee camps.[28]

On 5 April, UN Security Council Resolution 688 was passed, calling for Iraq to end the repression of its people. President Bush determined that the United States would join in the international effort to bring aid to the hundreds of thousands of refugees believed to be in danger of starvation in northern Iraq. On 10 April, the 24th Marine Expeditionary Unit (Special Operations Capable), which was deployed to the Mediterranean under U.S. European Command, was ordered to join Combined Task Force Provide Comfort on 16 April. The expeditionary unit entered northern Iraq on 20 April.[29]

The 24th Marine Expeditionary Unit (Special Operations Capable), the main Marine unit for Operation Provide Comfort, was commanded by Colonel James L. Jones Jr. Its ground combat element was Battalion Landing Team 2/8; the air element was a composite squadron formed from Marine Medium Helicopter Squadron 264; and logistics were handled by Marine Expeditionary Unit Service Support Group 24. Beyond Colonel Jones's command, many other Marines served with the combined task force. Brigadier General Anthony C. Zinni served as both deputy commanding general and chief of staff. In addition, the Contingency Marine Air-Ground Task Force 1-91 and detachments from the 2d Remotely Piloted Vehicle Company and the 4th Civil Affairs Group served in the combined task force. Fire control teams from the 2d ANGLICO served alongside the allied British, French, Spanish, and Italian NATO units that were also stationed in northern Iraq.

The Iraqi military chose not to respond to Operation Provide Comfort with military force, and after several months of providing security and supplies to the refugees, the 24th Marine Expeditionary Unit departed Iraq on 15 July 1991. Operation Provide Comfort then entered its second phase, which focused on aerial responses to Iraqi military aggression against Kurdish areas. This second phase in turn transformed in January 1997 into Operation Northern Watch. The Marine Corps committed detachments of KC-130 Hercules aerial refuelers and EA-6B Prowler electronic warfare aircraft to the support of Operation Northern Watch, which continued until Operation Iraqi Freedom in 2003.

In the south, Joint Task Force Southwest Asia

Painted with graffiti by Coalition troops, an Iraqi T-55 main battle tank lies amidst other destroyed vehicles along the highway between Kuwait City and Basrah, Iraq.

Photo by TSgt Joe Coleman, USAF. Defense Imagery, DF-ST-92-08469

Defense Imagery DN-ST-91-08410

Barbed wire, mines, and other obstacles were erected along the shoreline during the Iraqi occupation of Kuwait to prevent or slow attacks by sea.

was established under U.S. Central Command in August 1992 to enforce a no-fly zone over southern Iraq, which also lasted until Operation Iraqi Freedom began in 2003. Marine aircraft from land bases and aircraft carriers flew often in support of Operation Southern Watch.

In 1998, Marine Fighter Attack Squadron 312—commanded by Lieutenant Colonel Stephen M. Pomeroy and flying off the USS *Enterprise* (CVN 65)—flew strike missions into Iraq as part of Operation Desert Fox, a four-day bombing campaign conducted by the United States and Great Britain in response to Iraq's defiance of the United Nation's resolutions.[30]

Reflections

Liberating Kuwait from the Iraqi forces occupying it was not a victory free from cost. During Operations Desert Shield and Desert Storm, 383 American servicemembers lost their lives in the theater of war. Of those, 68 were Marines: 44 non-battle-related deaths and 24 battle-related deaths. A further 92 Marines were wounded in action. Five Marines, as mentioned above, were captured and repatriated following the conflict.[31]

There are no reliable estimates of Iraqi losses during the campaign. Iraqi records are unclear, for example, on exactly how many Iraqi troops were in Kuwait when the liberation began. Most estimates indicate that 20–30 percent of each Iraqi division had deserted or been given leave prior to the invasion; it is thus very difficult to determine how many Iraqis were slain in the fighting. Tens of thousands of Iraqis surrendered to Coalition forces, and thousands, perhaps tens of thousands, were slain resisting the liberation. And, of course, Iraqi casualties in the invasion of Kuwait are unclear, though they were not heavy. Saddam believed that if he could achieve a ratio of one American slain for every four Iraqis slain, he would win the war. He does not seem to have achieved that ratio, but he believed he won the war anyway.[32]

Indeed, Saddam was convinced that he won the Gulf War, that the tenacity and stubborn defense of Iraqi forces under fire persuaded the Americans to end the conflict earlier then they intended. As Kevin Woods notes in his examination of the Iraq side of the conflict, *The Mother of All Battles*, Saddam declared that

I am very sure the criminal Bush did not expedite the cease-fire until he realized that our armor was [resisting]. . . . He probably said to himself, "It is very apparent that he [Saddam] is going to cause us damage." He worried that the so-called victory would take an unfavorable turn; therefore he rushed alone, before the [UN] Security Council discussed the situation with him and decided on a cease-fire, in order for him to control the cease-fire situation.[33]

Saddam's primary criteria for victory was that he end the conflict alive and in command of Iraq. He began the war as a response to what he saw as an American conspiracy to destroy Saddam Hussein, and he saw no meaningful distinction between Iraq and himself. After the war, the Iraqi military undertook a series of studies and conferences devoted to learning the lessons of the Gulf War, lessons they put to immediate practical use against the ongoing Northern and Southern Watch air campaigns.[34]

The U.S. Army saw the Gulf War as a vindication of the training methods and doctrine developed in response to the crisis it experienced in the immediate aftermath of the Vietnam War. For the U.S. Navy, the war emphasized its ability to project power but highlighted its relative isolation from the post–Goldwater-Nichols joint command environment. For the U.S. Air Force, the Gulf War was the culmination of its fervent belief in airpower's ability to win wars.[35]

For their part, Marines began evaluating the Gulf War's impact on international relations, military affairs, and interservice politics even before it ended. Brigadier General Granville Amos, assistant commander of the 3d Marine Aircraft Wing, had some prophetic words and an admonition for those historical writers who would inevitably follow this war: "We are going to discuss it for years. Books are going to be written. The Marines . . . will self-flagellate and point fingers. . . . But I think that we've got to be careful of, as we are writing things down, that we don't lose sight of what our mission was and the fact that we did it." His warning was echoed by Marine Aircraft Group 13 commander Colonel John Bioty, who later stated, "Things worked better over there than we made them out to be back here. The real war was fought when we started to write the books about Desert Storm."[36]

Looking back at the conflict, the Marine commanders felt the role of the amphibious deception needed to be emphasized. Major General James Myatt, commander of the 1st Marine Division, recalled: "I think what we can't dismiss is the level of

effort put into the defenses along the beaches by the Iraqis. . . . Probably 40% to 50% of the Iraqi artillery pieces were pointed to the east in defense of this perceived real threat—an attack from the Gulf. There were literally hundreds of antiaircraft weapon systems laid in a direct-fire mode from Saudi Arabia all the way up way above Kuwait City to defend against the amphibious threat. . . . I think it [the amphibious feint] saved a lot of Marine lives."[37]

Major General William Keys, commander of the 2d Marine Division, believed that the Marines erred in overestimating the Iraqis:

I guess that our biggest overall intelligence shortcoming was in building Saddam Hussein and his forces into a monster that just wasn't there. Going into the battle, this made us more gun-shy than we should have been. Certainly, the Iraqis had more equipment and capability than any force we've ever faced. But the fighting spirit just was not there. The individual foot-soldiers were badly abused by their leaders—not necessarily their military leaders, but their government—and low morale was the result. I think their senior military leaders knew what they were doing. After we seized Kuwait City, we uncovered several sand tables depicting their defenses that were incredibly detailed. They were fully prepared for us. They had thousands of weapons and millions of rounds of small-arms and tank ammunition—so they could have put up one hell of a fight if they had wanted to. Their defensive areas were well organized, and had they chosen to put their hearts into it, we would have had a real fight on our hands.

He concluded that "I guess it all boils down to the fact that the individual Iraqi soldier did not measure up to, say, the North Vietnamese soldier. The Iraqis were not ready to die for what they believed in—whatever that was. And that's it in a nutshell."[38]

Lieutenant General Walter Boomer noted particularly the important role that the relatively new light armored vehicle battalions had in the war:

The LAVs [light armored vehicles] performed extremely well, in some cases very courageously. A lesson that I learned as far as LAVs is concerned is that you've got to stress to them that they need to be careful about what they take on. Part of the problem is that

Photo by LtCol Charles H. Cureton

A herd of camels continues across the desert, ignoring the military preparations around them during Operation Desert Shield.

you've got Marines manning them, and they don't think anything can defeat them. They can't go up against armor and they need to be really careful when they do. So, I think it's just a matter of talking to them about their mission what you expect of them and what you don't expect of them. In our case, it all turned out okay but on a couple of occasions I think it could have gotten a little dicey for them. It's hard for me to fault Marines for being aggressive. So, you've just got to be careful. But, conceptually it worked well and the vehicle served us well.[39]

Brigadier General James Brabham, commander of the 1st Force Service Support Group, noted that logistically the Corps had sent two-thirds of its combat power overseas, fought a war, and returned successfully. He continued: "But the equipment is now back, and it's ready to go, although residual cleanup efforts continue. Training has resumed at our bases, and we have no significant holes in our readiness or our capability to deploy again, when called. When you consider the hard, round-the-clock use that much of the equipment got for eight months, including combat, that's pretty phenome-

nal. And there are a lot of wonderful people out there in the logistics system who made that happen."[40]

Lieutenant General Boomer felt that despite the needed process of institutional self-criticism, "the campaign was successful, and I wouldn't do things much differently." He attributed that success to his junior Marines:

The young lance corporal would take a look, see something 75 or 100 meters out in front that needed to be done, and go out and do it without being told. As I read through award citations from Desert Shield and Desert Storm, this theme reappears, time and time again. That aggressive spirit comes from being well-trained, and confident in your professional knowledge. It is young Marines with that aggressive spirit who take their divisions ahead. When you say that the division is moving forward, you are really saying that thousands of Marines are forging ahead as individuals and in small units. They are the real heroes of any battle. You can have the best battle plan in the world, but without the right people to execute that plan it is no more than a pipe dream. It's the well-trained Marine who turns that plan into reality.[41]

The combined defense of Saudi Arabia and liberation of Kuwait was one of the most successful Marine operations in the twentieth century. One dead Marine is too many, but boldness, superior training, and superior technology made Desert Storm the least costly operation of its scale in Marine Corps history. It did not end conflict with Iraq, however: Marines returned to Kuwait several times in the following decade, and Saddam Hussein was not removed from power until 2003 by Operation Iraqi Freedom. Nevertheless, the Gulf War victory, while incomplete, still stands as a victory, one in which the Marine Corps played a significant part.

Notes

Chapter 1
Background to a Flashpoint

1. This section is based on material from Albert Hourani, *A History of the Arab Peoples* (Cambridge: Belknap Press, 2002), hereafter Hourani, *Arab Peoples*; John L. Esposito, ed., *The Oxford History of Islam* (Oxford: Oxford University Press, 1999), hereafter Esposito, *History of Islam*; Helen C. Metz, ed., *Iraq: A Country Study* (Washington, DC: Department of the Army, 1990); Phebe Marr, *The Modern History of Iraq*, 2d ed. (Boulder, CO: Westview Press, 2004), hereafter Marr, *History of Iraq*.

2. Hourani, *Arab Peoples*, p. 19.

3. Esposito, *History of Islam*, p. 12.

4. Ibid., pp. 14–18; Hourani, *Arab Peoples*, pp. 36–40.

5. Esposito, *History of Islam*, pp. 24–61; Hourani, *Arab Peoples*, pp. 32–59, 83–85.

6. This section is based on material from Marr, *History of Iraq*, pp. 21–60.

7. Ibid., pp. 53–60.

8. Ibid., pp. 61–176.

9. Ibid., p. 92.

10. Ibid., pp. 107–110.

11. Ibid., pp. 113–130.

12. Ibid., pp. 131–134.

13. Ibid., pp. 134–176.

14. Ibid., pp. 178–180.

15. Ibid., pp. 152–158.

16. Hourani, *Arab Peoples*, pp. 253, 280–281, 408–458; Helen C. Metz, ed., *Persian Gulf States: A Country Study* (Washington, DC: Department of the Army, 1994), hereafter Metz, *Persian Gulf States*; Richard Schofield, *Kuwait and Iraq: Historical Claims and Territorial Disputes* (London: Royal Institute of International Affairs, 1994).

17. Marr, *History of Iraq*, pp. 110–111; Metz, *Persian Gulf States*.

18. Metz, *Persian Gulf States*.

19. This section is based on material from Lawrence R. Benson and Jay E. Hines, *The United States Military in North Africa and Southwest Asia Since World War II* (MacDill Air Force Base, FL: United States Central Command, History Office, 1988), p. 1, hereafter Benson and Hines, *Since World War II*; Michael A. Palmer, *On Course to Desert Storm: The United States Navy and the Persian Gulf* (Washington, DC: Naval Historical Center, 1992), pp. 3–18, hereafter Palmer, *On Course;* Michael A. Palmer, *Guardians of the Gulf* (New York: Free Press, 1992), hereafter Palmer, *Guardians;* Jay E. Hines, "Confronting Continuing Challenges: A Brief History of U.S. Central Command," paper presented to the 2d International Conference of Saint Leo College's Center for Inter-American Studies, March 1997, hereafter Hines, "Challenges."

20. Benson and Hines, *Since World War II*, pp. 1–2; Palmer, *On Course*, pp. 19–40, 61–65.

21. Palmer, *On Course*, pp. 66–80.

22. Benson and Hines, *Since World War II*, pp. 19–21.

23. Palmer, *On Course*, pp. 75–88.

24. Ibid., pp. 76–79.

25. Ibid., pp. 80–81; Bruce R. Nardulli, "Dance of Swords: U.S. Military Assistance to Saudi Arabia, 1942–1964" (PhD dissertation, The Ohio State University, 2002), hereafter Nardulli, "Dance of Swords."

26. Palmer, *On Course*, pp. 89–100.

27. Ibid., p. 108.

28. Ibid., pp. 101–105; Dr. E. Asa Bates, "The Rapid Deployment Force—Fact or Fiction," *RUSI Journal*, Jun81, pp. 23–33; Gen P. X. Kelley, "Progress in the RDJTF," *Marine Corps Gazette*, Jun81, pp. 38–44; John Clementson, "Mission Imperative: The Rapid Deployment Joint Task Force," *Armed Forces*, Jul83, pp. 260–265, and Aug83, pp. 304–308.

29. Gen Robert H. Barrow intvw with BGen Edwin H. Simmons, 17Dec91 (MCHC, Quantico, VA), hereafter Barrow intvw; Allan R. Millett and Jack Shulimson, *Commandants of the Marine Corps* (Annapolis: Naval Institute Press, 2004), pp. 451–455, hereafter Millett and Shulimson, *Commandants*; Allan R. Millett, *Semper Fidelis: The History of the United States Marine Corps* (New York: The Free Press, 1991), pp. 607–635.

30. Barrow intvw; Millett and Shulimson, *Commandants*, pp. 451–455.

31. P. X. Kelley, *A Discussion of the Rapid Deployment Force* (Washington, DC: American Enterprise Institute, 1980), pp. 3–4, hereafter Kelley, *Rapid;* Palmer, *Guardians*, p. 114.

32. Palmer, *On Course*, pp. 105–106; Kelley, *Rapid*, p. 6.

33. Benson and Hines, *Since World War II*, pp. 39–43; Jay E. Hines, "From Desert One to Southern Watch: The Evolution of U.S. Central Command,"

Joint Forces Quarterly, Spring 2000, pp. 44–48, hereafter Hines, "Evolution."

34. Benson and Hines, *Since World War II*, p. 43; Hines, "Evolution," p. 44.

35. Gen George B Crist intvw with Benis M. Frank, 9–10Jan89 (MCHC Quantico, VA), hereafter Crist intvw 9–10Jan89.

36. Crist intvw 9–10Jan89; Hines, "Evolution," p. 44.

37. Crist intvw 9–10Jan89; Hines, "Evolution," p. 44.

38. Benson and Hines, *Since World War II*, p. 47; Robert C. Kingston, "The United States Central Command," *Defense '84*, Apr84, pp. 4–9; Hines, "Challenges."

39. This section is based on material from Kenneth M. Pollack, *Arabs at War: Military Effectiveness 1948–1991* (Lincoln and London: University of Nebraska Press, 2002), pp. 182–235, hereafter Pollack, *Arabs at War*; Kevin M. Woods, *The Mother of All Battles* (Annapolis: Naval Institute Press, 2008), pp. 36–40, hereafter Woods, *Mother*; Marr, *History of Iraq*, pp. 181–214; Stephen C. Pelletiere, *The Iran-Iraq War: Chaos in a Vacuum* (New York: Praeger, 1992), hereafter Pelletiere, *Chaos*; Stephen C. Pelletiere, Douglas V. Johnson II, and Leif R. Rosenberger, *Iraqi Power and U.S. Security in the Middle East* (Carlisle Barracks, Pennsylvania: Strategic Studies Institute, 1990), hereafter Pelletiere et al., *Iraqi Power*; Efraim Karsh, *The Iran-Iraq War, 1980–1988* (Oxford: Osprey, 2002), hereafter Karsh, *Iran-Iraq*; Dilip Hiro, *The Longest War: The Iran-Iraq Military Conflict* (New York: London: Routledge, 1991).

40. Pollack, *Arabs at War*, pp. 182–235; Marr, *History of Iraq*, pp. 181–216.

41. Pollack, *Arabs at War*, pp. 182–235; Marr, *History of Iraq*, pp. 181–216.

42. Pollack, *Arabs at War*, pp. 182–235; Marr, *History of Iraq*, pp. 181–216.

43. Pollack, *Arabs at War*, pp. 182–235; Marr, *History of Iraq*, pp. 181–216; Michael Knights, *Cradle of Conflict* (Annapolis: Naval Institute Press, 2005), p. 5, hereafter Knights, *Cradle*.

44. Pollack, *Arabs at War*, pp. 182–235; Marr, *History of Iraq*, pp. 181–216.

45. Pollack, *Arabs at War*, pp. 182–235; Marr, *History of Iraq*, pp. 181–216.

46. Maj Ronald E. Bergquist, *The Role of Airpower in the Iran-Iraq War* (Maxwell Air Force Base, AL: Air University Press, 1988); Tom Cooper and Farzad Bishop, *The Iran–Iraq War in the Air 1980–1988* (Atglen, PA: Schiffer Publishing, 2003); Pollack, *Arabs at War*, pp. 182–235; Marr, *History of Iraq*, pp. 181–216.

47. Bergquist, *Airpower*; Pollack, *Arabs at War*, pp.

182–235; Marr, *History of Iraq*, pp. 181–216.

48. Bergquist, *Airpower*; Pollack, *Arabs at War*, pp. 182–235; Marr, *History of Iraq*, pp. 181–216; Knights, *Cradle*, pp. 25–27.

49. Bergquist, *Airpower*; Pollack, *Arabs at War*, pp. 182–235; Marr, *History of Iraq*, pp. 181–216; Woods, *Mother*; Kevin M. Woods, et al., *Iraqi Perspectives Project: A View of Operation Iraqi Freedom from Saddam's Senior Leadership* (Norfolk, VA: Joint Center for Operational Analysis, n.d.), p. 15, hereafter Woods et al., *Iraqi Perspectives*.

50. Pollack, *Arabs at War*, pp. 182–235; Marr, *History of Iraq*, pp. 181–216.

51. Pollack, *Arabs at War*, pp. 182–235; Marr, *History of Iraq*, pp. 181–216.

52. Pollack, *Arabs at War*, pp. 182–235; Marr, *History of Iraq*, pp. 181–216; Karsh, *Iran-Iraq*, pp. 57–58; Pelletiere et al., *Iraqi Power*, pp. 24–25.

53. This section is based on material from Palmer, *On Course*; Palmer, *Guardians*; Hines, "Challenges"; David B. Crist, "Before Desert Storm: Marines in the Persian Gulf and the Beginning of U.S. Central Command," *Fortitudine* 29, no. 4 (2003): pp. 9–12, hereafter Crist, "Before Desert Storm"; David B. Crist, "Joint Special Operations in Support of Earnest Will," *Joint Forces Quarterly*, Autumn/Winter 2001–2002, pp. 15–22, hereafter Crist, "Joint Special Operations"; Danny J. Crawford, "Historical Overview of Marines in the Persian Gulf Region" (Washington, DC: Hist&MusDiv, HQMC, Aug91); Stephen Andrew Kelley, "Better Lucky than Good: Operation Earnest Will as Gunboat Diplomacy" (MA thesis, Naval Postgraduate School, 2007), hereafter Kelley, "Better Lucky"; John Partin, ed., *United States Special Operations Command History* (Tampa, FL: USSOCOM History and Research Office, 1998), hereafter Partin, *Special Operations*; Edward J. Marolda and Robert J. Schneller Jr., *Shield and Sword: The United States Navy and the Persian Gulf War* (Washington, DC: Naval Historical Center, 1998), pp. 3–43, hereafter Marolda and Schneller, *Shield and Sword*.

54. Palmer, *On Course*, pp. 112–119.

55. Ibid., p. 124.

56. David B. Crist, "A Low Intensity Conflict at Sea: U.S. Marines in the Persian Gulf, 1987–1988" (ms, MCHD, Quantico, VA, 2000), hereafter Crist, "Low Intensity."

57. Crist, "Joint Special Operations," pp. 15–22.

58. Ibid., pp. 15–22; Palmer, *On Course*, pp. 127, 130–132.

59. Palmer, *On Course*, pp. 142–146; Kelley, "Better Lucky."

60. Palmer, *On Course*, pp. 142–146; Kelley, "Better Lucky."

61. Palmer, *On Course*, pp. 142–146; Kelley, "Better Lucky"; Crist, "Before Desert Storm."

62. Pollack, *Arabs at War*, pp. 228–229; Palmer, *On Course*; Kelley, "Better Lucky"; Crist, "Before Desert Storm."

63. Woods, *Mother*, pp. 31–43; Pollack, *Arabs at War*, pp. 232–235; Marr, *History of Iraq*, pp. 212–215.

CHAPTER 2
Kuwait Invaded

1. This section is based predominantly on material from Woods, *Mother*, pp. 31–59; Pollack, *Arabs at War*, pp. 232–235; Marr, *History of Iraq*, pp. 217–227; Knights, *Cradle*, pp. 3–12; Peter Vine and Paula Casey, *Kuwait: A Nation's Story* (London: Immel Publishing, 1992), pp. 133–149, hereafter Vine and Casey, *Kuwait*; John Levins, *Days of Fear: The Inside Story of the Iraqi Invasion of Kuwait* (Dubai: Motivate Publishing, 1997), pp. 22–50, hereafter Levins, *Days of Fear*; Michael R. Gordon and LtGen Bernard E. Trainor, *The Generals' War* (Boston: Little, Brown and Company, 1995), pp. 4–30, hereafter Gordon and Trainor, *Generals' War*; Marolda and Schneller, *Shield and Sword*, pp. 43–59; BGen Robert H. Scales Jr., et al., *Certain Victory: The U.S. Army in the Gulf War* (Washington, DC: Office of the Chief of Staff, United States Army, 1993), pp. 39–69, hereafter Scales et al., *Certain Victory*; Richard W. Stewart, *War in the Persian Gulf: Operations Desert Shield and Desert Storm, August 1990–March 1991* (Washington, DC: U.S. Army Center of Military History, 2010), pp. 1–10, hereafter Stewart, *Persian Gulf*.

2. Marr, *History of Iraq*, pp. 217–22; Woods, *Mother*, pp. 31–59.

3. Marr, *History of Iraq*, p. 22.

4. Ibid., pp. 221–223; Woods, *Mother*, p. 72.

5. Marr, *History of Iraq*, p. 223; Woods, *Mother*, p. 41.

6. Woods, *Mother*, pp. 31–36.

7. Ibid., pp. 31–59; Marr, *History of Iraq*, pp. 218–225; quote from Barzan Ibrahim al-Tikriti ltr to Saddam Hussein 4Sept1989 (ISGZ-2004-00147), hereafter al-Tikriti ltr.

8. Woods et al., *Iraqi Perspectives*, p. 6.

9. Woods, *Mother*, p. 51; Saddam Hussein mtg w/Yasser Arafat, 19Apr1990 (ISGQ-2003-M0006048), hereafter Arafat mtg.

10. Woods, *Mother*, p. 51; Arafat mtg.

11. Woods et al., *Iraqi Perspectives*, pp. 15–16, 20.

12. Ibid., p. 95.

13. Woods, *Mother*, p. 49; Marr, *History of Iraq*, p. 227; Gordon and Trainor, *Generals' War*, pp. 20–23.

14. Woods, *Mother*, p. 77; Marr, *History of Iraq*, p. 227–228; mentioned in Saddam Hussein mtg w/president of Yemen, 4Aug1990 (ISGQ-2003-00044897), hereafter Yemen mtg.

15. Woods, *Mother*, pp. 60–62; Pollack, *Arabs at War*, pp. 182–235.

16. Woods, *Mother*, p. 62; Saddam mtg w/Baath officials, 17Nov1991 (ISGQ-2003-M0005371); "Role of the General Military Intelligence Directorate in Um Al-Ma'arik Battle and in Controlling Riots," 15Jul2001 (ISGP-2003-00033136), hereafter "Role of the GMID."

17. Woods, *Mother*, pp. 62–64.

18. Knights, *Cradle*, p. 7; Woods, *Mother*, p. 63; Charles E. Allen, "Warning and Iraq's Invasion of Kuwait: A Retrospective Look," *Defense Intelligence Journal*, 1998; Marolda and Schneller, *Shield and Sword*, pp. 42–43.

19. Woods, *Mother*, pp. 62–67; "Military Seminar on the Republican Guard during the Invasion of Kuwait, ca. 1993" (ISGQ-2003-M0006038).

20. Woods, *Mother*, pp. 62–67.

21. Ibid., pp. 70–73; "Role of the GMID"; Aerial Photograph of Kuwait City (ISGP-2003-00038232); Aerial Photograph of Saudi Arabian Naval Base (ISGP-2003-00037981); aerial photograph of Kuwaiti Desalination Plant (ISGP-2003-00038524); "Role of the Air Force and Air Defense in the Mother of All Battles," 5Oct1991 (ISGP-2003-00031468).

22. Woods, *Mother*, pp. 72–73; "5th Scientific Seminar on the Strategic Role of Umm al-Ma'arik Battle," Al-Bakir University for Military Studies, 15May1992 (ISGQ-2003-M0006198), hereafter al-Bakir seminar.

23. Woods, *Mother*, p. 78.

24. Ibid., pp. 78–81.

25. Ibid.

26. Ibid., p. 81.

27. Ibid., pp. 80–81; Vine and Casey, *Kuwait*, p. 140.

28. Woods, *Mother*, pp. 81–88.

29. Ibid., p. 88.

30. Vine and Casey, *Kuwait*, pp. 134–137.

31. Martin Stanton, *Road to Baghdad* (New York: Ballantine Books, 2003), pp. 47–71, quotes from pp. 52 and 54, hereafter Stanton, *Road to Baghdad*.

32. Woods, *Mother*, pp. 78–81.

33. Ibid., pp. 73–78; al-Bakir seminar; Robert O. Freeman, "Moscow and the Iraqi Invasion of Kuwait," *The Middle East after Iraq's Invasion of Kuwait* (Gainesville: University Press of Florida, 1993), pp. 88–90.

34. Woods, *Mother*, pp. 73–78.

35. Ibid.

36. Ibid., pp. 87–88.

37. Marine Security Guard (MSG) Bn rpt to HQ USMC, "Sequence of Events in Kuwait and Baghdad," 27Aug1990 (MSG Bn S-3 Archives, Quantico, VA), hereafter MSG Bn, "Sequence of Events"; MSG Bn ComdC, Jan–Dec90 (Gray Research Center, Quantico, VA), hereafter MSG Bn ComdC; Leo J. Daugherty III, *The Marine Corps and the State Department: Enduring Partners in United States Foreign Policy, 1798–2007* (Jefferson, NC: McFarland, 2009), hereafter Daugherty, *Enduring Partners*; Joseph Wilson, *The Politics of Truth* (New York: Carroll & Graf Publishers, 2004), pp. 106–174, hereafter Wilson, *Politics*; U.S. News & World Report staff, *Triumph Without Victory: The History of the Persian Gulf War* (New York: Random House, 1992), pp. 7–90, hereafter U.S. News, *Without Victory*.

38. Wilson, *Politics*, p. 130.

39. Ibid.; Daugherty, *Enduring Partners*; MSG Bn, "Sequence of Events"; MSG Bn ComdC.

40. *Without Victory*, p. 7; MSG Bn ComdC; Daugherty, *Enduring Partners*; Sgt Paul G. Rodriguez, AAR for Iraq's Invasion of Kuwait (MSG Bn S-3 Archives, Quantico, VA), hereafter Sgt Rodriguez, AAR; SSgt J. B. Smith, AAR for MSGDET, Kuwait, 2Aug90 to 11Dec90 (MSG Bn S-3 Archives, Quantico, VA), hereafter SSgt Smith, AAR.

41. SSgt Smith, AAR.

42. Sgt Rodriguez, AAR; the account of the alleged Kuwaiti murder of two Iraqi soldiers is also reported by Maj Feeley in U.S. News, *Without Victory*, p. 13.

43. Sgt Rodriguez, AAR.

44. U.S. News, *Without Victory*, p. 78.

45. SSgt Smith, AAR.

46. Ibid.

47. Ibid.; MSG Bn, "Sequence of Events"; MSG Bn ComdC.

48. SSgt Smith, AAR.

49. Ibid.; Sgt Rodriguez, AAR.

50. SSgt Smith, AAR; MSG Bn, "Sequence of Events"; MSG Bn ComdC; Daugherty, *Enduring Partners*.

51. This section is based primarily on material from Woods, *Mother*, pp. 103–118; Marr, *History of Iraq*, pp. 229–235; Gordon and Trainor, *Generals' War*, pp. 31–53; Marolda and Schneller, *Shield and Sword*, pp. 54–57.

52. Gordon and Trainor, *Generals' War*, pp. 36–37.

53. Woods, *Mother*, pp. 104–105; Saddam Hussein discussing right of Iraq in Kuwait, 1990 (Harmony document folder ISGP-2003 10151576).

54. Ibid., pp. 105–106.

55. Ibid., pp. 106–108.

56. LtGen Walter E. Boomer intvw with author, 27Jul06 (MCHC, Quantico, VA), hereafter Boomer intvw.

Chapter 3
Desert Shield

1. Department of Defense, *Conduct of the Persian Gulf War: Final Report to Congress* (Department of Defense: Washington, DC: 1992), p. 38, hereafter Department of Defense, *Final Report*; Scales et al., *Certain Victory*, pp. 49–51; Frank N. Schubert and Theresa L. Kraus, eds., *The Whirlwind War The United States Army in Operations Desert Shield and Desert Storm* (Washington, DC: U.S. Army Center of Military History, 1995), pp. 52–53, hereafter Schubert and Kraus, *Whirlwind War*; Marolda and Schneller, *Shield and Sword*, pp. 61–65.

2. Gordon and Trainor, *Generals' War*.

3. Barrow intvw.

4. Marolda and Schneller, *Shield and Sword*, pp. 63–64; Gordon and Trainor, *Generals' War*, pp. 49–51; LtGen Joseph P. Hoar, lecture at Marine Corps Historical Center, Washington, DC: 1Apr91 (Gray Research Center, Quantico, VA), hereafter Hoar lecture.

5. Ibid.

6. Gordon and Trainor, *Generals' War*, p. 50; Hoar lecture.

7. This section based on material from the relevant Marine command chronologies archived at the Gray Research Center, Quantico, VA, as well as Maj Steven M. Zimmeck, *U.S. Marines in the Persian Gulf, 1990–1991: Combat Service Support in Desert Shield and Desert Storm* (Washington, DC: Hist&MusDiv, HQMC, 1999), hereafter Zimmeck, *Combat Service Support*; LtCol Charles H. Cureton, *U.S. Marines in the Persian Gulf, 1990–1991: With the 1st Marine Division in Desert Shield and Desert Storm* (Washington, DC: Hist&MusDiv, HQMC, 1993), hereafter Cureton, *1st Marine Division*; LtCol Leroy D. Stearns, *U.S. Marines in the Persian Gulf, 1990–1991: With the 3d Marine Aircraft Wing in Desert Shield and Desert Storm* (Washington, DC: Hist&MusDiv, HQMC, 1999), hereafter Stearns, *3d Marine Aircraft Wing*; Col Charles J. Quilter II, *U.S. Marines in the Persian Gulf, 1990–1991: With the I Marine Expeditionary Force in Desert Shield and Desert Storm* (Washington, DC: Hist&MusDiv, HQMC, 1993), hereafter Quilter, *I Marine Expeditionary Force*.

8. Hoar lecture.

9. 7th Marines ComdC, Jul–Sep90 (Gray Research Center, Quantico, VA); Col Verle E. Ludwig, *U.S. Marines at Twentynine Palms, California* (Washington, DC: Hist&MusDiv, HQMC, 1989); Zimmeck, *Combat Service Support*, pp. 3–4, 215.

10. Stearns, *3d Marine Aircraft Wing*, pp. 5–15.

11. H&HS-38 ComdC, Jan91 (Gray Research Center, Quantico, VA).

12. Zimmeck, *Combat Service Support*, p. 7; Marolda and Schneller, *Shield and Sword*, pp. 63–65; MALS-16 ComdC, 4 Aug–3 Sept 1990 (Gray Research Center, Quantico, VA).

13. Maj Mike F. Applegate intvws with LtCol Charles H. Cureton, 6 and 13Dec90 (MCHC Quantico, VA), hereafter Applegate intvws; Cureton, *1st Marine Division*, p. 3; Quilter, *I Marine Expeditionary Force*, pp. 7–8.

14. MajGen John I. Hopkins, "This Was No Drill", *U.S. Naval Institute Proceedings*, Nov91, reprinted in Maj Charles D. Melson, Evelyn A. Englander, and Capt David A. Dawson, eds., *U.S. Marines in the Persian Gulf, 1990–1991: Anthology and Annotated Bibliography* (Washington, DC: Hist&MusDiv, HQMC, 1992), p. 25, hereafter Melson et al., *Anthology*.

15. Ibid.

16. This section based on material from the relevant Marine command chronologies archived at the Gray Research Center, Quantico, VA, as well as LtCol Ronald J. Brown, *U.S. Marines in the Persian Gulf, 1990–1991: With Marine Forces Afloat in Desert Shield and Desert Storm* (Washington, DC: Hist&MusDiv, HQMC, 1998), hereafter Brown, *Marine Forces Afloat*; Melson et al., *Anthology*; Marolda and Schneller, *Shield and Sword*; 13th MEU (SOC) ComdC, Jul–Dec90 (Gray Research Center, Quantico, VA), hereafter 13th MEU (SOC) ComdC.

17. Brown, *Marine Forces Afloat*, p. 12.

18. 13th MEU (SOC) ComdC; Brown, *Marine Forces Afloat*, pp. 15–16.

19. 4th MEB ComdC, Aug90 (Gray Research Center, Quantico, VA); Brown, *Marine Forces Afloat*, pp. 16–22; Operation Sharp Edge, the Liberian evacuations conducted 1990–1991, is described fully in Majs James G. Antal and R. John Vanden Berghe, *On Mamba Station: U.S. Marines in West Africa, 1990–2003* (Washington, DC: Hist&MusDiv, HQMC, 2004).

20. 4th MEB ComdC, Aug90.

21. Brown, *Marine Forces Afloat*, pp. 22–23, 230; 4th MEB ComdC, Aug90.

22. Brown, *Marine Forces Afloat*, pp. 21–25, 28; 4th MEB ComdC, Aug90.

23. Brown, *Marine Forces Afloat*, pp. 30–33; 4th MEB ComdC, Aug90.

24. Brown, *Marine Forces Afloat*, pp. 34–36, 42; Marolda and Schneller, *Shield and Sword*, p. 84.

25. ComUSNavCent, OpOrd 1-90, "Desert Shield Amphibious Operations" (msg 311200Z Aug 90); Brown, *Marine Forces Afloat*, pp. 41–45.

26. Brown, *Marine Forces Afloat*, pp. 42–43; Marolda and Schneller, *Shield and Sword*, pp. 117–118; Bernard C. Trainor, "Amphibious Operations in the Gulf War," *Marine Corps Gazette,* Aug94, p. 56.

27. 4th MEB AAR (Gray Research Center, Quantico, VA); Brown, *Marine Forces Afloat*, pp. 42–43; Marolda and Schneller, *Shield and Sword*, pp. 117–118.

28. Brown, *Marine Forces Afloat*, pp. 46–50; 13th MEU (SOC) ComdC, Oct90; 4th MEB ComdC, Oct90 (Gray Research Center, Quantico, VA).

29. Brown, *Marine Forces Afloat*, p. 48; 13th MEU (SOC) ComdC, Oct90.

30. Brown, *Marine Forces Afloat*, pp. 54–59; MajGen Harry W. Jenkins, Comments on draft ms, 24Feb2012 (MCHC, Quantico, VA).

31. 13th MEU (SOC) ComdC; Marolda and Schneller, *Shield and Sword*, pp. 83–96; Brown, *Marine Forces Afloat*, pp. 59–61.

32. Brown, *Marine Forces Afloat*, pp. 61–62.

33. This section based on material from the relevant Marine command chronologies archived at the Gray Research Center, Quantico, VA, as well as Zimmeck, *Combat Service Support*; Cureton, *1st Marine Division*; Stearns, *3d Marine Aircraft Wing*; Quilter, *I Marine Expeditionary Force*; Melson et al., *Anthology*; Marolda and Schneller, *Shield and Sword*.

34. Cureton, *1st Marine Division*, pp. 6–15; 1st MarDiv ComdC, Aug–Dec90 and Jan–Feb91 (Gray Research Center, Quantico, VA).

35. Stearns, *3d Marine Aircraft Wing*, pp. 44–45, 55.

36. Zimmeck, *Combat Service Support*, pp. 35–37; 1st FSSG ComdC, 3–30Sep90 (Gray Research Center, Quantico, VA).

37. Thomas E. Leard, "Marine Corps Intelligence for War as it Really Is" (master's thesis, Naval Postgraduate School, 1991), pp. 52–57; Quilter, *I Marine Expeditionary Force*, pp. 17–18; 1st SRIG SAR to I MEF, 10Jun91.

38. CO Naval Construction Battalions, U.S. Pacific Fleet, ltr to CNO, Subj: Naval Construction Force Support of Operation Desert Shield\Desert Storm, dtd 23 Jan92, hereafter "Naval Construction Force Support."

39. Scales et al., *Certain Victory*, pp. 90–97; Gordon and Trainor, *Generals' War*, pp. 66–70.

40. Scales et al., *Certain Victory*, pp. 90–97; Gordon and Trainor, *Generals' War*, pp. 66–70; Cureton, *1st Marine Division*, pp. 21–22.

41. Nardulli, "Dance of Swords."

42. Mohamed Heikal, *Illusions of Triumph* (New York: HarperCollins, 1992).

43. Quilter, *I Marine Expeditionary Force*, pp. 6, 27–28.

44. Otto J. Lehrack, *America's Battalion: Marines in the First Gulf War* (Tuscaloosa: University of Alabama Press, 2005), pp. 36–37, hereafter Lehrack, *America's Battalion*.

45. Boomer intvw.

46. Anthony H. Cordesman, *Saudi Arabia*, (Boulder: Westview Press, 1997), p. 122, hereafter Cordesman, *Saudi Arabia*; LtCol Peter J. Palmer, "Battle of Khafji: A Gulf State Perspective" (paper, Marine Corps University, u.d.), hereafter Palmer, "Gulf State."

47. Cordesman, *Saudi Arabia*, p. 137; Palmer, "Gulf State"; Stanton, *Road to Baghdad*.

48. Palmer, "Gulf State"; Stanton, *Road to Baghdad*, pp. 14–18; LtCol James R. Braden, "The Battle of Khafji: A Coalition Air Ground Task Force Victory" (paper, USMC Command and Staff College, 1999), pp. 5, 23, 29–30, hereafter Braden, "Khafji."

49. Gen Khaled bin Sultan with Patrick Seale, *Desert Warrior: A Personal View of the Gulf War by the Joint Forces Commander* (New York: HarperCollins, 1995), hereafter Khaled, *Desert Warrior*.

50. Col Joseph Molofsky intvws with author, 30Jun06 and 16Aug06 (MCHC, Quantico, VA), hereafter Molofsky intvw, 30Jun06, or Molofsky intvw, 16Aug06; Stanton, *Road to Baghdad*, pp. 23–25.

51. BGen Thomas V. Draude intvw with author and Dr. Fred Allison, 21Jun06 (MCHC, Quantico, VA), hereafter Draude intvw, 21Jun06.

52. Col John A. Admire intvw, CD 10234 (Grey Research Center, Quantico, VA), hereafter Admire intvw.

53. Molofsky intvws, 30Jun06 and 16Aug06; Braden, "Khafji," p. 8.

54. Lehrack, *America's Battalion*, pp. 55–56.

55. BGen Thomas V. Draude intvw with LtCol Charles H. Cureton, 29Dec90 (MCHC, Quantico, VA), hereafter Draude intvw, 29Dec90; 1st MarDiv ComdC, Oct90; Admire intvw; Cureton, *1st Marine Division*, pp. 21–24; Transcripts, I MEF Daily Staff Briefings, Sept–Nov90 (MCHC, Quantico, VA).

56. Draude intvw, 29Dec90.

CHAPTER 4
Preparing for War

1. Woods, *Mother*, pp. 103–117.

2. I MEF ComdC, Nov90; BGen Paul K. Van Riper, "Observations During Operation Desert Storm," *Marine Corps Gazette*, Jun91, pp. 54–61; Quilter, *I Marine Expeditionary Force*, pp. 24–27.

3. Stenographer's transcript of I MEF morning briefing, 19–21Nov90; 4th MEB ComdC, Nov90; Brown, *Marine Forces Afloat*, pp. 64–69; Marolda and Schneller, *Shield and Sword*, p. 150.

4. Braden, "Khafji," p. 8; Stearns, *3d Marine Aircraft Wing*, pp. 60–63, 72–75.

5. Brown, *Marine Forces Afloat*, pp. 69–70.

6. 4th MEB ComdC, Nov90; 4th MEB ComdC, Dec90; Marolda and Schneller, *Shield and Sword*, pp. 83–96; Brown, *Marine Forces Afloat*, pp. 62–64.

7. 4th MEB ComdC, Dec90; Marolda and Schneller, *Shield and Sword*, pp. 151–152; Brown, *Marine Forces Afloat*, pp. 62–64.

8. 4th MEB ComdC, Nov90; I MEF ComdC, Nov90; Quilter, *I Marine Expeditionary Force*, p. 30; Marolda and Schneller, *Shield and Sword*, p. 161.

9. Lehrack, *America's Battalion*, pp. 49–54; Marolda and Schneller, *Shield and Sword*, pp. 160–161.

10. Lehrack, *America's Battalion*, p. 52.

11. Henry Allen, "Saudi Christmas: the Marines Banter and Brave the Cold," *Washington Post*, 26Dec1990, reprinted in Melson et al., *Anthology*, pp. 43–45; Lehrack, *America's Battalion*, pp. 49–54.

12. Stenographer's transcript of I MEF morning briefing, 17Dec90; Marolda and Schneller, *Shield and Sword*, p. 163.

13. BGen Thomas V. Draude, comments on draft ms, 12Jan12 (MCHC, Quantico, VA).

14. Author(s) uncertain, I MEF ComdC Jan–Feb91.

15. 2d MarDiv ComdC, Jul–Dec90; LtCol Dennis P. Mroczkowski, *U.S. Marines in the Persian Gulf, 1990–1991: With the 2d Marine Division in Desert Shield and Desert Storm* (Washington, DC: Hist&Mus-Div, HQMC, 1993), pp. 3–7, hereafter Mroczkowski, *2d Marine Division*.

16. Zimmeck, *Combat Service Support*, p. 75.

17. 2d MarDiv ComdC, Jan–Apr91; Mroczkowski, *2d Marine Division*, pp. 10–11.

18. CG 3d MAW msg to CMC, Subj: Third MAW Reinforcement List, 0317 14ZDec90; Stearns, *3d Marine Aircraft Wing*, pp. 64–67.

19. 3d MAW ComdC, Jan–Feb91; Stearns, *3d Marine Aircraft Wing*, pp. 67–71.

20. 1st FSSG ComdC, Dec90–Feb91; DSC ComdC Dec90–Feb91; Zimmeck, *Combat Service Support*, pp. 63–67.

21. DSC ComdC Dec90–Feb91; Zimmeck, *Combat Service Support*, pp. 77–80.

22. 5th MEB ComdC Jul–Dec90; Brown, *Marine Forces Afloat*, pp. 73–76.

23. 5th MEB ComdC Jul–Dec90.

24. Ibid.

25. Ibid.; Brown, *Marine Forces Afloat*, p. 78.

26. Brown, *Marine Forces Afloat*, pp. 96–97; LtCol Darrell L. Stewart, MCRC PAM-92-0001, "Amphibious Operations in Southwest Asia" (MCCDC, Quantico, VA, 1992).

27. 11th MEU ComdC Jan–Jun91; Brown, *Marine Forces Afloat*, p. 76.

28. Brown, *Marine Forces Afloat*, pp. 98–103; Marolda and Schneller, *Shield and Sword*, pp. 121–122.

29. Brown, *Marine Forces Afloat*, pp. 106–107.

30. Ibid., pp. 74–76; Quilter, *I Marine Expeditionary Force*, pp. 21–23, 72; BGen Edwin H. Simmons, "Getting Marines To the Gulf," *U.S. Naval Institute Proceedings*, May 1991 reprinted in Melson et al., *Anthology*, pp. 13–14.

31. Woods, *Mother*, pp. 124–162.

32. Ibid., pp. 130–134, 144–149; Knights, *Cradle*, pp. 25–27; *A Statistical Compendium and Chronology—Gulf War Air Power Survey*, vol. 5 (Washington, DC: U.S. Government Printing Office, 1993), pp. 18–19, hereafter *GWAPS, Statistics; Weapons, Tactics, and Training and Space Operations—Gulf War Air Power Survey*, vol. 4 (Washington, DC: U.S. Government Printing Office, 1993), pp. 10–17, hereafter *GWAPS, Weapons*.

33. Woods, *Mother*, pp. 144–149; *GWAPS, Statistics*, pp. 18–19; *GWAPS, Weapons*, pp. 17–29.

34. Woods, *Mother*, pp. 134–137; Marolda and Schneller, *Shield and Sword*, pp. 67–69.

35. Woods, *Mother*, pp. 139–141; *3d Armored Division*, Maneuver Plan no. 3, 29Nov1990 (FM8625).

36. Woods, *Mother*, pp. 142–143.

37. "Iraqi Divisions & Independent Brigades," 24Feb1991, History Division Reference Files (MCHC, Quantico, VA); Woods, *Mother*, p. 204.

38. Pollack, *Arabs at War*, pp. 182–235; Woods, *Mother*, p. 141; Iraqi *III Corps* commander discusses the Gulf War (ISGQ-2003-M0003323).

39. Woods, *Mother*, pp. 139–140; Iraqi *III Corps* commander discusses the Gulf War (ISGQ-2003-M0003323).

40. Woods, *Mother*, pp. 156–159.

41. Ibid., pp. 149–156; Norman Cigar, *Saddam Hussein's Nuclear Vision: An Atomic Shield and Sword for Conquest* (Quantico, VA: Marine Corps University Press, 2011).

42. Woods, *Mother*, pp. 159–163.

43. Diane T. Putney, *Airpower Advantage: Planning the Gulf War Air Campaign 1989–1991* (Washington, DC: Air Force History and Museums Program, 2004), pp. 34–59, hereafter Putney, *Airpower Advantage*; Williamson Murray, *Air War in the Persian Gulf* (Baltimore: Nautical and Aviation, 1995), pp. 7–44, hereafter Murray, *Air War*; Gordon and Trainor, *Generals' War*, pp. 75–101.

44. Gordon and Trainor, *Generals' War*, pp. 75–101; Putney, *Airpower Advantage*, pp. 34–59.

45. Richard G. Davis, *On Target: Organizing and Executing the Strategic Air Campaign against Iraq* (Washington, DC: Air Force History and Museums Program, 2002), p. 37, hereafter Davis, *On Target*; Putney, *Airpower Advantage*, pp. 119–178.

46. Stearns, *3d Marine Aircraft Wing*, p. 46.

47. Ibid., pp. 46–47.

48. Ibid., pp. 46–49; Boomer intvw; Davis, *On Target*, pp. 97–98.

49. Scales et al., *Certain Victory*, pp. 108–133; Gordon and Trainor, *Generals' War*, pp. 123–141.

50. Quilter, *I Marine Expeditionary Force*, pp. 20–21.

51. Scales et al., *Certain Victory*, pp. 108–133; Quilter, *I Marine Expeditionary Force*, pp. 37–39.

52. Scales et al., *Certain Victory*, pp. 108–133; Quilter, *I Marine Expeditionary Force*, pp. 37–39.

53. Scales et al., *Certain Victory*, pp. 108–133; Boomer intvw.

54. LtGen Bernard E. Trainor, "Brief on Iraqi Forces," 10Dec1990.

55. Quilter, *I Marine Expeditionary Force*, pp. 37–39.

56. Sir Peter de la Billière, *Storm Command: A Personal Account of the Gulf War* (Abu Dhabi: Motivate Publishing, 1992), p. 88, hereafter de la Billière, *Storm Command*.

57. Ibid., p. 89; Gordon and Trainor, *Generals' War*, pp. 166–168; Boomer intvw.

58. de la Billière, *Storm Command*, pp. 89–90.

59. Boomer intvw.

60. Ibid.

61. Ibid.

62. Ibid.; Gordon and Trainor, *Generals' War*, pp. 175–177.

63. Boomer intvw; Brown, *Marine Forces Afloat*, p. 115.

64. Danny J. Crawford, "Activation of a Marine Expeditionary Corps for Operation Desert Storm," 30Jan1991, History Division Reference Files (MCHC, Quantico, VA).

65. Boomer intvw; Brown, *Marine Forces Afloat*, p. 115.

CHAPTER 5
The Air War

1. This section based on material from Murray, *Air War*; Gordon and Trainor, *Generals' War*; Woods, *Mother*; Stearns, *3d Marine Aircraft Wing*; Davis, *On Target*; *GWAPS, Statistics*; Stenographer's transcript of I MEF morning briefings, Jan91; Quilter, *I Marine Expeditionary Force*; Putney, *Airpower Advantage*; Marolda and Schneller, *Shield and Sword*.

2. Stearns, *3d Marine Aircraft Wing*, pp. 104–105.

3. Jay A. Stout, *Hornets over Kuwait* (Annapolis: MD:

Naval Institute Press, 1997), p. 69, hereafter Stout, *Hornets*; Stearns, *3d Marine Aircraft Wing*, p. 106.

4. Jon Stewart, "US Arsenal's 'Smart Weapons' Passing Combat Tests in Gulf," *San Francisco Chronicle*, 19Jan1991; Marvin Pokrant, *Desert Storm at Sea: What the Navy Really Did* (Westport, CT: Greenwood Press, 1999), pp. 10–13.

5. Woods, *Mother*, p. 181.

6. Stearns, *3d Marine Aircraft Wing*, p. 106; VMA-224 ComdC, 1–31Jan91 (Gray Research Center, Quantico,VA), hereafter VMA–224 Comd C; Quilter, *I Marine Expeditionary Force*, p. 49.

7. Stearns, *3d Marine Aircraft Wing*, p. 106; VMA-224 ComdC, 1–31Jan91; Quilter, *I Marine Expeditionary Force*, p. 49.

8. LtCol W. Beanan Cummings Jr., "Around the World to the Storm," *Marine Corps Gazette*, May92, p. 58.

9. Capt David W. Deist award citation (Ref MCHC, Quantico, VA).

10. VMFA-333 ComdC, Jan91 (Gray Research Center, Quantico, VA), hereafter VMFA-333 ComdC.

11. *GWAPS, Statistics*, p. 653; SSgt Robert M. Sexton, USAF, "Marine Aviator Scores Aerial Victory," *Marines,* May93, pp. 5–7; Davis, *On Target*, pp. 200–201.

12. Col John R. Bioty intvw, 15May95, hereafter Bioty intvw; Stearns, *3d Marine Aircraft Wing*, pp. 104–105; Lon Nordeen, "The Marines AV-8B Gulf Deployment," *AFM Magazine,* Feb92, pp. 42–43; LtCol Richard M. Barry, "In Praise of Close Air Support," *Marine Corps Gazette,* May92, p. 56; Stenographer's transcript of I MEF morning briefings, 17Jan91.

13. Bioty intvw; LtCol Richard M. Barry, "In Praise of Close Air Support," *Marine Corps Gazette,* May92, p. 56, hereafter Barry, "In Praise."

14. Barry, "In Praise."

15. Stenographer's transcript of I MEF morning briefings, 17Jan91.

16. Stearns, *3d Marine Aircraft Wing*, pp. 107–108; Stout, *Hornets*, pp. 72–73.

17. Stout, *Hornets*, pp. 80–81.

18. Ibid., p. 75–83.

19. Woods, *Mother*, pp. 241–242; *GWAPS, Statistics*, p. 161.

20. Northrop Grumman, "Joint Stars Data Analysis: The Battle of Khafji" (paper, USAF Studies and Analysis Agency, 1997), p. 18; James Titus, "The Battle of Khafji: An Overview and Preliminary Analysis" (Maxwell AFB, AL: School of Advanced Airpower Studies, 1996), p. 7.

21. Stearns, *3d Marine Aircraft Wing*, pp. 110–111.

22. Table 204 Desert Storm Coalition Aircraft Attrition

found in *GWAPS, Statistics*, pp. 642–649; Cynthia B. Acree with Col Clifford M. Acree, *The Gulf between Us: Love and Terror in Desert Storm* (Washington, DC: Brassey's, 2000), pp. 5–6, hereafter Acree et al., *Gulf between*; Stearns, *3d Marine Aircraft Wing*, p. 111.

23. Stearns, *3d Marine Aircraft Wing*, p. 111. For an extended, in-depth description of Col Acree's captivity, see Acree et al., *Gulf between Us*.

24. Stearns, *3d Marine Aircraft Wing*, pp. 111–112.

25. Ibid., p. 109; BGen Granville R. Amos intvw, 5Mar91 (MCHC, Quantico, VA).

26. Stearns, *3d Marine Aircraft Wing*, p. 114.

27. Ibid., p. 112–118; *GWAPS, Statistics*, pp. 469–511.

28. Stearns, *3d Marine Aircraft Wing*, pp. 109–110; Col Manfred A. Rietsch BAT intvw, Mar91 (MCHC, Quantico, VA), hereafter Rietsch intvw.

29. Col Donald A. Beaufait intvw with Alexander Hinman, 8Jul08 (MCHC, Quantico, VA).

30. Col William R. Jones intvw with Dr. Fred Alison, 8Mar02 (location unknown), hereafter Jones intvw.

31. Woods, *Mother*, p. 185.

32. Dr. Youssef Abdul-Moati, *A Diary of an Iraqi Soldier* (Center for Research and Studies on Kuwait, 1992), pp. 13–14, hereafter Abdul-Moati, *A Diary*.

33. Jones intvw.

34. I MEF, "Tiger Team Anti-Fratricide Report," 10Feb1991; Stenographer's transcript of I MEF briefing, 23Jan90.

35. Woods, *Mother*, pp. 189–191; Stearns, *3d Marine Aircraft Wing*, p. 118.

36. Stenographer's transcript of I MEF briefing, 21–26Jan90; Stearns, *3d Marine Aircraft Wing*, p. 118; Stout, *Hornets*, pp. 97–103.

37. Woods, *Mother*, pp. 192–193.

38. Putney, *Airpower Advantage*, p. 175.

39. Stenographer's transcript of I MEF briefings, Jan90.

40. Marolda and Schneller, *Shield and Sword*, pp. 182–192.

41. Rietsch intvw.

42. Stearns, *3d Marine Aircraft Wing*, pp. 120–121.

43. Ibid., p. 119; Table 204 Desert Storm Coalition Aircraft Attrition found in *GWAPS, Statistics*, pp. 642–649.

44. VMFA-333 ComdC; VMFA-235 ComdC, Jan91 (Gray Research Center, Quantico, VA).

45. Quilter, *I Marine Expeditionary Force*, pp. 51–52; Stenographer's transcript of I MEF briefing, 29Jan90.

46. Quilter, *I Marine Expeditionary Force*, pp. 51–52; Captured Iraqi War College Study, Al-Khafji Conflict (ISGQ-2003-00046031), hereafter Iraqi War College Study.

47. Stenographer's transcript of I MEF morning briefings, 28Jan91.

48. Woods, *Mother*, pp. 22–23; Iraqi War College Study.

49. Woods, *Mother*, pp. 22–23.

50. Iraqi War College Study.

51. Abdul-Moati, *A Diary*, p. 14.

CHAPTER 6
Preludes to al-Khafji

1. DSC ComdC, Dec90–Feb91; Zimmeck, *Combat Service Support*, pp. 77–80.

2. Zimmeck, *Combat Service Support*, p. 80.

3. Ibid., pp. 84–85.

4. Ibid., pp. 85–86.

5. Adam B. Siegel, "An American Entebbe," *U.S. Naval Institute Proceedings*, May92, p.100. For a more thorough description of Operation Eastern Exit, see Brown, *Marine Forces Afloat*, pp. 80–94.

6. Ibid., pp. 107–109.

7. Table 204 Desert Storm Coalition Aircraft Attrition found in *GWAPS, Statistics*, pp. 642–649; VMA-331 ComdC, Jan–May1991 (Gray Research Center, Quantico, VA); Maj Ben D. Hancock, "The Day The Magic Died," *Marine Corps Gazette*, May95, pp. 73–81.

8. Brown, *Marine Forces Afloat*, pp. 107–109.

9. Woods, *Mother*, pp. 180–184.

10. Ibid., p. 185.

11. Stenographer's transcript of I MEF morning briefing, 22Jan90; 1st LAI ComdC, Jan–Feb1991 (Gray Research Center, Quantico, VA), hereafter 1st LAI ComdC.

12. LtCol James L. Sachtleben, "Artillery Raids in Southwestern Kuwait," reprinted in Melson et al., *Anthology*, pp. 173–182, hereafter Sachtleben, "Artillery Raids."

13. Stearns, *3d Marine Aircraft Wing*, p. 122; Cureton, *1st Marine Division*, pp. 26–28; Sachtleben, "Artillery Raids."

14. 11th Marines ComdC, Jan–Feb1991 (Gray Research Center, Quantico, VA); Stenographer's transcript of I MEF morning briefing, 21Jan90.

15. 1st LAI ComdC; Stenographer's transcript of I MEF morning briefing, 26Jan90; Sachtleben, "Artillery Raids."

16. Stenographer's transcript of I MEF morning briefing, 28Jan90; Mroczkowski, *2d Marine Division*, p. 12.

17. Sachtleben, "Artillery Raids"; 1st LAI ComdC; Stenographer's transcript of I MEF morning briefing, 29Jan90.

18. This section based on material from LtCol James R. Braden, "The Battle of Khafji: A Coalition Air Ground Task Force Victory" (paper, USMC Command and Staff College, 1999), pp. 11–12, hereafter Braden, "Khafji"; see also Murray, *Air War*; Gordon and Trainor, *Generals' War*; Woods, *Mother*; Paul W. Westermeyer, *U.S. Marines in Battle: Al-Khafji, 28 January–1 February 1991* (Washington, DC: Marine Corps History Division, 2008), hereafter Westermeyer, *Al-Khafji*; Woods, et al., *Iraqi Perspectives*; Iraqi War College Study; Pollack, *Arabs at War*.

19. Iraqi War College Study.

20. Ibid.

21. Ibid., p. 96.

22. Edgar O'Ballance, *The Gulf War* (New York: Brassey's, 1988), summary of discussion on pp. 94, 143–145, 164–166, 173–174, 194; Gordon and Trainor, *Generals' War*, pp. 268–269; Palmer, "Gulf State."

23. *How They Fight: Desert Shield Order of Battle Handbook*, AIA-DS-2-90 (1990); Department of Defense, *Iraq Country Handbook*, DOD-2600-642794 (1994).

24. Iraqi War College Study; Captured Iraqi Training Pamphlet, Battle of al-Khafji (ISGQ-2003-00054592), hereafter Iraqi Training Pamphlet.

25. Iraqi War College Study, pp. 104–105.

26. Air War College Study, "EPW Interviews" (Maxwell AFB, AL: Air Force Historical Research Agency); Palmer, "Gulf State."

27. Iraqi War College Study, p. 101.

28. Draude intvw, 21Jun06.

29. Molofsky intvws, 30Jun06, 16Aug06; Braden, "Khafji," pp. 8–9.

30. Ibid., pp. 6–7.

31. Titus, "Khafji," p. 9; Gordon and Trainor, *Generals' War*, pp. 268–269.

32. Molofsky intvw, 16Aug06.

33. 1st Air-Naval Gunfire Liaison Company/1st Surveillance, Reconnaissance, Intelligence Group After Action Report for the Battle of Khafji, 29Jan91–1Feb91 (MCHC, Quantico VA), hereafter ANGLICO AAR.

34. LtCol Clifford O. Myers intvw by LtCol Charles H. Cureton, 8Mar91 (MCHC, Quantico, VA), hereafter Myers intvw.

35. Khaled, *Desert Warrior*; Braden, pp. 7–8; Palmer, "Gultate."

36. Zimmeck, *Combat Service Support*, p. 108.

37. Molofsky intvw, 16Aug06.

38. Braden, "Khafji," p. 8.

39. Iraqi War College Study, p. 97.

40. Ibid., pp. 99–101.

41. Ibid., p. 98.

42. Ibid., p. 99.

43. Ibid., p. 103; Gordon and Trainor, *Generals' War*, p. 269.

44. Iraqi War College Study, pp. 104–107.
45. Titus, "Khafji," p. 7.
46. Braden, "Khafji," p. 13.
47. Ibid., pp. 13–14; ANGLICO AAR.
48. David J. Morris, *Storm on the Horizon* (New York: Free Press, 2004), p. 145, hereafter Morris, *Storm*; Iraqi War College Study.
49. Morris, *Storm*, p. 145.
50. Iraqi War College Study, pp. 108–109.
51. Ibid., pp. 144–146.
52. Ibid., pp. 108–109.
53. Braden, "Khafji," p. 14.
54. Ibid.; ANGLICO AAR.
55. Morris, *Storm,* pp. 31–32.
56. Ibid., Ch. 1.
57. Ibid., pp. 3, 31–34.
58. Morris, *Storm,* p. 50; Roger Pollard, "The Battle for Op-4: Start of the Ground War," *Marine Corps Gazette*, Mar92, hereafter Pollard, "Op-4"; Myers intvw; 1st LAI ComdC.
59. Pollard, "Op-4"; Myers intvw; 1st LAI ComdC.
60. Operation Desert Sting is described in great detail in Brown, *Marine Forces Afloat*, pp. 139–143.

CHAPTER 7
The Battle of al-Khafji

1. Iraqi War College Study, pp. 120–125.
2. Morris, *Storm*, pp. 1–6; Pollard, "Op-4"; Myers intvw.
3. Morris, *Storm*, pp. 66–68, 68–73.
4. Pollard, "Op-4."
5. Ibid.; 1stLt David Kendall intvw, 7Feb91 (Gray Research Center, Quantico, VA), hereafter Kendall intvw.
6. Pollard, "Op-4."
7. Ibid.; Capt Roger L. Pollard intvw with LtCol Charles H. Cureton, CD# 10441 (Gray Research Center, Quantico, VA), hereafter Pollard intvw.
8. Kendall intvw.
9. Pollard, "Op-4"; 1st LAI ComdC; Fratricide: Investigation into USAF Attack on Marine LAV, SWA-0062, Seq. No. 01980 (MCLLS, Quantico, VA), hereafter Fratricide Investigation.
10. Pollard intvw; Myers intvw.
11. Pollard, "Op-4"; Pollard intvw; Myers intvw.
12. Iraqi War College Study, pp. 120–125, 144–146.
13. Ibid., pp. 120–125.
14. 2d LAI ComdC, Jan–Feb91 (Gray Research Center, Quantico, VA).
15. Ibid.; Titus, "Khafji," p. 12; Mroczkowski, *2d Marine Division*, pp. 20–23; Gordon and Trainor, *Generals' War*, pp. 274–275.
16. Morris, *Storm,* pp. 114–118.
17. Titus, "Khafji," p. 12; Gordon and Trainor, *Generals' War*, p. 275; Morris, *Storm*, pp. 119–125.
18. Titus, "Khafji," p. 12.
19. Pollard, "Op-4"; 1st LAI ComdC.
20. ANGLICO AAR; Braden, "Khafji," p. 15.
21. ANGLICO AAR; Braden, "Khafji," p. 14.
22. Khaled, *Desert Warrior*, p. 366.
23. Palmer, "Gulf State"; Titus, "Khafji," p. 13; Gordon and Trainor, *Generals' War,* pp. 279–286; Khaled, *Desert Warrior*, pp. 381–387; Rick Atkinson, *Crusade: The Untold Story of the Persian Gulf War* (Boston: Houghton Mifflin, 1993), pp. 208–213, hereafter Atkinson, *Crusade*.
24. Braden, "Khafji," p. 14.
25. ANGLICO AAR.
26. Molofsky intvw, 16Aug06; Khaled, *Desert Warrior*, p. 368.
27. Khaled, *Desert Warrior*, pp. 365, 368.
28. Braden, "Khafji," p. 15.
29. Titus, "Khafji," p. 11; Gordon and Trainor, *Generals' War*, pp. 273, 278.
30. HMLA-367 ComdC, Jan91, and HMLA-369 ComdC, Jan91 (Gray Research Center, Quantico, VA); Stearns, *3d Marine Aircraft Wing*, pp. 124–125.
31. Morris, *Storm*, p. 150–158.
32. Clifton A. Barnes, "In Every Clime and Place," *Leatherneck*, Aug91, pp. 16–20.
33. Titus, "Khafji," p. 10; Friedman, pp. 160, 197–198; Gordon and Trainor, *Generals' War*, pp. 268–269; Marolda and Schneller, *Shield and Sword*, pp. 227–229.
34. ANGLICO AAR; Braden, "Khafji," p. 15.
35. ANGLICO AAR; Braden, "Khafji," p. 15.
36. ANGLICO AAR; Braden, "Khafji," p. 15.
37. Iraqi War College Study, p. 111.
38. Ibid., pp. 120–125, 147–148.
39. Ibid., pp. 125–126.
40. Morris, *Storm*, pp. 166–169.
41. 1st Recon ComdC, Jan–Mar91, and 3d Recon ComdC, Jan–Feb91 (Gray Research Center, Quantico, VA).
42. Molofsky intvw, 30Jun06.
43. Morris, *Storm*, pp. 159–166.
44. I Marine Expeditionary Force Commander's Morning Briefing, 30Jan91; Boomer intvw.
45. Khaled, *Desert Warrior*, pp. 364, 376.
46. ANGLICO AAR.
47. Ibid.
48. Ibid.
49. Braden, "Khafji," p. 16; ANGLICO AAR.
50. ANGLICO AAR; Braden, "Khafji," pp. 16–17.
51. 1/12 ComdC, Jan–Feb91 (Gray Research Center,

Quantico, VA), hereafter 1/12 ComdC; HMLA-367 ComdC, Jan91 (Gray Research Center, Quantico, VA).

52. Braden, "Khafji," pp. 19–20.

53. Ibid.

54. Admire intvw.

55. Morris, *Storm,* pp. 193–196.

56. Ibid., pp. 196–197.

57. R. R. Keene, "In Every Clime and Place," *Leatherneck,* Mar91, pp. 22–27; Morris, *Storm,* pp. 196–198; Lehrack, *America's Battalion,* pp. 128–131.

58. David H. Mould, "Press Pools and Military-Media Relations in the Gulf War: A Case Study of the Battle of Khafji, January 1991," *Historical Journal of Film, Radio & Television,* Jun96, p. 133.

59. Khaled, *Desert Warrior,* p. 374.

60. Gordon and Trainor, *Generals' War,* pp. 279.

61. Khaled, *Desert Warrior,* p. 374; Boomer intvw.

62. Khaled, *Desert Warrior,* p. 378.

63. Braden, "Khafji," p. 20; Khaled, *Desert Warrior,* pp. 362–390; LtCol Martin N. Stanton, "The Saudi Arabian National Guard Motorized Brigades," *Armor,* Mar–Apr96, pp. 6–11.

64. Molofsky intvw, 16Aug06.

65. Ibid.

66. ANGLICO AAR.

67. Stanton, *Road to Baghdad,* pp. 261–262; Molofsky intvw, 16Aug06.

68. Stanton, *Road to Baghdad,* pp. 262–264; Braden, "Khafji," pp. 20–22; Molofsky intvw, 30Jun06.

69. Braden, "Khafji," pp. 22–23; Stanton, *Road to Baghdad,* p. 266.

70. Palmer, "Gulf State."

71. Titus, "Khafji," pp. 13–14.

72. Titus, "Khafji," pp. 17–20; Gordon and Trainor, *Generals' War,* p. 284. The most detailed secondary account of the downing of this AC-130 is in Atkinson's *Crusade,* p. 210.

73. Gordon and Trainor, *Generals' War,* pp. 283, 285–87.

74. Morris, *Storm,* p. 253; ANGLICO AAR; 1/12 ComdC.

75. Morris, *Storm,* pp. 253–258.

76. ANGLICO AAR; Braden, "Khafji," p. 17.

77. Braden, "Khafji," pp. 22–23; ANGLICO AAR.

78. Morris, *Storm,* pp. 258–266.

79. Braden, "Khafji," pp. 23–24.

80. ANGLICO AAR.

81. Titus, "Khafji," pp. 17–20; Gen Salah Aboud Mahmoud's comments and the references to Iraqi radio communications are taken from Gordon and Trainor, *Generals' War,* pp. 283, 285–87; the "cockroach" analogy appears in H. Norman Schwarzkopf, *It Doesn't Take a Hero* (New York: Linda Grey, Bantam, 1992), p. 429.

82. ANGLICO AAR.

83. Iraqi Training Pamphlet; ANGLICO AAR.

84. Myers intvw; Braden, "Khafji," p. 32.

85. Admire intvw; Molofsky intvw, 30Jun06.

86. Boomer intvw; Molofsky intvw, 16Aug06.

87. Titus, "Khafji"; Barry D. Watts, et al., "Effects and Effectiveness," *Operations and Effects and Effectiveness,* vol. II of *The Gulf War Air Power Survey,* Eliot A. Cohen, et al., eds. (Washington, DC: U.S. Government Printing Office, 1993), p. 240.

88. Khaled, *Desert Warrior,* p. 390.

89. Iraqi War College Study, p. 97.

90. Gordon and Trainor, *Generals' War,* p. 288.

91. Fratricide Investigation.

CHAPTER 8
The Final Preparations

1. Boomer intvw.

2. Mroczkowski, *2d Marine Division,* pp. 23–25; "Rolling With the 2d Marine Division: Interview with Lieutenant General William M. Keys, USMC," reprinted in Melson et al., *Anthology,* pp. 146–155, hereafter Keys, "Rolling with the 2d."

3. Keys, "Rolling with the 2d."

4. Boomer intvw.

5. BGen Charles C. Krulak intvw with Dr. David B. Crist, 17Oct00 (MCHC, Quantico, VA), hereafter Krulak intvw; Keys, "Rolling with the 2d"; Mroczkowski, *2d Marine Division,* pp. 25–26; Zimmeck, *Combat Service Support,* pp. 115–116.

6. Boomer intvw.

7. Brown, *Marine Forces Afloat,* pp. 130–133; Marolda and Schneller, *Shield and Sword,* p. 254.

8. Brown, *Marine Forces Afloat,* pp. 162–163.

9. Stenographer's transcript of I MEF briefing, 6Feb91.

10. Zimmeck, *Combat Service Support,* pp. 116–117.

11. Ibid., pp. 117–118.

12. Stearns, *3d Marine Aircraft Wing,* p. 145.

13. Krulak intvw.

14. LtGen James A. Brabham, comments on draft ms, 16Jan2012 (MCHC, Quantico, VA), hereafter Brabham comments; Zimmeck, *Combat Service Support,* pp. 120–124.

15. Sachtleben, "Artillery Raids"; Stearns, *3d Marine Aircraft Wing,* p. 122; Cureton, *1st Marine Division,* pp. 26–28; Mroczkowski, *2d Marine Division,* p. 12.

16. 1st MarDiv ComdC, Jan–Feb1991 (Gray Research Center, Quantico, VA), hereafter 1st MarDiv ComdC; 5/11 ComdC, Jan–Feb1991 (Gray Research Center, Quantico, VA), hereafter 5/11 ComdC.

17. Sachtleben, "Artillery Raids"; 5/11 ComdC.

18. I MEF to USCINCCENT "Friendly Fire Incident Report," 13Aug1991 (Box 26, Southwest Asia Archive, Gray Research Center, Quantico, VA), hereafter I MEF, "Friendly Fire"; Fratricide—Aircraft Incidents and Marine Air Command and Control Issues (Box 61, Southwest Asia Archive, Gray Research Center, Quantico, VA), hereafter Fratricide—Aircraft Incidents; 5/11 ComdC; 1st MarDiv ComdC.

19. 1st LAI ComdC; 1st MarDiv ComdC.

20. Stenographer's transcripts of I MEF briefings, 6–9Feb91; Marolda and Schneller, *Shield and Sword*, pp. 256–257.

21. Stenographer's transcript of I MEF briefing, 7Feb91.

22. 1st MarDiv ComdC; 1st LAI ComdC; Stenographer's transcript of I MEF briefing, 9Feb91.

23. 1st Recon ComdC, Jan–Mar1991 (Gray Research Center, Quantico, VA); Stenographer's transcripts of I MEF briefings, 10–12Feb91.

24. Stenographer's transcripts of I MEF briefings, 9–11Feb91; 1st MarDiv ComdC; 11th Marines ComdC, Jan–Feb1991 (Gray Research Center, Quantico, VA), hereafter 11th Marines ComdC.

25. 2d MarDiv ComdC, Jan–Apr1991 (Gray Research Center, Quantico, VA), hereafter 2d MarDiv ComdC; Stenographer's transcript of I MEF briefing, 12Feb91.

26. Abdul-Moati, *A Diary*, p. 14.

27. Ibid., p. 15.

28. Stearns, *3d Marine Aircraft Wing*, pp. 130–131; Col Manfred A. Rietsch BAT intvw, Mar91 (MCHC, Quantico, VA).

29. Quilter, *I Marine Expeditionary Force,* pp. 52–54.

30. Stearns, *3d Marine Aircraft Wing*, pp. 150, 192; HMLA 369 ComdC, Feb1991 (Gray Research Center, Quantico, VA); HMA 775 ComdC, Feb1991 (Gray Research Center, Quantico, VA).

31. Stearns, *3d Marine Aircraft Wing*, p. 132.

32. Col John R. Bioty Jr. intvw with Maj John T. Quinn II, 16May96 (MCHC, Quantico, VA); Stearns, *3d Marine Aircraft Wing*, pp. 139–140.

33. Stearns, *3d Marine Aircraft Wing*, pp. 134–136.

34. Table 204, Desert Storm Coalition Aircraft Attrition, found in *GWAPS, Statistics,* pp. 642–649, hereafter Table 204; Stearns, *3d Marine Aircraft Wing*, p. 133.

35. Table 204; Stearns, *3d Marine Aircraft Wing*, p. 133.

36. Paula Chin, "Home After 26 Days in Iraqi Hands, Pilot Russell Sanborn Celebrates His Freedom and Counts His Blessings," *People*, 01Apr91.

37. Col William R. Jones intvw with Fred Alison, 8Mar02 (location unknown).

38. Table 204; Stenographer's transcript of I MEF briefing, 12Feb91.

39. Marolda and Schneller, *Shield and Sword*, pp. 246–247; *GWAPS, Chronology*, p. 212.

40. Stenographer's transcript of I MEF briefing 17Feb91; Adam B. Sigel, "Missile Defense at the Waterfront: Implications of the SCUD Missile Attack on Al Jubayl Port, 15–16 February 1991," *Defense & Security Analysis* 19, no. 1, 2003, pp. 15, 17–18; Marolda and Schneller, *Shield and Sword*, p. 197.

41. Table 204; LtCol John Scanlan intvw with Fred Allison, 26Oct06 (Gray Research Center, Quantico, VA); Col Stephen F. Mugg intvw with Fred Allison, 17May10 (Gray Research Center, Quantico, VA); Capt R. A. Padilla, "F/A-18Ds Go to War," *U.S. Naval Institute Proceedings,* Aug91, p. 40; Stearns, *3d Marine Aircraft Wing*, p. 150.

42. Table 204; Stearns, *3d Marine Aircraft Wing*, pp. 144–145.

43. Table 204; Stearns, *3d Marine Aircraft Wing*, pp. 144–145.

44. I MEF "Excerpts from a Conversation with an Iraqi: Major, (Fathi) Imad B, Commander 159th Field Artillery Battalion, 7th Division, 3rd Corps, Concerning His Point of View on the War," 2Mar91.

45. Woods, *Mother*, p. 202.

46. Brown, *Marine Forces Afloat*, pp. 144–149.

47. G. J. Michaels, *Tip Of The Spear: U.S. Marine Light Armor in the Gulf* (Annapolis: Naval Institute Press, 1998), p. 155.

48. Stearns, *3d Marine Aircraft Wing*, pp. 126–128; Quilter, *I Marine Expeditionary Force*, pp. 63–64; Tiger Team Anti-Fratricide Report, 10Feb91 (Box 61, Southwest Asia Archive, Gray Research Center, Quantico, VA).

49. Stenographer's transcript of I MEF briefing, 12Feb91.

50. Marolda and Schneller, *Shield and Sword*, pp. 247–268; Brown, *Marine Forces Afloat*, pp. 149–154.

51. Ibid.

52. Woods, *Mother*, p. 134; Marolda and Schneller, *Shield and Sword*, pp. 247–268; Brown, *Marine Forces Afloat*, pp. 149–154.

53. Draude intvw; 1st MarDiv ComdC.

54. Draude intvw.

55. 11th Marines ComdC; 1st MarDiv ComdC; Stenographer's transcript of I MEF briefing, 20Feb91.

56. 1st MarDiv ComdC; Stenographer's transcript of I MEF briefing, 21Feb91; 11th Marines ComdC.

57. Woods, *Mother,* pp. 198–199.

58. Anthony Swofford, *Jarhead: A Marine's Chronicle*

of the Gulf War and Other Battles (New York: Scribner, 2003), pp. 189–190, hereafter Swofford, *Jarhead.*

59. 2d MarDiv ComdC; Mroczkowski, *2d Marine Division*, pp. 31–33; 2d LAI ComdC, Jan–Mar1991 (Gray Research Center, Quantico, VA).

60. Mroczkowski, *2d Marine Division*, p. 34.

61. Woods, *Mother*, p. 209.

62. Capt Kenneth W. Amidon Silver Star award citation (MCHC, Quantico, VA).

63. Capt Troy A. Ward Distinguished Flying Cross award citation (MCHC, Quantico, VA); 1stLt Kevin G. Mechler Distinguished Flying Cross award citation (MCHC, Quantico, VA).

64. 4th Marines ComdC, Jan–Mar1991 (Gray Research Center, Quantico, VA), hereafter 4th Marines ComdC; 3/7 ComdC, Jan–Mar1991 (Gray Research Center, Quantico, VA); 2/7 ComdC, Jan–Mar1991 (Gray Research Center, Quantico, VA).

65. Woods, *Mother*, p. 210.

66. Stenographer's transcript of I MEF briefing, 22Feb91; Quilter, *I Marine Expeditionary Force*, p. 75.

67. Cureton, *1st Marine Division*, p. 61.

68. 1st MarDiv ComdC; Stenographer's transcripts of I MEF briefings, 22–23Feb91; Cureton, *1st Marine Division*, pp. 58–61.

69. 4th Marines ComdC; 3/7 ComdC, Jan–Mar1991 (Gray Research Center, Quantico, VA); 2/7 ComdC, Jan–Mar1991 (Gray Research Center, Quantico, VA).

70. Col Charles J. Quilter II, "Anecdotes from the Ground Campaign," I MEF ComdC, Jan–Feb1991, hereafter Quilter, "Anecdotes."

71. SSgt Charles T. Restifo Silver Star award citation (MCHC, Quantico, VA).

72. Draude intvw; Cpl Gregory R. Stricklin Silver Star award citation (MCHC, Quantico, VA).

73. Phillip Thompson, *Into the Storm: A U.S. Marine in the Persian Gulf War* (Jefferson, NC: McFarland & Company, 2001), pp. 160–163, hereafter Thompson, *Into the Storm.*

74. I MEF, "Friendly Fire"; Fratricide—Aircraft Incidents; 1/12 ComdC, Jan–Feb1991 (Gray Research Center, Quantico, VA); Maj Richard Danchak, "Friendly Radars + Friendly Missiles = Fratricide" (Marine Corps Command and Staff College, Quantico, VA 1993).

75. Woods, *Mother*, pp. 210–212.

Chapter 9
Breaking the Saddam Line

1. This section is based primarily on the relevant unit command chronologies and the following works: Quilter, *I Marine Expeditionary Force*, pp. 73–90; Cureton, *1st Marine Division*, pp. 58–89; Mroczkowski, *2d Marine Division*, pp. 39–58; Zimmeck, *Combat Service Support*, pp. 142–149; Stearns, *3d Marine Aircraft Wing*, pp. 151–152; Brown, *Marine Forces Afloat*, pp. 137–170; Woods, *Mother*, pp. 211–249; Marolda and Schneller, *Shield and Sword*, pp. 279–306; Stewart, *War in the Persian Gulf*, pp. 35–44.

2. Stewart, *War in the Persian Gulf*, p. 35–44.

3. 1st MarDiv ComdC; Cureton, *1st Marine Division*, pp. 68–69.

4. 1st MarDiv ComdC; Cureton, *1st Marine Division*, p. 70.

5. Swofford, *Jarhead.*

6. Ibid., p. 219.

7. I MEF "Friendly Fire"; Cureton, *1st Marine Division*, p. 70; Swofford, *Jarhead*, p. 219; Sgt Gordon T. Gregory Silver Star award citation (MCHC, Quantico, VA); 4th Marines ComdC.

8. 1st MarDiv ComdC; Cureton, *1st Marine Division*, p. 71.

9. 1st MarDiv ComdC; Cureton, *1st Marine Division*, p. 72.

10. 1st MarDiv ComdC; Cureton, *1st Marine Division*, pp. 74–75.

11. Draude intvw; Cureton, *1st Marine Division*, pp. 75–76.

12. 1st MarDiv ComdC; Cureton, *1st Marine Division*, pp. 72, 76–77.

13. 1st MarDiv ComdC; Cureton, *1st Marine Division*, pp. 77–78.

14. 1st MarDiv ComdC; Cureton, *1st Marine Division*, pp. 78–80.

15. 1st MarDiv ComdC; Cureton, *1st Marine Division*, pp. 78–80.

16. 1/7 ComdC, Jan–Feb1991 (Gray Research Center, Quantico, VA), hereafter 1/7 ComdC.

17. 1st MarDiv ComdC; Cureton, *1st Marine Division*, p. 82.

18. 1st MarDiv ComdC; Cureton, *1st Marine Division*, p. 83; 1st LAI ComdC.

19. 1st LAI ComdC.

20. 1st MarDiv ComdC; Cureton, *1st Marine Division*, pp. 84–85.

21. LCpl Kasey A. Krock Silver Star award citation (MCHC, Quantico, VA).

22. 1st Marines ComdC; Cureton, *1st Marine Division*, pp. 85–87.

23. 1st MarDiv ComdC; Cureton, *1st Marine Division*, p. 87.

24. 2d MarDiv ComdC; Mroczkowski, *2d Marine Division*, p. 44.

25. 2d MarDiv ComdC; Mroczkowski, *2d Marine Division*, p. 45; Quilter, *I Marine Expeditionary Force*, pp. 86–87.

26. SSgt Daniel A. Kur Silver Star award citation (MCHC, Quantico, VA).

27. Mroczkowski, *2d Marine Division*, p. 45.

28. Ibid., p. 46.

29. Cpl Robert L. Novak Silver Star award citation (MCHC, Quantico, VA).

30. Mroczkowski, *2d Marine Division*, pp. 46–47.

31. Ibid., p. 48.

32. Ibid., pp. 48–51.

33. 8th Tank ComdC, Nov–Mar1991 (Gray Research Center, Quantico, VA); Mroczkowski, *2d Marine Division*, p. 51.

34. Khaled, *Desert Warrior*, pp. 391–99; Col David W. Landersman intvw with author, 27Jul08 (MCHC, Quantico, VA).

35. Marolda and Schneller, *Shield and Sword*, pp. 279, 288–289.

36. Ibid., p. 288.

37. MajGen James M. Myatt, "The 1st Marine Division in the Attack," reprinted in Melson et al., *Anthology*; Stearns, *3d Marine Aircraft Wing*, pp. 151–152.

38. *GWAPS, Statistics,* pp. 642–649; Stearns, *3d Marine Aircraft Wing*, p. 152.

39. Stearns, *3d Marine Aircraft Wing*, pp. 152–154.

40. Cureton, *1st Marine Division*, pp. 88–89; Stearns, *3d Marine Aircraft Wing*, p. 155.

41. Woods, *Mother*, pp. 220–225.

42. This section is based primarily on the relevant unit command chronologies and the following works: Quilter, *I Marine Expeditionary Force*, pp. 91–102; Cureton, *1st Marine Division*, pp. 90–102; Mroczkowski, *2d Marine Division*, pp. 39–58; Zimmeck, *Combat Service Support*, pp. 150–158; Stearns, *3d Marine Aircraft Wing*, pp. 152–161; Brown, *Marine Forces Afloat*, pp. 137–179; Woods, *Mother*, pp. 211–249; Marolda and Schneller, *Shield and Sword*, pp. 279–306; Stewart, *War in the Persian Gulf*, pp. 44–49.

43. Woods, *Mother*, p. 225.

44. Cureton, *1st Marine Division*, p. 90.

45. Ibid., p. 91; SSgt Joseph A. LeGarde Silver Star award citation (MCHC, Quantico, VA).

46. LCpl Chris A. Sweeney Silver Star award citation (MCHC, Quantico, VA).

47. Quilter, "Anecdotes."

48. Cureton, *1st Marine Division*, p. 91.

49. Ibid., p. 92.

50. Cpl Bryan K. Zickefoose and LCpl Michael S. Kilpatrick Silver Star award citations (MCHC, Quantico, VA); Cureton, *1st Marine Division*, p. 92.

51. Cureton, *1st Marine Division*, p. 93.

52. Ibid., pp. 94–95.

53. Woods, *Mother*, p. 226.

54. Cureton, *1st Marine Division*, p. 95.

55. 2dLt Thomas O. O'Connor Silver Star award citation (MCHC, Quantico, VA).

56. Cureton, *1st Marine Division*, pp. 94–95; Cpl Bryan R. Freeman Silver Star award citation (MCHC, Quantico, VA).

57. Cureton, *1st Marine Division*, p. 96.

58. Ibid., pp. 99–100.

59. Ibid., p. 96.

60. Woods, *Mother*, p. 226.

61. Cureton, *1st Marine Division*, p. 97.

62. Ibid., p. 101.

63. Mroczkowski, *2d Marine Division*, pp. 55–56.

64. Cpl Robert L. Novak Silver Star award citation (MCHC, Quantico, VA).

65. Quilter, *I Marine Expeditionary Force*, pp. 93, 95.

66. Molly Moore, "Storming the Desert with the Generals," reprinted in Melson et al., *Anthology,* hereafter Moore, "Storming."

67. Ibid.

68. Brown, *Marine Forces Afloat*, pp. 155–156.

69. Quilter, "Anecdotes"; Table 204; Stearns, *3d Marine Aircraft Wing*, p. 161.

70. Table 204; Woods, *Mother*, p. 227; Joseph Hanneman, "Eye of the Storm," *Perspective*, vol. 3, no. 1 (Spring 2003), p. 6.

71. Capt David W. Landersman Silver Star award citation (MCHC, Quantico, VA); Col David W. Landersman intvw with author, 27Jul08 (MCHC, Quantico, VA), hereafter Landersman intvw.

72. Landersman intvw.

73. Woods, *Mother*, p. 227.

Chapter 10
Liberating Kuwait

1. This section is based primarily on the relevant unit command chronologies and the following works: Quilter, *I Marine Expeditionary Force,* pp. 103–106; Cureton, *1st Marine Division*, pp. 103–117; Mroczkowski, *2d Marine Division,* pp. 59–71; Zimmeck, *Combat Service Support,* pp. 159–167; Stearns, *3d Marine Aircraft Wing,* pp. 162–165; Brown, *Marine Forces Afloat,* pp. 137–170; Woods, *Mother,* pp. 211–249; Marolda and Schneller, *Shield and Sword,* pp. 279–306; Stewart, *War in the Persian Gulf,* pp. 49–63.

2. Cureton, *1st Marine Division*, p. 103.

3. 1/7 ComdC.

4. Ibid.

5. Col Richard W. Hodory, comments on draft ms, 15Feb12 (MCHC, Quantico, VA).

6. Cureton, *1st Marine Division*, p. 112.

7. Ibid., pp. 115–116.

8. Ibid., pp. 115–116.

9. Ibid., pp. 115–116.

10. Ibid., pp. 115–117.

11. MajGen John H. Admire, comments on draft ms, 1Jan12 (MCHC, Quantico, VA).

12. Stewart, *War in the Persian Gulf*, p. 55.

13. Col John B. Sylvester, USA, intvw with LtCol Charles H. Cureton, 7Mar91 (MCHC, Quantico, VA), hereafter Sylvester intvw.

14. Ibid.

15. Mroczkowski, *2d Marine Division*, p. 65.

16. Stewart, *War in the Persian Gulf*, p. 56.

17. Moore, "Storming."

18. Brown, *Marine Forces Afloat*, pp. 155–156.

19. Stearns, *3d Marine Aircraft Wing*, p. 163.

20. Sylvester intvw.

21. Quilter, "Anecdotes."

22. Stearns, *3d Marine Aircraft Wing*, pp. 163–164.

23. Brown, *Marine Forces Afloat*, pp. 156–157.

24. Ibid., pp. 156–157.

25. Ibid., p. 173.

26. Stearns, *3d Marine Aircraft Wing*, pp. 166–168.

27. Quilter, *I Marine Expeditionary Force*, p. 103.

28. Marolda and Schneller, *Shield and Sword*, p. 300; *United States Special Operations Command History: 15th Anniversary* (Tampa, FL: USSOCOM History and Research Office, 2002), p. 44.

29. Boomer intvw.

30. This section is based primarily on the relevant unit command chronologies and the following works: Quilter, *I Marine Expeditionary Force*, pp. 103–106; Cureton, *1st Marine Division*, pp. 118–120; Mroczkowski, *2d Marine Division*, pp. 59–71; Zimmeck, *Combat Service Support*, pp. 168–172; Stearns, *3d Marine Aircraft Wing*, pp. 166–167; Brown, *Marine Forces Afloat*, pp. 137–179; Woods, *Mother*, pp. 211–249; Marolda and Schneller, *Shield and Sword*, pp. 279–306; Stewart, *War in the Persian Gulf*, pp. 49–63.

31. 1/7 ComdC.

32. 2d MarDiv ComdC; Mroczkowski, *2d Marine Division*, p. 66.

33. Molly Moore, "Porous Minefields, Dispirited Troops and a Dog Named Pow," reprinted in Melson et al., *Anthology*, pp. 95–100.

34. Table 204.

35. Maj Ben D. Hancock, "The Day the Magic Died," *Marine Corps Gazette*, May95, p. 73.

36. LtCol Michael B. Parkyn intvw with Fred Allison, 16Jun10, (Oral HistColl, Gray Research Center, Quantico, VA).

37. Quilter, "Anecdotes."

38. Boomer intvw.

39. Zimmeck, *Combat Service Support*, p. 172.

40. Brabham comments.

41. Quilter, *I Marine Expeditionary Force*, pp. 106–107.

42. Moore, "Storming."

43. Molly Moore, *A Woman at War* (New York: Macmillan Publishing, 1993), pp. 294–295.

44. Ibid., pp. 297–298.

45. I MEF ComdC, Jan–Feb1991 (Gray Research Center, Quantico, VA).

46. Gen H. Norman Schwarzkopf, "CENTCOM News Briefing," reprinted in Melson et al., *Anthology*, p. 53.

CHAPTER 11
Standing Down after Victory

1. Stearns, *3d Marine Aircraft Wing*, p. 167.

2. Col William R. Jones intvw with Dr. Fred Allison, 8Mar02 (location unknown).

3. Thompson, *Into the Storm*, pp. 175–176.

4. Ibid., pp. 176–177.

5. Sean T. Coughlin, *Storming the Desert: A Marine Lieutenant's Day-by-Day Chronicle of the Persian Gulf War* (Jefferson, NC: McFarland, 1996), pp. 90–96.

6. Thompson, *Into the Storm*, pp. 177–178.

7. Quilter, *I Marine Expeditionary Force*, pp. 106–104.

8. Brown, *Marine Forces Afloat*, pp. 173–180.

9. 13th MEU (SOC) ComdC, Mar91; Brown, *Marine Forces Afloat*, pp. 157–160.

10. 13th MEU (SOC) ComdC, Mar91; MSSG 13 ComdC, Feb–Mar91; Brown, *Marine Forces Afloat*, pp. 160–162.

11. H. Norman Schwarzkopf with Peter Petre, *It Doesn't Take a Hero* (New York: Bantam, 1992), pp. 88–489.

12. Stenographer's transcripts of I MEF briefings, 1–3Mar91; Quilter, *I Marine Expeditionary Force*, pp. 107–112.

13. Stenographer's transcripts of I MEF briefings, 1–3Mar91; Quilter, *I Marine Expeditionary Force*, pp. 107–112.

14. Stenographer's transcripts of I MEF briefings, 3Mar91.

15. Ibid.; Herbert Edwards Jr., "Awards during Desert Shield/Storm," email to author, 4Nov11.

16. Quilter, *I Marine Expeditionary Force*, p. 11.

17. Brown, *Marine Forces Afloat*, pp. 180–182.

18. 5th MEB ComdC, July90–Jun91; Brown, *Marine Forces Afloat*, pp. 180–182.

19. 11th MEU ComdC, Jan–Jun91; Brown, *Marine Forces Afloat*, pp. 186–188.

20. For an in-depth history of the Bangladesh humanitarian intervention, see Charles R. Smith, *U.S. Marines in Humanitarian Operations: Angels from the Sea: Relief Operations in Bangladesh, 1991* (Washington, DC: Hist&MusDiv, HQMC, 1995).

21. Cureton, *1st Marine Division*, p. 121.

22. Jay A. Stout, *Hornets over Kuwait* (Annapolis: Naval Institute Press, 1997), pp. 225–256; Quilter, *I Marine Expeditionary Force*, pp. 110–111.

23. Mroczkowski, *2d Marine Division*, pp. 70–72.

24. Zimmeck, *Combat Service Support*, p. 182; Gen Charles C. Krulak, comments on draft ms, 5Feb12 (MCHC, Quantico, VA).

25. Zimmeck, *Combat Service Support*, pp. 176–190.

26. Woods, *Mother*, pp. 246–250; for the uprisings, see Eric Goldstein and Andrew Whitley, *Endless Torment: The 1991 Uprising in Iraq and Its Aftermath* (New York: Human Rights Watch, 1992); for the history of Iraq following the Gulf War, including the uprisings, see Marr, *History of Iraq*; for the history of conflict between the United States and Iraq from 1991 through the 2003 invasion of Iraq, see Knights, *Cradle*.

27. Woods, *Mother*, p. 248.

28. Knights, *Cradle*, pp. 119–124.

29. For an in-depth examination of Marine operations in support of Operation Provide Comfort, see LtCol Ronald J. Brown, *Humanitarian Operations in Northern Iraq, 1991: With Marines in Operation Provide Comfort* (Washington, DC: Hist&MusDiv, HQMC, U.S. Marine Corps, 1995).

30. Dr. Fred Allison, unpub ms, author's files (Gray Research Center, Quantico, VA).

31. U.S. Congressional Research Service, *American War and Military Operations Casualties: Lists and Statistics*, 26 February 2010, p. 12.

32. Woods, *Mother*, p. 26.

33. Ibid., p. 240.

34. The best coverage of the Iraqi military in the Gulf and the subsequent years leading to Operation Iraqi Freedom in 2003 can be found in the works of Kevin Woods and Michael Knights. Specifically, see Knights, *Cradle*; Woods, *Mother*; and Woods et al., *Iraqi Perspectives*.

35. For the U.S. Army's take on the conflict, see Scales, *Certain Victory*. The U.S. Navy has covered its Gulf War experience very well in Marolda and Schneller, *Shield and Sword*. The U.S. Air Force is covered in-depth in the massive, five volume *Gulf War Air Power Survey* (Washington, DC: U.S. Government Printing Office, 1993), but the Air Force's own view of the war is found in Putney, *Airpower Advantage,* and Davis, *On Target*.

36. BGen Granville R. Amos intvw, 5Mar91; Stearns, *3d Marine Aircraft Wing*, p. 171.

37. "The 1st Marine Division in the Attack: Interview with Major General J. M. Myatt, USMC," reprinted in Melson et al., *Anthology*, p. 145.

38. "Rolling With the 2d Marine Division: Interview with Lieutenant General William M. Keys, USMC," reprinted in Melson et al., *Anthology*, p. 155.

39. Boomer intvw.

40. "Training, Education Were the Keys: Interview with Brigadier General James A. Brabham, USMC," reprinted in Melson et al., *Anthology*, p. 40.

41. "Special Trust and Confidence Among the Trail-Breakers: Interview with Lieutenant General Walter E. Boomer, USMC," reprinted in Melson et al., *Anthology*, p. 94.

Command and Staff List

U.S. Marine Forces Central Command

I Marine Expeditionary Force

Commanding General, I Marine Expeditionary Force, and Commander, U.S. Marine Forces Central Command	LtGen Walter E. Boomer
Deputy Commanding General, I Marine Expeditionary Force	MajGen John I. Hopkins (to 7Jan91) MajGen Richard D. Hearney (from 8Jan91)
Commanding General, I Marine Expeditionary Force (Rear)	MajGen John I. Hopkins
Deputy Commander, U.S. Marine Forces Central Command	MajGen Jeremiah W. Pearson III (to 17Jan91) MajGen Norman E. Ehlert (from 18Jan91)
Commander, U.S. Marine Forces Central Command (Forward)	MajGen John J. Sheehan
Chief of Staff	Col Eric E. Hastings
G-1	Col Alice B. Marshall (to 7Oct90) Col Robert K. Redlin (from 8Oct90)
G-2	LtCol Bruce E. Brunn (to 24Dec91) Col Forest L. Lucy (from 25Dec90)
G-3	Col Charles M. Lohman (to 13Dec90) Col Billy C. Steed (from 14Dec90)
G-4	Col Raymond A. List
G-6	Col Robert G. Hill

Command Element

Headquarters and Service Company I Marine Expeditionary Force (-) (Reinforced)	Maj Gary R. Ing
1st Surveillance, Reconnaissance, and Intelligence Group (-) (Reinforced)	Col Michael V. Brock
1st Radio Battalion (-) (Reinforced)	LtCol Thomas A. Flaherty
3d Naval Construction Regiment	Capt Michael R. Johnson, USN

1st Marine Division

Commanding Officer	MajGen James M. Myatt
Assistant Division Commander	BGen Thomas V. Draude

Chief of Staff	Col John F. Stennick
G-1	LtCol William MacGhee (to 6Oct90) Col Joseph R. Holzbauer (from 7Oct90)
G-2	LtCol Joseph Waldron (to 1Dec90) LtCol John D. Counselman (from 2Dec90)
G-3	Col James A. Fulks (to 21Jan91) LtCol Jerome D. Humble (from 22Jan91)
G-4	Col Jasper C. Lilly Jr.
G-6	LtCol Rodney N. Smith
Division Sergeant Major	SgtMaj Charles W. Chamberlain
Headquarters Battalion (-)	LtCol Michael L. Rapp (to 31Dec90) LtCol James P. O'Donnell (from 1Jan91)
1st Marines (-) (Reinforced) (Task Force Papa Bear)	Col Richard W. Hodory
1st Battalion, 1st Marines	LtCol Michael O. Fallon
3d Battalion, 9th Marines	LtCol Larry W. Wright (to 28Dec90) LtCol Michael H. Smith (from 31Dec90)
1st Tank Battalion	LtCol Michael M. Kephart
3d Marines (-) (Reinforced) (Task Force Taro)	Col John H. Admire
1st Battalion, 3d Marines	LtCol Michael V. Maloney
2d Battalion, 3d Marines	LtCol Robert W. Blose Jr.
3d Battalion, 3d Marines	LtCol John C. Garrett
4th Marines (-) (Reinforced) (Task Force Grizzly)	Col Ross A. Brown (to 21Jan91) Col James A. Fulks (from 22Jan91)
2d Battalion, 7th Marines	LtCol Roger J. Mauer
3d Battalion, 7th Marines	LtCol Timothy J. Hannigan
1st Battalion, 25th Marines	LtCol Stephen M. McCartney
7th Marines (-) (Reinforced) (Task Force Ripper)	Col Carlton W. Fulford Jr.
1st Battalion, 7th Marines	LtCol James N. Mattis
1st Battalion, 5th Marines	LtCol Christopher Cortez
1st Combat Engineer Battalion	LtCol Frank L. Kebelman III
3d Tank Battalion	LtCol Alphonso B. Diggs Jr.
11th Marines (-) (Reinforced)	Col Patrick G. Howard
1st Battalion, 11th Marines	LtCol John B. Sollis
3d Battalion, 11th Marines	LtCol Mark W. Adams
5th Battalion, 11th Marines	LtCol James L. Sachtleben
1st Battalion, 12th Marines	LtCol Robert W. Rivers
3d Battalion, 12th Marines	LtCol Joel L. Goza (to 31Oct90) LtCol Charles W. Adair (from 1Nov90)

1st Light Armored Infantry Battalion (-) (Reinforced) (Task Force Shepherd)	LtCol Clifford O. Myers III
3d Assault Amphibian Battalion (-) (Reinforced)	LtCol Ronald S. Eluk
1st Reconnaissance Battalion (-) (Reinforced)	LtCol Charles W. Kershaw (to 31Dec90) LtCol Michael L. Rapp (from 1Jan91)

2d Marine Division

Commanding Officer	MajGen William M. Keys
Assistant Division Commander	BGen Russell L. Sutton
Chief of Staff	Col James K. Van Riper
G-1	Col Mary K. Lowery
G-2	LtCol Christopher J. Gregor
G-3	Col Klaus D. Schreiber (to 14Oct90) Col Ronald G. Richard (from 15Oct90)
G-4	LtCol James D. Lenard (to 11Nov90) Col Morris O. Fletcher (from 12Nov90)
G-6	Col Sepp D. Ramsperger
Division Sergeant Major	SgtMaj Ronald A. Chamberlain
Headquarters Battalion (-) (Reinforced)	Col Roger C. McElraft
6th Marines (-) (Reinforced) (Task Force Breach Alpha)	Col Lawrence H. Livingston
1st Battalion, 6th Marines	LtCol Thomas S. Jones
3d Battalion, 6th Marines	LtCol Arnold Fields
2d Battalion, 2d Marines	LtCol Brian M. Youngs
8th Marines (-) (Reinforced) (Task Force Breach Bravo)	Col Larry S. Schmidt
1st Battalion, 8th Marines	LtCol Bruce A. Gombar
2d Battalion, 4th Marines	LtCol Richard L. Pugh (to 18Oct90) LtCol Kevin A. Conry (from 19Oct90)
3d Battalion, 23d Marines	LtCol Ray C. Dawson
10th Marines (-) (Reinforced)	Col Leslie M. Palm
2d Battalion, 10th Marines	LtCol Joseph R. Stewart
3d Battalion, 10th Marines	LtCol Philip E. Hughes
5th Battalion, 10th Marines	LtCol Harold W. Evans III (to 3Dec90) LtCol Andrew F. Mazzara (from 4Dec90)
2d Battalion, 12th Marines	LtCol Michael J. Swords
1st (Tiger) Brigade, 2d Armored Division	Col John B. Sylvester, USA
1st Battalion, 67th Armored Regiment	LtCol Michael T. Johnson, USA

3d Battalion, 67th Armored Regiment	LtCol Douglas L. Tystad, USA
3d Battalion, 41st Mechanized Infantry Regiment	LtCol Walter Wojdakowski, USA
1st Battalion, 3d Field Artillery	LtCol James R Kerin, USA
502d Forward Support Battalion	LtCol Coy R. Scroggins, USA
142d Signal Battalion	LtCol Henry C. Cobb Jr., USA
5th Air Defense Artillery	(no commander listed)

2d Light Armored Infantry Battalion (-) (Reinforced)	LtCol Keith T. Holcomb
2d Tank Battalion (-) (Reinforced)	LtCol Cesare Cardi
8th Tank Battalion (-) (Reinforced)	LtCol Michael D. Cavallaro
2d Assault Amphibian Battalion (-) (Reinforced)	LtCol Robert L. Williams
2d Combat Engineer Battalion (-) (Reinforced)	LtCol John D. Winchester
2d Reconnaissance Battalion (-) (Reinforced)	LtCol Scott W. McKenzie

3d Marine Aircraft Wing

Commanding General	MajGen Royal N. Moore
Assistant Wing Commander	BGen Harold W. Blot (to 4Oct90)
	BGen Granville R. Amos (from 5Oct90)
Chief of Staff	Col William A. Forney
G-1	LtCol Rudolph Lowery
G-2	LtCol Walter F. McTernan II
G-3	Col Terrance R. Dake
G-4	Col Robert W. Coop (to 20Oct90)
	LtCol Brian E. Dyck (to 31Oct90)
	Col Ronald M. Damura (from 1Nov90)
G-6	LtCol Philip J. O'Brien (to 11Oct90)
	Maj Les Duer (from 12Oct90)
Sergeant Major	SgtMaj Frederick T. Pattee
Marine Wing Headquarters Squadron 3 (-)	LtCol Cass D. Howell
Marine Aircraft Group 11	Col Manfred A. Rietsch
Marine Aviation Logistics Squadron 11 (Forward)	Maj Samuel L. Flores Jr. (date unknown)
	LtCol John J. Moyer (date unknown)
Marine All-Weather Attack Squadron 121	LtCol Stephen F. Mugg
Marine Fighter Attack Squadron 212	LtCol James M. Collins II
Marine Fighter Attack Squadron 232	LtCol Victor A. Simpson
Marine Fighter Attack Squadron 235	Col William C. McMullen III

Marine Fighter Attack Squadron 314   LtCol George G. Stuart
Marine Fighter Attack Squadron 333   LtCol Thomas A. Benes
Marine Fighter Attack Squadron 451   LtCol Andrew S. Dudley Jr.
Marine All-Weather Attack   LtCol William J. Horne
    Squadron 224
Marine All-Weather Attack   LtCol Waldo B. Cummings Jr.
    Squadron 533
Marine Tactical Electronic   LtCol Richard W. Bates
    Warfare Squadron 2
Marine Aerial Refueler   LtCol Arlen D. Rens
    Transport Squadron 352

Marine Aircraft Group 13   Col John R. Bioty Jr.
Marine Aviation Logistics   Maj Christopher D. Platt
    Squadron 13 (Forward)
Marine Aviation Logistics Squadron 14   LtCol Richard L. Owen Jr.
Marine Attack Squadron 231   LtCol William R. Jones
Marine Attack Squadron 311   LtCol Dickie J. White
Marine Attack Squadron 542   LtCol Theodore N. Herman
Marine Observation Squadron 1   LtCol Richard R. Lazisky
Marine Observation Squadron 2   LtCol Clifford M. Acree
    Maj Steven J. Antosh (acting from 19Jan91)

Marine Aircraft Group 16   Col Larry T. Garrett
Marine Aviation Logistics Squadron 16   LtCol Henry A. Commiskey Jr.
Marine Medium Helicopter   LtCol Gary J. Price
    Squadron 161
Marine Medium Helicopter   LtCol Marvin D. Hall
    Squadron 165
Marine Light Attack Helicopter   LtCol Terry J. Frerker
    Squadron 367
Marine Light Attack Helicopter   LtCol Michael M. Kurth
    Squadron 369
Marine Heavy Helicopter Squadron 462   LtCol Daniel R. Rose
Marine Heavy Helicopter Squadron 463   LtCol John R. Mills
Marine Heavy Helicopter Squadron 465   LtCol Ronnie S. Johnston
Marine Heavy Helicopter   LtCol Raymond L. Nymeyer
    Squadron 466 (-)

Marine Aircraft Group 26   Col Michael J. Williams
Marine Aviation Logistics   LtCol John F. Phelps
    Squadron 29 (Forward)
Marine Medium Helicopter   LtCol Emerson N. Gardner Jr.
    Squadron 261
Marine Medium Helicopter   LtCol John F. Pettine
    Squadron 266
Marine Medium Helicopter   LtCol Steven K. Bowman
    Squadron 774
Marine Heavy Helicopter Squadron 464   LtCol Richard J. Klinker (to 18Dec90)
    LtCol Ralph F. Tice (from 19Dec90)
Marine Heavy Helicopter Squadron 362   LtCol Robert A. Forrester
Marine Attack Helicopter Squadron 775   LtCol Paul W. Martin
Marine Light Helicopter Squadron 767   Col Al C. Boudreaux

Marine Air Control Group 38	Col Joseph Della-Corte
Headquarters and Headquarters Squadron 38	Maj Eric D. Zobel
Marine Air Control Squadron 2	LtCol William M. Prather (to 5Dec90)
	LtCol John R. Garvin (from 9Dec90)
Marine Air Control Squadron 6 (-)	LtCol Ronald J. Armstrong
Marine Air Traffic Control Squadron 38	Maj Robert J. Bozelli
Marine Air Support Squadron 3	LtCol Dennis C. Sorrell
Marine Wing Communications Squadron 38	LtCol Timothy J. Himes
2d Light Antiaircraft Missile Battalion	LtCol John E. Ryan
3d Light Antiaircraft Missile Battalion	LtCol Louis L. Boros
2d Low Altitude Air Defense Battalion (-)	LtCol Richard K. Bartzer
3d Low Altitude Air Defense Battalion (-)	LtCol George S. Fick
Marine Wing Support Group 37	Col Robert W. Coop
Headquarters and Headquarters Squadron 37	Maj Clifford C. Holbrook
Marine Wing Support Section 174	LtCol James P. Chessum
Marine Wing Support Section 271	LtCol Richard H. Zegar
Marine Wing Support Section 273	LtCol William L. Riznychok
Marine Wing Support Section 373	LtCol Stephen D. Hanson
Marine Wing Support Section 374	LtCol Stephen G. Hornberger (to 2Feb91)
	LtCol Brian E. Dyck (from 3Feb91)

Building Blocks of 1st Force Service Support Group
(August–September 1990)

Brigade Service Support Group 7	Col Alexander W. Powell
Combat Service Support Detachment 71	Capt Guido G. Aidenbaum
	Maj Allen Coulter
Combat Service Support Detachment 72	Capt Kerry K. Feldman
Combat Service Support Detachment 73	Capt Adrian W. Burke
Brigade Service Support Group 5	LtCol Ernest G. Beinhart III
Combat Service Support Detachment 31	Maj Thomas J. Nielsen

1st Force Service Support Group (-) (Reinforced)
(September 1990–April 1991)

Commanding General	BGen James A. Brabham Jr.
Chief of Staff	Col Thomas D. Stouffer
G-1	LtCol John M. Cassady
G-2	Capt Michael W. Oppliger
G-3	LtCol Hugh M. McIlroy Jr. (to 9Oct90)
	LtCol Kenneth W. Quigley (from 10Oct90)
	Col John J. Hully (from 23Nov90)

G-4	Maj Lowell K. Brueland (to 7Dec90)
	LtCol George M. Conroy (from 8Dec90)
G-6	Maj Christopher M. Weldon (to 7Oct90)
	LtCol Lawrence E. Troffer (from 8Oct90)
Sergeant Major	SgtMaj Phillip S. Williams
Headquarters and Service Battalion (-)	LtCol Henry T. Hayden
General Support Group 1	Col Thomas E. Hampton
	Col Paul A. Pankey
Combat Service Support	Maj Allen Coulter
Detachment 131	Capt Ritchie L. Rodebaugh
Combat Service Support	Capt Guido G. Aidenbaum
Detachment 132	Capt Tom D. Barna
2d Supply Battalion (-) (Reinforced)	LtCol Grant M. Sparks
2d Maintenance Battalion	Col Marlin D. Hilton
(-) (Reinforced)	
6th Motor Transport Battalion	LtCol Larry D. Walters
(-) (Reinforced)	
1st Landing Support Battalion	LtCol J. D. Burke (to 6Dec90)
(-) (Reinforced)	Maj J. E. McLean II (to 9Dec90)
	Capt C. Frazier Jr. (to 31Dec90)
	Maj Michael W. LaVigne (from 1Jan91)
1st Dental Battalion	Capt Robert A. Brunhofer, USN
General Support Group 2	Col Thomas E. Hampton
7th Motor Transport Battalion	LtCol Charlie F. Smith
(-) (Reinforced)	
2d Landing Support Battalion (-)	LtCol David B. Kirkwood
1st Medical Battalion (-)	Cdr Gary C. Breeden, USN
Combat Service Support	LtCol Linden L. Sparrow
Detachment 91 (enemy prisoners of war)	
Combat Service Support Detachment 82	LtCol David B. Kirkwood
Combat Service Support	Capt Eric R. Junger
Detachment 133	

Direct Support Command

Commanding General	BGen Charles C. Krulak
Chief of Staff	Col John A. Woodhead III
Headquarters and Service	LtCol James E. Vesely
Battalion (-), 2d Force Service Support Group	
7th Engineer Support Battalion	LtCol David L. John
(-) (Reinforced)	
8th Engineer Support Battalion	LtCol Charles O. Skipper
(-) (Reinforced)	
8th Motor Transport Battalion	LtCol Thomas S. Woodson
(-) (Reinforced)	
2d Medical Battalion (-) (Reinforced)	LCdr William G. Brown, USN
2d Dental Battalion (-)	(no commander listed)

Direct Support Group 1	Col Alexander W. Powell
Combat Service Support Detachment 141	Capt Adrian W. Burke
Combat Service Support Detachment 13	Capt William H. Ritchie III
Combat Service Support Detachment 142*	Capt Nello E. Dachman
Mobile Combat Service Support Detachment 17	Capt Edward J. Winter
Direct Support Group 2	Col Thomas P. Donnelly Jr.
Mobile Combat Service Support Detachment 26	LtCol David L. Wittle
Mobile Combat Service Support Detachment 28	LtCol James W. Head
Rear Area Security	
24th Marines (-)	Col George E. Germann
2d Battalion, 24th Marines	LtCol Francis A. Johnson
3d Battalion, 24th Marines	LtCol Ronald G. Guilliams

Commander Mobile Construction Battalions Forward
3d Naval Construction Regiment

Commanding Officer	Capt Michael R. Johnson, USN
Naval Mobil Construction Battalion 4	Cdr James T. Corbett, USN
Naval Mobil Construction Battalion 5	Cdr David F. Walsh, USN
Naval Mobil Construction Battalion 7	Cdr Gary M. Craft, USN
Naval Mobil Construction Battalion 24	Cdr James McGarrah, USN
Naval Mobil Construction Battalion 40	Cdr John R. Doyle, USN
Naval Mobil Construction Battalion 74	Cdr William P. Fogarty, USN

U.S. Naval Forces Central Command

4th Marine Expeditionary Brigade

Commanding General	MajGen Harry W. Jenkins Jr.
Chief of Staff	Col William W. Scheffler
G-1	Maj John R. Turner
G-2	LtCol Michael M. Bullen
G-3	LtCol Robert P. Mauskapf
G-4	LtCol Gary W. Collenborne
G-6	LtCol Glenn R. Williams

---

*Redesignated as Ammunition Company, 2d Supply Battalion, General Support Group 1, in December 1990.

Sergeant Major   SgtMaj Douglas E. Berry
Headquarters and Service Company   Capt Richard O. Bartch Jr.

Regimental Landing Team 2   Col Thomas A. Hobbs
    Headquarters Company, 2d Marines   Capt Richard B. Fitzwater
    1st Battalion, 2d Marines   LtCol Robert P. McAleer
    3d Battalion, 2d Marines   LtCol James T. Conway
    1st Battalion, 10th Marines   LtCol Douglas A. Okland
    2d Light Armored Infantry Battalion (-) (no commander listed)

Marine Aircraft Group 40   Col Glenn F. Burgess
    Marine Attack Squadron 331   LtCol Jerry W. Fitzgerald
    Marine Medium Helicopter   LtCol Robert J. Wallace
        Squadron 263
    Marine Medium Helicopter   LtCol Robert Saikowski
        Squadron 365
    Marine Heavy Helicopter Squadron 461   LtCol Daniel J. Moseler
    Marine Light Attack Helicopter   LtCol Kenneth W. Hill[*]
        Squadron 269 (-)
    Marine Aviation Logistics Squadron 14   LtCol Richard L. Owen Jr.
    Headquarters and Headquarters   LtCol Jackie K. Clark
        Squadron 28 (-)
    Marine Air Control Squadron 6 (-)   LtCol Ronald J. Armstrong
    Marine Wing Communications   LtCol William X. Spencer
        Squadron 28 (-)
    Marine Wing Support Squadron 274   LtCol T. J. Williams

Brigade Service Support Element 4   Col James J. Doyle Jr.

5th Marine Expeditionary Brigade

Commanding General   BGen Peter J. Rowe

Chief of Staff   Col Drake F. Trumpe

G-1   Maj Leslie E. Garrett

G-2   LtCol Malcolm Arnot

G-3   LtCol Thorys J. Stensrud (to 18Nov90)
                                    Col Robert J. Garner (from 19Nov90)

G-4   Col Eugene L. Gobeli

G-6   LtCol William V. Cantu

Sergeant Major   SgtMaj Elliot E. Harvey (to 19Nov90)
                                    SgtMaj Joseph I. Celestine (from 20Nov90)

---

[*]There were two Marine helicopter pilots named Kenneth W. Hill during the same period. Capt Kenneth W. Hill was killed in an accident in 1988 during Operation Praying Mantis.

Headquarters and Service Company	Maj Clifton R. Weyeneth
Regimental Landing Team 5	Col Randolph A. Gangle
Headquarters Company, 5th Marines	Maj Gary K. Schenkel
2d Battalion, 5th Marines	LtCol Kevin M. Kennedy
3d Battalion, 5th Marines	LtCol Donald R. Selvage
3d Battalion, 1st Marines	LtCol Robert S. Robichaud
2d Battalion, 11th Marines (-) (Reinforced)	LtCol Paul A. Gido
Marine Aircraft Group 50	Col Randall L. West
Marine Medium Helicopter Squadron 268	LtCol Melvin W. Forbush
Marine Medium Helicopter Squadron 265	LtCol John D. Holdstein
Marine Light Attack Helicopter Squadron 169 (-)	LtCol Theron D. Rogers
Marine Attack Helicopter Squadron 773	LtCol James M. Dunn
Brigade Service Support Group 5	LtCol Robert E. Lupton

13th Marine Expeditionary Unit (Special Operations Capable)

Commanding Officer	Col John E. Rhodes
Executive Officer	LtCol Rollin G. Napier
S-1	Capt Christopher G. Wright
S-2	Maj Steven J. Cash
S-3	LtCol John A. Clauer
S-4	Maj Russell O. Scherck
Sergeant Major	SgtMaj Anthony Reese
Communications Officer	Maj Marshall K. Snyder
1st Surveillance, Reconnaissance, and Intelligence Support Group	Capt Jon A. Stallings
2d Platoon, 2d Reconnaissance Company	Capt Ignatius P. Liberto
1st Platoon, 4th Reconnaissance Company	Capt Kenneth Grimes
Battalion Landing Team 1st Battalion, 4th Marines	LtCol George W. Flinn
Marine Medium Helicopter Squadron 164 (Composite)	LtCol Guy M. Vanderlinden
MEU Service Support Group 13	LtCol Bradley M. Lott

Selected Terms and Abbreviations from Operations Desert Shield/Desert Storm

A

AAA—Antiaircraft Artillery

AAFS—Amphibious Assault Fuel System

AAV—Amphibious Assault Vehicle

AB—Air Base

ABCCC—Airborne Battlefield Command and Control Center

A-Box—Fire Support Box

ACE—(1) Aviation Combat Element, or (2) Armored Combat Earthmover

ACR—Armored Calvary Regiment

AFCent—U.S. Air Forces Central Command

AI—Air Interdiction

AMALs—Authorized Medical Allowance Lists

ANGLICO—Air-Naval Gunfire Liaison Company

AO—Air Officer

AOR—Area of Responsibility

APC—Armored Personnel Carrier

APOD—Aerial Port of Debarkation

APS—Afloat Prepositioning Ships

ArCent—U.S. Army Forces Central Command

ASE—Air Support Element

ASOC—Air Support Operations Center

ASP—Ammunition Supply Point

ATACC—Advanced Tactical Air Command Center

ATC—Air Traffic Control

ATDL—Army Tactical Data Link

ATF—Amphibious Task Force

ATO—Air Tasking Order

AVLB—Armored Vehicle Launched Bridge

AWACS—Airborne Warning and Control System

AWC—Assistant Wing Commander

B

BAT—Battlefield Air Interdiction

BARCAP—Barrier Combat Air Patrol

BCP—Battery Command Post

BDA—Battle Damage Assessment

BDF—Bahrain Defense Force

BFV—Bradley Fighting Vehicle

BGen—Brigadier General

BSSG—Brigade Service Support Group

BW—Biological Warfare

C

C2—Command and Control

C3I—Command, Control, Communications, and Intelligence

CAAT—Combined Antiarmor Team

CAFMS—Computer-Assisted Force Management System

CAP—Combat Air Patrol

CAS—Close Air Support

CATF—Commander Amphibious Task Force

CAX—Combined Area Exercises

CE—Command Element

CEC—Civil Engineer Corps

CentCom—U.S. Central Command

CFR—Crash Fire and Rescue

CG—Commanding General

CIFS—Close-In Fire Support

CinC—Commander in Chief

CinCCent—Commander in Chief, U.S. Central Command

CJCS—Chairman of the Joint Chiefs of Staff

CLF—Commander Landing Force

CMC—Commandant of the Marine Corps

CNO—Chief of Naval Operations

CO—Commanding Officer

COC—Combat Operations Center

ComCBPac—Commander, Naval Construction Battalions Pacific Fleet

CommEx—Communications Exercise

ComUSNavCent—Commander, U.S. Naval Forces Central Command

CONUS—Continental United States

CP—(1) Control Point, or (2) Command Post

CRAF—Civil Reserve Air Fleet

CRC—Control and Reporting Center

CSAR—Combat Search and Rescue

CSP—Contingency Support Package

CSS—Combat Service Support

CSSA—Combat Service Support Area

CSSD—Combat Service Support Detachment

CSSE—Combat Service Support Element

CSSOC—Combat Service Support Operations Center

CUCV—Commercial Utility Cargo Vehicle

CV—Aircraft Carrier

CVN—Aircraft Carrier, Nuclear

CVW—Carrier Air Wing
CVWR—Reserve Carrier Air Wing
CWAR—Continuous Warning/Wave Acquisition Radar

D

DAS—Deep Air Strike
DASC(A)—Direct Air Support Center (Airborne)
DASC—Direct Air Support Center
DMAC—Division Mechanized Assault Course
DOD—Department of Defense
DOS—Days of Supply
DPICM—Dual-Purpose Improved Conventional Munitions
DSC—Direct Support Command
DSG—Direct Support Group

E

EAF—Expeditionary Airfield
ECM—Electronic Countermeasures
EDM—Engineering Development Module or Model
ELINT—Electronics Intelligence
EMCON—Emission Control
EOD—Explosive Ordinance Disposal
EPAC—Eastern Province Area Command
EPW—Enemy Prisoner of War
EW—Electronic Warfare
EW/C—Early Warning and Control

F

FAC—Forward Air Controller
FAC(A)—Forward Air Controller (Airborne)
FAE—Fuel Air Explosive
FARP—Forward Arming and Refueling Point
FASP—Forward Ammunition Storage Point
Fast FAC(A)—Fast Forward Air Controller (Airborne), F/A-18D
FAST—Fleet Antiterrorism Security Team
FEBA—Forward Edge of the Battle Area
FIE—Fly-In Echelon
FLIR—Forward Looking Infrared Radar
FMF—Fleet Marine Force
FMFLant—Fleet Marine Force Atlantic
FMFPac—Fleet Marine Force Pacific
FOB—Forward Operating Base
FOD—Foreign Object Damage
FRAGO—Fragmentary Order
FROG—Free Rocket Over Ground (missile)
FSCC—Fire Support Coordination Center
FSCL—Fire Support Coordination Line
FSSG—Force Service Support Group

G

GCE—Ground Combat Element
GPS—Global Positioning System
GSG—General Support Group

H

H_2S—Hydrogen Sulfide Gas
H&HS—Headquarters and Headquarters Squadron
H&SG—Headquarters and Support Group
HARM—High Speed Anti-Radiation Missile
HAWK—Homing All the Way Killer (MIM-23B surface-to-air missile)
HC—Helicopter Combat Support Squadron
HCS—Helicopter Combat Search and Rescue/Special Warfare Support Squadron
HDC—Helicopter Direction Center
HEAT—High Explosive Anti-Tank (munition)
HEFS—Helicopter Expeditionary Fuel System
HEMTT—Heavy Expanded Mobility Tactical Truck
HIDACZ—High Density Airspace Control Zone
HM—Helicopter Mine Countermeasures Squadron
HMA—Marine Attack Helicopter Squadron
HMH—Marine Heavy Helicopter Squadron
HMLA—Marine Light Attack Helicopter Squadron
HMM—Marine Medium Helicopter Squadron
HMMWV—High Mobility Multipurpose Wheeled Vehicle
HMX—Marine Helicopter Squadron
HPIR—High Power Illuminator Radar
HQMC—Headquarters Marine Corps
HS—Helicopter Antisubmarine Squadron
HSL—Helicopter Antisubmarine Squadron Light
HST—Helicopter Support Team
HT—Helicopter Training Squadron
HTACC—Helicopter Tactical Air Command Center
HUD—Head-Up Display
HUMINT—Human Intelligence
HVA—High Value Asset
HVU—High Value Unit

I

IADS—Integrated Air Defense System
ICM—Improved Conventional Munitions
IDASC—Improved Direct Air Support Center
IFASC—Interim Forward Automated Services Center
IFF—Identification, Friend or Foe
IMINT—Imagery Intelligence
INTEL—Intelligence
IOC—Initial Operational Capability
IR—Infra-Red

IRT—In Response To
ISO—In Support Of

J

JCS—Joint Chiefs of Staff
JFACC—Joint Force Air Component Commander
JFC—Joint Force Commander
JFC-E—Joint Forces Command–East
JFC-N—Joint Forces Command–North
JNAF—al-Jubayl Naval Air Facility
Joint STARS—Joint Surveillance Target Attack Radar System

K

KAANB—King Abdul Aziz Naval Base
KIA—Killed In Action
KTO—Kuwait Theater of Operations

L

LAAD—Low Altitude Air Defense
LAAM—Light Antiaircraft Missile
LAI—Light Armored Infantry
LAN—Local Area Network
LAV—Light Armored Vehicle
LCU—Landing Craft, Utility
LD—Line of Departure
LDT—Laser Detector Tracker
LGB—Laser-Guided Bomb
LLL—Low Light Level
LNO—Liaison Officer
LREOS—Long Range Electro Optical System
LRI—Long-Range International (passenger aircraft)
LSB—Landing Support Battalion
LtGen—Lieutenant General

M

MAC—Military Airlift Command
MACCS—Marine Air Command and Control System
MACG—Marine Air Control Group
MACS—Marine Air Control Squadron
MAG—Marine Aircraft Group
MAGTF—Marine Air-Ground Task Force
MajGen—Major General
MALS—Marine Air Logistics Squadron
MANPADS—Man Portable Air Defense System
MarCent—U.S. Marine Forces Central Command
MarDiv—Marine Division
MARFORSWA—Marine Forces, Southwest Asia
MASS—Marine Air Support Squadron

MATCS—Marine Air Traffic Control Squadron
MAW—Marine Aircraft Wing
M-Box—Maneuver Box
MCAS—Marine Corps Air Station
MCB—Marine Corps Base
MCCDC—Marine Corps Combat Development Command
MCLC—Mine Clearing Line Charge
MCSSD—Mobile Combat Service Support Detachment
MEB—Marine Expeditionary Brigade
MedEvac—Medical Evacuation
MedLog—Medical Logistics
MEF—Marine Expeditionary Force
MEU—Marine Expeditionary Unit
MEU (SOC)—Marine Expeditionary Unit (Special Operations Capable)
MHE—Materials Handling Equipment
MLRS—Multiple Launch Rocket System
MOPP—Mission Oriented Protective Posture. Protective equipment for chemical attack consists of a suit made of charcoal-activated cloth, overboots, gloves, and a gas mask with hood. There are four MOPP levels, depending upon the threat of a chemical attack, and each prescribes which items are to be worn. Level 1 consists of wearing the suit (trousers and jacket) and carrying the boots, gloves, and mask with hood. Level 2 involves wearing the overboots in addition to the suit, with the gloves and mask with hood still carried. At level 3 the mask with hood is worn. Level 4 requires the wearing of the entire outfit, including the gloves.
MP—Military Police
MPF—Maritime Prepositioning Force
MPS—Maritime Prepositioning Ship
MPSRON—Maritime Prepositioning Ship Squadron
MRE—Meal, Ready-To-Eat
MRL—Multiple Rocket Launcher
MRR—Minimum Risk Route
MSC—Major Subordinate Command
MSSG—Marine Expeditionary Unit Service Support Group
MULE—Modular Universal Laser Equipment
MV—(1) Merchant Vessel, or (2) Motor Vessel
MWCS—Marine Wing Control Squadron
MWHS—Marine Wing Headquarters Squadron
MWSG—Marine Wing Support Group
MWSS—Marine Wing Support Squadron

N

NAF—Naval Airfield
NAS—Naval Air Station

NATO—North Atlantic Treaty Organization
NATOPS—Naval Air Training and Operating Procedures Standardization
NAVCENT—Navy Component Central Command
NAVCHAPGRU—Naval Cargo Handling and Port Group
NBC—Nuclear, Biological, and Chemical
NBCB—Naval Base Construction Battalion
NM—Nautical Mile
NMCB—Naval Mobile Construction Battalion
NNOR—Non-Nuclear Ordnance Requirements
NSE—Navy Support Element
NVG—Night-Vision Goggles

O

OAS—Offensive Air Support
OP—Observation Post
OPEC—Organization of the Petroleum Exporting Countries
OpCon—Operational Control
OPP—Off-Load Preparation Party
OpRdy—Operational Readiness
ORF—Operational Readiness Float

P

PacFlt—Pacific Fleet
PACOM—Pacific Command
Pax—Personnel
PL—Phase Line
PLRS—Position Location Reporting System
PMO—Provost Marshal's Office; Military Police
POET—Primed Oscillator Expendable Transponder
POG—Port Operations Group
PTO—Pilot Training Officer

Q

QEP—Quick Exchange Program

R

RAF—Royal Air Force (United Kingdom)
RAP—Rocket Assisted Projectile
RAS—Rear Area Security
RCT—Regimental Combat Team
RGFC—*Republican Guard* Forces Command
ROE—Rules of Engagement
ROWPU—Reverse Osmosis Water Purification Unit
RPG—Rocket-Propelled Grenade
RPV—Remotely Piloted Vehicle
RSAF—Royal Saudi Air Force

RTB—Return to Base
RTCH—Rough Terrain Container Hauler
RWR—Radar Warning Receiver

S

SAAWC—Sector Antiair Warfare Coordinator
SAM—Surface-to-Air Missile
SAR—Search and Rescue
SASSY—Marine Corps Automated Supply Support System
SBT—Support Breach Team
SCUD—Soviet surface-to-surface missile
SEAD—Suppression of Enemy Air Defenses
SEAL—Sea, Air, and Land (Naval Special Warfare Team)
SecDef—Secretary of Defense
SecNav—Secretary of the Navy
SIGINT—Signals Intelligence
SIM—Simulated
SIMCAS—Simulated Close Air Support
SLEP—Service Life Extension Program
SLRP—Surveillance, Liaison, and Reconnaissance Party
SMCR—Selected Marine Corps Reserve
SOC—Special Operations Capable
SOP—Standard Operating Procedure
SPCC—Ships Parts Control Center
SRI—Surveillance, Reconnaissance, and Intelligence
SRIG—Surveillance, Reconnaissance, and Intelligence Group
SRISG—Surveillance, Reconnaissance, and Intelligence Support Group
SSM—Surface-to-Surface Missile
STOVL—Short Take-Off Vertical Landing
STT—Single Target Track
SWA—Southwest Asia
SWATG—Southwest Asia Training Group

T

TAC (A)—Tactical Air Coordinator (Airborne)
TACAIR—Tactical Air
TACAN—Tactical Air Navigation System
TACC—Tactical Air Command Center
TacEx—Tactical Exercise
TACP—Tactical Air Control Party
TADIL—Tactical Digital Information Link
TAFDS—Tactical Airfield Fuel Dispensing System
TALD—Tactical Air-Launched Decoy
TAMPS—Tactical Aircraft Mission Planning System
TAOC—Tactical Air Operations Center
TAOM—Tactical Air Operations Module

TAOR—Tactical Area of Responsibility
TAR—Tactical Air Response
TAVB—Aviation Logistics Support Ship
TERPES—Tactical Electronic Reconnaissance Processing and Evaluation System
TEWT—Tactical Exercise without Troops
TF—Task Force
TFW—Tactical Fighter Wing
T/O—Table of Organization
TOO—Target of Opportunity
TOS—Time on Station
TOT—Time on Target
TOW—Tube-launched, Optically-tracked, Wire-guided missile
TPFDL—Timed-Phase Force Deployment List
TWMP—Track Width Mine Plow
TWSEAS—Tactical Warfare Simulation Evaluation and Analysis System

U

UAV—Unmanned Aerial Vehicle
UDP—Unit Deployment Program
USNS—United States Naval Ship (civilian manned)
UW—Urban Warfare

V

VA—Attack Squadron

VAW—Carrier Airborne Early Warning System
VC—Fleet Composite Squadron
VF—Fighter Squadron
VFA—Strike Fighter Squadron
VFC—Fighter Composite Squadron
V/STOL—Vertical/Short Take-Off and Landing
VMA—Marine Attack Squadron
VMA(AW)—Marine All-Weather Attack Squadron
VMAQ—Marine Tactical Electronic Warfare Squadron
VMFA—Marine Fighter Attack Squadron
VMFA(AW) Marine All-Weather Fighter Attack Squadron
VMGR—Marine Aerial Refueler Transport Squadron
VMO—Marine Observation Squadron
VP—Patrol Squadron
VPU—Patrol Squadron Special Projects Unit

W

WIA—Wounded In Action
WTI—Weapons Tactics Instructor
WP—White Phosphorus

X

XO—Executive Officer

Chronology of Significant Events

1979

16 July   Saddam Hussein becomes president of Iraq.

4 November   Iranian militants seize U.S. embassy personnel, starting the Iranian hostage crisis.

1980

March   The U.S. Rapid Deployment Joint Task Force is established.

22 September   Iraq launches air strikes against Iran, beginning the Iran-Iraq War.

23 September   Iraq invades Iran.

1981

January   Iran launches first counteroffensive against Iraq.

20 January   The Iranian hostage crisis ends.

7 June   Israeli Air Force destroys Iraq's Osirak nuclear reactor.

1982

July   The first battle of Basrah between Iran and Iraq takes place.

1983

1 January   U.S. Central Command is established.

1985

27 November   Gen George B. Crist becomes commander of U.S. Central Command.

1987

January   The second battle of Basrah occurs.

17 May   USS *Stark* (FFG 31) is hit by two Iraqi Exocet missiles.

July	Operation Earnest Will, the U.S. Central Command's convoying of Kuwaiti tankers through the Persian Gulf, begins.
August	Detachment 2, 24th Marine Amphibious Unit (24th MAU), arrives in the Persian Gulf on board USS *Guadalcanal* (LPH 7), beginning Marine Corps involvement in Operation Earnest Will.
21 September	U.S. forces capture the Iranian vessel *Iran Ajr* as it lays mines in the Persian Gulf.
8 October	U.S. forces sink or destroy three Iranian motorboats after they fire on U.S. forces.
November	Contingency Marine Air-Ground Task Force (CMAGTF) 1-88 aboard USS *Okinawa* (LPH 3) relieves Detachment 2, 24th MAU, in the Persian Gulf.

1988

February	Iraq begins launching surface-to-surface missiles at Tehran in the final "War of the Cities." CMAGTF 2-88 aboard USS *Trenton* (LPD 14) relieves CMAGTF 1-88 in the Persian Gulf.
April	Iraqi forces drive the Iranians from the al-Faw Peninsula. USS *Samuel B. Roberts* (FFG 58) is severely damaged by an Iranian mine. In response, Operation Praying Mantis is conducted by U.S. forces, which sink an Iranian frigate, severely damage another, sink or destroy multiple Iranian small craft, and destroy two oil platforms. During the operation, a Marine AH-1T Sea Cobra crashes, and its crew members— Capts Stephen C. Leslie and Kenneth W. Hill—are killed.
May to July	Iraqis launch a series of offensives against the Iranians.
June	CMAGTF 3-88 relieves CMAGTF 2-88 in the Persian Gulf.
3 July	USS *Vincennes* (CG 49) mistakenly shoots down Iran Air Flight 655, killing its 290 civilian passengers.
8 August	Iran and Iraq announce a cease-fire, ending the Iran-Iraq War.
September	Operation Earnest Will ends.
23 November	Gen H. Norman Schwarzkopf, USA, becomes commander of U.S. Central Command.

1990

2 August	Iraqi military forces invade Kuwait. The U.S. government orders two carrier battle groups to the Persian Gulf.
6 August	Saudi Arabia requests U.S. assistance. The United Nations (UN) authorizes economic sanctions against Iraq.
7 August	President George H. W. Bush orders U.S. armed forces to Saudi Arabia. Operation Desert Shield begins.

I Marine Expeditionary Force (I MEF), 1st Marine Expeditionary Brigade (1st MEB), 4th Marine Expeditionary Brigade (4th MEB), and 7th Marine Expeditionary Brigade (7th MEB) receive warning orders for possible deployment to the Persian Gulf.

8 August	LtGen Walter E. Boomer assumes command of I MEF and U.S. Marine Forces Central Command.
10 August	The Commander-in-Chief Atlantic Fleet orders the 4th MEB from Camp Lejeune, North Carolina, to the Persian Gulf.
11 August	Brigade Service Support Group 7 arrives in Saudi Arabia to prepare the port of al-Jubayl, Saudi Arabia, for unloading Maritime Prepositioning Ship Squadron Two (MPSRON-2).
12 August	Three ships of MPSRON-2 arrive at the port of al-Jubayl.
14 August	First Marine helicopters (AH-1Ws) and fixed-wing aircraft depart El Toro, California. The 7th MEB, from the Marine Corps Air Ground Combat Center at Twentynine Palms, California, is the first Marine combat organization to arrive in the Persian Gulf.
15 August	Marine Light Attack Helicopter Squadron 369 (HMLA-369), comprising the first Marine Aircraft Group 70 (MAG-70) aircraft, arrives in theater.
	Headquarters Marine Corps announces the commitment of 45,000 troops to the Persian Gulf area. They consist of elements of I MEF, including units from the 1st Marine Division, 1st Force Service Support Group (1st FSSG), 3d Marine Aircraft Wing (3d MAW), and 7th MEB. Also en route are elements of the 4th MEB, including units from 2d Marine Division, 2d Force Service Support Group, and 2d Marine Aircraft Wing. Additionally, MPSRON-2 had been at Diego Garcia in the Indian Ocean. The five-ship squadron contains 7th MEB's equipment and enough supplies to sustain the 16,500-person force for 30 days.
	Ultimately, the Marines would comprise a portion of the approximately 200,000 U.S. ground troops.
16 August	Military Airlift Command begins flying missions to al-Jubayl Naval Air Facility.
20 August	Marine Attack Squadron 311 (VMA-311), with the first Marine fixed-wing aircraft (AV-8Bs), arrives in theater.
22 August	President Bush orders the first mobilization of U.S. military reserves in 20 years and declares the call-up "essential to completing our mission" of thwarting Iraqi aggression in the Persian Gulf.
24 August	MAG-70 begins combat air patrol missions over the northern Persian Gulf.
	The U.S. embassy in Kuwait is ordered closed. Marine security guards and approximately 100 U.S. officials and citizens are transferred to the U.S. embassy in Baghdad by the Iraqi government. They are among an estimated 1,000 Americans held hostage in Iraq during the crisis.
25 August	MajGen Hopkins reports 7th MEB is combat ready and ready to defend al-Jubayl, a week prior to expectations.

3 September	MAG-70 dissolves and 3d MAW stands up. BGen James A. Brabham assumes command of the 1st FSSG.
7 September	13th Marine Expeditionary Unit (Special Operations Capable) (13th MEU [SOC]) arrives in North Arabian Sea.
8 October	The first fatal accident for Marines in Operation Desert Shield claims eight lives when two UH-1N helicopters crash into the North Arabian Sea during a night training mission. The Marines were assigned to Marine Medium Helicopter Squadron 164, part of the 13th MEU (SOC).
13 October	The 13th MEU (SOC) interdicts and boards the Iraqi vessel *Al Mutanabbi*.
22 October	The 13th MEU (SOC) interdicts and boards the Iraqi vessel *Al Sahil Al Arabi*.
28 October	The 13th MEU (SOC) interdicts and boards the Iraqi vessel *Amuriya*.
8 November	President Bush announces that he plans to add more than 200,000 U.S. troops to those already deployed in Operation Desert Shield in the Persian Gulf area.
18 November	The 2d Marine Division receives orders to deploy to the Kuwait Theater of Operations.
22 November	President Bush addresses U.S. Marines, U.S. sailors, and British soldiers during his visit to Saudi Arabia. Standing before a crowd of more than 3,000 frontline forces, the president reaffirms his resolve to see Iraqi strongman Saddam Hussein ousted from Kuwait. The president and Mrs. Bush then join the Marines for a traditional Thanksgiving Day meal.
29 November	UN Security Council Resolution 678 authorizes the use of "all necessary means" to get Iraqi forces to leave Kuwait if they have not done so by 15 January 1991.
11 December	I MEF increases by 58 percent when air flow reinforcements start bringing an average of 945 Marines and sailors and 222 short tons of cargo every day for the remainder of the month.
24 December	The British 1st Armored Division is transferred to the operational command of U.S. Army Forces Central Command (ArCent); the U.S. Army's 1st (Tiger) Brigade, 2d Armored Division, is transferred to I MEF.
26 December	The 4th MEB interdicts and boards the Iraqi vessel *Ibn Khaldoon*.
30 December	The 4th MEB interdicts and boards the Iraqi vessel *Ain Zallah*.

1991

2 January	Operation Eastern Exit is launched when the 4th MEB contingency MAGTF departs Masirah, Oman, for Somalia.
5 January	Operation Eastern Exit continues. Two CH-53s launched from USS *Trenton* insert a 60-man evacuation force and then return to USS *Guam* (LPH 9) with 61 evacuees. Task Force 158/I MEF holds planning meeting.

6 January	Operation Eastern Exit, the Somalia evacuation, is completed.
6–15 January	Direct Support Command's (DSC's) engineers build a sprawling complex of more than 40 square kilometers at Kibrit, Saudi Arabia, directly west of al-Mishab, as a defensive measure against Iraqi air and artillery attack.
8 January	I MEF reports six Iraqi helicopters cross the border near Observation Post 4 (OP-4). The helicopters are in contact with Saudi and Marine interpreters on the ground. Helicopters requesting to land in Dhahran, Saudi Arabia, are refused and advised to land 30 miles south of the border. Four land at al-Khafji, Saudi Arabia, and two land near OP-4.
10 January	The U.S. Army's Tiger Brigade reports to the 2d Marine Division from ArCent.
11 January	Operation Eastern Exit ends; the 262 evacuees debark at Muscat, Oman.
12 January	Congress approves the president's use of military force against Iraq.
15 January	The UN deadline for Iraq to withdraw from Kuwait passes with Iraq still occupying that nation.
17 January	Operation Desert Shield becomes Operation Desert Storm as forces of the allied Coalition launch an air assault against targets in Iraq and occupied Kuwait in an effort to liberate Kuwait and enforce the UN Security Council's resolutions.
17–19 January	The Iraqis respond to the Coalition air bombardment by shooting FROG (free rocket over ground) missiles at al-Mishab.
18 January	Marine Observation Squadron 2 (VMO-2) loses an OV-10 Bronco flown by its commander, LtCol Clifford M. Acree. LtCol Acree and his observer, CWO-4 Guy L. Hunter, are captured by Iraqi forces. The last of the 2d Marine Division's units, the 2d Tank Battalion, completes its offload of equipment at al-Jubayl and moves forward to join the division. Iraq begins launching Scud missiles at Israel and Saudi Arabia.
21 January	1st Marine Division conducts an artillery raid against Iraqi forces in Kuwait. Baghdad airs footage of captured allied airmen. Marine prisoners are identified as LtCol Clifford Acree and CWO-4 Guy Hunter.
26 January	1st Marine Division conducts an artillery raid against Iraqi forces in Kuwait; Iraq begins dumping oil from Mina al-Ahmadi oil terminal into the Persian Gulf.
27 January	Saddam Hussein presents his plan for the attack on al-Khafji to the *III Corps* and *IV Corps* commanders in the Iraqi city of Basrah. Gen Salah Aboud Mahmoud promises to present Saddam with the city of al-Khafji as a present on the morning of 30 January. The 2d Marine Division conducts its first offensive operations with an artillery raid against Iraqi positions.
28 January	VMA-311 loses an AV-8B Harrier. Its pilot, Capt Michael C. Berryman, is taken prisoner by the Iraqis. Gen Salah Aboud Mahmoud meets with his division commanders at the *5th Mechanized Division* headquarters, beneath the al-Maqwa oil refinery.

The 3d Marine artillery raid into Kuwait is conducted.

E-8C Joint STARS aircraft note Iraqi movement on the Saudi-Kuwaiti border.

Coalition aircraft strike columns of the *3d Armored Division* moving through the al-Wafrah oil fields.

29 January	The Iraqi *5th Mechanized Division* and *3d Armored Division* assault the Kuwaiti-Saudi border, beginning the Battle of al-Khafji. Two Marine light armored vehicles are destroyed by friendly fire at OP-4 during the Iraqi assault. Eleven Marines are killed.
30 January	The *5th Mechanized Division* occupies al-Khafji. Iraqi forces assaulting the berm at OP-4 are repulsed. The 7th Battalion, 2d Brigade, Saudi Arabian National Guard, launches an attack to retake al-Khafji and is repulsed. A U.S. Air Force AC-130 attacking Iraqi reinforcements bound for al-Khafji is shot down by an Iraqi surface-to-air missile; the 14-man crew is lost.
31 January	7th Battalion, 2d Brigade, Saudi Arabian National Guard, launches another attack to retake al-Khafji and is repulsed.
1 February	The 7th and 8th Battalions, 2d Brigade, Saudi Arabian National Guard, secure al-Khafji and end Iraqi resistance in the city.
2 February	An AH-1 helicopter of Marine Attack Helicopter Squadron 775 crashes during an emergency MedEvac conducted using night-vision goggles; both pilots, Capt Jonathan R. Edwards and Maj Eugene McCarthy, die in the crash. U.S. Navy aircraft mistakenly bomb Battery S, 5th Battalion, 11th Marines, 30 kilometers north of al-Qaraah, killing one Marine, LCpl Eliseo C. Felix, and wounding two others.
3 February	HMLA-369 loses a UH-1N when it crashes into the ground; four fatalities result.
3–7 February	A Marine explosive ordnance disposal team clears al-Khafji, destroying a total of 4,000 pieces of ordnance and removing 80 armored vehicles in the process.
8 February	Khanjar forward logistics base established.
9 February	Marine Attack Squadron 231 loses an AV-8; the pilot, Capt Russell A. C. Sanborn, is taken prisoner.
9–20 February	DSC moves from Kibrit to Khanjar, approximately 160 kilometers northwest of Kibrit, in a massive supply buildup.
15 February	USS *Tarawa* (LHA 1) offloads AV-8Bs at al-Jubayl and is just missed by a Scud missile attack.
17 February	USS *Tripoli* (LPH 10) is disabled after it hits a mine.
18 February	Marine reconnaissance teams cross into Kuwait to conduct surveys of Iraqi minefields and obstacles and to identify any gaps and weaknesses.
20 February	The 2d Combat Engineer Battalion begins to make cuts through the berm along the Kuwaiti-Saudi border.

Marine Attack Squadron 331 (of Marine Aircraft Group 40) conducts 20 combat sorties from USS *Nassau* (LHA 4); this is the first fixed-wing combat strike from this class of ship.

21 February	The 2d Light Armored Infantry Battalion begins screening the 2d Marine Division in Kuwait.
22 February	The 2d Combat Engineer Battalion finishes the cuts through the berm. The 3d Battalion, 23d Marines, moves into Kuwait to provide security for artillery surveying parties.
23 February	Marine Attack Squadron 542 loses an AV-8; its pilot, Capt James N. Wilburn III, is killed in action. Four of the 2d Marine Division's artillery battalions move into Kuwait to provide fire support for the division's assault.
24 February	Marine Medium Helicopter Squadron 161 loses a CH-46 Sea Knight on a night-vision-goggle takeoff during the lift for Task Force X-Ray. I MEF begins the liberation of Kuwait. 1st and 2d Marine Divisions breach the Saddam Line.
25 February	Marine Attack Squadron 542 loses an AV-8; the pilot, Captain John S. Walsh, is recovered by friendly forces. VMO-1 loses an OV-10; Maj Joseph J. Small III is taken prisoner, and Capt David M. Spellacy, the pilot, is killed in action. 2d Marine Division assaults and secures its first objective, fighting through the "Ice Cube" and the "Ice Cube Tray." The Battle of Burqan, an Iraqi counterattack launched at the 1st Marine Division, ends with a Marine victory. Task Force X-Ray lands near Task Force Papa Bear.
26 February	Another counterattack is defeated on the 2d Marine Division's right flank. Iraqi units are reported to be withdrawing from Kuwait. The Tiger Brigade, 6th Marines, and 8th Marines attack to their final division objectives on the outskirts of al-Jahrah and Kuwait City. 1st Marine Division's Task Force Ripper reaches Kuwait International Airport. Eight thousand Iraqi prisoners of war (POWs) reach the holding compound at Kibrit.
27 February	Arab forces of the Joint Forces Command–North pass along the 2d Marine Division's front and participate in the liberation of Kuwait City. 2d Marine Division consolidates its positions outside of al-Jahrah and Kuwait and clears the last pockets of Iraqi resistance. 1st Marine Division consolidates its area and clears the last pockets of resistance around Kuwait International Airport.
28 February	Operation Desert Storm ends when the cease-fire declared by President Bush goes into effect.
3 March	Cease-fire accepted at Safwan airfield in Iraq.
4 March	13th MEU (SOC) captures more than 1,400 Iraqi POWs on Faylakah Island.
8 March	Marine Fighter Attack Squadron 212 loses two F/A-18s in a midair collision. 13th MEU (SOC) departs Persian Gulf.

9 March   4th MEB begins retrograde.

10 March   Five Marine POWs are among the 21 POWs who arrive at Andrews Air Force Base near Washington, DC. The Marine POWs were freed on 5 March and transported from Iraq by an International Red Cross aircraft. They are LtCol Clifford Acree, Maj Joseph Small III, Capts Michael Berryman and Russell Sanborn, and CWO-4 Guy Hunter.

Navy Cross and Unit Citations

THE SECRETARY OF THE NAVY
WASHINGTON

The President of the United States takes pleasure in presenting the NAVY CROSS to

LIEUTENANT COLONEL MICHAEL M. KURTH
UNITED STATES MARINE CORPS

for service as set forth in the following

CITATION:

For extraordinary heroism as Commanding Officer of Marine Light Attack Helicopter Squadron 369 during Operation Desert Storm on 26 February 1991. As the 1st Marine Division attacked north to prevent Iraqi forces from escaping, Lieutenant Colonel Kurth's repeated acts of bravery in providing close in fire support to embattled Marines helped collapse the Iraqi defenses. With visibility nearly impossible due to hundreds of burning oil field fires, and with total disregard for his own safety, he flew under and perilously close to high voltage powerlines. Placing himself at grave personal risk to intermittent Iraqi ground and antiaircraft fire, Lieutenant Colonel Kurth flew continuously for ten hours during the most intense periods of combat, twice having to control crash his aircraft. Employing a commercially borrowed Forward Looking Infrared Radar and Laser Designator, he flew through the al-Burqan Oil Field fires, between the AH-1W holding pattern and Task Force Ripper's forward lines, leading flight after flight of rearmed gunships to requesting units and then remaining dangerously exposed forward of friendly lines as he designated Iraqi armored vehicles for engagement. Lieutenant Colonel Kurth's courage and fearless dedication rallied fellow Marines and resulted in the destruction of as many as 70 Iraqi armored vehicles destroyed that day. By his outstanding display of decisive leadership, unlimited courage in the face of heavy enemy fire, and utmost devotion to duty, Lieutenant Colonel Kurth reflected great credit upon himself and upheld the highest traditions of the Marine Corps and the United States Naval Service.

THE SECRETARY OF THE NAVY
WASHINGTON

The President of the United States takes pleasure in presenting the NAVY CROSS to

CAPTAIN EDDIE S. RAY
UNITED STATES MARINE CORPS

for service as set forth in the following

CITATION:

For extraordinary heroism while serving as Commanding Officer, Company B, 1st Light Armored Infantry Battalion, Task Force Shepherd, 1st Marine Division, in the Emirate of Kuwait on 25 February 1991. During the early morning hours of G+I of Operation Desert Storm, an Iraqi mechanized division counterattacked elements of the 1st Marine Division in the vicinity west of the flame and smoke engulfed Burqan Oil Field in Southeastern Kuwait. As dense black smoke shrouded the battlefield, an Iraqi mechanized brigade engaged the 1st Marine Division Forward Command Post security forces. During the ensuing intense ten hour battle, Captain Ray repeatedly maneuvered his Light Armored Vehicle Company in harm's way, skillfully integrating his Light Armored Infantry weapons, reinforcing TOWs and AH-1W Attack Helicopters to decisively defeat main Iraqi counterattacks. Leading from the front and constantly exposed to large volumes of enemy fire, Captain Ray led swift, violent attacks directly into the face of the vastly larger enemy force. These attacks shocked the enemy, destroyed 50 enemy armored personnel carriers, and resulted in the capture of over 250 Iraqi soldiers. Operating perilously close to the attacking enemy, Captain Ray's courage, composure under fire, and aggressive war fighting spirit were instrumental in the defeat of a major enemy effort and the successful defense of the Division Forward Command Post. By his outstanding display of decisive leadership, unlimited courage in the face of heavy enemy fire, and utmost devotion to duty, Captain Ray reflected great credit upon himself and upheld the highest traditions of the Marine Corps and the United States Naval Service.

THE SECRETARY OF THE NAVY
WASHINGTON

The Secretary of the Navy takes pleasure in presenting the NAVY UNIT COMMENDATION to

I MARINE EXPEDITIONARY FORCE

for service as set forth in the following

CITATION:

For exceptionally meritorious service during Operations Desert Shield and Desert Storm from 14 August 1990 to 16 April 1991. An imminent Iraqi invasion of Saudi Arabia was deterred when the 7th Marine Expeditionary Brigade made the first Maritime Prepositioning Combat Deployment in history; moving 15,248 personnel, 194 aircraft, 548 tanks and heavy weapons, and more than 11,000 tons of supplies 12,000 miles in less than a week. During the next three months intensive training in the harsh desert prepared I Marine Expeditionary Force (I MEF) for combat action. On 17 January the 3d Marine Aircraft Wing initiated Marine participation in Operation Desert Storm. Marine aircraft flew 8,910 sorties and dropped 14,864 tons of ordnance while interdicting Iraqi command, control, and communications systems, striking strategic targets, isolating the future battlefield, and destroying Iraqi fortifications, weapons, and vehicles. The 1st and 2d Marine Divisions and the Direct Support Command secretly moved 100 kilometers west to occupy forward bases and assembly areas. Amphibious demonstrations held more than 50,000 Iraqis in static positions. From 18 to 23 February, Marine units entered Kuwait by stealth to prepare the battlefield. Combat engineers breached extensive minefields and barriers to allow mechanized forces, to swiftly penetrate enemy defenses. I MEF severed lines of communication, destroyed or captured enemy forces, aided the liberation of Kuwait City and then assumed defensive positions. The 1st Force Service Support Group and the Direct Support Command delivered more than 75,000 tons of supplies to forward units and detained 22,308 enemy prisoners of war. In 100 hours, I MEF won a stunning victory, captured all assigned objectives, destroyed 1,040 enemy tanks, 608 armored personnel carriers, and 432 artillery pieces. By their valiant fighting spirit, professional competence, and relentless devotion to duty, I Marine Expeditionary Force reflected great credit upon themselves and upheld the highest traditions of the Marine Corps and the United States Naval Service.

THE SECRETARY OF THE NAVY
WASHINGTON

The Secretary of the Navy takes pleasure in presenting the NAVY UNIT COMMENDATION to

OPERATIONS DESERT SHIELD AND DESERT STORM
AMPHIBIOUS TASK FORCE

for service as set forth in the following

CITATION:

For exceptionally meritorious service in support Operations Desert Shield and Desert Storm, including combat operations, as part of U.S. Naval Forces Central Command while deployed to Southwest Asia from August 1990 to April 1991. During this period, the Amphibious Task Force was involved in an unprecedented deployment of the largest and most capable Amphibious Task Force assembled in the last three decades. Consisting of 31 ships and more than 20,000 Marines from Atlantic and Pacific Fleet units, the Amphibious Force was fully integrated and capable of supporting a single, cohesive plan of attack. Execution of amphibious raids and demonstrations in the days prior to the ground offensive prevented the enemy from redeploying any part of the six divisions deployed to defend against an amphibious assault. In conjunction with these operations, Marine Harriers conducted their first combat operations from an Amphibious Assault Ship while other units harassed and confused the enemy. The U.S. Navy and Marine Corps Amphibious force contributed immeasurably to the victorious conclusion of Operation Desert Storm. By their superb professionalism, outstanding readiness, and inspiring devotion to duty, the officers and enlisted personnel of the Operations Desert Shield and Desert Storm Amphibious Task Force reflected great credit upon themselves and upheld the highest traditions of the United States Naval Service.

Aircraft Types, Distribution, and Call Signs

3d Marine Aircraft Wing

Unit	Aircraft Type (Quantity)	Tail Code/Call Sign
Marine Aircraft Group 11		
Marine All-Weather Attack Squadron 121	F/A-18D (12)	VK Green Knights
Marine Fighter Attack Squadron 212	F/A-18C (12)	WD Lancers
Marine Fighter Attack Squadron 232	F/A-18C (12)	WT Red Devils
Marine Fighter Attack Squadron 235	F/A-18C (12)	DB Death Angels
Marine Fighter Attack Squadron 314	F/A-18A (12)	VW Black Knights
Marine Fighter Attack Squadron 333	F/A-18A (12)	DN Shamrocks
Marine Fighter Attack Squadron 451	F/A-18A (12)	VM Warlords
Marine All-Weather Attack Squadron 224	A6-E (10)	WK Bengals
Marine All-Weather Attack Squadron 533	A6-E (10)	ED Hawks
Marine Tactical Electronic Warfare Squadron 2	EA-6B (12)	CY Playboys
Marine Aerial Refueler Transport Squadron 35	KC-130R (7)	QB Raiders
Marine Aircraft Group 13		
Marine Attack Squadron 231	AV-8B (19)	CG Ace of Spades
Marine Attack Squadron 311	AV-8B (19)	WL Tomcats
Marine Attack Squadron 542	AV-8B (18)	WH Tigers
Marine Observation Squadron 1	OV-10A/ OV-10D+ (11)	ER Sweet
Marine Observation Squadron 2	OV-10A/ OV-10D+ (7)	UU Hostage
Marine Aircraft Group 16		
Marine Medium Helicopter Squadron 161	CH-46E (12)	YR The First
Marine Medium Helicopter Squadron 165	CH-46E (11)	YW White Knights
Marine Light Attack Helicopter Squadron 367	AH-1W (10)/ UH-1N (12)	VT Scarface
Marine Light Attack Helicopter Squadron 369	AH-1W (17)/ UH-1N (5)	SM Gunfighters
Marine Heavy Helicopter Squadron 462	CH-53D (12)	YF Heavy Haulers
Marine Heavy Helicopter Squadron 463	CH-53D (8)	YH Pegasus
Marine Heavy Helicopter Squadron 465	CH-53E (8)	YJ Warhorses
Marine Heavy Helicopter Squadron 466 (-)	CH-53E (8)	YK Wolfpack
Marine Aircraft Group 26		
Marine Aviation Logistics Squadron 29 (Forward)		
Marine Medium Helicopter Squadron 261	CH-46E (12)	TV Raging Bulls
Marine Medium Helicopter Squadron 266	CH-46E (12)	ES Griffins
Marine Medium Helicopter Squadron 774	CH-46E (12)	MQ Wild Goose
Marine Heavy Helicopter Squadron 464	CH-53E (8)	EN Condors
Marine Heavy Helicopter Squadron 362	CH-53D (6)	YL Ugly Angels
Marine Attack Helicopter Squadron 775	AH-1J (11)	WR Coyotes
Marine Light Helicopter Squadron 767	UH-1N (12)	MM Nomads

4th Marine Expeditionary Brigade

Unit	Aircraft Type (Quantity)	Tail Code/Call Sign
Marine Aircraft Group 40		
Marine Attack Squadron 331	AV-8B (19)	VL Bumblebees
Marine Medium Helicopter Squadron 263	CH-46E (12)	EG Thunder Chickens
Marine Medium Helicopter Squadron 365	CH-46E (12)	YM Blue Knights
Marine Heavy Helicopter Squadron 461	CH-53E (12)	CJ Ironhorses
Marine Light Attack Helicopter Squadron 269 (-)	AH-1T (3)/ AH-1W (12)/ UH-1N (6)	HF Gunrunners

5th Marine Expeditionary Brigade

Unit	Aircraft Type (Quantity)	Tail Code/Call Sign
Marine Aircraft Group 50		
Marine Medium Helicopter Squadron 268	CH-46E (8)/ CH-53E (4)	YQ Red Dragons
Marine Medium Helicopter Squadron 265	CH-46E (12)	EP Dragons
Marine Light Attack Helicopter Squadron 169 (-)	AH-1W (6)/ UH-1N (12)	SN Vipers
Marine Attack Helicopter Squadron 773	AH1-J (14)	MP Red Dogs

Marine Corps Uniforms in the Gulf War

by LtCol Charles H. Cureton

The authority governing Marine uniforms and personal equipment is contained in the Marine Corps uniform regulations and Central Command–generated directives regarding wear. Neither Major General James M. Myatt nor Lieutenant General Walter E. Boomer officially authorized changes to the prescribed uniform. Differences existed among the Services, however. Unit insignia, name tags, and branch or specialty insignia characteristic of Army and Air Force dress were much in evidence. By mid-September 1990, Marines began applying the distinctive eagle, globe, and anchor USMC pocket insignia to the desert battle dress uniform. In addition, the green, and later tan, flight clothing; medium green "nomex" flame-retardant tracked vehicle and helicopter crew clothing; and green coveralls continued in use by those Marines authorized to wear such clothing. The use of those items added variety to the basic desert uniform and contributed to the gradual emergence of sometimes obvious, sometimes subtle, differences among the Marines, their units, and their commands.

Departures from the prescribed desert uniform and regulation equipment partly resulted from supply shortages which took place during the massive increase in American forces beginning in December 1990. For several weeks the desert battle dress uniform remained in short supply. The onset of cold weather and the lengthy period of field deployment contributed to the emergence of nonregulation sweat suits worn as undergarments, as well as various colored watch caps. Some of the differences proved to be idiosyncratic ("selective disobedience" as one officer noted) in nature, which Generals Boomer and Myatt tacitly permitted by their silence on the subject of dress—so long as everyone retained a semblance of uniformity.

During Operation Desert Shield the manner of wearing the pistol emerged as one obvious example of individualism and, to a lesser extent, of status and unit affiliation. Many of the officers and staff noncommissioned officers deploying with the 7th Marine Expeditionary Brigade wore the black leather shoulder belt designed for tank crews. On the I Marine Expeditionary Force staff the tanker shoulder belt distinguished former 7th Marine Expeditionary Brigade members from later arrivals. This distinction disappeared in time. The shoulder belt's convenience and comfort made it universally popular. Its use in the 1st Marine Division by persons authorized to carry the pistol centered on tracked vehicle personnel, division staff, and regimental staffs. Some battalion officers wore the shoulder belt, but it was uncommon in infantry units.

The tanker shoulder belt proved difficult to obtain as supplies of the belt disappeared. By December 1990, privately purchased belts made an appearance, but most aviation personnel held to their issue aviator shoulder belt. A variation to the shoulder belt was to affix the Beretta pistol holster to the upper nylon straps on the desert camouflage flak jacket cover and slide the holster's base into the jacket's breast pocket. Some members of the I Marine Expeditionary Force staff performing essentially office work, combined with the perceived remoteness from serious attack, dispensed with shoulder and waist belts and attached the holster and magazine pouches to the wide strap of the gas mask. They either wore this arrangement from around the waist in the prescribed manner for wearing the gas mask, or created a sort of quasi-shoulder holster rig with the gas mask case. Some members of the Marine expeditionary force staff merely slung the gas mask and pistol combination over their shoulder like a carry bag. Two members of the 4th Civil Action Group wore the holster attached to their trouser waist belts, thus making it inconspicuous and more suitable for their work with Saudi nationals. This configuration was not seen in the 1st Marine Division.

Regardless of the manner Marines carried the pistol, they normally had it attached to the green regulation nylon pistol lanyard. The prescribed method of wearing the lanyard was over the opposite shoulder from the pistol (if worn on the waist belt) and across the body. In time it proved more convenient to simply loop the lanyard through the metal bar at the base of the holster and attach the snap to the pistol, thereby dispensing with having to remove the lanyard every time the pistol belt came off. With shoulder belts, the lanyard looped around a con-

Originally published as appendix D in *U.S. Marines in the Persian Gulf, 1990–1991: With the 1st Marine Division in Desert Shield and Desert Storm* by LtCol Charles H. Cureton.

Desert Camouflage
Utilities

Nuclear, Biological, and
Chemical Warfare (NBC)
Defense Ensemble

Flying Ensemble
(F/A–18 Pilot)

Desert Camouflage
Utilities with Weapon

Nighttime Desert
Camouflage Utilities

Desert Camouflage
Utilities with
Field Equipment

Uniforms worn during Operations Desert Shield/Desert Storm.
Painting by Maj Donna I. Neary

U.S. Marines in the Middle East, 1991

Full-Color Plate

by

Major Donna J. Neary
U.S. Marine Corps Reserve

Shown in this plate are the various uniforms worn by Marines participating in Operations Desert Shield and Desert Storm. These uniforms are current as of 16 January 1991, D-Day for Desert Storm. It should be noted, however, that uniform regulations are never static, but reflect changing situations and requirements.

In the past, the Marine Corps has had little need for uniforms specifically designed for the desert environment. Historically, the closest predecessor to a desert uniform was a camouflage uniform, printed with a green pattern on one side and brown on the other, issued to Marine raiders, parachutists, and scout-snipers during World War II. The modern-day desert camouflage utility uniforms are part of the "Battle Dress Uniform" system adopted by the Army in 1979 to provide suitable field and combat uniforms for varying environments. Marines are issued these uniforms as special-purpose clothing when needed. Although the desert uniform has been worn for desert training and field exercises since its adoption, it was not actually worn in a hostile environment until the deployment of Marines to the Middle East during Operation Desert Shield, which began in August 1990 as a prelude to Operation Desert Storm.

At the far left is a woman Marine lance corporal in the standard six-color "chocolate chip" desert utility uniform for daytime wear. The 50 percent cotton/50 percent nylon coat, trousers, and flat-top bush hat are worn with a brown undershirt and black leather boots. Efforts are underway to make this uniform lighter in weight and thus more comfortable. Additionally, steps have been taken to procure utilities of a three-color tan camouflage pattern which studies have shown to be superior to the present six-color

pattern. A desert camouflage field jacket in the three-color pattern will be added to the desert wardrobe for wear during inclement weather. Although Marines may wear the black leather combat boots with this uniform, most opt to wear the jungle boots because of their lighter weight. Due to the threat of chemical or biological agent warfare, a carrying case containing the hooded M17A2 gas mask is worn on the left hip at all times.

Second from left is a Marine carrying an M16A2 rifle and attired in the M17A2 gas mask and special clothing designed to afford protection against contamination from nuclear, biological, or chemical (NBC) warfare. The layered fabric of the two-piece overgarment consists of a wind-resistant cotton poplin outer shell lined with a polyester tricot knit material which has been impregnated with charcoal to soak up any chemical agent before it comes in contact with the skin. It should be noted that while the fabric has the green woodland camouflage pattern used for the standard utility uniform, new NBC suits will be in the six-shade desert coloration. They also will be lighter in weight than the current clothing. Special gloves and overshoes shield the hands and feet. All these items are part of the Marine's Mission Oriented Protective Posture (MOPP) gear. An M258 skin decontamination kit is carried for emergency use.

In the center background is an F/A-18 pilot wearing a tri-service (Air Force/Navy/Marine Corps) Clothing Special Unit (CSU-13/P) cutaway anti-gravity garment ("G suit"). Basic survival equipment is contained in the modified Parachute Component Unit (PCU) series torso harness and Life Preserver (LPU). Flight boots with a leather

upper body, steel "safety toes," and non-slip soles are an essential part of flight clothing, as is the lightweight Helmet Gear Unit (HGU 55/P). A pistol and shoulder holster are worn on his left side.

In the center foreground is a lieutenant general participating in Desert Storm wearing the standard desert utility uniform, with the addition of a 9mm pistol and cartridge belt. Unlike the others shown in this uniform, this figure is wearing recently approved tan desert combat boots which are modeled after the jungle boots. However, they are lighter in weight, unvented to keep sand out, have no metal plate insteps, incorporate speed lacing, and have built-in ankle supports to prevent sprains while operating in sandy terrain.

The Marine second from right is dressed in the cotton-and-nylon poplin nighttime desert uniform in the "desert green grid pattern" which affords camouflage protection for desert operations after dark. Consisting of a hooded parka with removable quilted liner and drawstring trousers, this uniform is designed to be worn over the standard desert uniform to provide extra warmth.

At far right is a Marine in full combat gear with weapon. The lightweight body armor and field pack are the same worn with other combat uniforms and have desert utility covers to make them color compatible. Essential accessories include the standard Kevlar anti-fragmentation helmet with desert camouflage cover and ballistic laser eye protection goggles which will shield the wearer's eyes from harmful ultraviolet rays from the desert sun during the day. The field neckerchief worn over the face offers added protection from blowing sand.

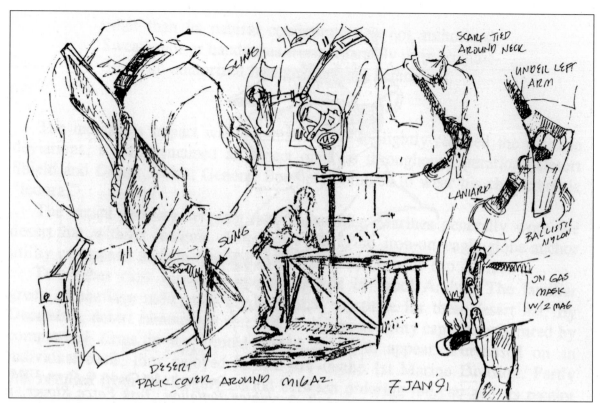

Some ways of carrying the pistol and M-16.

venient strap. Though rare, some officers adopted the British method of wearing the lanyard from the neck rather than across the body. A few officers, Lieutenant Colonel Frank L. Kebelman III of the 1st Combat Engineer Battalion chief among them, managed to obtain British Army lanyards. Since the cord proved too wide for the metal bar on the Beretta holster, Lieutenant Colonel Kebelman tied the loop of his lanyard around his waist belt.

Every member of the 1st Marine Division was issued desert battle dress uniform hat. The desert hat was part of the basic uniform made up of hat, boots, trousers, blouse, and green T-shirt. With the hat's capacity of being styled in a variety of ways, its proper wear was one of the few uniform matters to receive official guidance. The prescribed manner of wear was with the brim turned down along its entire circumference. Yet, immediately upon issue every conceivable interpretation emerged, some less subtle and outrageous than others. Popular styles included the rolled up "cowboy" brim, the flat hat with its absolutely level brim and flat crown (the latter achieved by a cardboard insert), the completely upturned brim, and the "fedora" worn by General Boomer.

The shaped battle dress hat typified Marines belonging to the force service support group, 3d Ma-

rine Air Wing units, or Marine expeditionary force headquarters. Its existence proved less common in the 1st Marine Division where field conditions, and some commanders, proved a natural deterrent. Within the division, styled hats appeared among rear echelon personnel rather than with Marines assigned to maneuver units. In October 1990 it would be a hat worn by a member of the division that prompted a Central Command directive against styling. In a visit to forward deployed units, Marine expeditionary force Sergeant Major Rafe J. Spencer spotted the one hat that went too far. While the hat in question merely had its front and back brims turned up, what pushed Sergeant Major Spencer into taking action was the fact that its owner was a gunnery sergeant and he used one of his metal collar rank insignia to pin the front brim to the crown. The resulting commander-in-chief of Central Command directive of 21 October prohibited all but regulation wear:

When the desert battle dress uniform floppy hat is worn, the chin strap will be tucked into the hat so it does not show and the brim of the floppy hat will be worn down. Curling or bending the brim of the hat, other than its nat-

Drawing by Sgt Charles G. Grow

1stSgt Wimer, Company D, 3d Assault Amphibian Battalion, Task Force Ripper, is wearing the desert hat in the correct manner, 7 January 1991.

Drawing by Sgt Charles G. Grow

The "fedora" style favored by LtGen Walter E. Boomer was often seen, 9 January 1990.

ural configuration, is not authorized. Sweat bands or bandannas worn separately or in conjunction with authorized headgear are not authorized.

The message's impact was minimal. While it slightly reduced the extreme deviations, styling remained an aspect of dress throughout Operations Desert Shield and Desert Storm. General Boomer continued to wear his characteristic "fedora."

The errant gunnery sergeant notwithstanding, Marines generally wore the desert hat without insignia. Exceptions were the iron-on eagle, globe, and anchor utility cap stencil and, in rare instances, the metal service cap device.

Two other caps appeared among Marines in Saudi Arabia. The familiar green camouflage utility cap was the usual substitute for their desert hat. By December, desert camouflage versions of the green utility cap (manufactured by commercial firms in the United States) began to appear. Purchased on an individual basis, they enjoyed limited use in the 1st Marine Division. Partly this resulted from the lengthy period between ordering the cap and its receipt via the very slow mail service. Also, by December the well-worn desert hat marked the

veteran from the newly arriving reinforcements, a number of whom had the desert camouflage utility cap. General Myatt preferred the desert utility cap and wore it constantly during the latter part of Operation Desert Storm.

Each service used the same pattern desert battle dress uniform, distinguishable only by insignia peculiar to each organization. Air Force personnel assigned to I Marine Expeditionary Force wore name tags, and their specialty and insignia embroidered in black thread on green backings as designed for the green utility uniform. Some managed to obtain these items done with brown thread letters on a tan backing. Army officers and enlisted men wore the same insignia and badges authorized for use on the green utility uniform. After December 1990, some examples of brown devices on tan cloth came into use, but those proved rare. Rank insignia consisted of the subdued style, either pin-on or embroidered on green backing.

Until mid-September 1990 Marine desert uniforms did not carry the eagle, globe, and anchor USMC pocket insignia. After 15 September, a large supply of iron-on labels arrived in Saudi Arabia and within a few weeks most utilities, but not all, carried this insignia. Typically, Marine desert battle dress uniforms went without unit patches of any kind. A notable exception was the I Marine Expeditionary Force liaison officers assigned to the British 7th Armored Brigade. They wore the brigade's red on

Photo by LtCol Charles H. Cureton
A Marine from 3d Battalion, 3d Marines, is shown in the dress worn at the start of Desert Storm, 17 January 1991. The camouflage netting on the helmet characteristic of that battalion is clearly evident.

Painting by LtCol Donna J. Neary
Marine Tanker.

uniforms. Marines assigned to the 1st Force Service Support Group working in the port at Jubayl largely gave up their desert uniforms and reverted to green camouflage utility dress. That alleviated the more pressing requirements and, by February, all Marines in the 1st Marine Division were entirely clothed in desert camouflage.

Correct wear of the desert battle dress uniform, sometimes referred to as the "chocolate chip" uniform, included the desert hat and either the jungle boot; black leather combat boot; or, by late February and March, the tan desert boot. When in combat dress during Operations Desert Shield and Desert Storm, prior to the ground offensive, the full uniform consisted of appropriate equipment as well as the green camouflage flak jacket or armored vest and Kevlar helmet, both of which came with special issue desert camouflage covers. With the onset of hostilities, General Myatt required everyone to wear the flak jacket and helmet. The pack also had a desert cover provided. The desert cover was sometimes used as a field expedient cover for the M16.

By December, the onset of cooler weather brought with it increasing use of the cold-weather night desert camouflage parka, a loose coat com-

black desert rat patch on the upper right sleeve. Some Marines assigned to Central Command wore name and service tags over their breast pockets. The service identifying tag consisted of "U.S. MARINE CORPS" in brown thread on tan cloth. These patches came in the same shape and dimensions and were worn in the same manner as Air Force name and service tags.

By December a crisis occurred in the availability of desert uniforms. The extensive buildup of American forces exhausted supplies, and some arriving units went without the desert battle dress for awhile. Complaints from General Myatt and other commanders resulted in a redistribution of desert plete with a removable liner. General Myatt left it as a matter of choice whether Marines wore the parka under or over the flak jacket. Matching trousers came with the parka. Most Marines, however, used the night desert camouflage trousers infrequently. Instead, in addition to the parka coat, many wore civilian sweat suit tops and bottoms under their desert utilities. Most sweat suits were gray in color, but it was not unusual to find division Marines wearing red, yellow, and blue suits. Since the weather had grown very cool and wet in January and little of the color showed anyway, unit commanders generally permitted the wearing of sweat suits and nonregulation watch caps of various colors without comment.

Supply shortages made it difficult for commanders to achieve total uniformity. From the beginning of Operation Desert Shield, items of green camouflage utility uniform were acceptable substitutes for missing desert items. All combinations proved possible, but there occurred no simultaneous wearing of desert jackets with green utility trousers or desert trousers with the green utility jacket. The mixing of green and desert items remained limited to caps and hats, the wearing of black, jungle, or tan boots, and occasionally the green camouflage field jacket. In addition, maintenance personnel frequently wore the issue green overalls. Tracked vehicle personnel wore fire-retardant "nomex" suits.

During the ground offensive all forward deployed I Marine Expeditionary Force personnel put on the mission-oriented protective posture jacket and trousers as well as chemical protective boots of various styles. In the 1st Marine Division, the flak jacket generally went over the mission-oriented protective posture jacket. The feeling in the division was that while everyone was vulnerable to chemical attack at all times, the flak vest frequently needed to be removed. In contrast, General William M. Keys, commanding the 2d Marine Division, directed that the mission-oriented protective posture jacket be worn over the flak vest. He felt that if contamination occurred, the flak jacket would not then require cleaning or replacement. After the first 24 hours of the ground offensive, General Keys saw that the chemical threat in the division's zone was sufficiently remote that he had the 2d Marine Division cease wearing mission-oriented protective posture suits. General Myatt saw the situation differently, and the 1st Marine Division continued using mission-oriented protective posture suits throughout the ground offensive. The mission-oriented protective posture suit, and the manner in which Marines wore the suit, became a manner of identifying to which division a Marine belonged.

The practice of personalizing equipment and clothing differed from unit to unit. Though largely confined to the division's artillery battalions, in those units, graffiti appeared on the covers of flak vests and helmets. Graffiti took the form of calendars, names of girlfriends, pithy comments, religious symbols, cartoon characters, and the 1st Marine Division's World War II patch in outline. In one instance the blue patch with its red number "1" appeared on the well-worn pocket of a flak jacket cover. Otherwise, marking clothing and equipment seldom went beyond that allowed by Marine Corps Uniform Regulations MCO P1020.34, which specified ink stamping the owner's name in certain inconspicuous locations. Some individuals, however, followed the practice of stenciling their names in one-inch-high letters across the back of utility jackets and flak vests.

A few units adopted organizational symbols for the uniform. Marines in Task Force Papa Bear stenciled the task force's paw print symbol on the back of flak vest covers as well as on the sides of vehicles. The 3d Battalion, 3d Marines, was distinctive in its use of camouflage netting on all helmets.

Marines used three types of boots in Saudi Arabia. During the extreme hot weather, the jungle boot surpassed the all-leather black boot in comfort, and it became the only boot available through unit supply. The boot proved generally adequate, eyelets located on the lower portion trapped sand, and it did not keep the foot particularly warm during the winter months. General Boomer recognized the boot's shortcomings, and in December 1990 the Marine Expeditionary Force G-4, Colonel Raymond A. List, announced that the tan desert boot would be available by January 1991. The desert boot was essentially the same as the jungle boot, but it was made of roughened tan leather and without eyelets. Since the desert boot initially appeared among Marines assigned to Central Command headquarters in Riyadh, Saudi Arabia, it was viewed as an affectation and called the "tinkerbell boot."

The abrasiveness of desert sand tended to wear off the black dye of the leather combat boot and the jungle boot; eventually the entire boot came apart as the result of abrasion and constant use. Replacing worn-out boots proved difficult because of the strained supply situation during the allied build up. Frustrated by the slowness of resupplies of any boots, division Marines frequently acquired commercially made desert boots from catalogs. However, quantities of desert boots began arriving in late January. First issues went to Task Forces Shepherd, Grizzly, and Taro. The rationale was that the Marines of Task Force Shepherd deserved the boot because of the length of time they had spent as the division's forward element. General Myatt felt that the Marines of Task Forces Taro and Grizzly needed the boots for their long desert march. Complete issue of the desert boot to the entire division occurred following its return from Kuwait.

Other items typical of Marine dress include the regulation tan web trouser belt with its brass open buckle and the khaki green tee shirt. The web belt proved durable, yet some Marines preferred belts made from nylon parachute straps. In one instance, a staff noncommissioned officer in the 1st Battalion, 7th Marines, wore a parachute cord around the waist in combination with two cloth straps as a sort of field expedient suspenders.

Nonstandard dress never gained official sanction. In September 1990, General Boomer stated his position that every I Marine Expeditionary Force Marine and sailor needed assurance that the frame of reference for himself and for unit discipline had not changed simply by virtue of serving under the unique circumstances of Saudi Arabia. He saw "squared away uniforms" and well-kept appearances as a demonstration that Marines were taking care of themselves. Dress and appearance acted as an outward indicator of unit morale and discipline. Yet, General Boomer recognized that conditions varied from one unit to another, and he allowed commanders the flexibility to authorize "temporary deviations due to unusual circumstances." Those deviations that occurred remained within parameters established by General Boomer or resulted from the "unusual circumstances" inherent in a lengthy field campaign.

Military Map Symbols

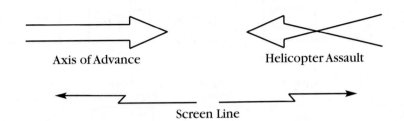

Axis of Advance   Helicopter Assault

Screen Line

Division Boundary

Corps Boundary

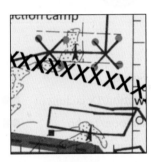

Defensive
Entrenchments

Fortification Breech

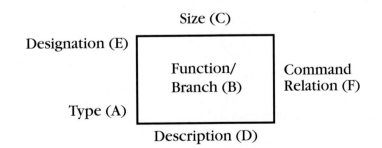

Size (C)

Designation (E)

Function/
Branch (B)

Command
Relation (F)

Type (A)

Description (D)

Military Units—Identifications

Headquarters	Infantry	Tracked Armor	Aircraft	Helicopter	Airborne (US)	Light Armored Infantry

Service Support Area	Mechanized Infantry	Artillery	Naval Infantry	Marine Expeditionary	Airborne (Air Assault)	Special Forces

---

Unit Size and Symbols

Squad	●	Regiment/Group				
Section/Detachment	●●	Brigade	X
Platoon/Troop	●●●	Division/Wing	XX
Company/Battery			Force/Corps	XXX
Battalion/Squadron				Army/Air Force	XXXX

Color Code

Blue = U.S. Forces   Green = Allied Forces   Red = Enemy Forces

---

The following abbreviations are used for the Iraqi Republican Guard units:

Nebuchadnezzar Infantry Division = NEB
al-Fao Infantry Division = FAW
Tawakalna Mechanized Division = TAW
Medina Armored Division = MED
Adnan Mechanized Division = ADN
Baghdad Mechanized Division = BAG

Examples

Combat Service Support Area Kibrit

6th Light Armored Division (FR)

1st Marines (-) (Reinforced) (Task Force Papa Bear)

2d Saudi Arabian National Guard Brigade

4th Marine Expeditionary Brigade

Hammurabi Armored Division (Republican Guard)

Brief on Iraqi Forces

by LtGen Bernard E. Trainor

On 10 December 1990, Lieutenant General Walter E. Boomer's staff and senior commanders received a briefing on the Iraqi military from retired Lieutenant General Bernard E. Trainor. General Trainor retired from the Marine Corps in 1985 after a career that included combat service in Korea and Vietnam, and then he went on to become a war correspondent for the New York Times. *General Trainor went to Iraq in the winter of 1987–88 to report on the Iran-Iraq War, and his status as a retired senior officer convinced the Iraqis to grant him unusual access to the front lines and their operational units.*

GEN TRAINOR: I went to Iraq during the winter of 1987–88 during what was known as the Cobla 5/6 Offensive by the Iranians. The Iranians called it their final offensive, and indeed it was the final offensive, but not in the way that the Iranians intended. They intended it to be the final offensive wherein they would have toppled the regime of Saddam Hussein. It turned out it was the final offensive before the collapse of the Iranian armed forces. But I got a good look at the Iraqis, and that's what I would like to address today. I'll give you an assessment, and then I think more importantly in the Q&A [question and answer], we can develop some of these things.

One of the beauties of going and becoming a military correspondent—or analyst as I was for the *New York Times*—was that when I went out to all of these Third World wars that I covered, and I covered just about every one of them during the period I was with the *Times*, once I made contact with military people I was running free; I was able to do things and go places that attachés could never go, or other journalists would go. There's kind of a brotherhood—a military brotherhood that exists—and it transcends national boundaries and ideologies, and once you are able to contact a military guy, in the position that I was in, all sorts of doors opened up to you, and that's what happened when I went to Iraq.

It [Iraq] is a very closed society, a paranoid society, a real police state, and you have attached to you a "bird dog" [close observer] and he never lets you out of his sight. When you go there and you say you are a retired three-star general from the Marine Corps who is now a journalist, you see the flicker in their eyes which essentially says "b——t," and the assumption is that you're a CIA [Central Intelligence Agency] agent and your military rank is a political

rank. But once you get down and talk to another soldier and talk about soldierly things that only another military man would talk about, then your bona fides are established at least with the military fellow, if not the political guy bird-dogging you, and that's what I was able to do. And they brought me down to—and I'm sure you all have a reasonable familiarity with the southern portion of Iraq. I went down to the area of al-Amarah, al-Majarr, as-Sulayb, down to al-Basrah and the Fish Lake* area where most of these offensives were taking place over the period of the four years of defensive operations that the Iraqis conducted.

There was no greater intention than letting me get below division level, but when I got talking with the division commander and he recognized that I was in fact a military man, then he was very anxious for me—he was typical military, "I want to show you what my guys do," and there was some business of compare and contrast—and I found this throughout the Third World. People, when they find out you were in Vietnam, well, everybody in the world knows about Vietnam, and they want to know how you did it in Vietnam and how you did it differently than the way they are fighting. The fact that I fought in Korea didn't mean a thing; nobody even knew what a Korea was, but they knew what Vietnam was.

This was a marvelous entrée. Whether I was talking with a young private in the Sandinista army or a major general in the Iraqi Army, this opened doors. So, this division commander, because he not only had military clout but he also had considerable political clout—and the two of them go together in the senior ranks of the Iraqi armed forces—he was able to go to the bird dog and get me down to where the fighting was and get right up on the lines. And I spent 45 minutes in an artillery OP [observation post] during an artillery exchange between the Iraqis and the Iranians—and you couldn't get much farther forward than that.

So I did get a good look at them, and what I'm going to tell you now is a judgment of their capability and their liabilities as I judged them during

---

*Fish Lake was a barrier created by Iraq on its border with Iran that was intended to prevent an Iranian assault. In addition to water, the lake was filled with mines, concertina wire, and high-voltage electrical lines.

the period from 1987 to 1988. Now, recognize that there have been some improvements. They have been qualitative improvements, but I think the improvements are just in a matter of degree. We can go into that maybe in the Q&A.

Let me start off with their officer corps and those generals that I talked about. The senior generals of the Iraqi Army are now skilled professional soldiers. This was not always true. During the eight or so years of the Iran-Iraq War, there were a lot of incompetent but politically loyal generals who led the Iraqi forces into Iran and got themselves whipped. Then these fellows were relieved and more competent professional military officers started to emerge or were appointed but were politically suspect, so therefore the direction of the war was conducted by Saddam Hussein and his small group, and that led to military incompetence regardless of the professional competence of the senior commanders.

Well, because of this interference, in 1985–86 the Iraqi Army was nearly defeated by the Iranians, and the military finally—they didn't revolt, obviously you don't revolt against Saddam Hussein—but they convinced Saddam Hussein, "We are loyal, but you have to leave the business of fighting the war to us." Saddam Hussein is not a military man, and he's very suspicious of his military because the military constitutes the only institution that can overthrow him or threaten him. So the competent generals who were politically loyal now were the final outcome of the original case where you had incompetent generals who were politically loyal.

The senior officers owe their positions and their prestige and their power—which is considerable—to the fact that they are on Saddam Hussein's "team." And oh, by the way, don't get too big for your britches or Saddam Hussein will remove you, and remove you physically, as may have been the case here just in the past week or so with the chief of staff of the armed forces.

What I am trying to imply is that while they are loyal to Saddam Hussein and they are very nationalistic Iraqis, they are also scared to death of Saddam Hussein. All the horror stories that you've ever heard about Saddam Hussein are probably true—and there are probably a lot more that we don't even know about—so these guys are going to stay close to Saddam Hussein. They are very competent. Most of them have been trained not only in Iraqi professional military schools—these are two-stars and above—but they have also been trained in foreign schools. They have been to professional schools in the Soviet Union and Britain, in France,

in Pakistan and India and other countries, so they have a broad amalgam of military concepts and doctrine. But make no mistake about it, the Iraqi military doctrine is not a Soviet doctrine, it's not a British doctrine, it's not a French doctrine; it's Iraqi and it developed out of the eight years of war. It's peculiarly theirs, but it has features of the experiences of other military forces.

Now let me drop down to the brigade level, brigade and battalion level. Oddly enough, these officers—and these now are the fellows who have grown up in the war and grew up as part of Saddam Hussein's regime. These are the fellows that survived the war as the platoon leaders, and now they are battalion commanders and/or brigade commanders. This was again at the same time frame I was there. None of these fellows have been to foreign schools, and that was probably because they were too busy fighting the war, but they have all been through the professional schools within Iraq and they, too, are very competent.

The company commanders and the platoon commanders, needless to say, have not been to any foreign schools, but they were very competent. That artillery position that I was in, the young lieutenant that was the FO [forward observer]—big strapping fellow, good looking guy, other than his hair being about as long as mine, you'd take him for a Marine—he knew his stuff, knew how to employ his artillery. And I couldn't speak any Arabic, but he had his maps out in front of him and we were able to point and touch and communicate with one another, and so he was competent.

Now, in terms of a danger to Saddam Hussein, it probably comes less from the senior officers than it does from the brigade and battalion commanders. He doesn't have a firm a grip on these people as he does the senior ones.

One of the things he would do during the Iran-Iraq War, during the lull when there wasn't any activity, fighting corps and divisions were kind of permanently established all along the 800-mile front, but the brigades would constantly move. Divisions and corps were wired in—all of their communications were underground—they have radios to use, but they normally would communicate via landlines, which is, as I said, were buried. So these guys have these permanently well-established positions, but the brigades would move every 30 days. Now, he did this for three reasons.

[The] number one reason [was] to keep the troops from getting too bored. They are looking at the same piece of terrain all the time, their fighting edge leaves, and [they get] the feeling that the grass is always greener on the other fellow's yard, so every 30 days they switch them around. And they may only go 5 miles, 10 miles, 200 miles, but they would constantly move them every 30 days for morale purposes.

Now, there was another reason he did it. From a professional standpoint, it gave the staff good training in the tactical movement of the troops, because when these brigades would move, they would move tactically. So it was good staff training.

And the third reason—and this is the political reason—Saddam Hussein, with his paranoia and his fear of conspiracy, he wanted to move these brigades so the young Turks would not get to know each other too well and perhaps conspire against him.

Well, those are the three reasons that they moved them around.

In my analysis and judgment on the Iraqi staff, their staff work is very good. Now, I would give it an outstanding to off-the-page for what they were doing facing the Iranians, but then again, they had enough practice of doing that because the Iranians did the same thing to them move after move after move, so they got the business of fighting a defensive war with their peculiar tactics. They got it down to a fine art.

Now, how does that translate when they are fighting a different type of enemy and a different type of war? Well, the fundamental soundness of their staff procedures will stand them in good stead, but the thing that they know how to do so well when they are facing the Iranians will no longer apply, so obviously their staff work is not going to be that good. But still don't think of them as a bunch of "rag heads" who can't put their act together. They are good.

Okay. Now let me talk about the individual military arms within the armed forces. Let me start off with their air force and disposal of it.

Now I will talk about their aviation element. It came in basically two packages—strategic aviation, designed to go deep into Iranian territory and take out deep targets and carry out terror bombings, and psychological, to break the morale of the Iranians. Those guys were in French planes, trained by the French, [and were] very good. These are the fellows that brought the Exocet [missile] into the [USS] *Stark*. They were quite good, but the Iraqis were so concerned about losing those aircraft and losing those pilots that the campaigns were spurts. They would launch the aircraft and carry on an air campaign for anywhere from days to maybe a week, and then

they would cut it off before the Iranians learned how to deal with the air attacks and started to trip their aviation. So those fellows are very good and one should keep that in mind—not that I have any concern that we would not, with the massive amount of early warning and aircraft we have out here—but I feel they could really effectively use that strategic arm very well. They are very good at cover and deception and you always have to worry about a leaker [undetected aircraft] getting through. But let me dispose of those. I didn't see that much of them. I just know more about them than I do of having seen them.

On the tactical side, battlefield interdiction, close air support—they were very, very poor, and I don't think they have improved particularly on it. Very poor. The close air support and interdiction aircraft didn't really give the Iranians that much trouble, and the pilots were poorly trained. They did not have the desire to close in battle. And the tactical helicopters were absolutely ridiculous. They would be well behind their lines and they would just fire their rockets in the direction of the Iranians, and then they drop down and feel they have satisfactorily done their job. So that, in a nutshell, is my assessment of the aviation side of the house.

Now let me go to that which I saw in much greater detail. Let me start off with their infantry. The infantry was basically conscript. Some of them would go on and stay on. Those that were bright went on for awhile, then they were sent off to college, but always subject to recall.

The infantry that I saw in the Iraqi Army reminded me very much of the infantry that I saw in the Soviet forces in Germany facing the NATO [North Atlantic Treaty Organization] forces. They were obedient, competent soldiers with very limited military knowledge beyond that which they themselves were assigned. In other words, if he's an RPG [rocket-propelled grenade] man, he knew how to use the RPG. If he had an AK-47 [assault rifle], he knew how to use an AK-47. If you ask one of them to move on to a crew-served weapon, he wouldn't have any particular tactical sense of how to employ it; they were simple guys but reasonably competent infantrymen.

Now, those of you who faced the North Koreans or the Chinese in the Korean War, or the VC [Viet Cong] or the NVA [North Vietnamese Army] in the Vietnam War, they do not come up to any of the enemies that we have fought in the past. Their infantry, they just don't match them [the VC or NVA], but they are still pretty good guys and know how to fire the weapons.

I'd go down—and this would be both in support positions on the second line, or even up on the line itself—you look in the eye, see whether there's fire there, whether they have any fight in their belly, and you didn't get too bright a look. They were there and they just wanted to survive, praise Allah they would. But you check their weapons: the weapons would be clean, and check the magazines, take out some of the rounds, magazines were clean, good to go. You look at their face mask—chemical mask, open the thing up, didn't find pogey-bait [candy] in there, you found the mask, it was ready to go, in good shape. Field sanitation, one of the things I looked as I went around the Third World to assess some of these forces and given frontline positions, it was pretty damn good. So that's kind of the picture of the infantryman in the Iraqi Army.

Their NCO [noncommissioned officer] system is a little queer. It's kind of like the Soviet system, kind of like a warrant officer, and he—this large bevy of all conscripts is too large for this sort of fellow, but they depend mostly on the platoon leaders to keep the forces together.

Now, they would withstand these Iranian attacks simply because they didn't have any choice, and their only job was to sit there and shoot, but I have to tell you, they were scared to death of the Iranians.

The Iranians—first, they never knew when the Iranians were coming, literally never knew, and they were afraid they were coming every night. And those that used to go out on outpost duty would be absolutely scared to death because when the Iranians attacked, they didn't signal their attack with artillery barrages or concentrations or prep[aration] fires of any sort. They didn't give anything away by SIGINTs [signals intelligence] because the Iranians really didn't have any radios and they did all their planning face-to-face and by sending messengers. And the Iranian Army, the regular army was simply in a support role.

The major fighting and the major planning was done by the [Iranian] Revolutionary Guard, and they would start off their attacks with these 12s- and 14-year-old kids called "Bahais," and these kids were going to go to Allah—that's what they wanted—and they would have two hand grenades and their job was to go out, not screaming, but they would infiltrate to get through the minefields, get through the wire, and blow up the outpost position which provided the main battle positions—and I'll describe those momentarily—to blow those fellows up in there and clear the minefields either by blowing them up, that was usually the way, and cutting

through the barbed wire. Then the Revolutionary Guards, the older fellows, they would start the charge and come at them [the Iraqis] like a bunch of Indians [Native Americans].

Well, this scared the hell out of the Iraqis. The Iranians were able to concentrate large numbers of forces at the breakthrough point, and the Iranians outnumbered the Iraqis, population-wise, 3 to 1 as it was, and at the point of contact, they would outnumber them 50 to 1. So, when these Iranians came, they came, and for some poor fellow sitting in that outpost, why he's going to go to Allah. So they were very, very nervous about that sort of thing, and if they ever tried to go to the rear, they were through because their own officers would shoot them. So there wasn't much joy among these fellows. They would stay there and literally be overrun.

Now let me move on to their armored forces, their tanks. They had lots of tanks, and we know they have the T-72, but they also have a lot of junk, and among that junk was the T-62, which the Iraqis considered useless. When I was out there, they were using them basically as a pillbox, too, because the maintenance on the thing was always breaking down, so they put them in these positions and pointed the tube [gun barrel] at the Iranian side.

Now, the supposedly best [Iraqi] units were the *Republican Guards*, and this was kind of a special force created by Saddam Hussein, really, for his own protection against a coup by the rest of the army, but they were used in the latter part of the war in kind of a semicounterattack role after these Iranian offenses started to lose their momentum. I was not at all impressed and I never saw any of the *Republican Guard* units in action, but I saw their other armored units in action and the maintenance was poor, the crews were poorly trained, [and] they didn't have the know-how to coordinate. I just was not impressed by their armor.

Now, subsequent to my presence out there and the very last stages of the war, the Iraqis went on the offensive and went against Iranian positions at a place called al-Faw—which I'm sure some of you are aware of, and it was a pretty impressive armored attack. But when I was there they were very poor, and they tried to put together a combined arms operation supporting the infantry and the tanks to go against the salients over by Fish Lake that the Iranians had supported by tanks that were on the Iraqi side on the Shatt al-Arab, and it was, I think, their first attempt at a combined arms approach in the attack, and it worked. But it was so primitive and so clumsy that going up to Twentynine Palms, California, they would have been laughed out of the corridor.

Now, presumably they have improved since then, but I can't imagine they have improved that much in either the use of the armor or their ability to combine the armor. I think they were successful at al-Faw, and I think they were successful at Mehran, and when they went into Kuwait, which was pretty impressive because it was a set piece battle that they had set there and planned it and rehearsed it, then they moved, and they didn't have that much opposition. At al-Faw they caught the Iranians by surprise. At Mehran there was minimum resistance, and of course in Kuwait there was minimum resistance, but in terms of having to use their armor forces with any sort of flexibility, I don't think they are going to do that well with it.

Now about the so-called *Republican Guard*, I haven't seen them, but I do know this. During the war there were only four of those divisions, and now they have expanded them. It depends on who you have talked to, whether they have six or eight of them—you may have a better handle on that than I do—but you just can't double your number and maintain the same sort of quality. So, I think they may have more of these *Republican Guard* units, but they probably deleted the quality.

Armor. Sure, it's going to be a problem, armor's always a problem, but I wouldn't think you'll have [German Field Marshal Erwin] Rommel roaring at you from these guys. They are going to make a lot of targets.

That's another thing I should say. I didn't see this so much in the Iran-Iraq War, but in some of the other conflicts that I have observed, Third World soldiers, if a tank is hit, they don't consider it a stationary pillbox that you can stay in and fight out of. The first it's hit, [all] they want to do is haul ass, they got to get out. You really don't even need a catastrophic kill, just a mobility kill and most of them are going to abandon the tanks.

Another interesting thing is you—and this was clearly brought out in Angola [in Africa]—you get the lead tank, everyone else tends to panic because that's the leader. He goes and everybody else finds convenient reasons to go into holy defilade someplace. Might be something to keep in mind. Mind you, I don't know if it applies to the Iraqi, but I have seen it in other venues, including the Soviets. This is what was happening to the Soviets in Afghanistan, and I also saw it in Chad with the Libyans, so it's a point to keep in mind.

Let me move on from the armor to what I really think is going to be the casualty-maker capability within the Iraqi armed forces. That's their artillery. They have lots of it, they know how to use it, and they don't operate the way we do. Where we have kind of an economy of force measure—you look for a point destruction mission, you try to get the target, adjust your rounds on to it, destroy it—their whole approach—and this, I guess is kind of an adoption from the Soviet model—is just throw that stuff out there. Put enough of it out there with all the tubes that you have, saturate the area and get the target you're aiming at. So that artillery is going to come, both the gun artillery and their rockets. They are going to crank that stuff out, and that will be a problem unless you get the artillery out. And they do have, probably, the best gun in the world that they bought from the South Africans, the G5 [155mm howitzer]. I don't know if they have any of the G6s, which is the SP [self-propelled] version of it. They also have another 210[mm howitzer], which they manufactured themselves [that] is supposed to be a pretty good artillery piece.

So, there's a lot of it, but the point is the way they employed it against the Iranians was based on the fact that they were sitting in these defensive positions for so long that they had these enormous stockpiles of ammunition behind them. And they have probably duplicated that sort of concept in their fixed positions up along the Kuwaiti border, that they brought lots of bullets with them. So, in order to get their supply point and get the guns themselves—but after that they are going to have an enormous problem of resupply just because of that concept of excess . . . they are going to have terrible ones up there, but I think the artillery is going to be a bugaboo for you.

Now let me talk about what I think is their best arm, and it's not a combat arm, it's their combat engineers. Their combat engineers, they put the best people in it, the best officers. You got these guys who are civil engineers and graduates of the universities, and you're not dealing with a peasant army up there. They are a pretty well-educated group of people.

These guys are just magnificent. They have lots of equipment and lots of capability, and very innovative, and they can put up positions so fast under fire it can make your head swim. I saw them doing this under those tremendous barrages they were being subjected to by the Iranians. So they can build roads, build obstacles, they can build defenses very, very quickly, and they have lots of equipment to do it with.

Now, to kind of put some of this together for

you, let me show you the way they have their defenses, then you can tell me how this matches up with what your intelligence is telling you up north.

[Uses a chalkboard]

Basically, this would be north—as I recall it's always at the top of the map—and this would be the Iranian positions. What they would do in their defenses, they would have an outpost line, and these basically were little strongpoints that almost look like some of those trench and even berm positions that we had in Vietnam, which were triangular in shape with strongpoints at each of the apex. These would be in supporting position of one another. This is ideally—what I'm describing to you—what would exist throughout the entire front, but obviously it doesn't, but it's notional and will give you an example of the way they conduct their defense.

So these will be the fellows that would give early warning when the Bahais go get them, and they would have wire and mines in front of them, and they would have wire and mines behind them. These, generally speaking, were in supporting distance, and in some instances, crew-served distance from the MLR—their main line of resistance—and the main line of resistance was usually conducted on a ridgeline, and what you saw here was basically the same sort of thing that you would see in pictures of World War I. They would have . . . trench lines in front, connecting trenches to the back, lateral trench line back there with bunkers and fighting positions here.

Now, normally they would do this on a natural piece of terrain, but if they didn't have a natural piece of terrain—and that was a likely avenue of approach—then they would construct one and their combat engineers would go in and use these earth movers. And when I was there they had about 1,300 of these enormous Japanese earth movers, and they would come in and build a ridge, and they would stabilize the soil with, I don't know, I guess it was epoxy and cement and some other synthetics, and literally build a ridge. Then they would put their trenches in it just as I have shown here on the natural ridge.

The trench line would run seven or eight feet deep, and they would have chicken wire on either side of them. They would be very narrow for just enough for one man to get through—and let me digress a moment. That was how I got into the artillery FO position. I had spotted it as we moved up—I could see the antenna sticking up and I knew there was an OP there—and we were on the back slope of this defensive position, and I could see the

antenna sticking up on the forward slope. When we got to the connecting trench that went up there, I simply took a left and went on up there, and my bird dog behind me was trying to grab me to stop me, but he couldn't catch up, so I got into the bunker. Their overhead cover—there's just really room for two people in there, the FO and I guess presumably the radioman—so I was able to duck in there and my bird dog was caught outside in the connecting trench shouting for me to come out, but he was in somewhat of an untenable position because the artillery was coming in and he was exposed, so I was able to spend 45 minutes in there. So they would construct these positions.

Now, back here you would have another position identical to these, and what they would do is sometimes they have two up, one back, and sometimes they have one up and two back, but basically these first two lines would be identical. This would be in supporting distance of this position; these would be in supporting position of the outpost; the outpost would be able to give mutual support, one to the other, so you see they had an integrated defense, and they would set these things up to try to channelize the attacks into a killing sack, and they would either make use of the natural terrain or when they would construct these hill lines, these ridgelines, they would angle them to try to create that sack.

Now, back here they would have another line. This, of course, would be occupied. This would be identical to these two, but unoccupied, but the trenches are there, the bunkers are there. Back here they would simply have sand berms, would have revetted positions in there that you could drive tanks into the fire, and . . . they would have these things as far back as you wanted to go, and if they didn't have enough—if this was the main attack, and you can obviously see what their game plan was when the Iranians would attack, the idea was to just trip them, bring them deeper into these defensive positions. And while these were reasonably rightly held, they kept their reserves back, and back here, coming all the way from Baghdad down to al-Amarah down to Basrah, was this marvelous road network and they could speed these lowboys [semi-trailers] carrying the earth movers, the lowboys carrying the tank reinforcements, they would be coming down these roads to move into these pre-prepared positions, and the engineers would simply stop and build successive positions, so eventually the Iranian attack would start to peter out.

Now, back here on the far side of the road they

would have all the supply and water points, ammunition points to support these defenses, and they had been developed over the years—they had more damn ammunition and stuff than you could imagine. When I was out there they had so much of it and from so many different countries and such a mixed bag that they had hired a Japanese firm to computerize their inventory control, and I presume that they have accomplished that by now, but they would just wear them out coming in like that.

But because he was afraid of taking too many casualties, he didn't want to take casualties—he being Saddam Hussein—there was rarely a counterattack. They would simply absorb the blow and then use their massive artillery and tank fire to reduce these Iranian positions, just literally beat them into the ground. The Iranians had very poor tactical logistics, and pretty soon these guys were hung out there and eventually crushed. It was only after the resistance was completely gone that the Iraqis would launch their counterattacks to restore the position. That was mainly their defense.

Now let me talk a little bit about—and I'll conclude on this and open it up to questions—the psychology. This is a police state in Iraq. Everybody is fearful, but everybody pretends life is lovely. Let me give you an illustration of that.

When the Iraqis would launch one of the strategic air campaigns of theirs and then shut it off, the Iranians would then respond, but of course they didn't have the capability. The way they responded was by popping off some Scuds, and normally they fired three Scuds at a time at Baghdad. Right after one of these Iraqi air campaigns ceased, everybody knew the Iranian Scuds were coming and they would be walking around on eggshells, and people shopping or talking to the guy, the market man or the fellow in the suit, everybody was looking over their shoulders, keeping an ear cocked for the Scuds to come in.

I said, they come in with three. I was in Baghdad one night—I didn't hear two of them but I heard the third one and the thing made a hell of a racket. And immediately after it, I heard sirens, and I heard bells and whistles and horns honking, pots, and pans. I said, "Jesus, what the hell did this hit to cause such a reaction?" You know what it was? They were all out celebrating because the three rounds had come in; they knew it would be the end until the next Iraqi air campaign. They were out celebrating: "The other guy got blown away, but that's his problem, not mine."

There's this unreal sense of normalcy—the cities were all hit up, but Amarah, which was right behind the line, everybody was acting as if nothing is wrong. You never saw a wounded or maimed Iraqi soldier in any of the main cities. They had sanitariums for them. They were kept out in sanitariums because he [Saddam] didn't want to upset the populace with this view of wounded people, even though every family had a relative either killed or wounded or captured, but they had to pretend everything was perfectly normal. The families would be taken out there, but their sons could not come into the cities. It was an eerie unreal sort of world, which I think shows you a degree of fragility in the morale of the Iraqis.

Let me give you a rather gruesome example of the extent to which Saddam Hussein went to maintain this facade of normalcy.

As you know, the war was not a constant war, it was a cyclical war. The Iranians would gear up and launch a massive offensive, then peter out, go build up their logistics, and come at them again. They did this year after year. Well, the Iranians always took more casualties than the Iraqis took—a substantial number of casualties—but Saddam Hussein, during one of these campaigns, was reluctant to let the families know that their sons had been killed in action, so back here on the far side of the road, out beyond where all the supply and water points and ammo [ammunition] points were, he also had these warehouses which were refrigerated, and that's where the bodies were put, put on ice. And during the period of the lull, the bodies would be taken out and sent on home to the families for burial, and along with a very, very handsome indemnity on the part of a grateful government—anything to [lessen] the shock of war to the Iraqi people.

Now, part of this was political, because the leadership of the Iraqi Army was made up of Sunni Muslims, and the foot soldiers were basically Shiite Muslims; and the Iranians were basically Peshites [Shiites] co-religionists, and Saddam Hussein was very much afraid of the revolt against the Sunni rule. So, for that reason he didn't want to suffer many casualties and didn't want people to realize how desperate the war was, and he went to this extent to hide it.

Now, I think that sort of mentality still exists, and let me give you the evidence of that. You probably know that as part of a deception plan to indicate that our blockade was hurting him, he instituted gas rationing in Iraq. That was two months ago, and it lasted about a week. There was such public outcry and upset over this that he was afraid of this delicate morale balance and he said, "Okay, no more gas ration[ing]." That was a mistake, and he fired the minister of energy.

You probably haven't seen that much out here, being in somewhat remote area, but back in the [United] States on all the networks, and CNN [Cable News Network], you see these "man in the street" interviews in beautiful downtown Baghdad: "Oh, no war, no war. If there is a war, we are battle-hardened, we ought to be able to beat the Americans." These guys are wrestling in the dark. Saddam Hussein himself constantly talks about, "The Americans can't take casualties; we can take hundreds of thousands of casualties. We have done it in the Iran[-Iraq] War; we are battle-hardened. We can stand these casualties, [but] the Americans can't stand to bleed." Again, it's all a psyche thing.

It's my judgment, although it's just to this incorrect evidence that I recently cited and also my observation of [them] during the war, that while they [the Iraqi Army] are a large and a very competent force in many respects, I think they tend to be a very fragile force. They have never had visited upon them the sort of firepower that we can deliver against them. If it comes to that, I think you're not going to find—you're certainly not going to find them fighting like the Japanese, or the North Koreans, or the VC or the NVA, and they may not fight well at all. I think they may collapse very quickly. I wouldn't plan on that sort of thing, but I think it's a distinct possibility.

Okay, I talked long enough and now it's your opportunity to ask me questions. Any of those that I can answer, I'll be happy to do it.

QUESTION: What is your assessment of their rear area security?

GEN TRAINOR: Rear area security was reasonably good. At least they had the guys there guarding all of these positions. The Iranians didn't have much of a capability to get at them, but they still had them pretty well guarded. How alert these guys were? I don't know.

One thing that I have to tell you on their mobile reserves—they were used to moving these reserves, and not only the *Republican Guards*, but also they did have reserve units. Because with that 800-mile front, what they had to do, they would hold the forces back until they found out where the main attack was coming because when the Iranians launched one of their offensives—not all of them were like this, some of them were deceptions, and the Iraqis could not afford to make a mistake—so they let the attacks develop until they determined which was the main one. That's when they would converge on the position, when all the earth movers

come barreling down the highways, and tanks and trucks full of infantry to fill up these positions. So that was the basic idea of their defense in depth, that they could take the time in making the decision on the reserves until the battle developed sufficiently.

But your question brings up something I seriously omitted. This may not go too well in the [Marine aircraft] wing, for those of you going in helicopters. I think in terms of the business of gaining air superiority, that's a doable job. It's going to cost some effort, obviously, and we will take some losses, but I think electrically controlled or radar controlled we will be able to take out their low and intermediate altitude defense. . . . But let me tell you, anybody falling below 10,000 feet is in harm's way because they have so many SAM-7s [surface-to-air missiles], ZSU-23s [23mm self-propelled anti-aircraft guns], so many garden-variety antiaircraft pieces that they will just make hell.

There's a mistaken belief that there was an Iranian plane during this period of just before the Scud came in. There was a report that there was an Iranian plane coming, and the antiaircraft opened up from downtown Baghdad and it was absolutely staggering. You have seen the displays at the Washington Monument on the Fourth of July? All you could see were tracers going up there, and driving down the road to Basrah, and in the most unlikely places there's a ZSU-23 crew sitting out there at a gas station or just sitting out by a small oasis.

They [have] all sorts of antiaircraft stuff and all of their armored forces where they are disposed right now, I would suspect are under an umbrella of that antiaircraft, and you're going to have to get it out. It's not going to be easy because no targeteer could target all that they have, and they will be able to move it around. So helicopter operations, unless they were properly planned, good cover and deception, good attack support that goes along with it, it could be very hazardous to the infantryman's health. And just flying the helicopter at an altitude below 10,000 feet is also going to be harmful.

QUESTION: You didn't talk about CBR [chemical, biological, radiological weapons].

GEN TRAINOR: Well, he's got the chemical weapons. I think once you accept the fact that he's going to use them, it would be foolish to say he would never use them. So, yeah, I think he would use them if he found value to them, but the question is how much value is he going to get out of them? How is he going to deliver: by artillery or rocket, or by airplane? An aerosol version in a bomb version, or if he manages to be able to fit something on the nose of a Scud? And I think the intelligence community is a little undecided about that.

But okay, let's give him that. So what is he going to use? The artillery and rockets would be against frontline troops. What forces are probably the best prepared to cope with something like that? The frontline troops. A real good target will be a target in the rear—an airfield or logistics base, and that would be a good sort of chemical target, but how is he going to deliver it: airplane or the Scud? [The] Scud is notoriously inaccurate—he may hit it, he may not, it may not land in Saudi Arabia. And in terms of the aircraft, presumably we are going to be able to take out most of his aircraft. However, as I say, he may get a leaker in there.

But then again, how much damage is that going to do? It's going to be more psychological than anything else. There will be casualties, but not mass casualties. On top of that, our intelligence community, I would hope, has made this a priority of EEIs [essential elements of information], and then we preempt, so I don't see that the chemical thing would be a problem. I think it's something that has been kind of overrated in terms of the anxiety factor, but let me tell you, this guy [Saddam] is a shrewd son of a b——h, and we talk about what we will do when we go to war, but it takes two to tango, and this guy has a few surprises up his sleeve. I'm sure he has a few technical surprises, and maybe a few tactical surprises, but this guy, knowing the fact that his air force is going to be decimated if we can get through those hardened bunkers built to NATO specifications—but he might take out one of these aircraft and load it up with some super Exocets, fly it over Iran airspace and try to beat the AWACS [airborne warning and control system aircraft], the [Northrup Grumman] E-2 [Hawkeye], beat everything and pop one off. And boy, wouldn't that be nice to catch an amphibious ship with all those Marines sitting there waiting to go to shore? Lots of casualties.

This is the sort of thing he wants. He knows what happened to the American policy in 1983 when the Beirut barracks was blown up and the whole presidential policy in Lebanon collapsed. That's in the back of his mind, so he's looking for great casualties. How about some sort of a commando raid? He's got a good commando force. Commando attack even before we go to war, if he becomes convinced that we are going to war and it's coming within the next 48 hours, and he launches six or seven of these commando teams—not at the frontline troops, but gets back to the rear, the supply areas where there's support people, and

not quite as combat ready as they are up on the line, and causes a lot of destruction there. They may all die in the process, but a wonderful thing if CNN was to have this film [transmitted] to the United States, fire and smoke going up and all those women bleeding out there in the desert.

Boy, oh boy, the reaction of the United States is going to be enormous. So that would be a psychological coup de main. So this son of a b——h is a clever rascal, and you're not going up against a primitive army, and you're certainly not going up against a dunce. Next question?

QUESTION: Given the fact that he gave back all the gains from the Iran-Iraq War, how susceptible do you think a PSYOP [psychological operations] campaign against the [Iraqi] army would work?

GEN TRAINOR: I don't think the PSYOP campaign against the army would work right now at all. I think it should be tried, not against the army but against the population, that "this guy is leading you down the path of national suicide." The only thing he [Saddam] has to worry about is the army turning against him, and the army is not going to turn against him if they are not suffering anything. I say the possibilities go up dramatically once the fighting starts and anguish and destruction is visited upon that army. Then they might have second thoughts about it; but until that happens, I don't think there's any chance of turning that one institution that can threaten Saddam Hussein into a real threat.

But one of the things that Saddam Hussein could do at the eleventh hour is, you know, if he really is convinced after January 15 we are coming at him, he says, "Okay, I'll back off, I'll back off," and pulls out, and then everybody is standing there waiting to go—and don't anticipate the command. So there we are. Now he pulls out. "Oh, he loses face and all that." Loses face? What do you mean? He controls the country; he's got an iron grip on the country. Is the army going to turn against him? He just saved them from getting their head handed to them, so they are not going to turn against him. Then what does he do? He's left us. He might do it. He might do it.

On the other hand, the Saudis, who are urging us to go get him, and the Israelis, who are in rare agreement with the Saudis, are saying he's got to go and saying to the United States, "If you don't get him, we will do it, we will provoke it and make you do it." So that's a possibility, but all crises eventually come to an end. This one, I think you're going to see the resolution of the current crisis sometime between now and the middle of March. Now, in the process, it may be creating another crisis, but that's another subject.

QUESTION: General, you alluded to use of a commando technique that they would apply. What did you see in their application of special forces brigades and commando companies?

GEN TRAINOR: I didn't see any. This was just a straight war, but I know he does have the commando forces. They come in by helicopter and do a reasonably good job. I think they are probably good for this reason: the Arab states have been able to develop very good commando-type forces. The Syrians have had good ones as far back as the '73 war with the Israelis [the Yom Kippur War; also known as the 1973 Arab-Israeli War]. The PLO [Palestine Liberation Organization] has very good commandos, so by extension I'm saying Saddam Hussein and these professional military leaders that run the Iraqi armed forces have probably turned out a pretty good special operations commando organization, but I did not see them in action.

QUESTION: General Trainor, did you get a feel for how low they would delegate authority to make tactical decisions to commit counterattacks, shift their axis of attack, that sort of thing?

GEN TRAINOR: The corps commander kind of set the tone, but within the desires of the corps commander, the division commanders would maneuver their brigades. Brigade commanders had tactical authority, so on down the line, but in the type of war they were fighting, the only significant decisions were really the allocation of resources, where they are going to reinforce. But down on the tactical level there wasn't much for these guys to do other than defend their positions. So in a sense, the question is moot.

I don't know. He gave greater tactical flexibility to his senior leaders in the last three years of the war than he did before that. Below that, I know the tactical commanders are capable of exercising considerable initiative, but they didn't have to do it in the type of war that they were fighting. But their command and control remains very vulnerable; their logistics remain vulnerable, as long as we have the air superiority.

QUESTION: Do you think we will see a lot of POWs [prisoners of war]?

GEN TRAINOR: Well, he has 450,000 troops and 29 divisions in Kuwait, and I assume that there are basically divisions along the coast. Then, turning to defend against the amphibious operation, and turning westward across the Saudi border and refusing up their right flank, and behind those you have some armored forces, central reserve in the middle of Kuwait, and his general reserve of armored forces up around Basrah.

Now, 450,000—he's got supposedly a million-man army, but beyond that he can get some militia, but of that million-man army that's relatively available to him, maybe 534,000 are what you might call reasonably good troops, and he's in a geopolitically untenable position. He's got a potential enemy—certainly an enemy in terms of his habitual Persian Turks to the east, in Iran the political facade, and the Syrians to the west, to say nothing of the Israelis in the south, this army in the south ready to move north—this is a tough position for a guy to be in.

So how is he going to defend against all of these? He just can't ignore the Iranians, the Turks, or the Druze that are over in that area. Also, he's got to keep some of these forces, decent forces there. So, he put a lot of stuff down south. A lot of it is second-rate units, second-rate infantry. So in answering your question, what it comes down to is he's got a field army of 450,000 men, and 225,000 of them [are] KIA [killed in action] and you've destroyed his military capability.

And I don't know what the battle plans are—and I'm not interested in knowing, so I'm free to speak my mind—but it seems to me the way you conduct this war, you conduct an air campaign against military industrial-related targets in Iraq itself to bring the war home to Iraq. Then you conduct your air campaign, your ground campaign and amphibious campaign, as the opportunity presents itself, to destroy his field army in Kuwait. That's where you want to do it, in Kuwait; that's the killing zone; that's where he put the people. The more he sends down there, the more POWs and MIAs [troops missing in action] you can inflict on him. If he does that, he can't last. Like the *Republican Guard* unit bit, it would seem to me they would be the ones more than likely than any other part of the armed forces to turn against Saddam Hussein.

GEN WALTER E. BOOMER: The Iranians captured three times the number of POWs than the Iraqis captured, so I would think that would indicate that some units gave up—although I'm not certain about that, and that really is my question. Do you have a feel for that? What would we be faced with in terms of the numbers of POWs we have to deal with?

GEN TRAINOR: It would be enormous. The infantry—once you get through the infantry, what you're engaging then is his mech ID [mechanized infantry divisions], and all of these divisions, they are not going anywhere, they are dug in, and a lot of them are going to be dug in permanently if you drop a few arc lights on them. But once you get around them—and I presume you're smart enough to—then you cut off their logistics, their lifeline, you're pounding the hell out of them with naval air and gunfire. The large numbers of Iraqi prisoners that were taken by the Iranians were primarily in the initial part of the war when the Iraqis conducted a very inept campaign into Iran, and when the Iranians counterattacked they scarfed up a lot of them. Early in the Iranian counterattack phase, the Iraqis got smart and started to develop the defenses I've just described.

QUESTION: General, in your experience, what did you see as the most effective tactical-physical deception the Iraqis pulled?

GEN TRAINOR: I don't know what they were doing to deceive the Iranians. It was more the Iranians deceiving the Iraqis. But I would say the cover and concealment of the Iraqis were very good. I think if you were over on the Iranian side looking back at these positions, they would be very difficult to get them because I know, being in one of the front-line positions and looking back at these successive positions, it was almost like looking out at sea. You really couldn't identify distance and what exactly was there, so they were very good in their cover and concealment, but they had plenty of time to do that sort of thing. I don't think I can adequately answer your question.

Okay. Thanks for the opportunity to be with you. I hope it was some value to you.

GEN BOOMER: General, it was of value and we appreciate it. Thank you very much.

List of Reviewers

Marines

General Walter E. Boomer (Ret)
General Carlton W. Fulford (Ret)
General Charles C. Krulak (Ret)
General Michael J. Williams (Ret)

Lieutenant General John E. Rhodes (Ret)

Major General John H. Admire (Ret)
Major General Harry W. Jenkins Jr. (Ret)

Brigadier General James A. Brabham Jr. (Ret)
Brigadier General Thomas V. Draude (Ret)

Colonel James A. Fulks (Ret)
Colonel Richard W. Hodory (Ret)

Scholars

Dr. John F. Guilmartin
Dr. Kevin L. Osterloh
Dr. Kevin M. Woods

Index

ISBN 978-0-9911588-1-2